Stacy Tyler Young
Michael Givens
Dimitrios Gianninas

Adobe® AIR™
Programming

UNLEASHED

SAMS | 800 East 96th Street, Indianapolis, Indiana 46240 USA

ADOBE® AIR™ Programming Unleashed

ISBN-13: 978-0-672-32971-5

ISBN-10: 0-672-32971-9

Library of Congress Cataloging-in-Publication Data

Young, Stacy Tyler.
  Adobe AIR programming unleashed/Stacy Tyler Young, Michael Givens, Dimitrios Gianninas.
    p. cm.
  ISBN 978-0-672-32971-5
  1. Cross-platform software development.   2. Internet programming.   3. Web site development.   I. Givens, Michael.   II. Gianninas, Dimitrios.   III. Title.
  QA76.76.D47Y675 2008
  006.7'6—dc22

                                                                                                2008041640

Printed in the United States of America

First Printing November 2008

Trademarks

Warning and Disclaimer

Bulk Sales

Sams Publishing offers excellent discounts on this book when ordered in quantity for bulk purchases or special sales. For more information, please contact

> **U.S. Corporate and Government Sales**
> **1-800-382-3419**
> **corpsales@pearsontechgroup.com**

For sales outside of the U.S., please contact

> **International Sales**
> **international@pearson.com**

Associate Publisher
Greg Wiegand

Acquisitions Editor
Laura Norman

Development Editor
Songlin Qiu

Managing Editor
Kristy Hart

Project Editor
Betsy Harris

Copy Editor
Karen Annett

Indexer
Lisa Stumpf

Proofreader
San Dee Phillips

Tech Editor
Michael Givens

Publishing Coordinator
Cindy Teeters

Book Designer
Gary Adair

Senior Compositor
Jake McFarland

Contents at a Glance

Table of Contents

About the Authors

Stacy Tyler Young is a senior computer scientist for Adobe Systems in Ottawa, Canada. He's been at the forefront of web technologies since the early nineties. His passion for computing goes back further to the days of the Apple II and the first Macintosh. Rudimentary software development began at the age of seven when he was introduced to the Logo programming language. *"FD 60 RT 45"* anyone?

Coming from a server-side development background, Stacy dove into Flex prior to its first release and has now expanded into developing solutions built on the AIR platform. His focus today lies in Interaction Design and how it can be applied to emerging technologies like AIR to help improve the user experience.

In addition to hearing him speak at local BarCamps or development conferences, you can catch him discussing a mixed bag of technology, environmental issues, and tinfoil hats on his blog: http://stacyyoung.org.

Michael Givens is the CTO of U Saw It Enterprises, a web technology consulting firm based in Houston, Texas. He is an Adobe Community Expert in Adobe Flex and an Adobe Corporate Champion known to share his experience and evangelism of all things Adobe. Certified in both ColdFusion 5 and as an advanced CFMX developer, he has been using ColdFusion since the days of Allaire Spectra. He has written *Adobe Apollo in Flight (Digital Short Cut)*, for Sams Publishing, written articles for the *ColdFusion Developer's Journal* and the *Web Developer's & Designer's Journal*, and blogs regularly at www.flexination.info.

Dimitrios Gianninas is a lead RIA developer at Optimal Payments Inc. based in Montreal, Canada. His primary passion has always been UI development and has excelled in this realm using Flex for web applications and is now expanding his reach to the desktop using AIR. Dimitrios' work has been showcased at conferences and written about in IT publications across the globe. He has also been a guest speaker at Adobe conferences, written articles for the Adobe Developer Center, been a Flex Derby judge, and now maintains his own technical blog at http://jimmyflex.blogspot.com.

Dedication

*This book is dedicated to my folks, George and Marlene,
and my two brothers, Chris and Randy. Thanks for being
just the right amount of crazy.*

—Stacy

*This book is dedicated to my wife, Leny Dayrit Givens; our sweet
family in the Philippines; my parents, Floyd and Nila; my brother,
Pat; his wife, Gigi; my nieces, Chelsea and Leilani; and two special
daughters in China, Lin Wentao and Lin Chen; and their mother,
Chen Qiu Yun. Thanks for all of the encouragement and inspiration
along the way.*

—Michael

*This goes out to my parents, George and Elpiniki, for all the hard
work and caring they put into me over the years. And to my brother,
Alex, whom I am most proud of.*

—Dimitrios

Acknowledgments

I'd like to thank my brother Randy who acted as the inspirational drill sergeant and project manager on this title. Although I might have no food left in the fridge thanks to you, I couldn't have pulled it off without your help.

Thanks to all of my coworkers at Adobe here in Ottawa and in offices abroad, especially the AIR and Flex teams. In particular Arno Gourdol, the engineering manager for AIR and Alex Harui, the magic 8-ball of the Flex world. Also Dan Lesage and Alex Choy, big thanks for approving this project in the first place.

Another big thank you to my coauthors, Michael Givens and Dimitrios "Jimmy" Gianninas, a long-time partner in crime with all things Flex. Also Weyert de Boer for his unique creative talent and...interesting storytelling.

Thanks to the crew at OP: Danny Chazanoff, Andre Lyver, and John Arnold. Your support and experience over the years has meant a great deal.

I'd like to give a shout out to Fabrizio Clemente, a mentor for me early on in life. Here's that book I promised.

Last, but not least, the folks at Sams: Songlin Qiu, Betsy Harris, Cindy Teeters, and especially Laura Norman for her unbelievable patience and understanding with this first-time author.

—Stacy

I'd like to offer special thanks to my father, Floyd, who always encouraged me to write. Even at a young age, it was too late to run from the example he set.

Thanks to the best mom, Nila Jean, a son could ever hope to have. Send money now, Mom. Thanks to my brother, Pat, who sets a fine example in the way he lives his life.

Thanks to my technical editor, Stacy Tyler Young, for the great attention to detail and the advice when the help was embedded too deeply.

Special thanks to Laura Norman, whom I have worked with before and will again. I would also like to thank Songlin Qiu, Betsy Harris, and Cindy Teeters, for their dedication and advice along the way. You gals rock. :-)

—Michael

Without question the first thank-you is to Stacy Young who always gets me into trouble, and without question this is the biggest amount of trouble he's gotten me into. Thanks, Stace!

Goes without saying that a big thank-you goes out to all the people who have worked hard to give life to Adobe Flex and Adobe AIR over the years; it's because of you guys that we are able to usher in a new era of web development.

Thanks to my great friends over at Optimal Payments and especially to my several managers over the years for allowing me the opportunity to showcase my talent: Parvez, Marco, and Andre.

—Dimitrios

We Want to Hear from You!

As the reader of this book, you are our most important critic and commentator. We value your opinion and want to know what we're doing right, what we could do better, what areas you'd like to see us publish in, and any other words of wisdom you're willing to pass our way.

You can email or write me directly to let me know what you did or didn't like about this book—as well as what we can do to make our books stronger.

Please note that I cannot help you with technical problems related to the topic of this book, and that due to the high volume of mail I receive, I might not be able to reply to every message.

When you write, please be sure to include this book's title and author as well as your name and phone or email address. I will carefully review your comments and share them with the author and editors who worked on the book.

Email: feedback@samspublishing.com

Mail: Greg Wiegand
         Associate Publisher
         Sams Publishing
         800 East 96th Street
         Indianapolis, IN 46240 USA

Reader Services

Visit our website and register this book at informit.com/register for convenient access to any updates, downloads, or errata that might be available for this book.

For code downloads, go to http://code.google.com/p/air-unleashed/source/checkout (for more information, see Appendix C, "Downloading Source Code for *Adobe AIR Programming Unleashed*").

Introduction

Thanks for grabbing a copy of *Adobe® AIR™ Programming Unleashed*!

Adobe® AIR™ technology is dramatically changing the landscape of web development. Even prior to its 1.0 release, the excitement around this product even in beta was astounding. With each new build, more and more features were being baked into the Adobe AIR platform—pushing the reach of Web technologies further into the desktop world.

If you are a developer who has been locked inside the browser world along with the rest of us, this technology will breathe new life into both you and your projects.

The goals of this book are remarkably simple:

- ► Make broad strokes through the fundamentals of the Adobe AIR platform to help you get up and running as quickly as possible

- ► Explain concepts in plain English in an easy-to-read format

- ► Offer approachable standalone code samples you can download, compile, and execute to see features in action

Personally, I've always had trouble understanding concepts presented in software books on the first pass. Although the authors might be the supreme authorities on a subject, it's conceivable that they sometimes forget what's easy for them is not easy for someone just getting started.

I've done my best to keep the writing on the straight and narrow with regard to simplicity. I sincerely hope it serves you well.

Who Should Read This Book?

This book is for any web developers looking to leverage what they already know and apply those skills in desktop software.

The Adobe AIR platform supports applications developed with HTML, AJAX, Adobe® Flex™, Adobe® Flash®, PDF, or virtually any combination thereof. I should note, however, that this title leans more toward Adobe AIR application development with Adobe Flex serving as the primary citizen.

If you're also new to Adobe Flex, don't worry. The examples presented within the chapters are approachable for newcomers.

Software Requirements

Adobe Flex Builder 3 has everything you need to build applications for the Adobe AIR platform. It is a commercial product available in standard and professional versions. However, if you are an educator or student, you can obtain your copy free by visiting this Adobe website:

www.flexregistration.com

Standalone software development kits (SDK) are available for both Adobe Flex and Adobe AIR. Both are entirely free. Combined with your favorite IDE, you can build Adobe AIR applications at no cost beyond your own time. In addition, the Flex SDK is now open source! Nightly builds are available to the public. For information on downloads or submitting a patch or to simply peruse the bug database, visit

http://opensource.adobe.com/wiki/display/flexsdk/Flex+SDK

Adobe AIR

Adobe AIR is comprised of an SDK and a runtime component installed on the user's machine. It's similar to Adobe Flash, but, rather than operate within the browser context, the Adobe AIR platform offers a suite of native desktop functionality to applications. Another significant difference is that Adobe AIR applications are installed like native applications and offer direct access from the user's desktop.

Windows Requirements

- ▶ Intel Pentium 1GHz or faster processor
- ▶ Microsoft Windows 2000 with Service Pack 4; Windows XP with Service Pack 2; or Windows Vista Home Premium, Business, Ultimate, or Enterprise
- ▶ 512MB of RAM

Mac OS X Requirements

- ▶ PowerPC G4 1GHz or faster processor or Intel Core Duo 1.83GHz or faster processor

- ▶ Mac OS X v10.4.910 or 10.5.1 (PowerPC); Mac OS X v10.4.9 or later, 10.5.1 (Intel)

- ▶ 512MB of RAM

For Adobe AIR applications leveraging the full-screen video playback features of the integrated Adobe Flash player, the following configurations are recommended:

Windows

- ▶ Intel Pentium 2GHz or faster processor

- ▶ Windows 2000 with Service Pack 4; Windows XP with Service Pack 2; or Windows Vista Home Premium, Business, Ultimate, or Enterprise

- ▶ 512MB of RAM; 32MB of VRAM

Mac OS X

- ▶ PowerPC G4 1.8GHz or faster processor or Intel Core Duo 1.33GHz or faster processor

- ▶ Mac OS X v.10.4.9 or later or 10.5.1 (Intel or PowerPC; Intel processor required for H.264 video)

- ▶ 512MB of RAM; 32MB of VRAM

Adobe Flex

Adobe Flex Builder 3 is an Integrated Development Environment (IDE) based on Eclipse in which you can code, build, test, and optimize Adobe Flex applications. It also comes with built-in Adobe AIR support, including debug support that allows developers to quickly launch and test applications without having to package and deploy. Adobe Flex Builder offers a single environment no matter what the nature of your project.

Adobe Flex Builder 3 can be downloaded via the Adobe website:

www.adobe.com/products/flex/features/flex_builder/

For information on upgrades and an Adobe Flex feature comparison chart, visit

www.adobe.com/products/flex/upgrade/

Development of Adobe Flex Builder 3 for Linux is underway at the time of this writing. For more information, visit

http://labs.adobe.com/technologies/flex/flexbuilder_linux/

Adobe Flex Builder 3 for Windows (Standard and Professional) Requirements

- ▶ Intel Pentium 4 processor

- ▶ Microsoft Windows XP with Service Pack 2 or Windows Vista Home Premium

▶ 1GB of RAM (2GB recommended)

▶ 500MB of available hard-disk space (additional 500MB required for plug-in configuration)

▶ Java Virtual Machine: Sun JRE 1.4.2, Sun JRE 1.5 (included), IBM JRE 1.5, or Sun JRE 1.6

▶ Eclipse 3.2.2–3.4 for plug-in configuration (Eclipse 3.3–3.4 recommended for Windows Vista)

▶ Adobe Flash Player 10 software (see following note)

▶ BEA Workshop 10.1

▶ IBM Rational Software Architect 7.0.0.3 (Eclipse 3.3 plug-in configuration only)

Adobe Flex Builder 3 for Mac OS (Standard and Professional)

▶ PowerPC G4 1.25GHz or Intel processor

▶ Mac OS X v10.4.7–10.4.10 or 10.5

▶ 1GB of RAM (2GB of RAM recommended)

▶ 500MB of available hard-disk space

▶ Java Virtual Machine: JRE 1.5 or JRE 1.6 from Apple

▶ Eclipse 3.2.2–3.4 (for plug-in configuration)

▶ Adobe Flash Player 10 software

> **NOTE**
>
> When installing Adobe Flex Builder 3, the latest version of the Adobe Flash Player 10 is also installed. You can verify the version of the player by visiting Adobe's website: http://kb.adobe.com/selfservice/viewContent.do?externalId=tn_15507.

Adobe Flex 3 SDK

Although Adobe Flex Builder 3 offers a seamless environment for Adobe Flex and Adobe AIR development, they are not mandatory. The Adobe Flex SDK on its own contains everything needed to build Adobe Flex applications from a command line.

In other cases, even if you're developing applications in Adobe Flex Builder 3, you still need to download the SDK if you're planning on using a build process (for example, Apache ANT). The requirements for Adobe Flex 3 SDK are as follows:

- ▶ Windows 2000, Windows XP, or Windows Server 2003, Java 1.4 (Sun, IBM, or BEA) or 1.5 (Sun)

- ▶ Mac OS X v10.4.x, Java 1.5 (as shipped from Apple) on PowerPC or Intel processor

- ▶ Red Hat Enterprise Linux 3 or 4, SUSE 10, Java 1.4 (Sun, IBM, or BEA) or 1.5 (Sun)

- ▶ Solaris 9, 10, Java 1.4 or 1.5 (Sun) Compilers only

- ▶ 512MB of RAM (1GB recommended)

- ▶ 200MB of available hard-disk space

Code Samples for This Book

Every concept introduced in this book is backed up with a complete code sample. Each of these is available as a standalone Adobe AIR project that can be built and run inside of Adobe Flex Builder.

For your added convenience, all project files have been made available on Google Code. Simply install the Subversion Eclipse plug-in directly into Adobe Flex Builder, point to the code repository, and sync! See Appendix C, "Downloading Source Code for *Adobe AIR Programming Unleashed*," for instructions on checking out the code files.

Optionally, all code will also be available as a Zip archive at the following location: www.informit.com/title/9780672329715.

PART I

Getting Started with Adobe AIR

IN THIS PART

Introduction to Adobe AIR

Conceptual Overview

Welcome to the new and exciting world of the Adobe® AIR™ version 1.5!

I promised myself that when it came down to writing the introduction to this book, I would not succumb to the urge of going back in time and talking about "the birds and the bees" of modern-day computer programming. After sampling a variety of technical books on the market, you'd swear the "history talk" is some kind of right of passage for authors.

Thanks to a co-worker of mine, I've had to throw that plan out the window. He pointed out that scores of kids who have never known a world without the Internet are soon to be unleashed into our workforce. As mind-boggling as that fact might be, that day is, of course, inevitable. So I worried that the idea of Adobe AIR would not have the same impact on them as it has had on me. It needs to be explained in context. So yes, I *am* going to talk a little history.

In all seriousness, looking back at the evolution of computing can offer some perspective. We're all overloaded these days with little time for professional development. We need to invest our time wisely. Understanding the trends of the past can help point us to the future.

Mainframes were big and scary. All the brains of the system were contained in these monstrous towers. They offered small, monochrome screens (or dumb terminals) in which a small portion of the business population would rattle away at the command line or ASCII menus. Given the requirements of the day, they got the job done.

Enter the dawn of modern desktop computing. Computers sitting on users' desks were reaching a level of sophistication at which they could actually do something useful. Combined with the explosion of networking, it seemed like a logical choice to push software out to the edges of the network. History refers to this phase as the "fat" client/server architecture era.

These client/server applications were designed to do most of the work up front on the host computer. The back-end mainframes (and, eventually, modern-day database systems) more or less took on the role of providing mass storage.

I had the wonderful opportunity of entering the workforce at this period in time. Productivity was skyrocketing. The idea of taking a portable computer home (still monochrome, of course) and not needing a lifeline to operate it was exciting. It was a great time...for them.

I, on the other hand, served as the local geek responsible for the installation and *maintenance* of these software programs and machines. Imagine having to distribute a software update to 100 people by running up and down the halls, hijacking each person's machine for a couple of minutes to run an installer. (Back then, if you valued your life, you would never dream of having users do their own updates.) Now imagine getting a call the next day about a new "critical" patch being released to address issues with the *previous* patch from the day before. Lovely.

Enter the World Wide Web—my savior.

Back then, the impact of porting the tiniest slice of a desktop application to the web was astounding. Things snowballed so fast that no one even stopped to complain about the crappy experience. We had *just* finished introducing new levels of sophistication with client/server technology. The next thing you know, we're dropping everything to build web-based tools.

Initial projects were nothing more than barren-looking Hypertext Markup Language (HTML) pages made up of a collection of blue, underlined hyperlinks. It felt like we took two steps forward and then one step back with regard to the user experience. People just didn't care. Tell them changes can be deployed in minutes instead of days and you could have drawn the user interface (UI) in crayon. It wouldn't have mattered.

Now fast-forward to the nineties and this past decade to today. The Internet is still here. In fact, it's tied into just about anything we do these days. Client technology has graduated beyond collections of blue hyperlinks. With the advent of Adobe® Flash®, Adobe® Flex™, and DHTML/Asynchronous JavaScript and XML (AJAX), we developers have created some great things.

Amazingly, after all this time has passed, the experience of our users is still contained within the browser. Web technologies have evolved, but that finite disconnect between the web application and the desktop still exists. This is manifested into a lack of continuity in the user experience.

The reality of today is a hybrid environment between native software and its Internet counterparts. Simply delivering a web-based solution is not good enough anymore. That approach has been commoditized. Users are looking for what's next—an enhanced user experience.

I'm not talking about just throwing video and flashing lights up on a website. I'm referring to the *complete* user experience. Complete in that our software *empowers* users to reach their goals with the least amount of effort, in the least amount of time.

The purpose of me giving that backstory earlier is that it characterizes how technology, as with many things, tends to expand and contract over time. By this token, I believe we're going to see an expansion back out to the edges of the network. The untapped power of not just the PC but *all* devices in use today is just too inviting.

To do this, we have to extend the reach of our web applications out of the browser and blend it in to the desktop environment. This is where Adobe AIR comes into play (see Figure 1.1).

FIGURE 1.1　Adobe AIR increases the reach of Rich Internet Applications (RIA) and exposes native desktop functionality.

What Is Adobe AIR?

Adobe AIR is a cross-operating system runtime that allows developers to leverage their existing web development skills in HTML, AJAX, XML, Flash, and Flex to build and deploy rich Internet applications for the desktop.

But what does this really mean to you as a web developer? Because Adobe AIR allows existing code and tools to be used to build desktop applications, the possibility of a whole new breed of applications is opening up. Have you ever been in the position where a client has asked for a feature that was simply just not possible due to the constraints of the web browser (for example, read/write files to the file system, local storage, or launch on startup)? The Adobe AIR platform shatters these limitations by extending all those capabilities and more to your web applications.

Gone is the thinking that applications can be developed in only one language or technology. You can now work in a hybrid environment where you can use the right tool for the right job. Do you want Flash-based applications to include HTML-based content? Or perhaps a mash-up of Adobe Flex and AJAX. Maybe even integrate PDFs (Portable Document Format)? Adobe AIR does it all by providing a homogenous platform across Windows, Mac, and Linux.

With Adobe AIR, you can develop desktop applications using one or any combination of the following technologies:

- Flash/Flex/ActionScript
- HTML/JavaScript/AJAX
- PDF

Looking at the Adobe AIR Architecture

The architecture of Adobe AIR can be summed up quickly. Imagine all the functionality of the latest Flash Player; combine that with the HTML Webkit web browser engine, add the open source database capabilities of SQLite, and top it off with an impressive collection of application programming interfaces (APIs) that provide access to the users operating system, and you have Adobe AIR. Oh and I almost forgot, Adobe AIR also bridges to an installed copy of Adobe Reader or Acrobat for PDF support.

The Adobe AIR platform offers a powerful toolset for next generation rich *desktop* applications:

- The latest Flash Player
- The HTML Webkit engine
- SQLite Local Database
- Cross-platform ActionScript APIs for native desktop integration
- Adobe Reader or Acrobat for integrated PDF support

The added bonus is that you can leverage all these capabilities by using what you, the web developer, already know. Adobe Flash developers can now integrate and access with HTML without the same concerns of cross-browser quirks. Adobe Flex developers, using the built-in Adobe AIR capabilities in Adobe Flex Builder, can expand their projects on the Adobe AIR platform in a few clicks. Working solely with HTML and AJAX? That's also an option as HTML applications are considered primary citizens in Adobe AIR. Regardless of where you're coming from, chances are you will find immediate possibilities with Adobe AIR.

Don't forget the APIs that give you the functionality of a desktop application—they are the key to going beyond the browser. Want to build custom branded desktop applications that include native drag-and-drop support? How about including full right-click context menu control and system notifications? On top of all this, you have so many ways to customize the appearance of your application, you'll be foaming at the mouth.

Here are just a few of the possibilities that Adobe AIR APIs open up:

- Multi-windowed applications with native windows
- Native drag and drop into and out of your application
- Native clipboard support for transferring data to and from your application
- File I/O
- Auto-update framework for application updates

▶ Customizable window chrome including transparencies and nonrectangular shapes

▶ System integration with the dock, taskbar, file associations and customizable application icons

The Adobe AIR APIs contain platform-specific capabilities, which are simply ignored on platforms that don't support them. For example, applications have an API for accessing the Mac OS Dock, but calling it on Windows doesn't have any effect.

You can think of the Adobe AIR architecture like layers of a cake, where the applications are the icing. The Adobe AIR platform takes care of business at the lower layers by providing a collection of APIs that are common across all the supported operating systems. Above that lies a container that enables cross-communication between the major components of the runtime—WebKit browser, Adobe Flex/Flash, and Adobe Reader (see diagram shown in Figure 1.2).

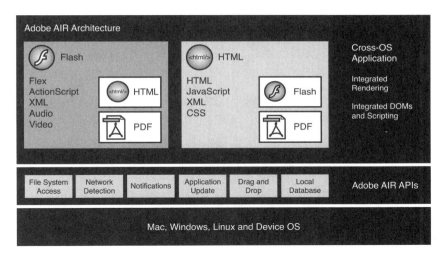

FIGURE 1.2   Adobe AIR architecture.

Summary

Adobe AIR dramatically changes how web applications can be created, deployed, and experienced. You have more creative control than ever before by extending the reach of your Adobe Flash, Adobe Flex, HTML, and AJAX applications to the desktop. If you are already an experienced web developer, you can leverage all these capabilities without having to learn yet another programming construct.

# CHAPTER 2

Setting Up the Development Environment

To develop Adobe® Flex™-based Adobe® AIR™ applications, you have a choice between using Adobe Flex Builder 3 or your favorite Integrated Development Environment (IDE) in combination with the Adobe AIR software development kit (SDK). We investigate both approaches in this chapter.

First, let's start with installing Adobe AIR—not the SDK but the actual runtime that will lay the foundation for future Adobe AIR application installations. This package will be installed on the end user's machine. At the time of this writing, the size of the Adobe AIR installer hovers around 16MB. This varies slightly between operating systems.

Installing Adobe AIR

The installation process is virtually identical on Windows and Mac OS X:

1. Download the runtime installation file for your platform from Adobe: http://get.adobe.com/air.

2. Double-click the Adobe AIR installer to begin (see Figure 2.1).

3. Follow the prompts to complete the installation (see Figures 2.2–2.4). Depending on your operating system, you might be prompted for your password to allow the install process to continue.

CAUTION

Administrative privileges are required to install Adobe AIR. If your user account does not have applications install permissions, contact your system administrator. Adobe AIR applications have access to the underlying operation system like any native application. For this reason, although inconvenient, it is an important security precaution.

Adobe AIR Installer

FIGURE 2.1   Adobe AIR installer.

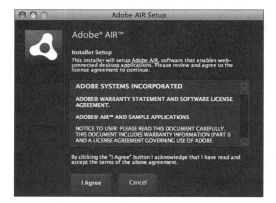

FIGURE 2.2   Start of the install process.

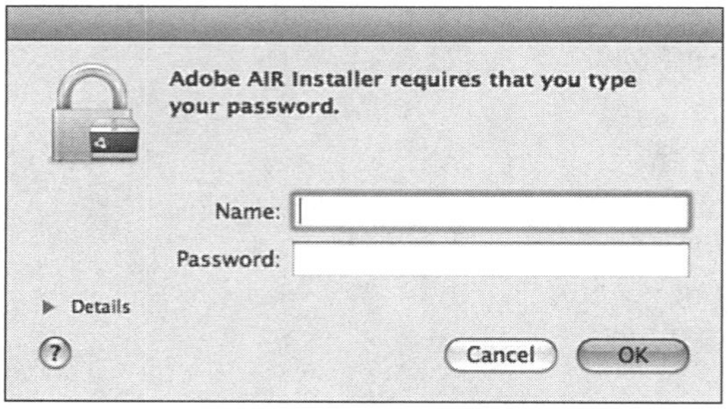

FIGURE 2.3   Install permission prompt on Mac OS X.

FIGURE 2.4   Installation complete.

When the installation of the runtime is completed, the operating system can install Adobe AIR applications. The applications themselves may originate from various sources such as via email, file download, or seamless installs from a website. Refer to Chapter 17, "Distributing Adobe AIR Applications," for more information.

Installing Adobe Flex Builder

Adobe Flex Builder 3 offers a number of productivity advantages when developing Adobe AIR applications. Significant features include

▶ Create AIR Project Wizard

▶ Step-through debugging capabilities

▶ Package Adobe AIR applications for distribution

▶ Publish application source code

Adobe Flex Builder 3 has everything you need in a single package. In addition, you have the choice of a standalone or plug-in installation. The standalone version is a branded version of Eclipse, whereas the plug-in integrates with an existing Eclipse installation.

The installation process is almost identical in both formats. When installing the plug-in version, be sure to have Eclipse already installed, as you will be prompted to provide its location during the Adobe Flex Builder 3 installation.

To install Adobe Flex Builder 3 for Windows or Mac OS X, follow these steps:

1. Download the installation file from the Adobe website: www.adobe.com/products/flex/.

2. Double-click the installer to begin the install process and follow the prompts.

NOTE

Be sure to uninstall any previous versions of Adobe Flex Builder prior to installing version 3. This latest version supports the use of different Flex SDKs, which is helpful if you have earlier Flex projects to support. This can be set in the properties of each Flex project.

3. Figure 2.5 depicts the initial screen of the install process. Select your language and click OK.

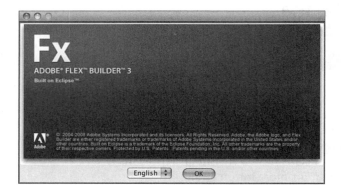

FIGURE 2.5   Initial Adobe Flex Builder 3 dialog.

4. Choose the install directory. The default value is the standard location for applications in the operating system (see Figure 2.6).

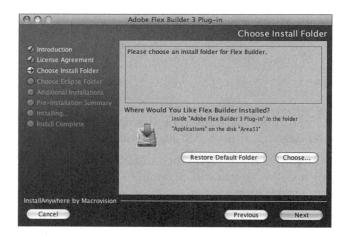

FIGURE 2.6   Select an install folder.

5. If you are installing the plug-in version of Adobe Flex Builder 3, you are prompted for the location of your pre-existing Eclipse installation. Verify the default location; the installer does not automatically locate the Eclipse folder (see Figure 2.7).

6. If you plan to use any HTML/JavaScript content in your Adobe AIR application, it's a good idea to install JSEclipse. This also applies if you do any development work with Adobe ColdFusion (see Figure 2.8).

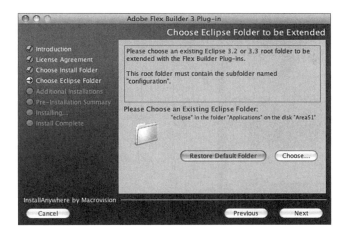

FIGURE 2.7   Prompt for existing Eclipse folder (plug-in version).

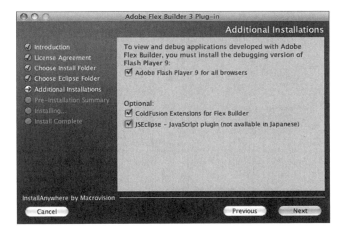

FIGURE 2.8   Additional install options.

7. At this point the installation begins (see Figure 2.9).

8. When installation has completed, start up Adobe Flex Builder 3 (or Eclipse) by accessing the Start menu in Windows or your chosen install location on Mac OS X.

When you open Adobe Flex Builder 3 standalone, the Adobe Flex perspective is immediately available. The plug-in install, however, requires you to turn on the Flex perspective. (Figure 2.10 depicts the default state of Eclipse after the Flex Builder plug-in installation.) This can be done via Window, Open Perspective, Other. You will find three perspectives available: Flex Development, Flex Debugging, and Flex Profiling (see Figure 2.11).

We'll be using all three at some point throughout this book, so feel free to add them all. The underlying Eclipse framework makes switching perspectives simple with the navigation bar at the top right.

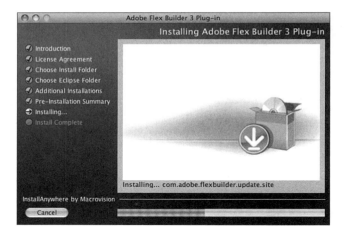

FIGURE 2.9   Installation process begins.

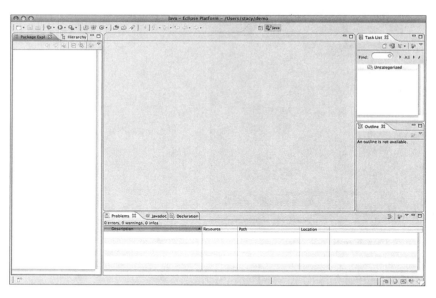

FIGURE 2.10   Initial view in Eclipse (plug-in install).

To create your first Adobe Flex-driven Adobe AIR application, access the File, New, Flex Project menu item, which launches a wizard (see Figure 2.12).

Select Desktop Application as the application type and click Finish.

Figure 2.13 shows the result of the new Flex Project Wizard. A default MXML file has been created and opened. At this point, you can compile and test your application. Of course, without having added new code, the compiled application will be a blank window. At least you will have confirmed your environment is properly configured!

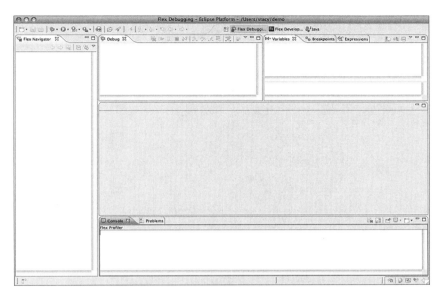

FIGURE 2.11   Adding the Adobe Flex perspective (plug-in install).

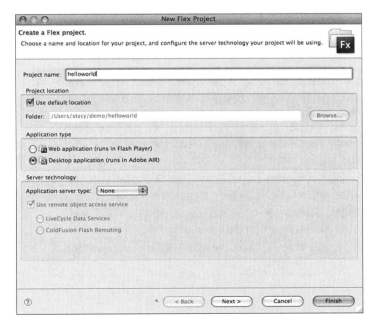

FIGURE 2.12   Creating a new Adobe AIR project using the New Flex Project Wizard.

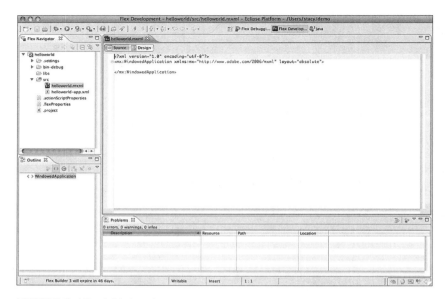

FIGURE 2.13   Initial project structure.

In the next chapter, we dissect the elements that make up an Adobe AIR application, including building our first simple project.

Perspectives in Adobe Flex Builder 3 and Eclipse

Every window in Eclipse contains one or more perspectives. A perspective is a particular layout of a collection of "views." Each view is a compartmentalized entity. For instance, the Flex Navigator on the left side of Adobe Flex Builder is a view, as is the Outline panel immediately beneath the navigator. All these views together make up the Adobe Flex Builder perspective.

You will also find additional perspectives, such as the Adobe Flex Debugger, defaults supplied by Eclipse, and of course any additional plug-ins you have installed.

Lastly, you can create your own perspectives and mix and match the views from various tools into a customized, super-productive development environment.

In Eclipse or Adobe Flex Builder 3, use Window, Open Perspective to browse available perspectives.

Installing the Software Development Kits (SDKs)

Downloading and working with the Adobe AIR and Adobe Flex SDKs is required if you want to use a development environment other than Adobe Flex Builder. They are also pertinent when setting up a formalized build process with Apache Ant and/or inclusion in a continuous integration environment.

Installing Java

Use of the SDKs requires that you have Java installed on your computer. You can use either the Java Runtime Environment (JRE) or the Java Development Kit (JDK) (version 1.4.2 or higher). Typically, if you're not planning to do any Java development, the JRE will do just fine. Either package can be downloaded and installed from http://java.sun.com. This is only required for Adobe AIR development environments. Users installing your Adobe AIR applications will only need Adobe's Integrated Runtime.

After Java is installed, open a console window (or command prompt on Windows) and type

```
java -version
```

If the computer spits back an error, you need to modify the system's PATH environment variable. Otherwise, if you see something similar to Figure 2.14, you know Java is installed and available via the systems PATH variable. Having the Java bin folder in the system path allows you to invoke the Java compiler from any directory without having to specify the entire directory path.

FIGURE 2.14   Checking installed Java version on OS X and Windows.

Adding Java to Your System Path

Environment variables are name/value pairs stored in memory. In our case, we're going to append a file path to a variable called PATH. The PATH environment variable is a string containing a series of system directory paths separated by colons or semicolons, depending on the OS. When you enter a command in a terminal window, the OS searches all these paths to locate the command in question. This avoids having to type the full path:

```
> java -version
```

Compared with

```
>/System/Library/Frameworks/JavaVM.framework/Versions/Current/Commands/java -version
```

One option on OS X is to create a small script file called .profile that sits in the root of your home directory. Inside this file, we append the PATH variable with the directory path containing our Java executable. Figure 2.15 outlines the contents of the .profile shell script.

FIGURE 2.15   Creating a .profile shell script on OS X.

PATH=$PATH simply means, "Take the existing PATH value and append our new value to the end." This prevents our script from eradicating any previous values that might already exist in the PATH variable. Figure 2.16 shows the directory contents of the path specified in our shell script.

On a Windows machine, you can alter the system PATH variable as well. Right-click on My Computer, select Properties, select the Advanced tab, and then click the Environment Variables button (see Figure 2.17).

You have the choice of setting a USER or SYSTEM variable in the Environment Variables dialog shown in Figure 2.18. USER variables exist only in memory when logged in under your user. SYSTEM variables exist for all users. We'll use the system PATH variable because it already exists and will not adversely affect any other users. Edit the PATH variable and append the path to the Java bin directory (see Figure 2.19).

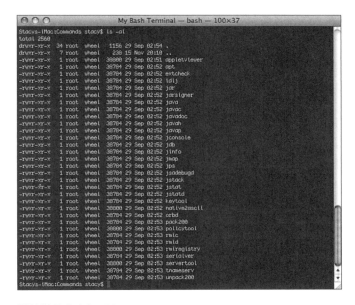

FIGURE 2.16   Directory contents.

FIGURE 2.17   System Properties dialog on Windows XP.

FIGURE 2.18   Locating the PATH variable in the Environment Variables dialog.

FIGURE 2.19   Appending the PATH variable.

Whether you're on Windows or Mac OS X, you need to close and re-open any command prompts or terminal windows for your environment variable changes to take effect.

Installing Adobe AIR and Adobe Flex SDKs

You can download the SDKs from their respective locations:

▶ Adobe AIR SDK

  http://www.adobe.com/products/air/tools/

▶ Adobe Flex SDK

  http://www.adobe.com/products/air/tools/

Aside from unzipping the archives into a convenient directory, you don't need to do anything specific in regard to installation. If you plan to use a build process (Apache Ant) and work in a team environment, you might want to consider additional environment variables to reference the locations of the SDKs. This avoids having to hard-code these paths in build scripts, which might differ among team members.

Summary

We've covered the installation process and basic system configuration for developing Adobe AIR applications. If you have previous Java development experience, you will feel right at home with this environment. If this is new for you, fear not; it's a straightforward process, so even newcomers can be up and running in a matter of minutes.

Next, we take a look at what constitutes an Adobe AIR project and the steps involved in building our first application.

CHAPTER 3

Creating an Adobe AIR Application

For many, the most exciting aspects of Adobe® AIR™ have to do with the new features that could only be made available outside of the browser. Although native system access is a major leap ahead for web application developers, several little gems are available in Adobe AIR that can help present your project in a more professional light.

In this chapter we touch on many of the odds and ends of the Adobe AIR platform that, although valuable, don't necessarily command their own dedicated chapter. If you are brand-spanking new to Adobe AIR, don't fret if you find yourself not understanding the intricacies of what's presented. The main goal is to give you an idea of what's possible on the outskirts of the runtime. Hopefully it might help trigger new ideas down the road as you begin to wrap your head around everything that's available to you on this platform.

Before we dive into the outlying aspects of the runtime, we first dive into a crash course in getting your first Adobe AIR application up and running.

Your First Adobe AIR Application

Let's start by creating a simple Adobe AIR Application called Hello World. Yes, original I know, but I'm hoping it will offer a feeling of familiarity as you dive into code for the first time.

First stop: walking through the basic steps needed to create an Adobe AIR project from scratch. For sake of simplicity we're going to be doing this in Adobe Flex Builder 3. We then get our Hello World example up and running using the Adobe Debug Launcher conveniently available within Flex Builder. Finally, we take a look at how to package our application and ready it for distribution. By the end of this process, you will have your own Adobe AIR file to pass around. It won't do much of anything yet, but at least you'll have your feet wet!

1. Open Adobe Flex Builder 3.
2. Select File, New, Flex Project.
3. Enter **Hello World** as the project's name.
4. Enter a location for your project to be stored. The default is just fine for our purposes.
5. There are two options for project type: a traditional Adobe® Flex™ application destined for browser deployment or an Adobe AIR desktop application (intended to run in Adobe AIR). Choose the latter.
6. For server technology, select None.
7. Click Finish to create the Adobe AIR project.

At this point the project is created. On the left side in the project browser, you can find your new project opened. On the right, the default MXML document is open. Your screen should look similar to the one shown in Figure 3.1.

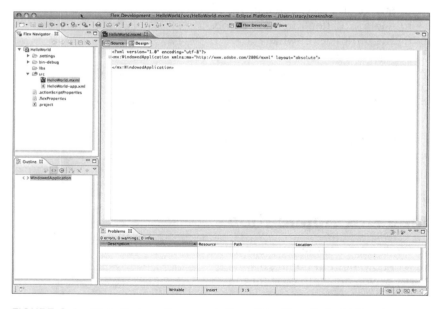

FIGURE 3.1   Default view after completion of the New Project Wizard.

If you look in the Adobe Flex Navigator window in the upper-left corner, you'll see that two files have been created under the src folder (see Figure 3.2). Every Adobe AIR application will require at least these two files.

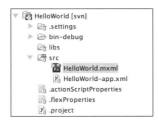

FIGURE 3.2   Source files created by default.

The first file found in the src folder is an MXML file. If you have done Flex development before, this will be familiar to you. This is a text-based file containing XML markup (called MXML) that will be interpreted into ActionScript by the Flex compiler and finally compiled into a Shockwave Flash (SWF) file. This file is the root content that serves as the base for your application. Although our example uses MXML, there is nothing stopping you from using an ActionScript class as the main document in an Adobe AIR project.

The second file found in the src folder is the application descriptor file. It has a specific name in the form of the main application file followed by a -app.xml. Notice that whenever you rename the main application file, Flex Builder automatically updates the name of the descriptor. If you are not using Flex Builder to author your Adobe AIR applications, you have to do this manually. The compiler follows this naming scheme to locate the descriptor when compiling the project.

Let's take a closer look at the descriptor file. Go ahead and double-click on the file marked HelloWorld-app.xml. At first glance the contents of the file might appear somewhat cryptic, but as you become more familiar with the anatomy of an Adobe AIR project, things will begin to fall into place.

We're only interested in a few of the tags at this point, so when you open the file, scroll down to about line 15 or 16. This is the section you should be looking at:

```
<!-- The application identifier string, unique to this application. Required. -->
<id>main</id>
<!-- Used as the filename for the application. Required. -->
<filename>main</filename>
<!-- The name that is displayed in the AIR application installer. Optional. -->
<!-- <name></name> -->
<!-- An application version designator (such as "v1", "2.5", or "Alpha 1").
Required. -->
<version>v1</version>
<!-- Description, displayed in the AIR application installer. Optional. -->
<!-- <description></description> -->
<!-- Copyright information. Optional -->
<!-- <copyright></copyright> -->
```

The first thing we have to do is give the application a unique identifier string. This needs to be unique, and many people simply use the reverse of their domain plus some extra identifier indicating the application's function. This is a machine-readable string; the end user never sees this text. For our example, use the following:

```
<!-- The application identifier string, unique to this application. Required. -->
<id>com.example.firstbreathofair/id>
```

Next, we add the information for the filename of the application. This is the name that your user sees. So for our example, use

```
<!-- Used as the filename for the application. Required. -->
<filename>First Breath of AIR</filename>
```

Now, change the tag for the name we want to appear as the title of the application installer:

```
<!-- The name that is displayed in the AIR application installer. Optional. -->
<!-- <name>First Breath of AIR Installer</name> -->
```

We leave the version designator to the default v1. This comes into play down the road with regard to distributing updates for deployed Adobe AIR applications. During the update process, the current and the update versions are presented to the user:

```
<!-- An application version designator (such as "v1", "2.5", or "Alpha 1").
Required. -->
<version>v1</version>
```

Next, add a short description for the application:

```
<!-- Description, displayed in the AIR application installer. Optional. -->
<!-- <description>This is an example of a simple Hello World AIR application built in
➥Flex</description> -->
```

And, finally, we have the copyright tag. This is exposed to the operating system (OS) and can be seen on a Mac by using Get Info. For now, leave it blank:

```
<!-- Copyright information. Optional -->
<!-- <copyright></copyright> -->
```

So now your block of text should look like this:

```
<!-- The application identifier string, unique to this application. Required. -->
<id>com.example.firstbreathofair/id>
<!-- Used as the filename for the application. Required. -->
<filename>First Breath of AIR</filename>
<!-- The name that is displayed in the AIR application installer. Optional. -->
<!-- <name>First Breath of AIR Installer</name> -->
<!-- An application version designator (such as "v1", "2.5", or "Alpha 1").
➥Required. -->
<version>v1</version>
<!-- Description, displayed in the AIR application installer. Optional. -->
<!-- <description>This is an example of a simple Hello World AIR application built
in Flex</description> -->
<!-- Copyright information. Optional -->
<!-- <copyright></copyright> -->
```

The rest of the tags control many of the properties of the main native application window as well as the application system icons and file associations. The native window properties correlate to the default `WindowedApplication` tag inserted by default into the main MXML document when the project was created.

Now open `HelloWorld.mxml` and add the code outlined in Listing 3.1.

LISTING 3.1   Creating a Hello World Example

```
<?xml version="1.0" encoding="utf-8"?>
<mx:WindowedApplication
    xmlns:mx="http://www.adobe.com/2006/mxml"
    horizontalAlign="center"
    verticalAlign="middle"
    layout="vertical">

    <mx:Button label="Hello World" />

</mx:WindowedApplication>
```

That's all there is to it! At this point we can actually compile and launch the application. Right-click `HelloWorld.mxml` in the source root of the project and select Run As, Adobe AIR Application. This invokes the compiler, and the application is launched inside the Adobe AIR Debug Launcher (ADL). The ADL allows developers to compile and run Adobe AIR applications without having to go through the trouble of packaging and signing every single time.

Upon launching the application, you should see a result that matches Figure 3.3.

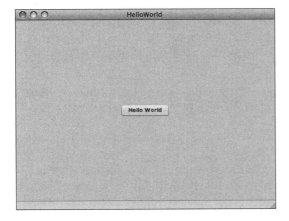

FIGURE 3.3   Hello World example running inside the ADL.

In Adobe Flex, the default tag is `Application`. In an Adobe AIR project, the default tag is `WindowedApplication`. This indicates the application is using a native window as its container. In other words it's telling the compiler to load your application inside a native operating system window. Looking at our Hello World example, notice the native window chrome and the standard window controls—just like any other application launched from the desktop.

Although Adobe Flex Builder creates a default MXML document with a `WindowedApplication` tag when creating an Adobe AIR project, there's nothing stopping you from reverting to using an `Application` tag instead. This tells the compiler that you don't want a default native window created for your application. If you were to make this change in our Hello World example and relaunch it, nothing would show onscreen. Your application is still running; there just isn't a viable container to host our Button control. You can verify this by looking at the running process via the task manager on Windows or the activity monitor on OS X.

Now why would we ever want to do this? Well, the most frequent use case might be that you want a custom window chrome rather than the system default. This approach would be your starting point, followed by creating your initial native window, with custom chrome, via script within your project—more on that in Chapter 5, "Working with Windows." Lastly, you also have the option of using a straight-up `ActionScript` class as your default application container, again creating your native window instance from within the constructor or subsequent method within the class.

At this point, you're ready to package and distribute your application.

From a bird's eye view, a packaged Adobe AIR application is just a zip-based file containing all the files and metadata of your project. The runtime will either already reside on the users machine or, through a detection mechanism, be installed just prior to installing your application. After Adobe AIR is on the machine, the operating system will associate `*.air` files and launch the Adobe AIR installer when the user opens a file with the Adobe AIR extension. The runtime then presents the user with an install sequence for a given Adobe AIR application and then copies the application files into the right directories. Next, it creates the tradition native hooks into the operating system, like shortcuts in the menu and/or desktop, and establishes file associations with your application (if you've specified any in your application descriptor).

Let's move on to creating our first Adobe AIR file! Either click on the Export Release Build button on the Flex Builder toolbar or go to Project, Export, Release Build. Figure 3.4 outlines the options that are presented to you.

Click Next to get to the Digital Signature dialog, as shown in Figure 3.5.

Digitally signing your Adobe AIR applications assures users that the application they're installing identifies you as the publisher. Adobe AIR displays the publisher's name during the installation process when the Adobe AIR application has been signed with a certificate that is trusted; otherwise, the publisher name is displayed as "Unknown."

To sign Adobe AIR files, you can use an existing Class 3, high-assurance, code-signing certificate, or you can obtain a new one. Certificates from Verisign or Thawte can be used. Don't worry about these details for now. We get into more details in Chapter 17, "Distributing Adobe AIR Applications."

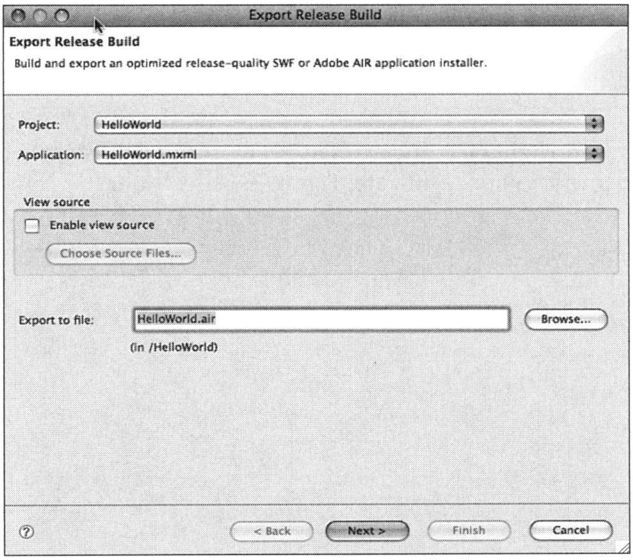

FIGURE 3.4   Initial options when exporting an Adobe AIR project.

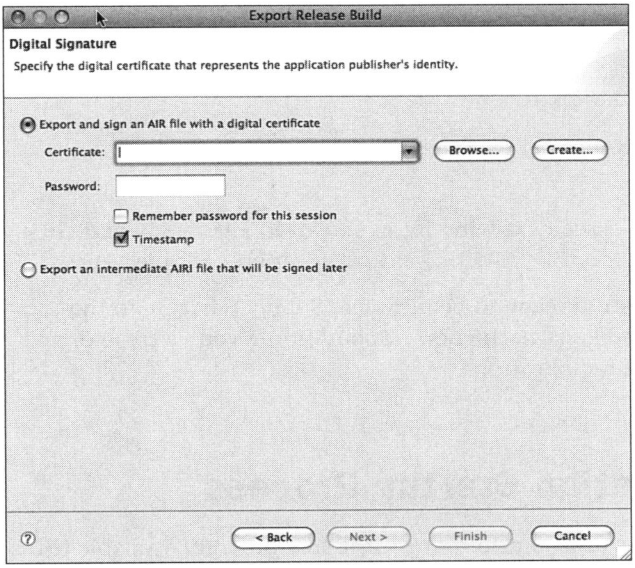

FIGURE 3.5   Providing a digital signature.

For development purposes you can generate a self-signed certificate using the Adobe AIR
Development Tool (ADT) used to package Adobe AIR installation files. A user can choose

to trust a self-signed certificate, and then any Adobe AIR applications signed with the certificate will display the value of the common name field in the certificate as the publisher name. Adobe AIR does not provide any means for a user to designate a certificate as trusted.

Click Create to get the Create Self-Signed Digital Certificate dialog. Fill in the Publisher Name and Password, and choose a name for your certificate. Figure 3.6 shows our completed sample form.

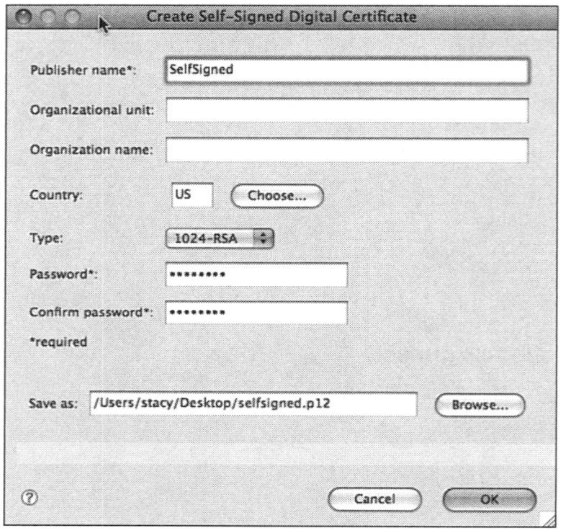

FIGURE 3.6   Creating a self-signed certificate.

Click OK and reenter the password in the next window, as shown in Figure 3.7, and click Finish to complete the export of your Adobe AIR project into an Adobe AIR file.

You now have an Adobe AIR application ready to be installed. Simply navigate to the folder where you stored the files, double-click the new Adobe AIR file you've created, and follow the instructions to install your application!

Exploring the Application Startup Process

In this section we explore the application startup process, the functionality available to you at runtime, and user scenarios you may need to accommodate. First, let's examine how Adobe AIR applications get launched.

Your application can be launched (invoked) in a number of ways:

- Launch on user login

- Launch from the desktop

- Launch from the command line

- Launch by file-type association (User opens a file type associated with your Adobe AIR application.)

- By clicking an Adobe AIR application icon in the Dock or Windows Start menu

- Launch after the install of an Adobe AIR application

- Launch after auto-detect of an available application update

- Launch from a website

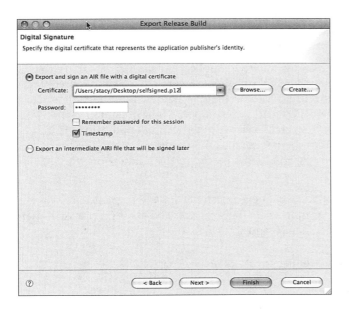

FIGURE 3.7   Finishing the export process.

Handling Application Invoke Events

Whenever an Adobe AIR application is invoked, whether it is the initial launch or when the application is already running, the NativeApplication object dispatches an InvokeEvent. The NativeApplication is a singleton object available in all Adobe AIR applications at runtime. This means we can add event listeners to this object to react to the InvokeEvent.

> **NOTE**
>
> If you run an Adobe AIR application from the browser, an `InvokeEvent` is only dispatched if the application isn't already running. This is not the case when the user attempts to launch the application again by opening the application in the dock or Start menu. Keep this in mind if you're relying on this event to execute critical startup logic routines.

To "hear" invoke events, you need to add an event listener to the `NativeApplication` instance. Any invoke events generated before the application has completed its initialization process are queued. When the application startup is complete and your event listener has registered itself, it will receive all invoke events that occurred prior the application being ready. It's also conceivable that a new invoke event is dispatched during the time the queued events are being processed and may "butt-in" and be fed to your event listener out of sequence. This typically isn't critical but good to know if you happen to have specific logic tied to the invocation of your application.

Application invocation does not necessarily equate to application startup. If you try to invoke an Adobe AIR application that is already running, a new invoke event is fired. It's the responsibility of the application to listen for and handle the new invoke event as desired. For example, the invoke event might be used to open a new document window in an Adobe AIR word processor or a new blank canvas in a drawing application. The event object carries a pertinent set of properties such as the residing directory of the Adobe AIR application in addition to any arguments passed to the application when it was invoked.

In Listing 3.2 we have an example of adding an event listener for the `InvokeEvent` that is registered when the application has completed its initialization and creation process—that is, instantiating all the objects for the display, and so on.

LISTING 3.2   Adding an Event Listener for the `InvokeEvent`

```
<?xml version="1.0" encoding="utf-8"?>
<mx:WindowedApplication
    xmlns:mx="http://www.adobe.com/2006/mxml"
    layout="vertical"
    verticalAlign="middle" horizontalAlign="center"
    creationComplete="init()">

    <mx:Script>
        <![CDATA[

        [Bindable]
        private var invokeArguments:Array = [];

        private function init():void
        {
```

```
      eventText.text += "init() \n";
      nativeApplication.addEventListener( InvokeEvent.INVOKE, onInvoke );
    }

    private function onInvoke( event:InvokeEvent ):void
    {
      eventText.text += "onInvoke( " + event.type + " ) \n";
      currentDir.text = event.currentDirectory.nativePath;
      argumentText.text += event.arguments.toString() + "\n";
    }

    ]]>
  </mx:Script>

  <mx:Label text="Current Directory:" />
  <mx:TextInput
    id="currentDir"
    width="80%" />
  <mx:Label text="Events Fired:" />
  <mx:TextArea
    id="eventText"
    width="80%"
    height="100"/>
  <mx:Label text="Event Arguments:" />
  <mx:TextArea
    id="argumentText"
    width="80%"
    height="100"/>
</mx:WindowedApplication>
```

NOTE

When multiple files are opened at the same time and are associated with an Adobe AIR application, the behavior differs between Windows and Mac OS X. On a Macintosh, your application receives a single `InvokeEvent` containing all the file references in `event.arguments`. On a Windows PC, an `InvokeEvent` is dispatched for each individual file with a reference to each respective file in `event.arguments`.

If you run this sample from within Adobe Flex Builder, you can see both the `init()` and `onInvoke()` functions being called (see Figure 3.8). If you export the sample to an Adobe AIR file and perform an install and then run the application, same result. Attempt to launch it a second time while the application is already running, and you will notice the `onInvoke()` trace log show up in the applications text field indicating it has fired.

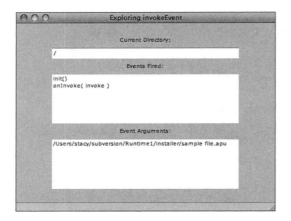

FIGURE 3.8   Sample application launched from a data file associated with the application.

> **TIP**
>
> Keep in mind that launching an Adobe AIR application from the Adobe Flex Builder 3
> debugger and ADL will quit any previously running instances and launch a new instance.
> To fully test `InvokeEvent` logic, package your application and install it as a user.

Launching on Login

You can set your Adobe AIR application to launch automatically when a user logs in. This
can be done by setting the following:

```
NativeApplication.nativeApplication.startAtLogin=true
```

The application continues to launch on login until the setting is changed to `false`. Take
note that this is not the same as launching on startup. Users have to actually log into
their machines for your Adobe AIR application to launch.

Launching Applications from the Command Line

Any command-line arguments specified when an Adobe AIR application is launched from
a command line are available in the arguments array inside `InvokeEvent`.

The arguments are whitespace-delimited strings unless enclosed in double quotation marks.

Launching from the Browser

A website can launch an Adobe AIR application. You can make this permissible using the
following:

```
<allowBrowserInvocation>true</allowBrowserInvocation>
```

NOTE

Be sure to consider the security factors when launching from a browser. Data can be sent via the `arguments` property of the `BrowserInvokeEvent` object, and you might not want to use this data in any sensitive operations.

Exploring the Application Shutdown Process

When a user attempts to shutdown your application, there are instances where you may want to interrupt the operation—perhaps prompt the user to save data or perform background tasks such as firing off a message to a server-side process or caching data locally in a database.

There are a number of ways an application can be closed:

- ▶ Last application window is closed. (`NativeApplication.nativeApplication.autoExit` must be set to `true`.)

- ▶ Select the Exit command from the File menu on Windows or the application menu on OS X.

- ▶ Computer shutdown.

- ▶ Programmatically from your application.

One approach would be to create a centralized callback function that handles all logic required for the shutdown process. Remember you might have multiple windows open performing all different sorts of operations and in different states. Blindly terminating the application may prove hazardous to the users data, even if it were the user that initiated the shutdown. Listing 3.3 provides a simplified example of listening for and reacting to events dispatched during shutdown.

Notice in the `init()` function we've added two listeners, one for an `EXITING` event and a second for the `CLOSING` event.

The `EXITING` event is fired from the `NativeApplication` when any of the shutdown actions previously listed are executed. The `EXITING` event is fired before the application is closed. This gives us the opportunity to catch the event and decide whether to proceed with the shutdown. In our example we're invoking a callback function called `onShutDown` that simply pops an alert window and asks the users to confirm that they'd like to close the application. Calling `preventDefault()` in the callback function stops the `EXITING` event and allows you to intervene. Selecting Yes or No in the alert dialog either closes the application or simply closes and returns the user to the application.

If your application has a number of active windows, you can provide centralized management in the same manner. You might want to cycle through the open windows and close them in a particular order after verifying each of their states—that is, unsaved data, and so on.

As for the second event listener for the CLOSING event, this is attached to the native window instance. If the user closes the last remaining window, the CLOSING event fires before the EXITING event. This is important to understand because if you're expecting to execute code before shutdown or include a confirmation dialog, your application will hang. The reason behind this is the last window will close and *then* dispatch an EXITING event. If the window is gone, there's no way for the user to interact with process such as confirming shutdown through a dialog. We've added a listener for the CLOSING event as well to account for this particular use case.

Every window instance fires its own CLOSING and CLOSE event. These events can be caught and handled within the context of each window, allowing each to operate independently. In your own global shutdown process, you might decide to simply cycle through all window instances and close each one by one. Then each window instance can handle its own preclosing logic (see Listing 3.3).

LISTING 3.3   Example of Interrupting an Application Exit Event

```
<?xml version="1.0" encoding="utf-8"?>
<mx:WindowedApplication
    xmlns:mx="http://www.adobe.com/2006/mxml"
    layout="vertical"
    title="Application Exit Example"
    creationComplete="init()">

    <mx:Script>
        <![CDATA[

        import mx.events.CloseEvent;
        import mx.controls.Alert;

        private function init():void
        {
            NativeApplication.nativeApplication.autoExit = true;
            NativeApplication.nativeApplication.addEventListener(
                Event.EXITING, onShutDown );
            nativeWindow.addEventListener( Event.CLOSING, onShutDown );
        }

        private function onShutDown( event:Event ):void
        {
            event.preventDefault();

            Alert.show( "Do you REALLY want to close this application?",
                "Wait! Don't go!", 3, null, onConfirmation );
```

```
      }

      private function onConfirmation( event:CloseEvent ):void
      {
         if( event.detail == Alert.YES )
            NativeApplication.nativeApplication.exit();
      }

      private function exitApplication():void
      {
         var event:Event = new Event( Event.EXITING, false, true );

         NativeApplication.nativeApplication.dispatchEvent( event );

         if( !event.isDefaultPrevented() )
         {
            NativeApplication.nativeApplication.exit();
         }
      }

   ]]>
   </mx:Script>
   <mx:Button label="Exit Application" click="exitApplication()" />
</mx:WindowedApplication>
```

When attempting to shut down an Adobe AIR application, you can call `exit()` on the `NativeApplication` object as follows:

```
NativeApplication.nativeApplication.exit();
```

Keep in mind that the user might have multiple native windows open at any given time (if your application supports such a scenario). When the exit command is executed, each window asks to close. As each window closes, both a `CLOSING` and `CLOSE` event is fired. If there are any event listeners on those events that interrupt the process via `preventDefault()`, the originating `exit()` call does not happen. This is good because it allows each window instance to establish whether it's safe to close down in its current state.

Reading Application Settings

Each Adobe AIR project has an application descriptor file. In Adobe Flex Builder, this is generated for you automatically when a new project is created. The file is located in the root source folder and is named after the default document in the project. For instance, if the default MXML is called `main.mxml`, the generated descriptor file is called `main-app.xml`.

The role of the descriptor is to provide publishing information, default native window parameters, and file associations—among other things for the compiler and the Adobe AIR runtime. The descriptor XML is accessible at runtime as a property of `nativeApplication` called applicationDescriptor. Our sample code in Listing 3.4 demonstrates how to access these properties via script. You can see the results at runtime in Figure 3.9.

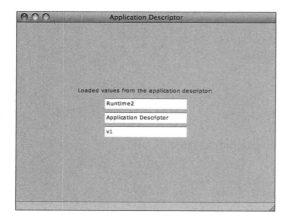

FIGURE 3.9   Reading descriptor properties at runtime.

LISTING 3.4   Reading Elements of the Application Descriptor

```
<?xml version="1.0" encoding="utf-8"?>
<mx:WindowedApplication
    xmlns:mx="http://www.adobe.com/2006/mxml"
    layout="vertical"
    verticalAlign="middle"
    horizontalAlign="center"
    creationComplete="init()">

    <mx:Script>
        <![CDATA[

        private function init():void
        {
            var descriptor:XML = nativeApplication.applicationDescriptor;
            var ns:Namespace = descriptor.namespace();

            filename.text = descriptor.ns::filename[0];
            appName.text = descriptor.ns::name[0];
            version.text = descriptor.ns::version[0];
        }

        ]]>
    </mx:Script>

    <mx:Label text="Loaded values from the application descriptor:" />
```

```
    <mx:TextInput id="filename" />
    <mx:TextInput id="appName" />
    <mx:TextInput id="version" />
</mx:WindowedApplication>
```

Establishing File Associations

This might be a small feature, but it's definitely one of my favorites: file associations. Having a dedicated Dock icon or shortcut on the desktop is cool, but being able to claim file extensions for your Adobe AIR application's own use is really cool. The idea is simple enough: Upon installation of your application, you can specify file extensions that should be linked to your application. This does a couple of things for you. First, your application can be launched when one of these files is opened, just as a file with the extension .xls launches MS Excel. Second, you can specify your own icons for these file extensions. Consider that free advertising!

File associations between your file type and your Adobe AIR application are declared in the descriptor file available in the source root of your project. The Adobe AIR installer associates the application as the default opening application for the declared file types during the installation process.

These associations can also be managed at runtime from your application. This might come in handy because existing file-type associations are not overridden during the installation process. To do that, you have to call the following method from your application:

```
NativeApplication.setAsDefaultApplication("db");
```

This creates an association between your application and all files with the extension .db on the file system—for example, foo.db (see Figure 3.10).

One thing to keep in mind is whatever extension you plan on specifying must be indicated in your applications descriptor file. Otherwise the setAsDefaultApplication() function throws an exception. Listing 3.5 is a snippet from a descriptor file.

LISTING 3.5   Specifying Associated File Types in the Application Descriptor

```
<!-- Listing of file types for which the application can register. Optional. -->
<fileTypes>
   <!-- Defines one file type. Optional. -->
   <fileType>
      <!-- The name that the system displays for the registered file type.
Required. -->
      <name>MyAIRFile</name>
      <!-- The extension to register. Required. -->
      <extension>myair</extension>
      <!-- The description of the file type. Optional. -->
      <description>My AIR File</description>
      <!-- The MIME type. Optional. -->
      <contentType></contentType>
```

```
    <!-- The icon to display for the file type. Optional. -->
    <icon>
        <image16x16></image16x16>
        <image32x32></image32x32>
        <image48x48></image48x48>
        <image128x128></image128x128>
    </icon>
  </fileType>
</fileTypes>
```

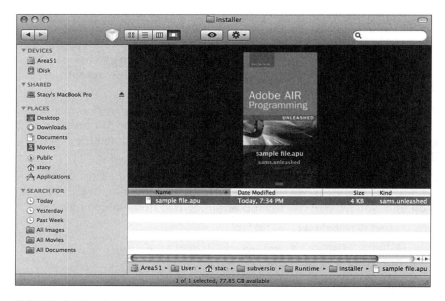

FIGURE 3.10   A file with an extension associated with our sample project.

Table 3.1 outlines available functions related to the management of file associations.

TABLE 3.1   Managing File Associations in Adobe AIR

Method	Description
isSetAsDefaultApplication()	Returns true if the Adobe AIR application is associated with the provided file type
setAsDefaultApplication()	Establishes an association between the Adobe AIR application and files with the provided file type
removeAsDefaultApplication()	Removes the association between the Adobe AIR application and the provided file type
getDefaultApplication()	Returns the path of the application that is currently associated with the provided file type

Detecting User Presence

Sometimes your application might need to take action based on whether users are present/idle at their computer. One use case might be a security requirement. If an application deals with sensitive information, it might be required that an application reverts to a login screen if the user has been idle (that is, no keyboard or mouse interaction) for a given amount of time.

Good news: This functionality is available right out of the box. There are three elements to this equation, all of which stem from `NativeApplication`:

- ▶ Set the idle time via `idleThreshold`.

- ▶ Add an event listener for `USER_IDLE`.

- ▶ Add an event listener for `USER_PRESENT`.

Listing 3.6 shows a simplified example. The `idleThreshold` is the time in seconds that the `nativeApplication` object will wait before dispatching an event signifying the user is idle. The second event listener executes its own callback function when user activity is detected.

LISTING 3.6   Detecting User Presence

```xml
<?xml version="1.0" encoding="utf-8"?>
<mx:WindowedApplication
    xmlns:mx="http://www.adobe.com/2006/mxml"
    layout="vertical"
    horizontalAlign="center"
    title="Detecting User Presence"
    creationComplete="init()">

    <mx:Script>
        <![CDATA[

        import mx.controls.Alert;

        private function init():void
        {
            NativeApplication.nativeApplication.idleThreshold = 10;
            NativeApplication.nativeApplication.addEventListener(
                Event.USER_IDLE, onUserIdle );
            NativeApplication.nativeApplication.addEventListener(
                Event.USER_PRESENT, onUserPresent );
        }

        private function onUserIdle( event:Event ):void
```

```
      {
         message.text = "You have been idle for 10 seconds.";
      }

      private function onUserPresent( event:Event ):void
      {
         message.text = "";
         Alert.show( "Welcome back!", "User Presence Detected" );
      }


      ]]>
   </mx:Script>
   <mx:Label id="message" />
</mx:WindowedApplication>
```

Retrieving Version and Patch Information

If you need to determine version and patch level information about the Adobe AIR platform currently installed on the user's machine, both elements are available as properties of
`nativeApplication` (see Listing 3.7). This can be accessed via a singleton object called
`NativeApplication`, which is instantiated automatically at runtime.

Although sometimes confusing, `NativeApplication` and `nativeApplication` are not the
same. `NativeApplication` is a singleton class used to obtain a reference to the native application instance itself via a property called `nativeApplication`. In most cases you would use

```
NativeApplication.nativeApplication.runtimeVersion;
```

If you are scripting directly within the `WindowedApplication` tag, then you can alternatively reference the native application instance directly, like so:

```
nativeApplication.runtimeVersion;
```

LISTING 3.7   Determining Version and Patch Level of the Runtime Environment

```
<?xml version="1.0" encoding="utf-8"?>
<mx:WindowedApplication
   xmlns:mx="http://www.adobe.com/2006/mxml"
   layout="absolute"
   creationComplete="init()">

   <mx:Script>
     <![CDATA[

     private function init():void
     {
        trace( "Runtime Version: " +
```

```
            NativeApplication.nativeApplication.runtimeVersion );
         trace( "Runtime Patch Level: " +
            NativeApplication.nativeApplication.runtimePatchLevel );
      }

      ]]>
   </mx:Script>
</mx:WindowedApplication>
```

Summary

In this chapter, we covered the anatomy of an Adobe AIR application—from creating a simple Hello World example to investigating some of the bits and pieces that differentiate Adobe AIR applications from their web-based cousins. Going forward, we'll build on this base.

Debugging Adobe AIR Applications

Debugging Adobe® AIR™ applications written in Adobe® Flex™ includes multiple approaches that range from the simple to the more complex. For example, simply using the Flex `Alert` class to pop up some debugging text or the `trace()` command are two simple types of debugging techniques:

```
mx.controls.Alert.show('Hey I made it here with no
➡problem.');
trace('Hey I made it here too - again with no
➡problem.');
```

As you can see, alerts and traces are limited to their application and usefulness. A stepwise, from code line to code line, more complex debugging can be performed with a debugger. The Adobe Flex Builder debugger and the command-line debugger, `fdb`, enable you to step through and debug the code used by your Flex-based AIR applications. Just as you might suspect, this debugger requires that you code your AIR application with Flex. For Adobe AIR applications built with HTML/JavaScript/AJAX, Adobe® Flash® CS3, Adobe Dreamweaver CS3, the Adobe AIR Debug Launcher (ADL) is a command-line debugger that you can use to debug these applications. You can also use the ADL to debug Flex-based applications if you do not have a license for Flex Builder or simply enjoy the command line. There is also the Adobe AIR HTML Introspector that can be used to debug your HTML or AJAX-based applications. Third-party tools or the Adobe Flex-based `<mx:TraceTarget/>` tag can be invaluable when analysis of network traffic between your Adobe AIR application and a server-side or data-related connection has issues. In this chapter you learn how to use these debugging tools to solve development bugs before they become live bugs in a deployed application.

Using the Adobe Flex Builder Debugger

Adobe Flex Builder provides full debugging support for Adobe AIR applications. To begin a debug session in Adobe Flex Builder, complete the following steps:

1. Open the source file for the Flex-based AIR application (such as an Extensible Markup Language [MXML] file) in Adobe Flex Builder.

2. Set one or more breakpoints by double-clicking in the left gutter (left side of the line numbers of the source code) while viewing the source code.

3. Click the Debug button on the main toolbar (see Figure 4.1). Switch to the Adobe Flex Debugging Perspective when prompted.

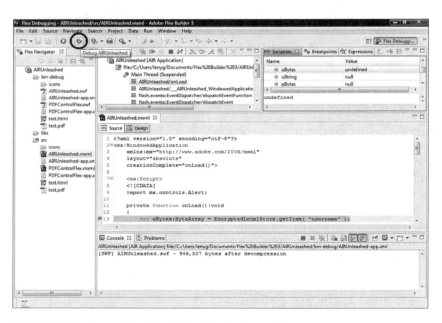

FIGURE 4.1   Launching the Adobe Flex Builder debugger.

4. Examine the Variables, Breakpoints, and Expressions sections of the resulting debug session (see Figure 4.2).

   You can also select Run, Debug.

The application launches and runs in the Adobe Flex Builder debugger, catching any breakpoints or runtime errors. You can debug the Adobe AIR application like any other Adobe Flex application by stepping into code, stepping over code, monitoring variables, or monitoring watches in Flex Builder.

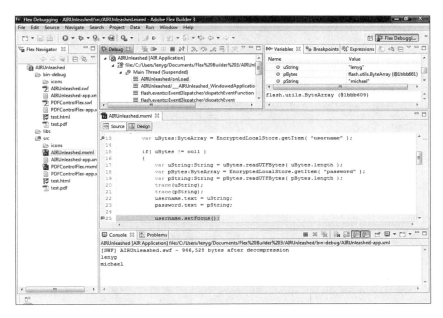

FIGURE 4.2   Viewing the variables of a debug session.

Figure 4.2 displays the variables, uString and pString, and because the breakpoint is past the code that sets these values, the variables are displayed—in this case, lenyg and michael, respectively. Also note that the trace results are displayed in the console window.

The Adobe Flex Builder debugger is a very powerful tool. The Adobe Flex Debugging Perspective provides all the debugging tools you would expect from a robust, full-featured development debugging tool. The debugging tools allow you to do the following:

▶ Set and manage breakpoints

▶ Step into and over code

▶ Watch variables

▶ Evaluate expressions (see Figure 4.3)

Figure 4.3 displays the expressions, uString and pString, and because the breakpoint is past the code that sets these values, the expressions are displayed—in this case, lenyg and michael, respectively. Also note that the trace results are again displayed in the console window.

Further information about the Adobe Flex Builder debugger can be found at the following site:

http://livedocs.adobe.com/flex/3/html/compile_debug_1.html

Free videos about debugging with Adobe Flex Builder are also available from Lynda.com:

http://movielibrary.lynda.com/html/modPage.asp?ID=290

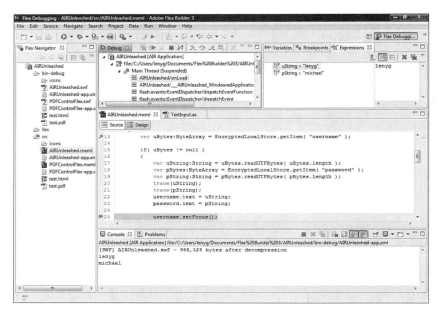

FIGURE 4.3   Example of watching expressions.

NOTE

Another MXML tag that might prove very useful is the `<mx:TraceTarget/>` tag. This tag can be placed anywhere in the Adobe Flex code; during debugging, it displays network traffic (flash-remoting type) data in the console window.

Using the Adobe AIR Debug Launcher (ADL) to Debug

If you do not use Adobe Flex Builder or your Adobe AIR applications are not Flex-based, you can use the Adobe AIR Debug Launcher (ADL). With the ADL, you can run either Adobe Flex-based or HTML-based applications during development. Keep in mind that you can perform only a certain amount of debugging with the ADL. Additionally, using the ADL, you can run an application without first packaging and installing it, saving you some time and effort during the development phase of your project.

NOTE

By default, the ADL uses the Adobe AIR runtime included with the AIR software development kit (AIR SDK) and with the Flex 3.0 SDK, which means you do not need to install the Adobe AIR runtime separately.

You should note that the ADL can print trace statements and runtime errors to the standard output log or console, but it does not support breakpoints or other debugging features. If you're developing an Adobe Flex-based application, you should use the Adobe Flash debugger (or the Adobe Flex Builder debugger) for complex debugging issues.

To launch an application with the ADL (for more information, go to http://livedocs.adobe.com/flex/3/html/CommandLineTools_4.html#1033678); use the following syntax from a command prompt (adl plus the Adobe AIR XML Descriptor file's name—include the file extension in the name):

```
adl myApp-app.xml
```

CAUTION

During the running of the ADL, if you see this warning/error in the command prompt

```
"initial content not found"
```

the initial content is specified in myApp-app.xml.

If you are using the myApp-app.xml file in the Adobe Flex src directory, the file content is not actually specified—instead, you will see <content>[This value will be overwritten by Flex Builder in the output app.xml]</content>

In this case, run the ADL for the myApp-app.xml file that Flex Builder autogenerates in the bin-debug directory—it has the correct value:

```
<content>AIRUnleashed.swf</content>
```

Optional ADL syntax includes that shown here and in Table 4.1:

```
adl [-runtime dir] [-pubid pub id] [-nodebug] Descriptor.xml [root-dir [-- arguments]
```

TABLE 4.1   ADL Optional Syntax

Option	Description
-runtime [dir]	The directory (specify the file system path) to use for launching the Adobe AIR runtime. If not specified, the default location of the runtime is used—either AIR SDK's or Flex 3 SDK's AIR runtime, depending on which of the ADLs you use.
-pubid [pub id]	Specifies a publisher ID for the Adobe AIR application for testing purposes.
-nodebug	Turns off debugging.
Descriptor.xml	XML-based Descriptor file for the Adobe AIR application. You can specify the file system path to this file.
root-dir	Root directory of the Adobe AIR application to run. You can specify the file system path to this directory.
— arguments	Passes any strings after the – as command-line arguments.

For more information about ADL syntax, refer to the documentation at http://livedocs.adobe.com/flex/3/html/CommandLineTools_4.html#1031951.

Figure 4.4 depicts the results of running the ADL for the Adobe Flex-based Adobe AIR application discussed in this chapter. Also note that the trace results are again displayed in the command window (in this case, lenyg and michael).

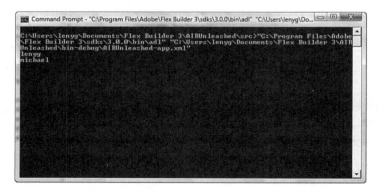

FIGURE 4.4   Running an Adobe AIR application with the ADL.

ADL error and exit codes can be reviewed here: http://livedocs.adobe.com/flex/3/html/ CommandLineTools_4.html#1041429.

Using the Adobe Flash Debugger (FDB) to Debug

To debug an Adobe Flex-based Adobe AIR application with the Adobe Flash debugger, follow these steps:

1. Start the FDB. The FDB program is located in the bin directory of the Flex SDK folder. The console displays the FDB prompt: <fdb>

2. Execute the Run command <fdb>**run** and press Enter.

3. In a different command or shell console, start your Adobe AIR application with the ADL:

    ```
    adl myApp-debug.xml
    ```

4. Using the FDB commands, set breakpoints as desired.

5. Type **continue** and press Enter.

Figure 4.5 depicts the results of running the FDB and the ADL for the Adobe Flex-based Adobe AIR application discussed in this chapter. Note that the trace results are again displayed in the FDB command window (in this case, lenyg and michael).

Using Third-Party Tools to Debug

Third-party tools, such as ServiceCapture, Charles, and Ethereal/Wireshark, allow the developer to capture the network traffic (flash-remoting) or data flow between the Adobe AIR application and any server-side infrastructure.

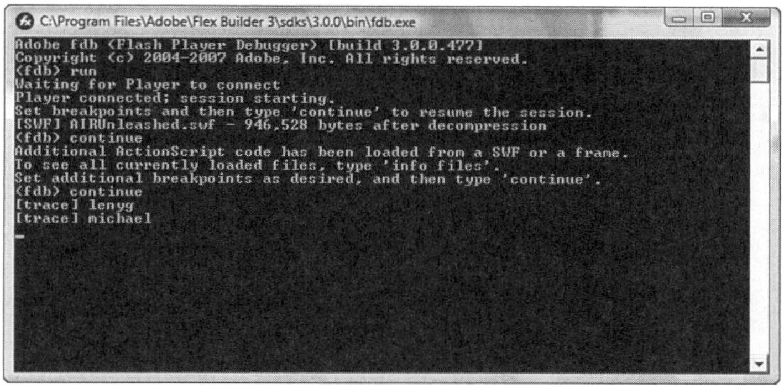

FIGURE 4.5   Running an Adobe AIR application with the FDB and the ADL.

NOTE

Flash-remoting provides a communication connection for data transfer between a Flash swf and a web application server. Flash-remoting is available for Adobe ColdFusion, .NET, and PHP server-side technologies (natively for ColdFusion).

Additionally, for an Adobe Flex-based Adobe AIR application, the <mx:TraceTarget/> tag can be placed anywhere in the Adobe Flex code, and during debugging, the network traffic (flash-remoting type) data will be displayed in the console window. These tools can be invaluable when you get stuck in a corner trying to figure out why your data seems to be missing. Syntax case-sensitivity issues are readily solved with this sort of debugging. In Figure 4.6, the data transferred between an Adobe AIR application and a ColdFusion server is shown using ServiceCapture.

Debugging with the Adobe AIR HTML Introspector

To develop HTML or AJAX-based Adobe AIR applications, you can use the Adobe AIR Extension for Dreamweaver, the Adobe AIR SDK command-line tools, or other Web development tools that support Adobe AIR. Debugging HTML or AJAX-based Adobe AIR applications presents a different sort of debug requirements. Fortunately, the Adobe AIR SDK includes an AIRIntrospector.js JavaScript file (called the Adobe AIR HTML Introspector) that you can include in your application to help debug HTML-based or AJAX-based Adobe AIR applications. The Adobe AIR HTML Introspector includes the following features:

▶ A tool that allows the developer to point to user-interface elements in an application and see its markup and DOM properties.

▶ A console for sending objects' references for introspection. You can adjust property values, execute JavaScript code, and serialize objects to the console, which limits you from editing the data. You can also copy and save text from the console.

▶ A tree-based view for DOM properties and functions.

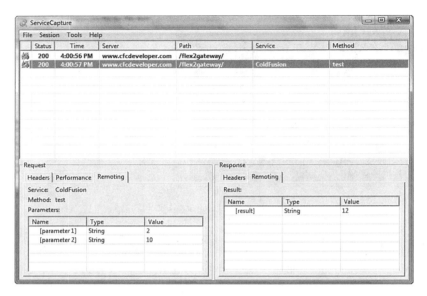

FIGURE 4.6   Adobe AIR and ServiceCapture.

▶ An edit capability for the attributes and text nodes of the DOM elements.

▶ A list of links, CSS styles, images, and JavaScript files loaded in your application.

▶ A view of the initial HTML source and the current markup source for the user interface.

▶ A view of the files in the application directory. (This feature is only available for the Adobe AIR HTML Introspector console opened in the application sandbox and is not available for consoles open for nonapplication sandbox content.)

▶ A viewer for XMLHttpRequest objects and their properties, including responseText and responseXML properties (when available).

▶ A way to search for matching text in the source code and files.

To leverage the Adobe AIR HTML Introspector, you should copy the AIRIntrospector.js file to the application's project directory and include the following code in the HTML main application file:

```
<script type="text/javascript" src="AIRIntrospector.js"></script>
```

NOTE

The AIRIntrospector.js file is included in the frameworks directory of the Adobe AIR SDK.

CAUTION

Include the `AIRIntrospector.js` file only when developing and debugging the application. Remove it in the packaged Adobe AIR application that you distribute.

You should also include the `AIRIntrospector.js` file in every HTML file that corresponds to a different native window in your application.

The `AIRIntrospector.js` file defines a class, `Console`, which you can access from JavaScript code by calling `air.Introspector.Console`. The `Console` class includes five methods: `log()`, `warn()`, `info()`, `error()`, and `dump()`. The `log()`, `warn()`, `info()`, and `error()` methods all let you send an object to the Console tab. The most basic of these methods is the `log()` method. Listing 4.1 shows a sample HTML-based application that includes the `AIRIntrospector.js` reference and a call to the log method. Running this application with the ADL reveals the application shown in Figure 4.7. Figure 4.8 shows another view within the console.

FIGURE 4.7   Adobe AIR HTML Introspector (HTML-view).

LISTING 4.1   HTML-Based Adobe AIR Application

```
<html>
    <head>
        <title>Source Viewer Sample</title>
        <script type="text/javascript" src="AIRIntrospector.js"></script>
```

```
    <script type="text/javascript">
        function logBtn()
        {
            var button1 = document.getElementById("btn1");
            air.Introspector.Console.log(button1);
        }
    </script>
</head>
<body>
    <p>Click to view the button object in the Console.</p>
    <input type="button" id="btn1"
        onclick="logBtn()"
        value="Log" />
</body>
</html>
```

FIGURE 4.8   Adobe AIR HTML Introspector (source-view).

The info(), error(), and warn() methods are similar to the log() method but simply provide different types of information.

To configure the Adobe AIR HTML Introspector, see the details at http://livedocs.adobe. com/air/1/devappshtml/AIR_Introspector_1.html#1050347. To utilize the Adobe AIR HTML Introspector with content in a nonapplication sandbox, review the following information: http://livedocs.adobe.com/air/1/devappshtml/AIR_Introspector_1.html#1051966.

The Adobe AIR HTML Introspector is a valuable tool to add to your tool belt for debugging your HTML or AJAX-based Adobe AIR applications. You might also want to look at a third-party tool, Aptana Studio, which is a free, open source Ajax development environment that offers features such as JavaScript debugging, full HTML/CSS/JS content assist, FTP support, and integrated samples.

Debugging Content Loaded into the HTML Control

The Adobe AIR HTML control is very easy to integrate into your application. It can be used to simply load in an external HTML file or URL by the location attribute as follows:

```
<?xml version="1.0" encoding="utf-8"?>
<mx:WindowedApplication xmlns:mx="http://www.adobe.com/2006/mxml"
➡layout="absolute">
    <mx:HTML location="http://www.google.com"/>
</mx:WindowedApplication>
```

But what happens if the URL is unavailable? How does the developer debug this control? Look at the following code with an obvious location problem:

```
<?xml version="1.0" encoding="utf-8"?>
<mx:WindowedApplication xmlns:mx="http://www.adobe.com/2006/mxml"
➡creationComplete="init()"
    layout="absolute">
    <mx:Script>
        <![CDATA[
            private function init():void {
                htmlControl.location = "http://www.google2.com";
            }
        ]]>
    </mx:Script>
    <mx:HTML id="htmlControl"/>
</mx:WindowedApplication>
```

Running this Adobe AIR application loads a blank application as the location URL is invalid. By running the code in the Adobe Flex Builder debugger, you can see the offending URL in the location property of the HTML control (see Figure 4.9).

Although not as intuitive as many errors or issues identified with the debugger, there is still value in seeing the information that the debugger provides. The trace() function and Alert class are available for a bit more help.

Performance and Memory Profiling

Although this topic might seem different from the debugging one discussed so far, a poorly performing, memory-leaking Adobe AIR application could arguably be said to contain one or more bugs. Performance and memory profiling for Adobe Flex-based Adobe AIR applications might prove useful if you are seeing these sorts of issues in your applications. The Adobe Flex Builder Profiler is an important feature for fully optimizing your Adobe Flex or Adobe AIR applications and should be added to your routine of predeployment checks. The Profiler can help you identify performance bottlenecks and memory leaks in your applications. The Profiler records data about the state of the application, including the number of objects, the size of those objects, the number of method calls,

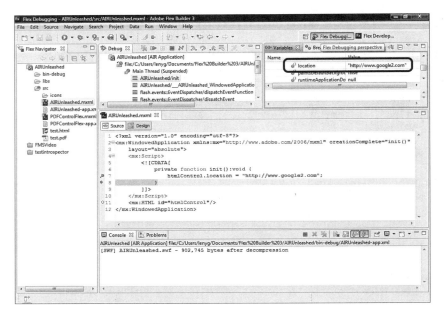

FIGURE 4.9   HTML control location property.

and the time spent in those method calls. Profiling an application can help you understand the following about your application: *call frequency, method duration, call stacks,
number of instances (object allocation), object size, and garbage collection.* To get started with
profiling, look for the Profiler button in the Adobe Flex Builder Development Perspective's
toolbar, as shown in the top left of Figure 4.10 (just to the right of the Debug button).
Figure 4.10 also shows the location of the Profiler output—the console is found in the
lower portion of the figure.

Clicking on the Profiler button should launch the application using the default browser.
You can configure profiling to use Microsoft Internet Explorer, Firefox, or the standalone
Flash Player. After launching, the Profiler pauses the application. Then the Profiler displays
a Configure the Profiler Agent dialog similar to that shown in Figure 4.11.

In the configuration dialog are four check box choices. The first, Enable Memory Profiling,
causes the Profiler Agent to collect information each time an object is created and garbage
collected. This information is useful when trying to find potential memory leaks and
when trying to find excessive object creation. As part of the first check box, the second
and the third ones are dependent on it being selected. The second check box, Watch Live
Memory Data, instructs Adobe Flex Builder to display the Live Objects panel. This panel
shows what classes have been instantiated, how many have been created, how many are
in the heap, how much memory they have taken up, and how much memory the active
objects are taking up. The third check box, Generate Object Allocation Stack Traces, causes

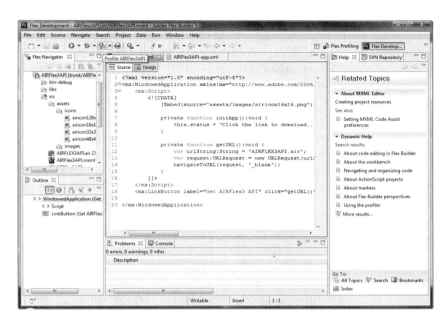

FIGURE 4.10   Profiler button.

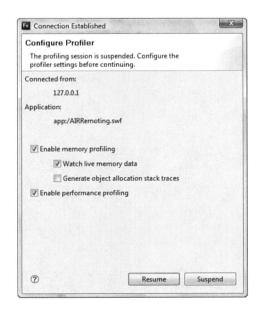

FIGURE 4.11   Configure the Profiler Agent dialog.

a stack trace to be captured each time a new object is created. This can cause profiling to run slower and use more memory, so it is recommended to use it only as needed. The last check box, Enable Performance Profiling, causes the Profiler to collect a sample, essentially a stack trace, at regular intervals. These samples can be used to determine where the bulk of the execution time in your application is spent. Sampling allows you to profile without noticeably slowing down the application. Profiling data can be saved and reloaded for later evaluation.

It is important to remember that profiling is not simply a single, discrete step in the process of developing an application. Profiling should be a routine step during application development. In fact, if possible, you should profile an application often during the application development phase so that you can quickly identify problem areas. Profiling is an iterative process, so you can gain the most benefit by profiling as often as possible.

Summary

Debugging Adobe AIR applications can be a bit tricky at times, but you now have a full arsenal of tools available. By leveraging the robust Adobe Flex Builder debugger, the Adobe AIR HTML Introspector, the minimalist approach of the ADL, or the FBD, or by leveraging the Adobe Flex Builder Profiler, as well as third-party tools such as ServiceCapture or the Adobe Flex-based `<mx:TraceTarget/>` tag, debugging can be a trivial issue.

PART II

Building Adobe AIR Applications

IN THIS PART

CHAPTER 5

Working with **Window**s

Creating windows in Adobe® AIR™ applications is a signifi-cant departure from traditional webcentric Adobe® Flex™ development. For starters, Adobe AIR applications run on the user's desktop. So the "windows" we're referring to originate from the underlying native operating system, as with any other desktop software. Web developers no longer need to rely on Adobe Flex TitleWindow, JavaScript pop-ups, or browser windows propped up as a poor substitute for the real thing.

Implementing any kind of windowlike container in Adobe Flex today serves as a reminder of the limitations imposed on the user experience by the browser environment. At first glance, a TitleWindow resembles the idiom of a "windowed interface," but users soon discover their artificial nature. They cannot be minimized to the taskbar or dragged to a secondary screen as with native windows.

For Adobe Flex Beginners

A TitleWindow is a layout container in the Adobe Flex framework (mx.containers.TitleWindow). It's most often used as a pop-up container. Although it can be moved independent of the underlying Adobe Flex appli-cation, its movement is limited to the confines of the browser window.

Another option in achieving a multiwindow interface is to launch additional browser windows. There is no arguing the fact that this approach *does* deliver native windows, but this approach brings about a new set of challenges.

First, browser pop-up windows offer limited control over their appearance and behavior. Second, and more important, there is a high cost in complexity when loading and communicating with content hosted in this context. In the case of Adobe Flex applications, we're talking about a Shockwave Flash (SWF) file compiled from MXML, hosted in a single browser window. Any additional Flash or Hypertext Markup Language (HTML) content loaded in a browser pop-up does not exist as part of your Adobe Flex application. Any communication between the two needs to be brokered by other means—either by maintaining a LocalConnection or by writing a whack of JavaScript code!

Windows in Adobe AIR

Coding my first `Window` examples in Adobe AIR gave me a warm and fuzzy feeling. Sure, they look and behave like native windows, but the real benefit resides in the application framework itself. All windows of an Adobe AIR application exist in the same context.

For example, picture a main application window designed as a drawing canvas with a second, smaller window off to the side as a floating tool palette. For the drawing canvas to "hear" and react to button click events in the tool palette, such as the user selecting a new drawing tool, an event listener can be added on the tool palette directly from the main canvas.

This is made possible in Adobe AIR by having all windows tied to our application available as an `Array` in an application scope.

```
var arrayOfOpenWindows:Array = NativeApplication.openedWindows;
```

In this chapter, we look at different methods of window creation and where they're applicable in an Adobe AIR application. In addition, we look at moving beyond the default system chrome and investigate what's involved in creating custom window chrome.

Let's start with three window classes available to us in Adobe AIR:

- ▶ **`flash.display.NativeWindow`**—The lowest common denominator in terms of windows in Adobe AIR. Content such as SWFs, images, and HTML can be added to them, whereas other window types wrap this base functionality and offer extended behavior.

- ▶ **`mx.core.WindowedApplication`**—An application container used to house Adobe Flex applications and deliver desktop functionality. This type can only serve as the root window of an application and is configured via the `application.xml` file.

- ▶ **`mx.core.Window`**—Also a container for housing Adobe Flex content but can be instantiated any number of times. Adobe Flex developers will rely on this type most of the time.

Creating Windows Using `NativeWindow`

`NativeWindow` can be used to host an array of content such as HTML, Adobe® Flash® SWF files, or images. It is not, however, intended for use with Adobe Flex components directly. Instead, please refer to "Creating Windows Using `mx.core.Window`" later in this chapter.

A special type of `NativeWindow`, `HTMLLoader.createRootContent()`, exists specifically for hosting HTML content. It includes the necessary machinery for loading HTML as well as support for scrolling content.

For now let's start with the basics. Here's how to go about creating and configuring a NativeWindow:

▶ Create and configure `NativeWindowInitOptions`.

▶ Create an instance of `NativeWindow`, passing in `NativeWindowInitOptions`.

▶ Open the Window onscreen.

Listing 5.1 outlines these steps in ActionScript code. If you have downloaded the source code for this book, then you will find the correlating project in your FlexBuilder called "Chapter05-01".

LISTING 5.1   Creating a `NativeWindow`

```
<?xml version="1.0" encoding="utf-8"?>
<mx:WindowedApplication
      xmlns:mx="http://www.adobe.com/2006/mxml"
      layout="vertical"
      verticalAlign="middle" horizontalAlign="center">

      <mx:Script>
       <![CDATA[

      private function openWindow():void
      {
              var windowOptions:NativeWindowInitOptions = new
➡NativeWindowInitOptions();
              windowOptions.systemChrome = NativeWindowSystemChrome.STANDARD;
              windowOptions.type = NativeWindowType.NORMAL;

              var newWindow:NativeWindow = new NativeWindow( windowOptions );
              newWindow.activate();
      }

      ]]>
      </mx:Script>

      <mx:Button label="Create Window" click="openWindow()" />

</mx:WindowedApplication>
```

Setting `NativeWindowInitOptions`

NativeWindow initialization options, `NativeWindowInitOptions`, describe the look and behavior of your window. Once set, these parameters are passed into the constructor when instantiating the `NativeWindow` instance. These options are not mandatory because they all have default values. For instance, not passing in `NativeWindowInitOptions` gives you a standard-looking window for your operating system with standard window controls. As we progress through this chapter, we explore how we can change this default behavior—but keep in mind that after the window is created, these options cannot be changed! Table 5.1 outlines the configurable options.

Let's explore what each of these `NativeWindowInitOptions` are and how they affect the characteristics of a new native window. First up is the `systemChrome`. The chrome is what frames the content of a native window.

TABLE 5.1   Properties of **NativeWindowInitOptions**

Property	Description
systemChrome	Specifies the type of system chrome used by the window
type	Specifies the type of the window to be created
maximizable	Specifies whether the window can be maximized
minimizable	Specifies whether the window can be minimized
resizable	Specifies whether the window can be resized
transparent	Specifies whether the window supports transparency and alpha blending against the desktop

NativeWindowInitOptions.systemChrome

The frame that encompasses a window is referred to as the chrome. The chrome typically offers controls to manipulate the window, such as minimize, drag, resize, and close.

There are three options for `systemChrome`, as shown in the following sections.

NativeWindowSystemChrome.STANDARD   This option creates a standard-looking native window as per the operating system the Adobe AIR application is running on (see Figure 5.1). Also, the `transparent` property of the window must be set to `false` (which is the default value). The following snippet demonstrates how to set the `systemChrome` to standard, which is also the default value if none is specified.

```
var windowOptions:NativeWindowInitOptions = new NativeWindowInitOptions();
windowOptions.systemChrome = NativeWindowSystemChrome.STANDARD;
```

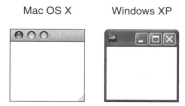

Mac OS X   Windows XP

FIGURE 5.1   Standard system chrome on Mac OS X and Windows XP.

> **NOTE**
>
> The standard chrome is managed by the operating system, and your application has no direct access to the controls themselves. You can, however, react to the events that are dispatched as a result of the user interacting with these controls. (See "Understanding Window Events" later in this chapter.)

NativeWindowSystemChrome.NONE   This option specifies that the window should not display any system chrome whatsoever. Creating a `NativeWindow` with no chrome generates a rectangle onscreen with no controls. This is the starting point for implementing custom chrome discussed later in this chapter. The following demonstrates how to specify no system chrome:

```
var windowOptions:NativeWindowInitOptions = new NativeWindowInitOptions();
windowOptions.systemChrome = NativeWindowSystemChrome.NONE;
```

NativeWindowInitOptions.type

Each window offers unique traits suited for different roles in an application. There are three `NativeWindowTypes` to choose from:

- ▶ NORMAL
- ▶ UTILITY
- ▶ LIGHTWEIGHT

NativeWindowType.NORMAL   This is the default window type. If nothing is specified for this parameter in your `NativeWindowInitOptions`, Figure 5.2 shows what is displayed.

Mac OS X   Windows XP

FIGURE 5.2   Default window type on Mac OS X and Windows XP.

NORMAL windows have typical controls such as minimize, maximize, and close. Their physical characteristics match that of any standard window on each respective operating system.

NativeWindowType.UTILITY   In Figure 5.3, you see the same system chrome but differences in both physical and behavioral aspects of NativeWindow.

Mac OS X   Windows XP

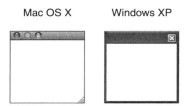

FIGURE 5.3   **UTILITY** windows have a slimmer title bar, and they don't show up in the Windows taskbar or the Mac OS X Dock (note the lack of a Minimize icon).

Often used as containers for supporting content or tool palettes, these windows do not serve as the primary focus of an application. Their content may change as events happen in the main application window, such as displaying properties of an object that has received focus.

> **NOTE**
>
> There are applications that utilize this window type as its primary user interface. These are typically smaller, more specialized applications such as instant messaging or media players. There isn't a need to crowd the user's Dock or taskbar with an application running in the background most of the time.

NativeWindowType.LIGHTWEIGHT   LIGHTWEIGHT NativeWindows have no chrome whatsoever. In fact, you'll get a runtime error unless you specifically set the systemChrome property to NONE. Creating a window in this fashion gives you a white box that can't be moved or even closed directly. Figure 5.4 demonstrates a native window with no chrome and uses a bitmap image as the window's background.

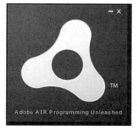

Mac OSX   Windows XP

FIGURE 5.4   An Adobe AIR application implemented with custom window chrome.

Uses for LIGHTWEIGHT NativeWindows range from custom system chrome implementations to toast messages (dialogs that temporarily slide up onscreen like toast out of a toaster) to drawer dialogs common on Mac OS X.

NativeWindowInitOptions.transparent
This property refers to the transparency of the window background window. A transparent window has no default background. Any area not occupied by a display object is invisible; for example, whatever lies beneath your application window shows through.

You can also change the alpha property of your display objects to allow underlying desktop content to show through.

CAUTION

Display objects with an alpha setting of less than .06 (approximately) prevent the window from capturing mouse events in that area. It will appear as though you have clicked the object *behind* the window.

NOTE

You cannot create transparent windows in combination with any system chrome.

NativeWindowInitOptions.maximizable
When this property is set to false, the window cannot be maximized. For a window with system chrome, this affects the appearance of the window Maximize button, such as making it appear disabled.

NOTE

On Mac OS X, you'll have to set both the maximizable *and* resizable options to false to prevent the window from being zoomed or resized.

NativeWindowInitOptions.minimizable
When this property is set to false, the window cannot be minimized. As with a window with system chrome, this affects the appearance of the window Minimize button.

NativeWindowInitOptions.resizable
When this property is set to false, the window cannot be resized.

NOTE

As with the NativeWindowInitOptions.maximizable property, on Mac OS X, you'll have to set both the maximizable and resizable options to false to prevent the window from being zoomed or resized.

Creating an Instance of the Window

Now we need to create a new `NativeWindow` instance. Remember that the properties defined in `NativeWindowInitOptions` cannot be changed after we instantiate the window. The default window size is determined by the operating system, but you can change it by setting the window bounds. (We'll look at this later in the chapter.)

```
var newWindow:NativeWindow = new NativeWindow( windowOptions );
```

The variable `windowOptions` refers to the `NativeWindowInitOptions` we constructed in the previous section.

Putting the Window Onscreen

If we were to stop at the previous step, the user would not see anything appear onscreen. After instantiating our `NativeWindow`, we need to specifically put it on the screen. There are two ways this can be accomplished:

```
NativeWindow.activate()
```

or

```
NativeWindow.visible = true
```

Using `NativeWindow.activate()`

Invoking the `activate()` method on the `NativeWindow` instance does the following:

▶ Makes the window visible

▶ Brings the window to the front

▶ Gives the window keyboard and mouse focus

The following snippet instantiates a new `NativeWindow`, passing in window options, followed by the `activate()` method.

```
var newWindow:NativeWindow = new NativeWindow( windowOptions );
newWindow.activate();
```

Using `NativeWindow.visible`

This property specifies whether the window is visible on the desktop. It affects only visibility and does not give the window focus or bring it to the front.

For example, you might want to open a supporting UTILITY type window for an application where focus must remain on the primary window. Rather than activating your window, simply set its `visible` property to `true`, and it appears onscreen without the primary window flashing in and out of focus.

By default, `visible` is set to `false`. To make the window visible, do the following:

```
var newWindow:NativeWindow = new NativeWindow( windowOptions );
newWindow.visible = true
```

> **NOTE**
>
> An invisible window isn't displayed on the desktop, but all the properties and methods are still available.
>
> On Mac OS X, turning off visibility on a minimized window does not remove it from the Dock. The user is still able to click that Dock icon, which causes the window to be visible, restore, and have focus.

Creating Windows Using `mx.core.Window`

The Adobe Flex `mx.core.Window` class essentially *wraps* `NativeWindow` and facilitates the addition of Adobe Flex content. As an Adobe Flex developer, you will find yourself using this class to create windows in most cases.

The steps to creating a `Window` differ slightly from `NativeWindow`:

- ▶ Create an instance of `Window`.

- ▶ Set `Window` properties (optional—there are defaults).

- ▶ Open the `Window` on the `Screen`.

> **NOTE**
>
> Rather than include full class path on each mention of `mx.core.Window`, we use "Window" instead—capitalizing the "W."
>
> If we're just referring to the generic term "window," it is not capitalized.

Let's take a look at a simplistic example of instantiating a `Window` instance and opening it onscreen. (See Listing 5.2)

LISTING 5.2   Simple Example of Using `mx.core.Window`

```
<?xml version="1.0" encoding="utf-8"?>
<mx:WindowedApplication
   xmlns:mx="http://www.adobe.com/2006/mxml"
   layout="vertical"
   verticalAlign="middle" horizontalAlign="center">

   <mx:Script>
      <![CDATA[
      import mx.core.Window;
```

```
    private function openWindow():void
    {
        var myWindow:Window = new Window();
        myWindow.systemChrome = NativeWindowSystemChrome.STANDARD;
        myWindow.type = NativeWindowType.NORMAL;
        myWindow.open( true );
    }
    ]]>
  </mx:Script>
  <mx:Button label="Create Window" click="openWindow()" />
</mx:WindowedApplication>
```

Creating an Instance of Window

Using the Adobe Flex `Window` class, we create an instance:

```
var myWindow:Window = new Window();
```

Notice there is no `NativeWindowInitOptions` object passed into the constructor of `Window`. You can now set those same properties directly on the `Window` instance itself, as you will see demonstrated in the following section.

> **NOTE**
>
> Although a number of window properties can now be set after the `Window` instance has been created, certain properties still follow the rule of having to be applied before a window is opened onscreen, for example, `systemChrome`, `type`, and so on. After they're set, they cannot be changed.

Setting Window Properties

Using `mx.core.Window` differs from `NativeWindow` in that we can set all parameters after it has been instantiated. The one exception is the `nativeWindow` property of `Window`; this is not accessible until we open it onscreen.

To create a window using `mx.core.Window`, do the following:

```
var myWindow:Window = new Window();
myWindow.systemChrome = NativeWindowSystemChrome.STANDARD;
myWindow.type = NativeWindowType.NORMAL;
```

> **NOTE**
>
> You can still use the same static variables from the `NativeWindow` classes because they are essentially just resolving to strings.

As with `NativeWindow`, you have the same options to choose from with regard to both the chrome of the window instance and the window type. There are some differences in the results of these options which we'll take a closer look at now.

Chrome Options for `mx.core.Window`

Creating a `Window` with standard window chrome yields the same result as with `NativeWindow`. After all, `mx.core.Window` is essentially a `NativeWindow` primed to host Adobe Flex content. The only visual difference visually is the gray background, which represents the Adobe Flex content area (see Figure 5.5).

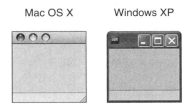

FIGURE 5.5   mx.core.Window of type NORMAL with standard system chrome.

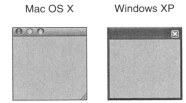

FIGURE 5.6   mx.core.Window of type UTILITY with standard system chrome.

FIGURE 5.7   mx.core.Window of type NORMAL with NONE system chrome. By default Adobe Flex displays its own chrome.

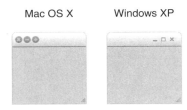

FIGURE 5.8   mx.core.Window of type UTILITY with NONE system chrome.

Mac OS X   Windows XP

FIGURE 5.9   mx.core.Window of type LIGHTWEIGHT with NONE system chrome.

> **NOTE**
>
> Although the options for window types are the same as NativeWindow, a difference lies
> in how you deal with windows with systemChrome set to NONE. When systemChrome is
> set to NONE, Adobe Flex displays its own system chrome. You can disable this by setting
> the showFlexChrome property to false on your Window instance.

At times, you will still need to access the underlying NativeWindow properties. For
example, moving a window from one location onscreen to another requires setting the x
and y coordinates of NativeWindow (see Listing 5.3). You won't find those properties on
the parent mx.core.Window class.

LISTING 5.3   Referencing nativeWindow Properties When Using mx.core.Window

```
var myWindow:Window = new Window();
myWindow.systemChrome = NativeWindowSystemChrome.STANDARD;
myWindow.type = NativeWindowType.NORMAL;
myWindow.open( true );
myWindow.nativeWindow.x = 100;
myWindow.nativeWindow.y = 100;
```

Opening a Window Onscreen

Finally, to open a Window onscreen, use the open() method. Although the Window defaults
to "active," you have the option to change this via a Boolean passed in with the method
call as follows:

```
newWindow.open( true );
```

Passing false into the open method will cause the Window to open but not make it active.
In other words, give the window focus.

Getting a Window Reference

Before you can work with a particular window, you first need to get a reference of that
Window instance. The following sections describe the various ways to obtain a Window reference.

Window Constructor

You can use the window constructor for a new `NativeWindow` to get a reference, like this:

```
var myWindow:NativeWindow = new NativeWindow();
```

Current Window Stage

You can get a reference directly from the current window stage, as follows:

```
stage.nativeWindow
```

Display Object on the Stage

Any display object on the stage can also give you a reference, as follows:

```
aDisplayObject.stage.nativeWindow
```

As an example, suppose you have an `mx.containers.Panel` in some window. To get the reference to the parent `NativeWindow` instance, you can do this:

```
myPanel.stage.nativeWindow
```

Referencing the Active Window

A desktop window that currently holds user focus is referred to as the "active" window. You can reference this window via `NativeApplication`, as follows:

```
var myWindow:NativeWindow = NativeApplication.nativeApplication.activeWindow;
```

> **NOTE**
>
> If the active window on the desktop is not associated with your application, `activeWindow` returns a null value.

Referencing All Opened Windows

All open windows can be referenced via the `nativeApplication` object. These can be cycled through like any `Array`. Each element will be a `NativeWindow` instance.

```
var myWindows:Array = NativeApplication.nativeApplication.openedWindows;
```

Window Operations

In this section we look into controlling a Window's dimensions, positioning and behaviors.

Resizing a Window

You can invoke a resize action on a window by calling the following method:

```
NativeWindow.startResize();
```

> **NOTE**
>
> The resize functionality only exists in `NativeWindow`. In your `Window` instance of type `mx.core.Window` or `mx.core.WindowedApplication`, you need to call the `startResize()` method on the `nativeWindow` property of your window. (`Window` and `WindowedApplication` are essentially just an Adobe Flex wrapper on `NativeWindow`.)

The next code example (as shown in Listing 5.4) demonstrates an `mx.core.Window` being created with a button that initiates the resize of that same window from the lower-right corner. (Click and hold the Start Resize button and drag your mouse to resize the window.)

LISTING 5.4   Initiating Window Resize

```
<?xml version="1.0" encoding="utf-8"?>
<mx:WindowedApplication
    xmlns:mx="http://www.adobe.com/2006/mxml"
    layout="vertical"
    verticalAlign="middle"
    horizontalAlign="center">

    <mx:Script>
        <![CDATA[
        import mx.controls.Button;
        import mx.core.Window;
        private var myWindow:Window;

        private function openWindow():void
        {        var dragButton:Button = new Button();
            dragButton.label = "Click, hold and drag mouse";
            dragButton.addEventListener( MouseEvent.MOUSE_DOWN, resizeWindow );

            myWindow = new Window();        myWindow.width = 300;
            myWindow.systemChrome = NativeWindowSystemChrome.STANDARD;
            myWindow.type = NativeWindowType.NORMAL;
            myWindow.setStyle( "horizontalAlign", "center" );
            myWindow.setStyle( "verticalAlign", "middle" );
            myWindow.addChild( dragButton );
            myWindow.open( true );
        }
```

```
      private function resizeWindow( event:MouseEvent ):void
      {
         myWindow.nativeWindow.startResize( NativeWindowResize.BOTTOM_RIGHT );
      }
      ]]>
   </mx:Script>
   <mx:Button label="Create Window" click="openWindow()" />
</mx:WindowedApplication>
```

Listing 5.4 is an oversimplified example for sake of clarity. A more realistic use case would involve having graphic elements within a custom window chrome initiate this resize behavior. (See "Creating Custom Window Chrome" later in this chapter.)

Moving a Window

To move a window, call the `startMove()`method on the `NativeWindow` instance. If you're using `mx.core.Window`, reference the underlying `NativeWindow` via the `nativeWindow` property:

```
var myWindow:Window = new Window();
myWindow.open();
myWindow.nativeWindow.startMove();
```

Maximizing, Minimizing, and Restoring a Window

Maximizing causes a window to expand to the bounds of the current screen. To maximize a window, use

```
NativeWindow.maximize();
```

To minimize a window, use

```
NativeWindow.minimize();
```

To restore a window, use

```
NativeWindow.restore();
```

Restoring a window simply means that the window will return to the size that it was before it was either minimized or maximized.

Closing a Window

To close a window, use

```
NativeWindow.close()
```

Closing a window empties the contents of the window, but if any other objects have references to that content, the content objects are not destroyed. You can check the `closed` property of a window to test whether a window has been closed. If the window being closed is the last one, and the `NativeApplication.autoExit` property is set to `true` (the default setting), the application quits.

Understanding Window Events

An event-based programming model is used to interact with `NativeWindows`, so let's take a look at what happens when an event takes place before we get into any specific operations.

For some `NativeWindow` operations, there are two associated events. The first dispatched event notifies you that something is *about to happen*, allowing you the opportunity to interject with a callback function. The second event tells you that something *has already happened*.

You'll have to register a listener with that particular window instance to handle these events. The listener catches any of the events and allows you to execute logic using a callback function. In other words, "when object xyz dispatches a certain event, execute this particular function I've defined."

Suppose a user clicks the Close button of a window. An event is dispatched to notify listeners that a window is about to close, giving our application a chance to react. We might want to prompt the users to save their work if they haven't done so already. If the users choose to save, we'd first invoke the necessary functionality to save, and after that's done, trigger the window to close. If our users don't want to save their work, our callback function logic simply does nothing, and the window closes. Now, a second event is dispatched signaling that the window has finished closing.

Listing 5.5 shows an example in which we add event listeners for both `Event.CLOSING` and `Event.CLOSE` on an instance of `mx.core.Window`.

LISTING 5.5   Exploring Window `CLOSE` and `CLOSING` Events

```
<?xml version="1.0" encoding="utf-8"?>
<mx:WindowedApplication
    xmlns:mx="http://www.adobe.com/2006/mxml"
    layout="vertical"
    verticalAlign="middle"
    horizontalAlign="center">

    <mx:Script>
        <![CDATA[
        import mx.core.Window;

        private function openWindow():void
        {
            var myWindow:Window = new Window();
```

```
            myWindow.systemChrome = NativeWindowSystemChrome.STANDARD;
            myWindow.type = NativeWindowType.NORMAL;
            myWindow.open( true );

            myWindow.nativeWindow.addEventListener( Event.CLOSE, onWindowClose );
            myWindow.nativeWindow.addEventListener( Event.CLOSING, onWindowClosing );
        }

        private function onWindowClosing( event:Event ):void
        {
            trace( "Window is about to close" );
        }

        private function onWindowClose( event:Event ):void
        {
            trace( "Window has closed" );
        }
        ]]>
    </mx:Script>

    <mx:Button label="Create Window" click="openWindow()" />
</mx:WindowedApplication>
```

NOTE

`Event.CLOSE` will not fire from `mx.core.Window`. You must listen to its parent `NativeWindow` to be notified of the event. This is because the Adobe Flex context is destroyed after the `CLOSING` event fires and is unavailable to dispatch the final `CLOSE` event.

Canceling a Window Event

Often you'll need to intercept an event and invoke conditional logic to determine whether you want that event to continue, such as in the example cited earlier in Listing 5.5. In that example we're simply tracing a message to the output console, but in the real world, you may want to prompt users that their work isn't currently saved and ask if they want to do so.

Listing 5.6 outlines how to interrupt the closing sequence by catching the CLOSING event and calling `preventDefault()` on the event object. This stops the event in its tracks. In this example we're only doing this if `isWorkSaved` is `false`, indicating the user has attempted to close the application without saving his or her work.

Our Alert dialog makes a callback to `onAlertClose`, upon which time we act on the users' decision to save their work. When that has been done, we can simply call the `close()` method on our `Window`. We're also calling `exit()` because this is our main application

Window we're closing. If we didn't call exit(), the Window would close but the application process would still be running, so it's important to keep that in mind!

Here's how we could add to our example in code Listing 5.5:

LISTING 5.6   Cancelling a Window CLOSING event

```
<?xml version="1.0" encoding="utf-8"?>
<mx:WindowedApplication
        xmlns:mx="http://www.adobe.com/2006/mxml"
        layout="vertical"
        verticalAlign="middle"
        horizontalAlign="center"
        initialize="init()">

    <mx:Script>
        <![CDATA[
            import mx.events.CloseEvent;
            import mx.controls.Alert;

            private var isWorkSaved:Boolean = false;

            private function init():void
            {
                nativeWindow.addEventListener( Event.CLOSING, onWindowClosing );
            }

            private function onWindowClosing( event:Event ):void
            {
                if( !isWorkSaved )
                {
                    event.preventDefault();
                    Alert.show( "Would you like to save your work?", "Warning!",
➥Alert.YES | Alert.NO, this, onAlertClose );
                }
            }

            private function onAlertClose( event:CloseEvent ):void
            {
                if( event.detail == 1 )
                {
                    // Save users work here
                    isWorkSaved = true;
                    trace( "Work has been saved" );
                }
                nativeWindow.close();
```

```
            exit();
        }
      ]]>
   </mx:Script>
</mx:WindowedApplication>
```

NOTE

If you are using a custom window chrome, then it will be up to you to programmatically dispatch the CLOSING and CLOSE events.

Creating Custom Window Chrome

Adobe AIR projects generated from the New Flex Project Wizard in Adobe Flex Builder output a default MXML file with a root tag called WindowedApplication. As outlined earlier in this chapter, this gives your application a standard native window as expected.

What if a project calls for a truly customized window chrome, such as a fully branded look and feel that includes custom icons for window controls and a nonrectangular shape?

No sweat—this can be accomplished by the following steps:

1. Set the window chrome to none and the transparency to true in the application's descriptor file (see Listing 5.6).
2. On WindowedApplication set the showFlexChrome to false.
3. Create a Canvas with an embedded background image (optional).

In Listing 5.6 we've changed the chrome and transparency properties in the application descriptor, which prevents Adobe AIR from opening a visible default Window when the application is launched. This, in combination with setting the showFlexChrome to false in our application code (see Listing 5.7) delivers the desired effect.

LISTING 5.7   Modifying **Window** Properties in the Application Descriptor File

```
<!— Settings for the application's initial window. Required. —>
<initialWindow>
    <!— The main SWF or HTML file of the application. Required. —>
    <!— Note: In Flex Builder, the SWF reference is set automatically. —>
    <content>[This value will be overwritten by Flex Builder in the output
➥app.xml]</content>

    <!— The title of the main window. Optional. —>
    <!— <title>Custom Chrome</title> —>
    <!— The type of system chrome to use (either "standard" or "none").
➥Optional. Default standard. —>
```

```
<systemChrome>none</systemChrome>
<!— Whether the window is transparent. Only applicable when systemChrome
➥is false. Optional. Default false. —>
<transparent>true</transparent>
<!— Whether the window is initially visible. Optional. Default false. —>
<visible>true</visible>
<!— Whether the user can minimize the window. Optional. Default true. —>
<!— <minimizable></minimizable> —>
<!— Whether the user can maximize the window. Optional. Default true. —>
<!— <maximizable></maximizable> —>
<!— Whether the user can resize the window. Optional. Default true. —>
<!— <resizable></resizable> —>
<!— The window's initial width. Optional. —>
<!— <width></width> —>
<!— The window's initial height. Optional. —>
<!— <height></height> —>
<!— The window's initial x position. Optional. —>
<!— <x></x> —>
<!— The window's initial y position. Optional. —>
<!— <y></y> —>
<!— The window's minimum size, specified as a width/height pair,
➥such as "400 200". Optional. —>
<!— <minSize></minSize> —>
<!— The window's initial maximum size, specified as a width/height pair,
➥such as "1600 1200". Optional. —>
<!— <maxSize></maxSize> —>
</initialWindow>
```

Embedding an image as your application's background is completely optional. At this point you literally have a blank slate to work with inside your Adobe Flex application. You can use a circular or square background image or perhaps draw your application background yourself via the ActionScript drawing APIs, it's up to you. See Figure 6.10.

FIGURE 5.10   Example of using a bitmap image as the custom chrome for a Window.

In Listing 5.8 we've opted to simply embed a bitmap image and used that as the background. In addition we've included a drop shadow filter on the Canvas that gives a floating perspective to the application.

LISTING 5.8   Creating a Window with Custom Chrome in Adobe Flex

```
<?xml version="1.0" encoding="utf-8"?>
<mx:WindowedApplication
        xmlns:mx="http://www.adobe.com/2006/mxml"
        layout="vertical"
        horizontalScrollPolicy="off"
        verticalScrollPolicy="off"
        showFlexChrome="false"
        creationComplete="init()">

    <mx:Style source="styles.css" />

        <mx:Script>
            <![CDATA[
            import mx.controls.Label;

             private function init():void
            {
               myCanvas.addEventListener( MouseEvent.MOUSE_DOWN, moveWindow );
               var dropShadow:DropShadowFilter = new DropShadowFilter();
               var glow:GlowFilter = new GlowFilter(0x000000,1,5,5,3);
               var filters:Array = new Array( dropShadow, glow );
               myCanvas.filters = filters;
            }

            private function moveWindow( event:MouseEvent ):void
            {
               stage.nativeWindow.startMove();
            }

            private function onMinimize():void
            {
               stage.nativeWindow.minimize();
             }

             private function onClose():void
            {
               stage.nativeWindow.close();
            }
```

```
      ]]>
   </mx:Script>

   <mx:Canvas
       id="myCanvas"
       width="200" height="200"
       backgroundImage="@Embed(source='assets/air.png')"
       horizontalScrollPolicy="off" verticalScrollPolicy="off">

       <mx:Image source="@Embed(source='assets/minimize.png')"
➥click="onMinimize()" x="168" y="6" alpha="0.8" />
       <mx:Image source="@Embed(source='assets/close.png')" click="onClose()"
➥x="180" y="6" alpha="0.8" />
       <mx:Label text="Adobe AIR Programming Unleashed" styleName="scores"
➥x="10" y="176" />
   </mx:Canvas>
</mx:WindowedApplication>
```

There is a little added work going this route because you have to create your own mecha-nisms for standard window controls such as minimize, maximize, and so on. In Listing 5.7 we've added listeners on our window control images and explicitly, via the event handlers, initiatied the desired window behavior.

Summary

We've explored how to create windows onscreen using both the flash.desktop.NativeWindow and mx.core.Window classes. In essence mx.core.Window is just a wrapper for the NativeWindow class, making it ready to host elements of an Adobe Flex application.

As for the look and feel of your application windows, the sky is the limit. If the standard operating system chrome won't do the trick, then you can build your own customized chrome from scratch.

# CHAPTER 6

Working with **Screen**s

Working with Screens is fairly straightforward. Adobe® AIR™ exposes an application programming interface (API) (flash.display.Screen) that enables you to determine the visual real estate of the runtime environment, such as the number of Screens available, their dimensions (or bounds), and a Screen's usable space.

We'll step through a number of examples to highlight the inner workings of Screens, but first we need to lock down the concept of the virtual desktop in Adobe AIR.

The Virtual Desktop

Whether a user has one or an array of five screens, they are all represented as a single, virtual space in the Adobe AIR Screen API. For example, a user with a dual-monitor setup with each screen running at 1024×768 resolution is, in most cases, represented as a virtual desktop of 2048×768, as illustrated in Figure 6.1.

Keep in mind that the number of screens and their physical location to one another does not necessarily coincide with the dimensions of the virtual desktop.

This virtual space is based on how the monitors are configured in the operating system (OS). For instance, although two monitors might sit side by side, one screen could be configured on top of the other via the display controls of the given OS. See Figure 6.2.

To position windows onscreen, you set the x and y coordinates within the virtual desktop. You can do this via the native window properties or by setting the bounds of a native window. We'll see examples of both in the sample applications that follow in this chapter (see Listings 6.1 and 6.2).

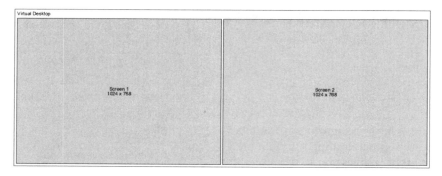

FIGURE 6.1   Virtual desktop representing two screens.

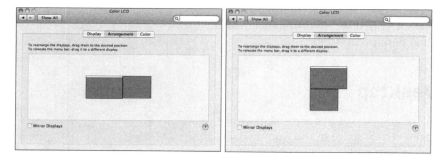

FIGURE 6.2   Screen arrangement on Mac OS X.

NOTE

If more than one monitor maps to the same screen, with one configured to mirror the other, then they will exist as a single screen within the virtual desktop. In the case of one desktop spanning (not extending) onto a second screen, they too will be treated as a single screen within the virtual desktop.

CAUTION

It's important *not* to cache screen information beyond local methods or functions as the user can change the configuration of their desktop and screens at any time.

Determining the Number of Screens

To determine the number of screens available at runtime, take a look at the static property in the `flash.display.Screen` class. It returns an `Array` of all `Screens` at the given time:

```
Screen.screens
```

It's important to keep in mind that the order of the screens in the `Screen.screens` array will not always correlate to the physical layout presented to the user. Listing 6.1 outlines how to determine the number of screens by measuring the length of the `Screen.screens` array.

LISTING 6.1   Retrieving the Number of Screens

```
<?xml version="1.0" encoding="utf-8"?>
<mx:WindowedApplication
    xmlns:mx="http://www.adobe.com/2006/mxml"
    layout="vertical"
    horizontalAlign="center" verticalAlign="middle">

    <mx:Script>
    <![CDATA[

    import mx.controls.Alert;

    private function getScreens():void
    {
        Alert.show( Screen.screens.length + " screen(s) detected." );
    }

    ]]>
    </mx:Script>

    <mx:Button label="Click to detect number of Screens" click="getScreens()" />
</mx:WindowedApplication>
```

Obtaining a Reference to the Main Screen

The main screen is the user's primary display. In Mac OS X, this translates to the window currently hosting the menu bar, whereas in Microsoft Windows, the screen is explicitly defined as primary in the desktop properties. We can reference this once again via a static property in `flash.display.Screen`:

```
Screen.mainScreen
```

NOTE

There is not always a direct correlation between `Screen.mainScreen` and a single, physical display. The user might have their primary display spanned across multiple monitors.

What is the purpose of singling out the primary display?

One example might be an application that offers an array of preset window configurations. Being able to reference the main screen makes positioning and sizing the application's main interface a snap.

With a little detective work, you can probably determine the primary display yourself. Looping through all the screens and examining their visible bounds would be a logical place to start, but as the saying goes, "Work smart, not hard."

NOTE

The visible bounds on an instance of a `Screen` object returns a `Rectangle` object that represents an area within that `Screen` in which your window(s) can occupy space and be completely visible. As you'll see later in the chapter (see Listing 6.4), this is an important concept to take into consideration when designing applications that will run on different operating systems.

Determining Screen Resolution

Let's take a look at a simple example, which loops through all the available `Screen` objects and measures the resolution of each instance. We can do so by examining the *bounds* of each `Screen`. See Listing 6.2.

LISTING 6.2   Screen Resolution

```
<?xml version="1.0" encoding="utf-8"?>
<mx:WindowedApplication
    xmlns:mx="http://www.adobe.com/2006/mxml"
    layout="vertical"
    horizontalAlign="center" verticalAlign="middle">

        <mx:Script>
        <![CDATA[

        import mx.controls.Label;

        private function measureScreenRes():void
        {
            var screens:Array = Screen.screens;
```

```
        for( var i:int=0; i < screens.length; i++ )
        {
           var screen:Screen = Screen.screens[i];
           var bounds:Rectangle = screen.bounds;
           var label:Label = new Label();
           label.text = "Screen [" + i + "]: " + bounds.width + " x "
➥+ bounds.height;
           this.addChild( label );
        }
     }


     ]]>
     </mx:Script>
     <mx:Button label="Analyze Screen Resolution" click=" measureScreenRes()" />
</mx:WindowedApplication>
```

What's the difference between the "visible bounds" and the "bounds" of a Screen? Whereas the visible bounds represent an area where content is unobstructed, the bounds encompass the entire screen, for example, the menu bar, the Dock, or the taskbar. Figure 6.3 highlights the visible bounds on Mac OS X.

FIGURE 6.3   The dashed line represents the visible bounds of the main screen on Mac OS X.

Positioning Windows Programmatically

By examining the bounds of a Screen, you can calculate the sizing and positioning of the application windows. Listing 6.3 outlines a basic technique that builds a specific user interface layout, which encompasses the entire screen.

LISTING 6.3   Positioning Windows Based on Screen Bounds

```xml
<?xml version="1.0" encoding="utf-8"?>
<mx:WindowedApplication
    xmlns:mx="http://www.adobe.com/2006/mxml"
    layout="vertical"
    creationComplete="init()">

    <mx:Script>
        <![CDATA[
        import mx.core.Window;

        private var paletteWidth:int = 200;
        private var numPalettes:int = 3;

        /**
         * Create a main window with x number of supporting
         * palette windows to the upper right of the screen
         */
        private function init():void
        {
            nativeWindow.x = nativeWindow.y = 0;
            nativeWindow.width = Screen.mainScreen.bounds.width - paletteWidth - 3;
            nativeWindow.height = Screen.mainScreen.bounds.height;

            var yCoord:int = Screen.mainScreen.visibleBounds.top;
            var xCoord:int = Screen.mainScreen.bounds.width - paletteWidth;
            var screen:Screen = Screen.mainScreen;
            var paletteHeight:Number = int( screen.visibleBounds.height / 3 );

            for( var i:int = 0; i < numPalettes; i++ )
            {
                var paletteWindow:Window = new Window();
                paletteWindow.type = NativeWindowType.UTILITY;
                paletteWindow.open( false );
                paletteWindow.nativeWindow.x = xCoord;
                paletteWindow.nativeWindow.y = yCoord;
                paletteWindow.nativeWindow.height = paletteHeight;
                paletteWindow.nativeWindow.width = paletteWidth;
                yCoord += paletteWindow.nativeWindow.height + 1;
            }
        }
    ]]>
    </mx:Script>
</mx:WindowedApplication>
```

Figure 6.4 shows Listing 6.3 in action with one large drawing canvas with a number of window palettes along side. Their locations onscreen are computed based on available real-estate at runtime.

FIGURE 6.4   Application with a supporting window palettes.

The next example outlined in Figure 6.5 highlights the potential differences in visible bounds between two operating systems.

FIGURE 6.5   Differences in window positioning between operating systems. (Mac OS X versus Windows XP).

Let's take a look at another challenge you might face when dealing with positioning on screens. Window 'snapping' is a common behavior in the software world. Again, it really comes down to some basic math at runtime. Ah, but wait—this is the land of Adobe AIR, where cross-platform differences occasionally creep up and bite you in the butt. In Listing 6.4, we make use of visibleBounds property for our calculations. This can differ between operating systems because the value of visibleBounds is the result of subtracting fixed items on the screen—that is, the Dock and menu bar on Mac OS X or the Start bar on Windows.

LISTING 6.4   Window Positioning Relative to Screen

```
<?xml version="1.0" encoding="utf-8"?>
<mx:Application
        xmlns:mx="http://www.adobe.com/2006/mxml"
        creationComplete="init()">

    <mx:Script>
    <![CDATA[

    import mx.core.Window;

    private var window:MyWindow;
    private var snapWidth:Number = 200;
    private var windowIsLocked:Boolean = false;

    private static var DIRECTION_RIGHT:String = "right";
    private static var DIRECTION_LEFT:String = "left";

    private function init():void
    {
     window = new MyWindow();
     window.systemChrome = NativeWindowSystemChrome.STANDARD;
     window.type = NativeWindowType.UTILITY;
     window.width = 460;
     window.height = 200;
     window.open( true );
     window.nativeWindow.addEventListener( NativeWindowBoundsEvent.MOVING,
➥onWindowMoving );
    }

    /**
     * Calculate the bounds of a snapped window every time
     * as the desktop dimensions may change.
     */
    private function getSnapBounds( screen:Screen, direction:String ):Rectangle
    {
     var bounds:Rectangle = new Rectangle();
     bounds.height = screen.visibleBounds.bottom;
```

```
        bounds.width = snapWidth;
        bounds.y = screen.visibleBounds.top;

        if( direction == DIRECTION_RIGHT )
        {
                bounds.x = screen.visibleBounds.width - bounds.width;
        }
        else
        {
                bounds.x = screen.visibleBounds.x;
        }
        return bounds;
    }

    /**
     * Determine the direction the window is being moved. If it's
     * offscreen, snap to the edge of the screen.
     */
    private function onWindowMoving( event:NativeWindowBoundsEvent ):void
    {
     var eventWindow:NativeWindow = event.target as NativeWindow;
     var currentScreen:Screen = deriveScreenFromPoint(
➥eventWindow.bounds.topLeft );

        if( event.afterBounds.x < event.beforeBounds.x ) // window moving left
        {
                if( eventWindow.bounds.x + eventWindow.bounds.width * 0.20
➥< currentScreen.visibleBounds.left )
                {
                        event.preventDefault();
                        eventWindow.bounds = getSnapBounds( currentScreen,
➥DIRECTION_LEFT );
                        window.nativeWindow.addEventListener
➥( NativeWindowBoundsEvent.MOVING, preventMove );
                        window.nativeWindow.removeEventListener
➥( NativeWindowBoundsEvent.MOVING, onWindowMoving );
                }
        }
        else // window moving right
        {
                if( eventWindow.bounds.x + eventWindow.bounds.width * 0.80 >
➥currentScreen.visibleBounds.right )
                {
                        event.preventDefault();
                        eventWindow.bounds = getSnapBounds( currentScreen,
➥DIRECTION_RIGHT );
```

```
                        window.nativeWindow.addEventListener
➡( NativeWindowBoundsEvent.MOVING, preventMove );
                        window.nativeWindow.removeEventListener
➡( NativeWindowBoundsEvent.MOVING, onWindowMoving );
                }
        }
    }

    private function preventMove( event:NativeWindowBoundsEvent ):void
    {
     event.preventDefault();
    }

    /**
     * Based on a given Point determine the screen that
     * Point is located on
     */
    private function deriveScreenFromPoint( point:Point ):Screen
    {
     var screens:Array = Screen.screens;
     for( var i:int=0; i < screens.length; i++ )
     {
             var bounds:Rectangle = screens[i].bounds;
             if( point.x < bounds.right && point.x > bounds.left && point.y
➡< bounds.bottom && point.y > bounds.top )
             {
                     return screens[i] as Screen;
             }
     }
     return Screen.mainScreen;
    }

            ]]>
        </mx:Script>

</mx:Application>
```

The application in Listing 6.4 showcases a window-snapping behavior exhibited by some instant messaging applications. When the user attempts to move the main window off-screen, it is automatically resized and repositioned along the edge of the screen.

This snapping behavior is accomplished by calculating the window's position each time it is moved. When the application is initialized, an eventListener is added to the underlying NativeWindow instance. As the user begins to drag the window, a NativeWindowBoundsEvent is fired, which, in turn, invokes the callback function.

A definite point of interest is the use of beforeBounds and afterBounds. These are available as properties of the NativeWindowBoundsEvent object passed into the callback function. Each of these properties represents the bounds of our window before and after the impending MOVE event. This is handy because we can leverage this information to determine which direction the window is being dragged and have the application react accordingly, for example, snapping to the left or the right of the screen.

Finally, after determining that the window is being moved offscreen, we can now trigger the window-snapping behavior. The getSnapBounds() function calculates the sizing and positioning needed to snap our window into position, as shown in Figure 6.5.

Using Full-Screen Mode

Feeling confined operating in the limited real estate of the visible bounds of the Screen? Not to worry; you can always take your application full screen!

Using the stage, accessed as a property of mx.core.Window or mx.core.WindowedApplication, complete the following:

▶ Create a Rectangle.

▶ Specify the area of the virtual desktop to be scaled to full screen.

▶ Set the Stage.fullScreenSourceRect.

▶ Set the Stage.displayState to FULL_SCREEN.

The source Rectangle to be scaled must always be set before triggering full-screen mode, even if it is the entire stage as there is no default. See Listing 6.5.

LISTING 6.5   Launching Full-screen Mode

```
<?xml version="1.0" encoding="utf-8"?>
<mx:WindowedApplication
    xmlns:mx="http://www.adobe.com/2006/mxml"
    layout="vertical"
    horizontalAlign="center" verticalAlign="middle">

    <mx:Script>
        <![CDATA[
        private function openInFullScreen():void
        {
            stage.fullScreenSourceRect = new Rectangle( 0, 0, stage.width,
➥stage.height );
            stage.displayState = StageDisplayState.FULL_SCREEN;
```

```
            escMessage.text = "Hit ESC to exit fullscreen mode";
     }


     ]]>
   </mx:Script>

   <mx:Button label="Fullscreen" click="openInFullScreen()" />
   <mx:Label id="escMessage" />
</mx:WindowedApplication>
```

Summary

Although this chapter hasn't touched on *every* aspect of how Screens are represented in Adobe AIR, hopefully the examples provided will at least help in achieving a "moment of Zen"—that wonderful feeling when new concepts sink into our brains and all the dots are connected.

As with anything else, after the basics are mastered, the options available to you are virtually limitless!

CHAPTER 7

Working with Files and Directories

With the `File` application programming interface (API), your Adobe® AIR™ applications can take advantage of an unprecedented level of access to the user's local file system. You can now access low-level functionality of working with files and directories through an ActionScript API.

Our main focus in this chapter is on the `flash.filesystem.*` package. See Table 7.1.

> **NOTE**
>
> Full class definitions are available in the ActionScript documentation (ASDocs) shipped with the Adobe® Flex™ 3 software development kit (SDK) or within Adobe Flex Builder via the Help documentation.

We use specific examples to show the functionality of specific methods, events, and properties for each particular class.

Let's take a look at common functionality performed under the covers of traditional native applications and how to accomplish the same feat in Adobe AIR. Some of these operations include the following:

▶ Determining file or directory paths

▶ Opening and reading files

▶ Creating files and directories

▶ Writing files

▶ Working with temporary files and directories

▶ Copying and moving files and directories

▶ Retrieving directory listings

▶ Retrieving file and directory properties

TABLE 7.1   ActionScript Classes Introduced

Class	Package	Description
File	flash.filesystem	An object that represents a path to a file or directory. May be a reference to an existing file or directory, or one that does not yet exist.
FileStream	flash.filesystem	Used to read or write File objects. Files can be accessed synchronously or asynchronously.
FileMode	flash.filesystem	A parameter specified when opening a FileStream object. A string constant that represents the capabilities of the FileStream object—that is, read, write, append.

NOTE

A set of Flex Adobe AIR components is available for working with files and directories such as FileSystemTree, among others. They extend their traditional Flex counterparts to facilitate working with the file system. They can be used with Adobe AIR's File I/O API to create sophisticated user interfaces with minimal effort. Please refer to Chapter 14, "Working with Adobe Flex AIR Components."

Determining File or Directory Paths

With the Adobe AIR file system API, OS-specific code isn't needed to reference a particular file. The syntax is platform-independent, so you can use the same components, classes, methods, and properties to access files in each operating system.

A File object points to the path of a file or directory. This can be an existing file or directory, or it can be one that doesn't exist yet, for example, a file you are intending to create.

A File object's path can be represented in a couple of ways: url or nativePath.

Understanding File.url

The first method of referencing a File object is via a URL scheme. In short, use the standard syntax across operating systems:

```
file:///C:/Documents%20and%20Settings/<username>/Desktop/example.txt
file:///System/Users/<username>/Desktop/example.txt
```
This format is what you will find when referencing the url property of flash.filesystem.File.

In most cases, however, it is a helpful practice to leverage static constants available in that same `File` class. (See Table 7.2) Using these variables obfuscates the file-system specifics of the operating system and provides reference to common locations. For example, a reference to the user's home directory would look identical on both Mac and PC:

```
var file:File = File.userDirectory.resolvePath("myFile.txt");
```

For example, Figure 7.1 makes reference to `document.txt` residing on a user's desktop. In using full paths in this manner, you would need to detect the runtime operating system and build the path accordingly. Thankfully, this is done for us in Adobe AIR via a set of static properties in `flash.filesystem.File`, all of which are outlined in Table 7.2.

NOTE

You cannot create, write, or delete any files or directories that use the URL scheme `app:`. In the spirit of security best practices, if you want to store data specific to your application, consider using `applicationStorageDirectory`.

To create a file on the user's desktop named `example.txt`, we can leverage `File.desktopDirectory` as follows:

```
var file:File = File.desktopDirectory.resolvePath( "example.txt" );
```

`File.desktopDirectory` references the proper path to the desktop based on the operating system the application is running and returns a `File` reference.

TABLE 7.2   Common Directories Available as Static Constants

Static Constant	URL Scheme	Description
applicationDirectory	app:	Location containing the installed files of an application.
applicationStorageDirectory	app-storage:	A place to store files needed by the application, such as settings or log files.
desktopDirectory	file:	The Desktop directory underneath the user directory.
documentsDirectory	file:	Starting from the user directory, this is the My Documents subdirectory on Windows and the Documents subdirectory on Mac OS X.
userDirectory	file:	The user's home directory. This is typically `C:\Documents and Settings\<username>` on Windows and `/Users/<username>` on Mac OS X.

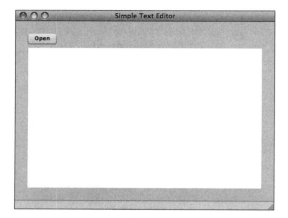

FIGURE 7.1   Initial screen of a simple text editor application.

Next, calling `resolvePath` creates a `File` object called `example.txt` in a location relative to the desktop. If we had used `File.documentsDirectory`, `example.txt` would be relative to the user's documents directory, and so on.

Now, the value passed into `resolvePath` can be a path itself. Suppose we want to create our file inside a new (or existing) directory named `AIR` residing on the desktop:

```
var file:File = File.desktopDirectory.resolvePath( "AIR/example.txt" );
```

The preceding statement resolves to the following on Microsoft Windows and Mac OS X, respectively:

```
file:///C:/Documents%20and%20Settings/<username>/Desktop/AIR/example.txt
file:///System/Users/<username>/AIR/Desktop/example.txt
```

This process is just about providing common points of file-system access for Adobe AIR developers, regardless of the operating system.

Understanding `File.nativePath`

It is also possible to create files and directories using native paths specific to the runtime operating system. Let's look at how we'd create the same `example.txt` `File` object using a native path:

```
var file:File = new File(
"C:\Documents%20and%20Settings\<username>\Desktop\AIR\example.txt" );
```

This works fine on Windows clients but fails miserably on any other platform, such as OS X (and, eventually, Linux). Still, the option is there if needed. Also keep in mind that regardless of how a file or directory is created, the native path is available via the `nativePath` property of the `File` class.

> **NOTE**
>
> Whereas the URL scheme utilizes the forward slash consistently across platforms, `nativePath` uses the backslash (\) on Windows and the forward slash (/) on Mac OS X.

Opening and Reading a File

Let's take a look at the steps involved in opening and reading a file (in this case, a text file):

- ▶ Create a `File` reference.

- ▶ Open a `FileStream`.

- ▶ Read the `File` into the `FileStream`.

- ▶ Read the `File` contents into a local variable.

- ▶ Close the `FileStream`.

In the example in Listing 7.1, the `File` reference is being created by the `browseForOpen` method, which opens a native file selection dialog (see Figure 7.2). When the user makes a selection, an event is passed into our established handler. The event target is a `File` reference with a URL pointing to the selected file:

```
var file:File = new File();
file.addEventListener( Event.SELECT, callback );
file.browseForOpen( message );
```

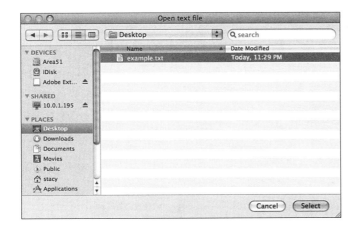

FIGURE 7.2   Native file dialog opened using `File.browseForOpen()`.

LISTING 7.1   Example of File Browser Prompt and Reading File Contents

```
<?xml version="1.0" encoding="utf-8"?>
<mx:WindowedApplication
        xmlns:mx="http://www.adobe.com/2006/mxml"
        layout="vertical"
        horizontalAlign="left"
        title="Simple Text Editor">
          <mx:Script>
        <![CDATA[

    private function browseForOpen( message:String, callback:Function ):void
    {
     var file:File = new File();
     file.addEventListener( Event.SELECT, callback );
     file.browseForOpen( message );
    }

    private function onFileOpen( event:Event ):void
    {
     var file:File = event.target as File;
     var fileStream:FileStream = new FileStream();
     fileStream.open( file, FileMode.READ );

     var fileContents:String = fileStream.readUTFBytes(
       fileStream.bytesAvailable );
     fileStream.close();

     fileText.text = fileContents;
    }

        ]]>
    </mx:Script>

        <mx:Button id="open" label="Open"
          click="browseForOpen( 'Open text file', onFileOpen )" />
        <mx:TextArea id="fileText" width="100%" height="100%" />
</mx:WindowedApplication>
```

This leads us to the onFileOpen method (our callback function), where the real work takes place.

Next, we're going to create a FileStream.

Think of a FileStream object as a sort of "container" to place the bits of your file into memory so you have something to work with programmatically.

Synchronous Versus Asynchronous File Operations

Although our example uses `FileStream.open()`, there is also `FileStream.openAsync()`. Using `open()` immediately reads the file while the application sits and waits for that task to complete. The technical term to describe this type of operation is *synchronous*.

On the other hand, `openAsync()` performs the same task—you guessed it—*asynchronously*. This is the equivalent of your application saying, "Hey, go read this file. When you're done, let me know as I've got other things to do in the meantime."

A consequence to the asynchronous approach is that you need to set up an event listener with a callback function that you want invoked when the read operation is completed.

Listing 7.2 shows how that would apply to our previous, synchronous example.

LISTING 7.2   Reading a File Asynchronously

```
<?xml version="1.0" encoding="utf-8"?>
<mx:WindowedApplication
        xmlns:mx="http://www.adobe.com/2006/mxml"
        layout="vertical"
        horizontalAlign="left">

   <mx:Script>
      <![CDATA[

      private var file:File;

      private function browseForOpen( message:String, callback:Function ):void
      {
       var file:File = new File();
       file.addEventListener( Event.SELECT, callback );
       file.browseForOpen( message );
      }

      private function onFileOpen( event:Event ):void
      {
       var myFilePath:String = event.target.url;
       file = new File( myFilePath );
       var fileStream:FileStream = new FileStream();
       fileStream.addEventListener( Event.COMPLETE, onFileOpenComplete );
       fileStream.openAsync( file, FileMode.READ );
      }

      private function onFileOpenComplete( event:Event ):void
      {
```

7

```
        var fileStream:FileStream = event.target as FileStream;
        var fileContents:String = fileStream.readUTFBytes(
          fileStream.bytesAvailable );
        fileText.text = fileContents;
        fileStream.close();
      }


      ]]>
  </mx:Script>

    <mx:HBox>
        <mx:Button id="open" label="Open"
            click="browseForOpen( 'Open text file', onFileOpen )" />
    </mx:HBox>
            <mx:TextArea id="fileText" width="100%" height="100%" />
</mx:WindowedApplication>
```

The difference in the asynchronous approach is the addition of the `onFileReadComplete`
handler. This gets invoked the moment the read operation is completed in `onFileOpen()`.
The callback (event handler) function now receives a `FileStream` object with our file
contents—after that, it's business as usual in regard to updating the text area to show the
file contents, as seen in Figure 7.3.

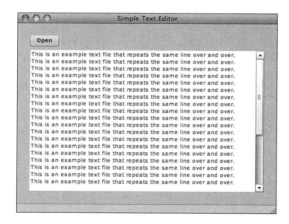

FIGURE 7.3   File content loaded into a TextArea control.

NOTE

Why use asynchronous methods? Large files can take time to load. Using asynchronous file operations allows you to deliver a more responsive user interface (UI) via
onscreen notifications, such as a progress bar, and so on.

Using `FileMode`

You might have noticed the use of the `FileMode` class in the file open/read examples. It is used in the `fileMode` parameter of the `open()` and `openAsync()` methods of the `FileStream` class. The particular `FileMode` chosen dictates the capabilities of the `FileStream` object.

Depending on which `fileMode` you use, you can do the following:

▶ Read data from the file.

▶ Write data to the file.

▶ Create a nonexistent file upon opening.

▶ Truncate a file, deleting all data upon opening before writing.

▶ Append a file, writing data to the end of the file.

▶ Update a file, writing data anywhere in the file.

Table 7.3 shows the capabilities each constant in the `FileMode` class provides when applied as the `fileMode` parameter of an `open()` method of a `FileStream` object.

TABLE 7.3   Available File Modes

File Mode	Read	Write	Create	Truncate	Append	Update
FileMode.READ	X					
FileMode.WRITE		X	X	X		
FileMode.APPEND		X	X		X	
FileMode.UPDATE	X	X	X			X

NOTE

You can read and write data in a number of different ways using the different methods included in the class. We'll be using several methods in our examples, but for more information see `flash.filesystem` in the Adobe Flex 3 Language Reference located at:

http://livedocs.adobe.com/flex/3/langref/index.html

Creating and Writing a File

Now let's look at creating and writing files. This time, we'll walk through an expanded version of our simple text editor application. This text editor has the capability to create a new file and save it locally on the computer (see Listing 7.3). This allows us to look at different parts of the `File` API being used in context.

LISTING 7.3   Expanded Version of a Simple Text Editor Application

```
<?xml version="1.0" encoding="utf-8"?>
<mx:WindowedApplication
      xmlns:mx="http://www.adobe.com/2006/mxml"
      layout="vertical"
      horizontalAlign="left"
      title="Simple Text Editor">
        <mx:Script>
      <![CDATA[

    [Bindable]
    private var saveOptionAvailable:Boolean = false;
    [Bindable]
    private var closeOptionAvailable:Boolean = false;
    private var file:File;

    private function browseForOpen( message:String, callback:Function ):void
    {
     var file:File = new File();
     file.addEventListener( Event.SELECT, callback );
     file.browseForOpen( message );
    }

    private function browseForSave( message:String, callback:Function ):void
    {
     var file:File = new File();
     file.addEventListener( Event.SELECT, callback );
     file.browseForSave( message );
    }

    private function onFileOpen( event:Event ):void
    {
     file = event.target as File;
     var fileStream:FileStream = new FileStream();
     fileStream.open( file, FileMode.READ );

     var fileContents:String = fileStream.readUTFBytes(
       fileStream.bytesAvailable );
     fileStream.close();

     fileText.text = fileContents;

     closeOptionAvailable = true;
    }
```

```
    private function saveFile():void
    {
     if( file != null )
     {
          saveFileToDisk();
     }
     else
     {
          browseForSave( "Select location to save text file", saveFileToDisk )
     }
     saveOptionAvailable = false;
     closeOptionAvailable = true;
    }

    private function saveFileToDisk( event:Event=null ):void
    {
     var fileToSave:File = ( event != null )? event.target as File: file;
     var fileStream:FileStream = new FileStream();
     fileStream.open( fileToSave, FileMode.WRITE );
     fileStream.writeUTFBytes( fileText.text );
     fileStream.close();

     file = fileToSave;
    }

    private function closeFile():void
    {
     file = null;
     fileText.text = "";
     closeOptionAvailable = saveOptionAvailable = false;
    }

    ]]>
  </mx:Script>

    <mx:HBox>
          <mx:Button id="openButton" label="Open" click="browseForOpen
➥( 'Open text file', onFileOpen )" />
          <mx:Button id="saveButton" label="Save" click="saveFile()"
➥enabled="{ saveOptionAvailable }" />
          <mx:Button id="closeButton" label="Close" click="closeFile()"
➥enabled="{ closeOptionAvailable }" />
      </mx:HBox>
          <mx:TextArea id="fileText" width="100%" height="100%"
➥change="saveOptionAvailable=true;" />
</mx:WindowedApplication>
```

Building on the previous version of our text editor, we've added the ability to open, edit, and save files now. In fact, we can even create new files and save them to the file system. Figure 7.4 shows a text file being loaded into the application, which is then modified and then saved back to disk.

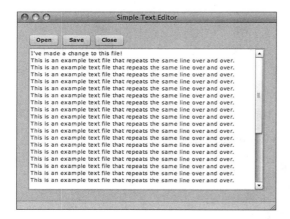

FIGURE 7.4   Editing and saving a file to the file system.

The significant difference in this updated version of the text editor is in its file-writing capabilities. Take a look at the saveFileToDisk() method:

```
private function saveFileToDisk( event:Event=null ):void
{
    var fileToSave:File = ( event != null )? event.target as File: file;
    var fileStream:FileStream = new FileStream();
    fileStream.open( fileToSave, FileMode.WRITE );
    fileStream.writeUTFBytes( fileText.text );
    fileStream.close();
    file = fileToSave;
}
```

We should highlight two items in this method: First, although we're using the same open() method on the FileStream as we used for reading a file, the FileMode is now WRITE. Second, we're using writeUTFBytes() and passing in our file contents, which is essentially the opposite of our read operation using readUTFBytes().

Although it's not all that intuitive from a user-interface perspective, the user can close an opened file and return to a blank document. If the user starts writing at that point, the Save option is made available. Clicking that button invokes a Save As dialog, which eventually leverages our same "write" logic with some minor differences.

Working with Directories

So far, there might seem to be a lack of support for directories. We've seen a `File` class, but no `Directory` class. Because files and directories share the same basic operations (copying, moving, deleting, and so on), the directory functionality is actually found in the `File` class.

The basic idea is to create a new `File` object reference and then perform directory-specific operations such as creating or listing directories (see Table 7.4).

TABLE 7.4   Directory-Specific Operations in `flash.filesystem.File`

Method Name	Description
`File.createDirectory()`	Creates the directory (and all parent directories) if it does not exist.
`File.createTempDirectory`	Returns a reference to a new temporary directory. This is a new directory in the system's temporary directory path.
`File.deleteDirectory()`	Removes the directory. Can be done asynchronously.
`File.getDirectoryListing()`	Lists the contents of a directory. Can be done asynchronously.
`File.getRootDirectories()`	Lists all of the root directories of the file system.

Creating a New Directory

Working with directories is almost identical to working with files with a couple of minor exceptions. For instance, creating a directory named `AIR` in the user's documents folder is as follows:

```
var myDirectory:File = File.documentsDirectory.resolvePath( "AIR" );
myDirectory.createDirectory();
```

Creating a Temporary Directory

You can also use Adobe AIR to create temporary directories. Temporary directories can be useful in many different situations, such as a temporary cache for downloaded media files.

```
var myTempDirectory:File = File.createTempDirectory();
```

The `createTempDirectory()` method generates a temp directory on the given operating system and returns a reference to that directory. As with the previous example, you can hold that reference in a local variable and use it as a relative path when you want to write to that directory.

When you're finished with it, simply set that local variable to `null`.

Deleting a Directory

Deleting a directory is straightforward. Create a reference to the target folder and call deleteDirectory:

```
var myDirectory:File = File.documentsDirectory.resolvePath( "AIR" );
myDirectory.deleteDirectory( true );
```

Retrieving a Directory Listing

It's easy to iterate through the contents of a directory using the getDirectoryListing() and getDirectoryListingAsync() methods.

This is a good example of a process that should be done asynchronously. Because a directory could have any number of subdirectories and files, anywhere from zero to thousands, the length of time for the operation is unpredictable. Performing it asynchronously ensures that your application won't look frozen while the directory contents are being retrieved.

The following code segment is an example to show how to get the contents of a directory and display various properties of each item:

```
var myDirectory:File = File.documentsDirectory;
var files:Array = myDirectory.getDirectoryListing();
for( var i:uint = 0; i < files.length; i++ )
{
   trace( files[i].name, files[i].nativePath, files[i].size );
}
```

Summary

This chapter explored the basic concepts of the Adobe AIR File API.

To the average Windows or Mac developer out there developing applications in native languages, working with files and directories is certainly nothing new and exciting. As for web developers, though, some might consider this feature-set to be the Holy Grail of the Adobe AIR platform. No longer are we cordoned off by the restrictions of the web browser when it comes to local file manipulation. It's been a long time coming.

CHAPTER 8

Understanding the Drag-and-Drop API

One of the more exciting features of Adobe® AIR™ is the drag-and-drop application programming interface (API). Although Adobe® Flex™ supports drag-and-drop, that support is limited to the context of your application; that is, objects can be moved within the container of the application and not beyond. With the expanded API in Adobe AIR, you can now drag data between your Adobe AIR application and the user's native operating system—for instance, dragging images, text, or even file references between your Adobe AIR application and other native programs such as Microsoft Word or simply moving data to and from the user's file system.

The concept behind the magic is quite simple. The Adobe AIR API provides access to the native Clipboard. When the user initiates a drag gesture, you can programmatically decide what information should be "carried" in the Clipboard. When the user terminates the action by dropping the object, the receiving application attempts to interpret the data in the Clipboard. For example, if we wanted to offer the user the ability to transfer data from a data grid in an Adobe AIR application to an Excel spreadsheet, the most reliable approach would be to populate the Clipboard with a comma-delimited version of the data residing in the data grid control. When the user completes the drop gesture, the spreadsheet recognizes that there is compatible data and attempts to incorporate the contents into the target document; that is, it inserts the data into the proper amount of rows and columns.

Another interesting aspect is the level of control over the gesture itself. You can control the proxy image used for the operation. A proxy image is the visual representation of the type of data the user is attempting to transfer out or into the Adobe AIR application. You've seen examples of this every day: Dragging a folder in Windows Explorer from one location to another carries an image of a folder next to the mouse pointer. This feedback helps users understand the implications of the action they're about to take. Again, this isn't exactly new in the world of Adobe Flex, but again the big difference with Adobe AIR applications is that these proxy images carry over onto the desktop. For instance, when dragging an image from your application, you might decide to use a scaled down version of that same image as the drag proxy image. When the user moves beyond the bounds of the Adobe AIR application, that drag image persists, just as it would if you were moving that same image from one location to another on the desktop.

Let's glance at elements of the drag-and-drop API introduced in this chapter (see Table 8.1).

TABLE 8.1   ActionScript Classes Introduced

Package	Class	Description
flash.display	BitmapData	Pixel data of a bitmap object. An image can be altered in various ways by manipulating its BitmapData.
flash.desktop	Clipboard	Container for objects to be transferred via user gestures like drag-and-drop.
flash.desktop	ClipboardFormats	Defines constants for data formats used in the Clipboard.
flash.desktop	NativeDragManager	Used to coordinate drag-and-drop operations between Adobe AIR and the native operating system.
flash.desktop	NativeDragOptions	Used to provide hints to the target object as to how the data should be used—move, copy, link, and so on.

Examining the Drag-Out Gesture

We'll start by outlining a bare-bones example to highlight what's involved in the drag-out gesture. The idea behind the example outlined in Listing 8.1 is to create a native window housing a drag-enabled image. When the image is dragged out of the application, we will assign a reference to the image file on disk. There is nothing stopping us from adding multiple data formats into the Clipboard, such as BitmapData or even a ByteArray. This increases the odds of success in the drop operation because the target object has a wider array of options when importing the data. For now, though, we will keep things simple.

If you have Listing 8.1 checked out of the repository, go ahead and launch it from Adobe Flex Builder to get a feel for how the drag-out operation works at runtime. Click and hold the mouse button on the image, then drag it to the desktop, and release the mouse button.

LISTING 8.1   Drag and Drop, Take 1

```
<?xml version="1.0" encoding="utf-8"?>
<mx:WindowedApplication
    xmlns:mx="http://www.adobe.com/2006/mxml"
    layout="vertical"
    horizontalAlign="center"
    verticalAlign="middle"
    width="600" height="400"
    title="Drag 'n Drop Example">

    <mx:Script>
    <![CDATA[

    [Bindable]
    private var imageUrl:String = "app:/assets/flex.png";

    private function onMouseDown( event:MouseEvent ):void
    {
        var image:Image = event.currentTarget as Image;
        var imageFile:File = new File( image.source as String );

        var clip:Clipboard = new Clipboard();
        clip.setData( ClipboardFormats.FILE_LIST_FORMAT, [ imageFile ], false );

        NativeDragManager.doDrag( image, clip );
    }

    ]]>
    </mx:Script>

    <mx:Image id="myImage" source="{ imageUrl }" mouseDown="onMouseDown( event )" />
</mx:WindowedApplication>
```

Figure 8.1 depicts the initial state of our drag-out sample application.

When you run the example, you see that the drag-out operation work in that image file is copied to the target location. Something is missing, though, because it is not clear just what exactly is being dragged out of the application. We'll get to that in a minute. First, let's look at what the application is doing behind the scenes.

Notice the Image MXML component at the bottom of Listing 8.1. We're kicking off our drag by calling the onMouseDown() event handler when the user clicks down on the image:

```
<mx:Image id="myImage" source="{ imageUrl }" mouseDown="onMouseDown( event )" />
```

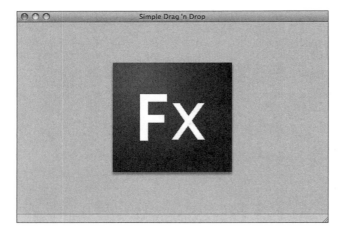

FIGURE 8.1   Drag-enabled image.

The onMouseDown event handler function is first creating a Clipboard instance and setting a reference to our image file used in the application as the Clipboard's data. This is done by passing in the image source into the constructor of the File object. This gives us a "handle" of the file that the drop target can use to locate that file on disk.

Next up is the doDrag() call on the NativeDragManager. Managers are typically singleton classes, meaning there's one instance for the entire application. The image, specified as the drag initiator, and the Clipboard instance are passed into the doDrag() call. The rest is history as far as the drag-out gesture goes. The drag manager itself is capable of handling the subsequent drop operation.

NOTE

In Adobe AIR, Flex objects that extend UIComponent have drag-and-drop events baked in that enable you to add logic at various stages of the operation. These include events such as nativeDragStart, nativeDragOver, nativeDragEnter, nativeDragExit, nativeDragDrop, and nativeDragComplete. Refer to the Adobe Flex ActionScript API reference.

As mentioned previously, the first example is missing visual feedback for the users to indicate what they are attempting to transfer out of the Adobe AIR application. Listing 8.2 outlines how to add such behavior.

LISTING 8.2   Drag and Drop, Take 2

```
<?xml version="1.0" encoding="utf-8"?>
<mx:WindowedApplication
        xmlns:mx="http://www.adobe.com/2006/mxml"
```

```
        layout="vertical"
        horizontalAlign="center"
        verticalAlign="middle"
        width="600" height="400"
        title="Drag 'n Drop Example">

        <mx:Script>
        <![CDATA[

        [Bindable]
        private var imageUrl:String = "app:/assets/flex.png";

        private function onMouseDown( event:MouseEvent ):void
        {
        var image:Image = event.currentTarget as Image;
        var imageFile:File = new File( image.source as String );

        var clip:Clipboard = new Clipboard();
        clip.setData( ClipboardFormats.FILE_LIST_FORMAT, [ imageFile ], false );

        // Copy our image, change its alpha and display during drag
        var bmData:BitmapData = (myImage.content as Bitmap).bitmapData.clone();
        var transform:ColorTransform = new ColorTransform();
        transform.alphaMultiplier = 0.3;
        var rect:Rectangle = new Rectangle(0, 0, bmData.width, bmData.height);
        bmData.colorTransform( rect, transform );

        // What drag options do we want to hint to the drop target?
        var dragOptions:NativeDragOptions = new NativeDragOptions();
        dragOptions.allowMove = false;
        dragOptions.allowCopy = true;
        dragOptions.allowLink = false;

        NativeDragManager.doDrag(
            myImage,
            clip,
            bmData,
            new Point( -myImage.mouseX, -myImage.mouseY ),
            dragOptions);
        }

        ]]>
        </mx:Script>
        <mx:Image id="myImage" source="{ imageUrl }" mouseDown="onMouseDown
➥( event )" />
</mx:WindowedApplication>
```

Although the example in Listing 8.1 succeeds in providing the drag-out behavior, it does not provide any visual feedback to indicate what the user is attempting to transfer out of the Adobe AIR application. In addition, the act of dragging from one application to another or to the desktop does not normally cause the object in question to be physically moved. Typically the user is expecting a copy to be made.

The second version of our application, as outlined in Listing 8.2, solves both problems. Figure 8.2 shows that a new proxy image is used throughout the drag-out gesture.

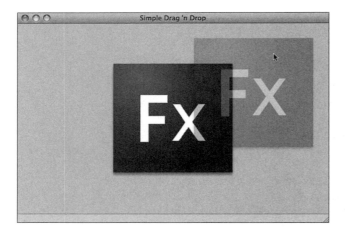

FIGURE 8.2   Drag-enabled image with proxy image.

To add a visual cue while the drag is in process, we've now added in bitmap data as the proxy image in the doDrag() call. By cloning the bitmap data, we can alter the alpha transparency without affecting the original image. This provides the effect of a matching, faded version of our graphic when the user performs a drag operation.

To position the proxy image properly, we need to provide a new Point (x and y coordinates). If we do not specify a value, the upper-left edge of the proxy image appears at the coordinates of the mouse click. A more natural experience would be to have the proxy image emerge from the exact coordinates of the original image, as if a copy were being peeled off. We can do this by using -mouseX and -mouseY of the underlying image. Subtracting these values gives us the onscreen location of the upper-left corner of the original image. Passing this Point into the doDrag() method causes the proxy image to appear at that Point.

> **NOTE**
>
> Adobe Flex Developers: When comparing `flash.desktop.NativeDragManager` and `mx.managers.DragManager`, you'll notice some subtle differences. One such difference is the proxy image used in the `doDrag()` operation. Rather than passing in an `IFlexDisplayObject`, the `NativeDragManager` is expecting a `BitmapData` object. Keep in mind that in Adobe AIR, Flex isn't the only game in town. The `NativeDragManager` has to interact with the OS to overlay your proxy image outside of your Adobe AIR application. In that context, there is no notion of Adobe Flex objects, hence the requirement for a raw image format like `BitmapData`, which is just an array of pixel data.

Examining the Drag-In Gesture

Now let's look at dragging items *into* an Adobe AIR application. Listing 8.3 is the start of a file preview application. The user can drag an image or text file into the drop zone and have the contents rendered onscreen. We look at how to interpret and use Clipboard data when objects are dragged from the desktop or other native applications.

LISTING 8.3   File Preview, Drag-In Example

```
<?xml version="1.0" encoding="utf-8"?>
<mx:WindowedApplication
    xmlns:mx="http://www.adobe.com/2006/mxml"
    layout="vertical"
    horizontalAlign="center"
    verticalAlign="middle"
    width="600" height="400"
    title="File Preview"
    creationComplete="init()">
        <mx:Script>
    <![CDATA[

    import mx.core.UIComponent;
    import mx.managers.DragManager;

     [Bindable]
    private var imageSource:String;
     [Bindable]
    private var fileText:String;

    private function init():void
    {
       this.currentState = "base";
```

```
        }

        private function onDragEnter( event:NativeDragEvent ):void
        {
           if( event.clipboard.hasFormat( ClipboardFormats.FILE_LIST_FORMAT ) )
           {
              var fileArray:Array = event.clipboard.getData
➥( ClipboardFormats.FILE_LIST_FORMAT ) as Array;
              var file:File = fileArray[0] as File;
              if( !file.isDirectory && !file.isSymbolicLink && !file.isPackage )
              {
                 NativeDragManager.acceptDragDrop( this.dropArea );
                 acceptState( true );
              }
           }
        }

        private function onDragExit( event:NativeDragEvent ):void
        {
            acceptState( false );
        }

        private function acceptState( bool:Boolean ):void
        {
           if( bool )
           {
              dropArea.setStyle( "borderColor", 0x629632 );
              dropArea.setStyle( "borderThickness", 2 );
           }
           else
           {
              dropArea.setStyle( "borderColor", 0x999999 );
              dropArea.setStyle( "borderThickness", 1 );
           }
        }

        private function onDragDrop( event:NativeDragEvent ):void
        {
            var fileArray:Array = event.clipboard.getData
➥( ClipboardFormats.FILE_LIST_FORMAT ) as Array;
            var file:File = fileArray[0] as File;

            switch( file.extension.toLowerCase() )
            {
```

```
            case "png":
              loadImage( file.url );
              break;
          case "jpg":
              loadImage( file.url );
              break;
          case "gif":
              loadImage( file.url );
              break;
          default:
              // Attempt to load as text
               loadText( file.url );
      }
      acceptState( false );
    }

    private function loadImage( url:String ):void
    {
       imageSource = url;
       currentState = "image";
    }

    private function loadText( url:String ):void
    {
       var file:File = new File( url );
       var fileStream:FileStream = new FileStream();
       fileStream.open( file, FileMode.READ );

        var fileContents:String = fileStream.readUTFBytes
➥( fileStream.bytesAvailable );
       fileStream.close();

        fileText = fileContents;
        currentState = "text";
    }

    ]]>
    </mx:Script>

    <!— TO-DO: This needs to be replaced with a simple viewstack —>
    <mx:states>
       <mx:State name="base">
         <mx:AddChild relativeTo="{ dropArea }">
            <mx:Label text="Drop Image or Text File Here" fontWeight="bold" />
```

```
            </mx:AddChild>
            <mx:AddChild relativeTo="{ dropArea }">
               <mx:Image source="@Embed(source='/assets/file_icon.png')" />
            </mx:AddChild>
         </mx:State>
         <mx:State name="image">
            <mx:AddChild relativeTo="{ dropArea }">
              <mx:Image source="{ imageSource }" />
            </mx:AddChild>
         </mx:State>
         <mx:State name="text">
            <mx:AddChild relativeTo="{ dropArea }">
               <mx:TextArea id="file" text="{ fileText }" width="100%"
➥height="100%" />
            </mx:AddChild>
         </mx:State>
      </mx:states>

      <mx:Box
         id="dropArea"
         width="100%" height="100%"
         borderStyle="solid" borderThickness="1"
         borderColor="#999999" backgroundColor="#FFFFFF"
         verticalAlign="middle" horizontalAlign="center"
         backgroundAlpha="0.3"
         nativeDragEnter="onDragEnter( event )"
         nativeDragDrop="onDragDrop( event )"
         nativeDragExit="onDragExit( event )" />

      <mx:Button label="Clear" click="this.currentState='base'" />
</mx:WindowedApplication>
```

Figure 8.3 shows the file preview application launched from Adobe Flex Builder. If you have Listing 8.3 checked out from the repository, try experimenting by dragging an image or text file into the application.

As with our drag-out examples earlier in the chapter, drag events generated by a drag-in gesture also contain a Clipboard object. This allows us to examine what the user is attempting to drag into the application before actually allowing the drop to take place.

Let's begin with the Box MXML component near the end of Listing 8.3:

```
<mx:Box
   id="dropArea"
   width="100%" height="100%"
   borderStyle="solid" borderThickness="1"
```

```
borderColor="#999999" backgroundColor="#FFFFFF"
verticalAlign="middle" horizontalAlign="center"
backgroundAlpha="0.3"
nativeDragEnter="onDragEnter( event )"
nativeDragDrop="onDragDrop( event )"
nativeDragExit="onDragExit( event )" />
```

We're leveraging the native drag events inherently available in the Box component to specify callback functions to invoke. The nativeDragEnter event fires when a drag operation enters the Adobe AIR application. This can originate from anywhere—the desktop or another application. When it's fired, the onDragEnter() method, defined in the script block above, is invoked.

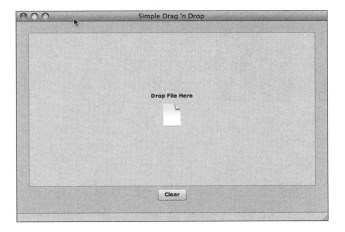

FIGURE 8.3   Screenshot of file preview application.

We're using the hasFormat() method on the Clipboard to determine whether a file list exists as that's all our sample application can handle. After determining that we've got a file to work with, grab that File reference and verify it's not a directory, a package (Mac only), or a symbolic link. (A File object can be many things!)

```
if( event.clipboard.hasFormat( ClipboardFormats.FILE_LIST_FORMAT ) )
{
   var fileArray:Array = event.clipboard.getData( ClipboardFormats.FILE_LIST_FORMAT
) as Array;
   var file:File = fileArray[0] as File;
   if( !file.isDirectory && !file.isSymbolicLink && !file.isPackage )
   {
      NativeDragManager.acceptDragDrop( this.dropArea );
      acceptState( true );
   }
}
```

Figure 8.4 highlights that after verifying we are indeed dealing with a `File` object, we can provide a visual cue to the user signaling the drop can be accepted by means of changing the border color of the `Box`.

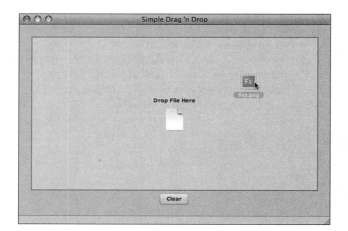

FIGURE 8.4   Providing visual cues on drag events.

```
private function acceptState( bool:Boolean ):void
{
    if( bool )
    {
        dropArea.setStyle( "borderColor", 0x629632 );
        dropArea.setStyle( "borderThickness", 2 );
    }
    else
    {
        dropArea.setStyle( "borderColor", 0x999999 );
        dropArea.setStyle( "borderThickness", 1 );
    }
}
```

Now if the user does decide to drop the file in our designated area, this fires off yet another event. The `Box` specifies a `nativeDragDrop` handler that is invoked.

In the drop handler function, we examine the contents a little more closely by verifying the file extensions and deciding whether we're capable of displaying the file onscreen:

```
var fileArray:Array = event.clipboard.getData( ClipboardFormats.FILE_LIST_FORMAT )
as Array;
```

After the contents of the `Clipboard` are cast to a `File` object, which is what we're expecting, we can now use any properties and/or methods from the `File` class to determine the file extension of the item being dropped. Based on the extension, we can set the state of the view accordingly and render the file contents:

```
switch( file.extension.toLowerCase() )
{
   case "png":
   case "jpg":
   case "gif":
      loadImage( file.url );
      break;
   default:
      // Attempt to load as text
      loadText( file.url );
}
```

Keep in mind that Listing 8.3 is a simplified example. You are not of course limited to working with file references. As mentioned previously, the possibilities are endless. You might need to work with multiple data formats in the Clipboard, depending on the specific type of Adobe Flex control, the user is attempting to drag into.

NOTE

As always, for the sake of simplicity when introducing Adobe AIR concepts, we've used straightforward examples in MXML. When implementing these features in your own applications, modeling logic into ActionScript classes in accordance with common programming design patterns will save you much heartache with respect to code maintenance and extensibility.

Summary

The concept of drag-and-drop is not new for those who have experience with the `DragManager` in Adobe Flex. However, we've touched on some significant differences when working with the `NativeDragManager` and `NativeDragEvents` in Adobe AIR. No longer are you limited to drag-and-drop interacts within the context of a browser window.

This new functionality alone is enough to get excited about Adobe AIR. It is time to break free of those boring file dialogs and deliver a much more fluid user experience through drag-and-drop functionality in your Adobe AIR applications.

# CHAPTER 9

Working with Copy and Paste

The copy and paste capabilities of an Adobe® AIR™ application are due to the Clipboard application programming interface (API) in the runtime. This small but powerful API is another convenient feature that allows the Adobe AIR developer to build powerful and full-featured desktop applications. It can be said that if you build for the desktop, you should provide copy and paste, as users have come to expect these capabilities in all desktop applications. The copy and paste features within an Adobe AIR application can handle the major data types and include the following: bitmaps, files, text, URL strings, serialized objects, and object references (only valid within the originating application).

In this chapter you learn how to add copy and paste functionality to your Adobe AIR applications. You see the major data types being moved in and out of the Clipboard in several examples. You also see a strategy for handling large amounts of data in a deferred manner to improve your application's Clipboard perceived performance. By the end of this chapter, you should be ready to add this must-have feature—copy and paste—to your Adobe AIR applications.

Meet the Adobe AIR Clipboard Classes

The three Clipboard classes are `Clipboard`, `ClipboardFormats`, and `ClipboardTransferMode`; they are found in the Adobe AIR package, `flash.desktop`.

> **NOTE**
>
> This package also contains the classes for drag-and-drop and icon features.

The first class, the `Clipboard` class, provides a repository for transferring data and objects through the operating system's Clipboard (the OS Clipboard is accessed through the static property, `generalClipboard`) and through drag-and-drop operations. Think of this as the "loading zone" or "memory" for the copy and paste operations. A code snippet that shows the Clipboard's `generalClipboard` property is

```
return String(Clipboard.generalClipboard.getData(ClipboardFormats.TEXT_FORMAT));
```

In this example, you see that the `getData` method is retrieving data that is text-based. (`TEXT_FORMAT` is a constant for the `ClipboardFormats` class.) This second class, the `ClipboardFormats` class, provides the constant definitions for all the data types used by its sister class, `Clipboard`, and includes those shown in Table 9.1

TABLE 9.1   `ClipboardFormats` Class Data Type Constants

Type	Description
BITMAP_FORMAT	Used for image data
FILE_LIST_FORMAT	Used for an array of files type of data
HTML_FORMAT	Used for HTML type of data
TEXT_FORMAT	Used for string data
URL_FORMAT	Used for URL string data

The final class, the `ClipboardTransferMode` class, provides the constant definitions for the transfer modes, `transferMode`, for the `Clipboard` class' method, `getData()`, and includes those shown in Table 9.2.

TABLE 9.2   `ClipboardTransferMode` Class Constants

Type	Description
CLONE_ONLY	Clipboard returns a copy.
CLONE_PREFERRED	Clipboard returns a copy if available or a reference.
ORIGINAL_ONLY	Clipboard returns a reference.
ORIGINAL_PREFERRED	Clipboard returns a reference if available or a copy.

The transfer modes can be thought of as the manner in which that data is transferred—a copy or by reference.

```
return String(Clipboard.generalClipboard.getData(ClipboardFormats.TEXT_FORMAT,
➥ClipboardTransferMode.ORIGINAL_ONLY));
```

Using the TEXT_FORMAT Data Type

Now that you have the package and class information memorized, a simple example using the TEXT_FORMAT is shown in Listing 9.1 (the custom ActionScript 3 class for this example) and Listing 9.2 (the Extensible Markup Language [MXML] for this Adobe AIR application). The resulting Adobe AIR application is shown in Figures 9.1 and 9.2.

FIGURE 9.1   Adobe AIR application—the Clipboard example (initial state of the application).

FIGURE 9.2   Adobe AIR application—the Clipboard example (pasting the Clipboard).

> **TIP**
>
> During a copy to the Clipboard, the existing Clipboard is automatically overwritten. However, it is a best practice to clear the system Clipboard before writing new data to it to make sure that unrelated data in any other formats is also deleted. See `Clipboard.generalClipboard.clear()` in Listing 9.1.

LISTING 9.1   ClipboardSample.as Using the TEXT_FORMAT Data Type

ActionScript class—ClipboardSample.as:

```
package info.flexination.air.actionscripts
{
    import flash.desktop.Clipboard;
    import flash.desktop.ClipboardFormats;

    public class ClipboardSample
    {
        public function ClipboardSample()
        {
            var basketball:String = "Basketball";
            var sport:String;

            copy(basketball);
```

```
            sport = paste();
            trace(sport); //traces: "Basketball"
        }

        public function getClipBoard():String {
            var myclip:ClipboardSample = new ClipboardSample();
            return myclip.paste();
        }

        private function copy(text:String):void{
            Clipboard.generalClipboard.clear();
            Clipboard.generalClipboard.setData(ClipboardFormats.TEXT_FORMAT, text);
        }

        private function paste():String{
            if(Clipboard.generalClipboard.hasFormat(ClipboardFormats.TEXT_FORMAT)){
                return String(Clipboard.generalClipboard.getData
➥(ClipboardFormats.TEXT_FORMAT));
            } else {return null;}
        }

    }
}
```

LISTING 9.2   Adobe AIR Application Using the ClipboardExample.as

MXML:
```
<?xml version="1.0" encoding="utf-8"?>
<mx:WindowedApplication xmlns:mx="http://www.adobe.com/2006/mxml" title="AIR™
➥Copy and Paste Example" applicationComplete="init()" layout="absolute">
    <mx:Script>
    <![CDATA[
    import info.flexination.air.actionscripts.ClipboardSample;
    import mx.controls.Alert;
    import mx.utils.ObjectUtil;

    private var myClip:ClipboardSample = new ClipboardSample();

    private function init():void {
        //Alert.show(ObjectUtil.toString((myClip.getClipBoard())));
    }
    ]]>
    </mx:Script>
    <mx:TextArea top="10" bottom="305" left="24.5" right="24.5"
➥toolTip="Paste into the textarea with CTRL + V"/>
</mx:WindowedApplication>
```

In Figure 9.1, the initial state of the application shows an empty `TextArea` control. However, the data is already in the Clipboard because of the way the AS3 class was written—during instantiation, the variable (`basketball`), is immediately copied into the Clipboard:

```
var basketball:String = "Basketball";
copy(basketball);
private function copy(text:String):void{
    Clipboard.generalClipboard.clear();
    Clipboard.generalClipboard.setData(ClipboardFormats.TEXT_FORMAT, text);
}
```

Figure 9.2 shows the results of simply issuing the `paste` command (Windows Ctrl-C or Mac OS X Command-C)—as mentioned, the Clipboard contains `basketball` as soon as the Adobe AIR application is running.

Another example, also using the `TEXT_FORMAT` data type, is shown in Listings 9.3 and 9.4. The resulting Adobe AIR application is shown in Figures 9.3 and 9.4. In this example, there are two `TextArea` controls in the MXML-based application. The first `TextArea` control has the contents of the current Clipboard loaded during the function handler for the `applicationComplete` event. The `getClipBoard()` function is called from the AS3 `ClipboardSample2` class:

```
private var myClip:ClipboardSample2 = new ClipboardSample2();
private function init():void {
    //Alert.show(ObjectUtil.toString((myClip.getClipBoard())));
    ta.text = myClip.getClipBoard();
}
```

In the `getClipBoard()` function, the `paste()` method is called:

```
public function getClipBoard():String {
    var myclip:ClipboardSample2 = new ClipboardSample2();
    return myclip.paste();
}
private function paste():String{
    if(Clipboard.generalClipboard.hasFormat(ClipboardFormats.TEXT_FORMAT)){
        return
String(Clipboard.generalClipboard.getData(ClipboardFormats.TEXT_FORMAT));
    } else {return null;}
}
```

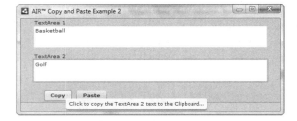

FIGURE 9.3   Adobe AIR application—the Clipboard example 2 (initial state of the Application).

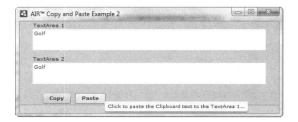

FIGURE 9.4   Adobe AIR application—the Clipboard example 2 (pasting the Clipboard).

LISTING 9.3   ClipboardSample2.as Using the TEXT_FORMAT Data Type

```
package info.flexination.air.actionscripts
{
    import flash.desktop.Clipboard;
    import flash.desktop.ClipboardFormats;

    public class ClipboardSample2
    {
        public function ClipboardSample2()
        {
        }

        public function getClipBoard():String {
            var myclip:ClipboardSample2 = new ClipboardSample2();
            return myclip.paste();
        }

        public function setClipBoard(inTxt:String):void {
            var sport:String;
            copy(inTxt);
            sport = paste();
            trace(sport); //traces: value of inTxt
        }
```

```
        private function copy(text:String):void{
            Clipboard.generalClipboard.clear();
            Clipboard.generalClipboard.setData(ClipboardFormats.TEXT_FORMAT, text);
        }

        private function paste():String{
            if(Clipboard.generalClipboard.hasFormat(ClipboardFormats.TEXT_FORMAT)){
                return
String(Clipboard.generalClipboard.getData(ClipboardFormats.TEXT_FORMAT));
            } else {return null;}
        }


    }
}
```

LISTING 9.4   Adobe AIR Application Using the ClipboardExample2.as

```
<?xml version="1.0" encoding="utf-8"?>
<mx:WindowedApplication xmlns:mx="http://www.adobe.com/2006/mxml" title="AIR™
➥Copy and Paste Example 2" applicationComplete="init()"
➥layout="absolute" height="185">
    <mx:Script>
    <![CDATA[
    import info.flexination.air.actionscripts.ClipboardSample2;
    import mx.controls.Alert;
    import mx.utils.ObjectUtil;

    private var myClip:ClipboardSample2 = new ClipboardSample2();

    private function init():void {
        //Alert.show(ObjectUtil.toString((myClip.getClipBoard())));
        ta.text = myClip.getClipBoard();
    }

    private function doCopy():void {
        myClip.setClipBoard(ta2.text);
    }

    private function doPaste():void {
        ta.text = myClip.getClipBoard();
    }
    ]]>
    </mx:Script>
    <mx:TextArea id="ta" top="15" bottom="124" left="24.5" right="24.5"
➥toolTip="Paste into the textarea with CTRL + V" width="300"/>
```

```
    <mx:TextArea id="ta2" toolTip="Paste into the textarea with CTRL + V" top="82"
➥bottom="57" left="24.5" right="24.5"/>
    <mx:Text x="24.5" y="0" text="TextArea 1" left="24.5" right="24.5"
➥width="300"/>
    <mx:Button x="45" y="143" label="Copy" click="doCopy()"
➥toolTip="Click to copy the TextArea 2 text to the Clipboard..."/>
    <mx:Button x="107" y="143" label="Paste" click="doPaste()"
➥toolTip="Click to paste the Clipboard text to the TextArea 1..."/>
    <mx:Text x="24.5" y="67" text="TextArea 2"/>
</mx:WindowedApplication>
```

Clicking the Copy button places any text that is in the second TextArea control into the Clipboard as it calls the doCopy() function in the MXML. The ClipboardSample2 class' setClipBoard() function accepts the second TextArea control's text:

```
private function doCopy():void {
    myClip.setClipBoard(ta2.text);
}
```

The setClipBoard() function calls the copy() function, passing in the text that was transferred from the second TextArea control:

```
public function setClipBoard(inTxt:String):void {
    var sport:String;
    copy(inTxt);
}
```

Same as you saw before, the data type is TEXT_FORMAT, and the data is placed in the Clipboard via the setData() method:

```
private function copy(text:String):void{
    Clipboard.generalClipboard.clear();
    Clipboard.generalClipboard.setData(ClipboardFormats.TEXT_FORMAT, text);
}
```

Clicking the Paste button calls the doPaste() function in the MXML that in turn calls the class' getClipBoard() function:

```
private function doPaste():void {
    ta.text = myClip.getClipBoard();
}
```

The getClipBoard() function calls the paste() function in the AS3 class:

```
public function getClipBoard():String {
    var myclip:ClipboardSample2 = new ClipboardSample2();
    return myclip.paste();
}
```

The paste() function uses the getData() function of the Clipboard class and returns the contents back to the getClipBoard() function, and ultimately, the first TextArea control:

```
private function paste():String{
    if(Clipboard.generalClipboard.hasFormat(ClipboardFormats.TEXT_FORMAT)){
    return String(Clipboard.generalClipboard.getData(ClipboardFormats.TEXT_FORMAT));
    } else {return null;}
}
```

Using the BITMAP_FORMAT Data Type

The next example shown in Listing 9.5 demonstrates passing the image data type, BITMAP_FORMAT, through the Clipboard and back into the Adobe AIR application. In this example, the Adobe AIR application, written in Adobe® Flex™, instantiates the ActionScript 3 class as follows:

```
private var myClip:ClipboardSample3 = new ClipboardSample3();
```

A button labeled Copy calls the doCopy() function:

```
private function doCopy():void {
    var bd:BitmapData = new BitmapData(img2.width,img2.height);
    bd.draw(img2);
    myClip.setClipBoard(bd);
}
```

The doCopy() function creates the BitmapData of an image, the variable is bd, and the id is img2. The AS3 class' setClipBoard() function passes the BitmapData of the image. The setClipBoard() function is shown:

```
public function setClipBoard(inImg:BitmapData):void {
    var image:BitmapData;
    copy(inImg);
}
```

The copy function of the AS3 class is passed the image BitmapData:

```
private function copy(imgData:BitmapData):void{
    Clipboard.generalClipboard.clear();
    Clipboard.generalClipboard.setData(ClipboardFormats.BITMAP_FORMAT, imgData);
}
```

The image is now stored in the Clipboard. Back in the Adobe AIR application, you can click the Paste button. This calls the doPaste() function:

```
private function doPaste():void {
    var pastedbd:BitmapData = myClip.getClipBoard();
```

```
    //Alert.show(ObjectUtil.toString(pastedbd));
    ta.text = String(ObjectUtil.toString(pastedbd));
    var ba:ByteArray = PNGEnc.encode(pastedbd);
    swf.load(ba);
}
```

The getClipBoard() function in the AS3 class is called and stored in a BitmapData variable:

```
public function getClipBoard():BitmapData {
    var myclip:ClipboardSample3 = new ClipboardSample3();
    return myclip.paste();
}
```

The paste() function from the AS3 class is called and returns the BitmapData stored in the Clipboard:

```
private function paste():BitmapData{
    if(Clipboard.generalClipboard.hasFormat(ClipboardFormats.BITMAP_FORMAT)){
        return
BitmapData(Clipboard.generalClipboard.getData(ClipboardFormats.BITMAP_FORMAT));
    } else {return null;}
}
```

Finally, the TextArea displays the BitmapData as an Object in a String utilizing the Adobe Flex ObjectUtil class toString() method. Leveraging a PNGEnc.as class, the BitmapData is converted to a ByteArray. The ByteArray is loaded into an Adobe Flex SWFLoader component and displayed. You should note that there is no loss of data, and so the image appears just like the original one.

LISTING 9.5   Adobe AIR Application Using BITMAP_FORMAT

AS3:

```
package info.flexination.air.actionscripts
{
    import flash.desktop.Clipboard;
    import flash.desktop.ClipboardFormats;
    import flash.display.BitmapData;

    public class ClipboardSample3
    {
        public function ClipboardSample3()
        {
        }

        public function getClipBoard():BitmapData {
            var myclip:ClipboardSample3 = new ClipboardSample3();
```

```
            return myclip.paste();
        }

        public function setClipBoard(inImg:BitmapData):void {
            var image:BitmapData;
            copy(inImg);
            image = paste();
        }

        private function copy(imgData:BitmapData):void{
            Clipboard.generalClipboard.clear();
            Clipboard.generalClipboard.setData(ClipboardFormats.BITMAP_FORMAT,
➡imgData);
        }

        private function paste():BitmapData{
            if(Clipboard.generalClipboard.hasFormat
➡(ClipboardFormats.BITMAP_FORMAT)){
                return BitmapData(Clipboard.generalClipboard.getData
➡(ClipboardFormats.BITMAP_FORMAT));
            } else {return null;}
        }

    }
}
```

CAUTION

You will need the `PNGEnc.as` file included in your Adobe AIR project code to run the Listing 9.5 MXML.

The `PNGEnc.as` class necessary to run this particular example is beyond the scope of this book but is shown in the following code. It appears here only for your reference because it converts `BitmapData` to a `ByteArray`. The Adobe Flex `SWFLoader` control chosen for this example requires `ByteArray` data and not `BitmapData`:

```
package {

    import flash.geom.*;
    import flash.display.*;
    import flash.utils.*;

    public class PNGEnc {
```

```
public static function encode(img:BitmapData):ByteArray {
    // Create output byte array
    var png:ByteArray = new ByteArray();
    // Write PNG signature
    png.writeUnsignedInt(0x89504e47);
    png.writeUnsignedInt(0x0D0A1A0A);
    // Build IHDR chunk
    var IHDR:ByteArray = new ByteArray();
    IHDR.writeInt(img.width);
    IHDR.writeInt(img.height);
    IHDR.writeUnsignedInt(0x08060000); // 32bit RGBA
    IHDR.writeByte(0);
    writeChunk(png,0x49484452,IHDR);
    // Build IDAT chunk
    var IDAT:ByteArray= new ByteArray();
    for(var i:int=0;i < img.height;i++) {
        // no filter
        IDAT.writeByte(0);
        var p:uint;
        if ( !img.transparent ) {
            for(var j:int=0;j < img.width;j++) {
                p = img.getPixel(j,i);
                IDAT.writeUnsignedInt(
                    uint(((p&0xFFFFFF) << 8)¦0xFF));
            }
        } else {
            for(var k:int=0;k < img.width;k++) {
                p = img.getPixel32(k,i);
                IDAT.writeUnsignedInt(
                    uint(((p&0xFFFFFF) << 8)¦
                    (p>>>24)));
            }
        }
    }
    IDAT.compress();
    writeChunk(png,0x49444154,IDAT);
    // Build IEND chunk
    writeChunk(png,0x49454E44,null);
    // return PNG
    return png;
}

private static var crcTable:Array;
private static var crcTableComputed:Boolean = false;

private static function writeChunk(png:ByteArray,
        type:uint, data:ByteArray):void {
```

```
            if (!crcTableComputed) {
                crcTableComputed = true;
                crcTable = [];
                for (var n:uint = 0; n < 256; n++) {
                    var c:uint = n;
                    for (var k:uint = 0; k < 8; k++) {
                        if (c & 1) {
                            c = uint(uint(0xedb88320) ^
                                uint(c >>> 1));
                        } else {
                            c = uint(c >>> 1);
                        }
                    }
                    crcTable[n] = c;
                }
            }
            var len:uint = 0;
            if (data != null) {
                len = data.length;
            }
            png.writeUnsignedInt(len);
            var p:uint = png.position;
            png.writeUnsignedInt(type);
            if ( data != null ) {
                png.writeBytes(data);
            }
            var e:uint = png.position;
            png.position = p;
            var d:uint = 0xffffffff;
            for (var i:int = 0; i < (e-p); i++) {
                d = uint(crcTable[
                    (d ^ png.readUnsignedByte()) &
                    uint(0xff)] ^ uint(d >>> 8));
            }
            d = uint(d^uint(0xffffffff));
            png.position = e;
            png.writeUnsignedInt(d);
        }
    }
}
```

The main application's MXML is as follows:

```
<?xml version="1.0" encoding="utf-8"?>
<mx:WindowedApplication xmlns:mx="http://www.adobe.com/2006/mxml" title="AIR™
➥Copy and Paste Example 3" layout="absolute" height="403">
    <mx:Script>
    <![CDATA[
```

```
import info.flexination.air.actionscripts.ClipboardSample3;
import mx.controls.Alert;
import mx.utils.ObjectUtil;

private var myClip:ClipboardSample3 = new ClipboardSample3();

private function doCopy():void {
    var bd:BitmapData = new BitmapData(img2.width,img2.height);
    bd.draw(img2);
    myClip.setClipBoard(bd);
}

private function doPaste():void {
    var pastedbd:BitmapData = myClip.getClipBoard();
    //Alert.show(ObjectUtil.toString(pastedbd));
    ta.text = String(ObjectUtil.toString(pastedbd));
    var ba:ByteArray = PNGEnc.encode(pastedbd);
    swf.load(ba);
}
]]>
</mx:Script>
<mx:Canvas id="canvas">
    <mx:TextArea id="ta" x="25" y="140" height="219" width="450"/>
    <mx:SWFLoader id="swf" x="103.5" y="30" width="50" height="50"/>
    <mx:Image id="img2" source="assets/jpgs/leprichaun.jpg" x="25" y="31"
➥width="50" height="50"/>
    <mx:Text y="10" text="Image 2" left="103.5" right="18.5"/>
    <mx:Button x="24" y="88" label="Copy" click="doCopy()"
➥toolTip="Click to copy the Image 1 to the Clipboard..."/>
    <mx:Text x="25" y="10" text="Image 1"/>
    <mx:Text x="25" y="123" text="Pasted Object"/>
    <mx:Button x="103" y="87" label="Paste" click="doPaste()"
➥toolTip="Click to paste the Clipboard Image to the Image 2..."/>
    </mx:Canvas>
</mx:WindowedApplication>
```

Figure 9.5 shows the Adobe AIR application that the Listing 9.5 code runs.

Using the HTML_FORMAT Data Type

The next data type examined is the HTML_FORMAT. Listing 9.6 and Figure 9.6 show an example of the HTML_FORMAT data type in use. This example enables you to browse to an HTML file (the HTML displays in an Adobe AIR HTML control), copy the HTML, and then paste it into a second HTML control. The usual instantiation of variables is loaded during the Adobe AIR application startup:

```
private var myClip:ClipboardSample4 = new ClipboardSample4();
private var htmlFile:File;
[Bindable] private var files:String = new String();
```

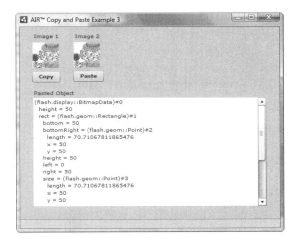

FIGURE 9.5   Adobe AIR Application using the BITMAP_FORMAT data type for copying and pasting an image.

FIGURE 9.6   Adobe AIR application using the HTML_FORMAT data type for copying and pasting HTML data.

Flex [Bindable] Metadata Tag

When a variable is the source of a data-binding expression, Adobe Flex automatically copies the value of the source to any destination variable when the source property changes. To signal to Adobe Flex to perform the copy, you use the `[Bindable]` meta-data tag to register the variable with Adobe Flex.

Clicking the Load File button runs the `loadHTML` function. An `addEventListener` triggers the `fileSelected` function after an HTML page is selected, and the page is displayed in the first HTML control:

```
private function loadHTML():void {
    var htmlFilter:FileFilter =
    new FileFilter("HTML", "*.htm;*.html;");
    htmlFile = new File();
    htmlFile.browseForOpen("Select a Web Page", [htmlFilter]);
    htmlFile.addEventListener(Event.SELECT, fileSelected);
}
private function fileSelected(event:Event):void {
    html.location = htmlFile.url;
}
```

Clicking the Copy button calls the `doCopy()` function, and the `setClipBoard()` function in the AS3 class is passed the `[Bindable]` variable, `files`, and data:

```
private function doCopy():void {
    files = html.location as String;
    myClip.setClipBoard(files);
}
```

As previously seen, the `setClipBoard` function accepts the files and calls the `copy()` function, but this time as `HTML_FORMAT`, and calls the `generalClipboard` property of the Clipboard's `setData()` method passing in the `files` variable:

```
private function copy(inFiles:String):void{
    Clipboard.generalClipboard.clear();
    Clipboard.generalClipboard.setData(ClipboardFormats.HTML_FORMAT, inFiles);
}
```

Now your HTML page is stored in the Clipboard. Clicking the Paste button triggers the `doPaste()` function, triggering the `getClipBoard()` function of the AS3 class that is stored in the variable, `pastedStringofFiles`. The returned value is placed in the `TextArea` as well as the location property of the second HTML control.

The MXML is as follows:

```
private function doPaste():void {
    var pastedStringofFiles:String = myClip.getClipBoard();
    //Alert.show(ObjectUtil.toString(pastedbd));
    ta.text = String(ObjectUtil.toString(pastedStringofFiles));
    html2.location = pastedStringofFiles;
}
```

The AS3 is as follows:

```
public function getClipBoard():String {
    var myclip:ClipboardSample4 = new ClipboardSample4();
    return myclip.paste();
}
private function paste():String{
    if(Clipboard.generalClipboard.hasFormat(ClipboardFormats.HTML_FORMAT)){
        return Clipboard.generalClipboard.getData(ClipboardFormats.HTML_FORMAT) as
➥String;
    } else {return null;}
}
```

LISTING 9.6   Adobe AIR Application Using the HTML_FORMAT Data Type

AS3:

```
package info.flexination.air.actionscripts
{
    import flash.desktop.Clipboard;
    import flash.desktop.ClipboardFormats;

    public class ClipboardSample4
    {
        public function ClipboardSample4()
        {
        }

        public function getClipBoard():String {
            var myclip:ClipboardSample4 = new ClipboardSample4();
            return myclip.paste();
        }

        public function setClipBoard(inFiles:String):void {
            var files:String = inFiles;
            copy(files);
        }
```

```
    private function copy(inFiles:String):void{
        Clipboard.generalClipboard.clear();
        Clipboard.generalClipboard.setData(ClipboardFormats.HTML_FORMAT,
➡inFiles);
    }

    private function paste():String{
        if(Clipboard.generalClipboard.hasFormat(ClipboardFormats.HTML_FORMAT)){
            return Clipboard.generalClipboard.getData
➡(ClipboardFormats.HTML_FORMAT) as String;
        } else {return null;}
    }


  }
}
```

MXML:

```
<?xml version="1.0" encoding="utf-8"?>
mx:WindowedApplication xmlns:mx="http://www.adobe.com/2006/mxml" title="AIR™
➡Copy and Paste Example 4" layout="absolute" height="414" width="372"
➡horizontalScrollPolicy="off" verticalScrollPolicy="off">
  <mx:Script>
  <![CDATA[
  import info.flexination.air.actionscripts.ClipboardSample4;
  import mx.controls.Alert;
  import mx.utils.ObjectUtil;
  import flash.filesystem.File;

  private var myClip:ClipboardSample4 = new ClipboardSample4();
    private var htmlFile:File;
    [Bindable] private var files:String = new String();

  private function loadImage():void {
      var htmlFilter:FileFilter =
      new FileFilter("HTML", "*.htm;*.html;");
      htmlFile = new File();
      htmlFile.browseForOpen("Select a Web Page", [htmlFilter]);
      htmlFile.addEventListener(Event.SELECT, imageSelected);
  }

  private function imageSelected(event:Event):void {
      html.location = htmlFile.url;
  }

  private function doCopy():void {
      files = html.location as String;
```

```
        myClip.setClipBoard(files);
    }

    private function doPaste():void {
        var pastedStringofFiles:String = myClip.getClipBoard();
        //Alert.show(ObjectUtil.toString(pastedbd));
        ta.text = String(ObjectUtil.toString(pastedStringofFiles));
        html2.location = pastedStringofFiles;
    }
    ]]>
    </mx:Script>
    <mx:Canvas id="canvas" width="412" height="411">
        <mx:TextArea id="ta" x="25" y="308" height="51" width="327"/>
        <mx:HTML id="html2" x="180.5" y="30" width="139" height="202"/>
        <mx:HTML id="html" x="25" y="31" width="139" height="201"/>
        <mx:Text y="10" text="HTML 2" left="180.5" right="-58.5"/>
        <mx:Button x="110" y="261" label="Copy" click="doCopy()"
➥toolTip="Click to copy the HTML 1 to the Clipboard..."/>
        <mx:Text x="25" y="10" text="HTML 1"/>
        <mx:Text x="25" y="291" text="Pasted Object"/>
        <mx:Button x="25" y="261" label="Load File" click="loadImage()"/>
        <mx:Button x="181" y="261" label="Paste" click="doPaste()"
➥toolTip="Click to paste the Clipboard HTML to the HTML 2..."/>
    </mx:Canvas>
</mx:WindowedApplication>
```

Using the FILE_LIST_FORMAT Data Type

The FILE_LIST_FORMAT data type usage differs from the other types discussed so far. The one notable difference is the FILE_LIST_FORMAT expects an array of files and not simple String data (as in TEXT_FORMAT, HTML_FORMAT, and URL_FORMAT) or BitmapData (as in BITMAP_FORMAT) to be passed into the Clipboard. In the following function, you see the inFiles variable is an Array:

```
private function copy(inFiles:Array):void{
    Clipboard.generalClipboard.clear();
    Clipboard.generalClipboard.setData(ClipboardFormats.FILE_LIST_FORMAT, inFiles);
}
```

In Adobe Flex, you can browse for one or more files with code similar to the following. A button is clicked that calls the loadFiles() function, and when one or more files is selected, the event listener triggers the fileSelected function that pushes the filenames into a TextArea control, ta1. The complete code listing is shown in Listing 9.7 and includes two files—the class file, ClipboardSample6.as, and the MXML file, AIRCopyPaste6.mxml. The resulting Adobe AIR application is shown in Figure 9.7.

```
[Bindable] private var files:FileReferenceList = new FileReferenceList();
private function loadFiles():void {
    var anyFileFilter:FileFilter =
    new FileFilter("All", "*.*;");
    files.browse([anyFileFilter]);
    files.addEventListener(Event.SELECT, fileSelected);
}
private function fileSelected(event:Event):void {
    // Create an array with the size of the selected files.
    var filesSelected:Array = new Array(files.fileList.length);
    var strFilesNames:String = '';
    // Loop through all the selected files and add their names to the List control
    for (var i:int=0;i<files.fileList.length;i++) {
      var fileReference:FileReference = files.fileList[i];
      filesSelected[i] = fileReference.name;
      if (i==0) {
        strFilesNames = filesSelected[i];
      } else {
        strFilesNames += ', ' + filesSelected[i];
       }
    }
    myString = "app:/" + strFilesNames;
    ta1.text = strFilesNames;
    btnCopy.enabled = true;
```

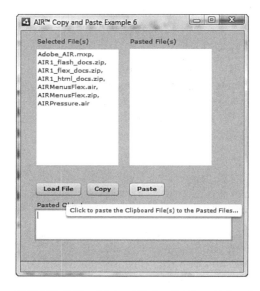

FIGURE 9.7   Adobe AIR Application Using the FILE_LIST_FORMAT Data Type to copy and paste one or more files.

LISTING 9.7   Adobe AIR Application Using the FILE_LIST_FORMAT Data Type to Copy and Paste One or More Files

ClipboardSample6.as is as follows:

```
package info.flexination.air.actionscripts
{
  import flash.desktop.Clipboard;
  import flash.desktop.ClipboardFormats;
  import flash.filesystem.File;

  import mx.controls.Alert;

  public class ClipboardSample6
  {
    public function ClipboardSample6()
    {
    }

    public function getClipBoard():Array {
      var myclip:ClipboardSample6 = new ClipboardSample6();
      return myclip.paste();
    }

    public function setClipBoard(inFiles:File):void {
      try {
            copy(inFiles);
      } catch(e:Error) {
        Alert.show(e.message);
      }
    }

    private function copy(inFiles:File):void{
      Clipboard.generalClipboard.clear();
      Clipboard.generalClipboard.setData(ClipboardFormats.FILE_LIST_FORMAT,
➥[inFiles], false);
    }

    private function paste():Array{
      if (Clipboard.generalClipboard.hasFormat(ClipboardFormats.FILE_LIST_FORMAT)){
        return Clipboard.generalClipboard.getData(ClipboardFormats.FILE_LIST
➥_FORMAT) as Array;
      } else {
        return null;
      }
    }

  }
}
```

The MXML for this example is as follows:

```
<?xml version="1.0" encoding="utf-8"?>
<mx:WindowedApplication xmlns:mx="http://www.adobe.com/2006/mxml" title="AIR"
Copy and Paste Example 6" layout="absolute" height="414" width="372"
horizontalScrollPolicy="off" verticalScrollPolicy="off">
  <mx:Script>
  <![CDATA[
  import info.flexination.air.actionscripts.ClipboardSample6;
  import mx.controls.Alert;
  import mx.utils.ObjectUtil;
  import flash.filesystem.File;

  private var myClip:ClipboardSample6 = new ClipboardSample6();
  [Bindable] private var files:FileReferenceList = new FileReferenceList();
  private var myString:String = new String();
  private var myFiles:File = new File(null);
  private function loadFiles():void {
    var anyFileFilter:FileFilter = new FileFilter("All", "*.*;");
    files.browse([anyFileFilter]);
    files.addEventListener(Event.SELECT, fileSelected);
  }

  private function fileSelected(event:Event):void {
    //Alert.show(ObjectUtil.toString(event));
    // Create an array with the size of the selected files.
    var filesSelected:Array = new Array(files.fileList.length);
    var strFilesNames:String = '';
    // Loop through all the selected files and add their names to the List control
    for(var i:int=0;i<files.fileList.length;i++)
    {
      var fileReference:FileReference = files.fileList[i];
      filesSelected[i] = fileReference.name;
      if (i==0) {
        strFilesNames = filesSelected[i];
      } else {
          strFilesNames += ', ' + filesSelected[i];
      }
    }
    myString = "app:/" + strFilesNames;
    ta1.text = strFilesNames;
    btnCopy.enabled = true;
  }
 private function doCopy():void {
   var myFiles:File = new File (myString);
   myClip.setClipBoard(myfiles);
   btnPaste.enabled = true;
 }
```

```
    private function doPaste():void {
      var pastedArrayofFiles:Array = myClip.getClipBoard();
      //Alert.show(ObjectUtil.toString(pastedArrayofFiles));
      ta.text = String(ObjectUtil.toString(pastedArrayofFiles));
      ta2.text = pastedArrayofFiles[0].nativePath;
    }
    ]]>
    </mx:Script>
    <mx:Canvas id="canvas" width="412" height="411">
        <mx:TextArea id="ta" x="25" y="308" height="51" width="327"/>
        <mx:TextArea id="ta2" x="180.5" y="30" width="139" height="202"/>
        <mx:TextArea id="ta1" x="25" y="31" width="139" height="201"/>
        <mx:Text y="10" text="Pasted File(s)" left="180.5" right="-58.5"/>
        <mx:Button id="btnCopy" x="110" y="261" label="Copy" click="doCopy()" toolTip=
➡"Click to copy the selected File(s) to the Clipboard..." enabled="false"/>
        <mx:Text x="25" y="10" text="Selected File(s)"/>
        <mx:Text x="25" y="291" text="Pasted Object"/>
        <mx:Button x="25" y="261" label="Load File" click="loadFiles()"/>
        <<mx:Button id="btnPaste" x="181" y="261" label="Paste" click="doPaste()"
➡toolTip="Click to paste the Clipboard File(s) to the Pasted Files..."
➡enabled="false"/>
    </mx:Canvas>
    </mx:WindowedApplication>
```

Using the URL_FORMAT Data Type

The URL_FORMAT data type usage is straightforward and technically not much different from the TEXT_FORMAT data type. The URL_FORMAT data type still expects a String, but in this case, the String is a URL and passed to the ClipboardFormats class constant URL_FORMAT as shown here:

```
private function copy(inURL:String):void{
    Clipboard.generalClipboard.clear();
    Clipboard.generalClipboard.setData(ClipboardFormats.URL_FORMAT, inURL);
}
private function paste():String{
    if (Clipboard.generalClipboard.hasFormat(ClipboardFormats.URL_FORMAT)){
        return Clipboard.generalClipboard.getData(ClipboardFormats.URL_FORMAT) as
String;
```

6

```
    } else {
        return null;
    }
}
```

FIGURE 9.8   Adobe AIR Application Using the URL_FORMAT data type to copy and paste a URL String.

The complete code listing is shown in Listing 9.8 and includes two files—the class file, ClipboardSample7.as, and the MXML file, AIRCopyPaste7.mxml. The resulting Adobe AIR application is shown in Figure 9.8.

LISTING 9.8   Adobe AIR Application Using the URL_FORMAT Data Type to Copy and Paste a URL

ClipboardSample7.as is as follows:

```
package info.flexination.air.actionscripts
{
    import flash.desktop.Clipboard;
    import flash.desktop.ClipboardFormats;
    import mx.controls.Alert;

    public class ClipboardSample7
    {
```

```
        public function ClipboardSample7()
        {
        }

        public function getClipBoard():String {
            var myclip:ClipboardSample7 = new ClipboardSample7();
            return myclip.paste();
        }

        public function setClipBoard(inURL:String):void {
            try {
                    copy(inURL);
            } catch(e:Error) {
                Alert.show(e.message);
            }
        }

        private function copy(inURL:String):void{
            Clipboard.generalClipboard.clear();
            Clipboard.generalClipboard.setData(ClipboardFormats.URL_FORMAT, inURL);
        }

        private function paste():String{
            if (Clipboard.generalClipboard.hasFormat(ClipboardFormats.URL_FORMAT)){
                return Clipboard.generalClipboard.getData
➥(ClipboardFormats.URL_FORMAT) as String;
            } else {
                return null;
            }
        }


    }
}
```

The MXML for this example is as follows:

```
<?xml version="1.0" encoding="utf-8"?>
mx:WindowedApplication xmlns:mx="http://www.adobe.com/2006/mxml" title="AIR™
➥Copy and Paste Example 7" layout="absolute" height="414" width="372"
➥horizontalScrollPolicy="off" verticalScrollPolicy="off">
    <mx:Script>
    <![CDATA[
    import info.flexination.air.actionscripts.ClipboardSample7;
    import mx.controls.Alert;
    import mx.utils.ObjectUtil;
    import flash.filesystem.File;
```

```
    private var myClip:ClipboardSample7 = new ClipboardSample7();

    private function doCopy():void {
        myClip.setClipBoard(ta1.text);
        btnPaste.enabled = true;
    }

    private function doPaste():void {
        var pastedURL:String = myClip.getClipBoard();
        //Alert.show(ObjectUtil.toString(pastedURL));
        ta.text = String(ObjectUtil.toString(pastedURL));
        if (pastedURL!=null) {
            ta2.text = pastedURL as String;
        }
    }
    ]]>
    </mx:Script>
    <mx:Canvas id="canvas" width="412" height="411">
        <mx:TextArea id="ta" x="25" y="308" height="51" width="327"/>
        <mx:TextArea id="ta2" x="180.5" y="30" width="139" height="202"/>
        <mx:TextArea id="ta1" text="http://www.flexination.info" x="25" y="31"
➥width="139" height="201"/>
        <mx:Text y="10" text="Pasted URL" left="180.5" right="-58.5"/>
        <mx:Button id="btnCopy" x="110" y="261" label="Copy" click="doCopy()"
➥toolTip="Click to copy the selected File(s) to the Clipboard..."
➥enabled="{(ta1.text!='')?true:false}"/>
        <mx:Text x="25" y="10" text="URL&#xa;"/>
        <mx:Text x="25" y="291" text="Pasted Object"/>
        <mx:Button id="btnPaste" x="181" y="261" label="Paste" click="doPaste()"
➥toolTip="Click to paste the Clipboard File(s) to the Pasted Files..."
➥enabled="false"/>
    </mx:Canvas>
</mx:WindowedApplication>
```

Clipboard Deferred Rendering

In special cases, copying to the Clipboard is an expensive proposition (computationally expensive) due to data size or even data transfer or network latency. In these cases, instead of "holding" your Adobe AIR application in an apparent pause state, you can defer the Clipboard rendering by supplying a function that supplies the data on demand. The rendering function is added to the Clipboard using the setDataHandler() method. The function must return the data in the appropriate format (for example, for the TEXT_FORMAT data type, the rendering function must return a String). Listing 9.9 shows an example of the TEXT_FORMAT and the use of a rendering function.

The main difference in this code and the code you have seen previously is in this special case, you see the `setDataHandler()` method and a rendering function (`renderData` in this code) that defers the handling of the data handoff to the Clipboard. This could prove beneficial if the amount of data loaded into the Clipboard is as large as our fake large data string pretends to be. You can see the effect of this simulated example by first clicking on the Copy button; but before clicking the Paste button, change the text in the top `TextArea`. Now click on the Paste button. Without the deferred rendering, you would see the original text in the second `TextArea` despite your changes in the first `TextArea`. However, because of the deferred rendering, you will see the "changed" text that you typed, even though you did not click the Copy button again. The rendering was delayed until it was actually needed.

LISTING 9.9   Adobe AIR Application Using the Deferred Rendering (`setDataHandler`)

```xml
<?xml version="1.0" encoding="utf-8"?>
mx:WindowedApplication xmlns:mx="http://www.adobe.com/2006/mxml" title="AIR™
➥Copy and Paste Example 7" layout="absolute" height="414" width="372"
➥horizontalScrollPolicy="off" verticalScrollPolicy="off">
    <mx:Script>
    <![CDATA[
    import info.flexination.air.actionscripts.ClipboardSample7;
    import mx.controls.Alert;
    import mx.utils.ObjectUtil;
    import flash.filesystem.File;

    private var myClip:ClipboardSample7 = new ClipboardSample7();

    private function doCopy():void {
        myClip.setClipBoard(ta1.text);
        btnPaste.enabled = true;
    }

    private function doPaste():void {
        var pastedURL:String = myClip.getClipBoard();
        //Alert.show(ObjectUtil.toString(pastedURL));
        ta.text = String(ObjectUtil.toString(pastedURL));
        if (pastedURL!=null) {
            ta2.text = pastedURL as String;
        }
    }
    ]]>
    </mx:Script>
    <mx:Canvas id="canvas" width="412" height="411">
        <mx:TextArea id="ta" x="25" y="308" height="51" width="327"/>
        <mx:TextArea id="ta2" x="180.5" y="30" width="139" height="202"/>
        <mx:TextArea id="ta1" text="http://www.flexination.info" x="25" y="31"
➥width="139" height="201"/>
```

```
        <mx:Text y="10" text="Pasted URL" left="180.5" right="-58.5"/>
        <mx:Button id="btnCopy" x="110" y="261" label="Copy" click="doCopy()"
➥toolTip="Click to copy the selected File(s) to the Clipboard..."
➥enabled="{(ta1.text!='')?true:false}"/>
        <mx:Text x="25" y="10" text="URL&#xa;"/>
        <mx:Text x="25" y="291" text="Pasted Object"/>
        <mx:Button id="btnPaste" x="181" y="261" label="Paste" click="doPaste()"
➥toolTip="Click to paste the Clipboard File(s) to the Pasted Files..."
➥enabled="false"/>
    </mx:Canvas>
</mx:WindowedApplication>
```

Figure 9.9 shows the resulting Adobe AIR application from Listing 9.9.

FIGURE 9.9   Adobe AIR application using deferred rendering (setDataHandler) to improve perceived performance.

NOTE

For more information on copy and paste for Adobe AIR applications, check out the Adobe documentation available on its website or as separate downloads (as PDFs or in HTML format) located at the following URL:

www.adobe.com/support/documentation/en/air/

The Adobe Flex 3/Adobe AIR API is also available as an Adobe AIR application in the code samples for this book (see Appendix C, "Downloading Source Code for *Adobe AIR Programming Unleashed*," for more information on how to download the code).

Summary

The Adobe AIR runtime and the Clipboard API enable the feature that users know as copy and paste to be an integral part of your Adobe AIR applications. For you, the developer, leveraging the three integral classes (`Clipboard`, `ClipboardFormats`, `ClipboardTransferMode`) in the `flash.desktop` package is now in your toolkit of Adobe AIR skills. You can provide your users the professional-quality, rich desktop application they have come to expect that includes interaction with the Clipboard of the OS.

CHAPTER 10

Working with Native Menus

Operating systems provide the means for creating custom menus in applications created for their systems, as long as you know the intricacies of the operating system (OS), but now with Adobe® AIR™, you can create your custom menus much more easily than working with a particular OS programming's learning curve. The Adobe AIR NativeMenu application programming interface (API) allows you to leverage the Native Menu features of the particular OS on which your Adobe AIR application runs, and because of the Adobe AIR runtime, you can do this in a rapid development fashion. Adobe AIR supports the following types of menus:

▶ Application Menus

▶ Window Menus

▶ Context Menus

▶ Dock and System Tray Menus

▶ Pop-Up Menus

▶ Flex Menus

This ability to build your Adobe AIR applications with custom menus is a powerful capability for developing professional desktop applications. In this chapter, you learn how and where the different menu types are used (in some cases, some are available only on a particular OS) and see examples of their usage.

Meeting the `NativeMenu` Class

The new class that we meet in this chapter is the `NativeMenu` class (an Adobe AIR class), shown in Table 10.1.

TABLE 10.1 NativeMenu API

Package	Class	Description
flash.display	NativeMenu	The NativeMenu class contains methods and properties for creating menus.

Adobe AIR menus include the following types, shown in Table 10.2. Each menu type is important but may not be used in every Adobe AIR application. It is up to the developer to decide which types are important to the users of the application.

TABLE 10.2 Adobe AIR Menu Types

Menu	Supported OS	Description
Application	Mac OS X	Accesses the OS-supplied default application menu
Window	Windows	Creates desktop windows and menu items
Context	All	Creates the "right-click" menu
Dock icon	Mac OS X	Creates the dock icon and corresponding menu items
System tray	Windows	Creates the system tray icon and corresponding menu items icon
Pop-Up	All	Creates a pop-up menu (similar to the Context Menu type but not initiated with a right-click user event)
Flex	All	Creates Adobe® Flex™-based menu items

Menus that you create, except for the Adobe Flex, Application, and Windows Menus, respond to two events, as shown in Table 10.3.

TABLE 10.3 Adobe AIR Menu Events

Event	Description
displaying	Dispatched just before the menu is displayed. Use to initiate any code that you want to launch with the menu display event.
select	Dispatched when a menu item is selected. Add a listener and function to handle each menu item selected.

The Flex Menus include the `itemClick` and `menuShow` events only. Application Menus include those shown in Table 10.4.

TABLE 10.4   Application Menu Events

Event	Description
activate	Dispatched when the application has the focus (active)
deactivate	Dispatched when the application loses focus
exiting	Dispatched when exiting the application
invoke	Dispatched when the application is called
networkChange	Dispatched when a network connection is detected or an existing network connection is lost
userIdle	Dispatched when a user's inactivity surpasses a certain idleThreshold time period
userPresent	Dispatched when mouse or keyboard activity is detected after the idleThreshold time period has been reached

Windows Menus respond to the events shown in Table 10.5.

TABLE 10.5   Windows Menu Events

Event	Description
activate	Dispatched when the application has the focus (active)
deactivate	Dispatched when the application loses focus
close	Dispatched after the window has been closed
closing	Dispatched immediately before the window is closed
displayStateChange	Dispatched after the window's displayState property has changed
displayStateChanging	Dispatched immediately before the window's displayState property has finished changing
move	Dispatched after the window has been moved on the desktop
moving	Dispatched as the window is moving on the desktop
resize	Dispatched after the window has been resized
resizing	Dispatched as the window is being resized

Application Menus

An *Application Menu* is a default and all-inclusive menu that applies to the entire application on the Mac OS X.

CAUTION

Application Menus are only supported on the Mac OS X.

The Mac OS X automatically creates this Application Menu, so you can use the Adobe AIR menu API to either add menu items and other submenus to these automatically generated menus or to remove existing menu items. You simply add event listeners for handling

10

how the menu item commands respond to the events that are dispatched. Listing 10.1 shows an example of an Adobe AIR application that demonstrates an Application Menu. The `creationComplete` event calls the init() function where a new `NativeMenu()` is instantiated—myNativeMenu.

```
private function init():void {
    // create main menu
    var myNativeMenu:NativeMenu = new NativeMenu();
    // other code omitted for brevity
}
```

Next a couple of `NativeMenuItem` menus are created.

```
    // create a couple of menu items
    var menuItem1:NativeMenuItem = new NativeMenuItem("Hello AIR World");
    menuItem1.data = "You selected 'Hello AIR World' from the menu.";
    var menuItem2:NativeMenuItem = new NativeMenuItem("Buy Now");
    menuItem2.data = "You selected 'Buy Now' from the menu.";
```

These menu items are then added to the main menu, myNativeMenu.

```
    // add the menu items
    myNativeMenu.addItem(menuItem1);
    myNativeMenu.addItem(menuItem2);
```

An event listener is added to respond to the menu item's selection and the event handler, onMenuSelection is triggered to show an `Alert`. Finally a submenu is added—Custom Menu.

```
    NativeApplication.nativeApplication.menu.addEventListener( Event.SELECT,
➥onMenuSelection );
    NativeApplication.nativeApplication.menu.addSubmenu( myNativeMenu,
➥"Custom Menu" );
private function onMenuSelection( event:Event ):void {
    Alert.show( event.target.data );
}
```

The complete application code is shown in Listing 10.1.

LISTING 10.1   Adding a Custom Application Menu to a Mac OS X

```
<?xml version="1.0" encoding="utf-8"?>
mx:WindowedApplication
    xmlns:mx="http://www.adobe.com/2006/mxml"
    creationComplete="init()"
    layout="vertical"
    horizontalAlign="center"
    verticalAlign="middle">
```

```
    <mx:Script>
    <![CDATA[
        import mx.controls.Alert;

        private function init():void
        {
            // create main menu
            var myNativeMenu:NativeMenu = new NativeMenu();

            // create a couple of menu items
            var menuItem1:NativeMenuItem = new NativeMenuItem("Hello AIR World");
            menuItem1.data = "You selected 'Hello AIR World' from the menu.";
            var menuItem2:NativeMenuItem = new NativeMenuItem("Buy Now");
            menuItem2.data = "You selected 'Buy Now' from the menu.";

            // add the menu items
            myNativeMenu.addItem(menuItem1);
            myNativeMenu.addItem(menuItem2);

            NativeApplication.nativeApplication.menu.addEventListener(
➥Event.SELECT, onMenuSelection );
            NativeApplication.nativeApplication.menu.addSubmenu( myNativeMenu,
➥"Custom Menu" );
        }

        private function onMenuSelection( event:Event ):void
        {
            Alert.show( event.target.data );
        }
    ]]>
    </mx:Script>

    <mx:Label text="Please select an option from the 'Custom Menu' above." />
</mx:WindowedApplication>
```

Figure 10.1 shows the resulting Adobe AIR application with a Mac OS X Application Menu.

Window Menus

Window Menus are associated with a window and appear below the title bar. Window Menus can be added to a window by creating a NativeMenu object, adding one or more NativeMenuItem objects, and assigning them to the menu property of the NativeWindow object (or in Adobe Flex, the FlexNativeMenu object). See Listing 10.2 for a code example. The resulting Adobe AIR application for this code is shown in Figure 10.2.

10

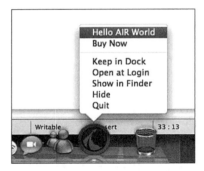

FIGURE 10.1   Adobe AIR example—`NativeMenu` added to a Mac OS X Application Menu.

FIGURE 10.2   Adobe AIR example—`NativeMenu` added to a `NativeWindow`.

CAUTION

Window Menus are only supported on the Windows OS.

NOTE

It should also be noted that Native Menus can only be used with windows that have system chrome.

In creating a Windows Menu, the first step is to create the main menu, as shown by the following code:

```
// create main menu
var myNativeMenu:NativeMenu = new NativeMenu();
```

Next, you should create one or more menu items using the `NativeMenuItem` class as shown here. (This class expects a `String`, representing the menu's label.)

```
// create a couple of menu items
var menuItem1:NativeMenuItem = new NativeMenuItem("Hello AIR World");
var menuItem2:NativeMenuItem = new NativeMenuItem("Buy Now");
```

Now, you should add the menu items to the main menu you initially created, as shown:

```
// add the menu items to the main menu
myNativeMenu.addItem(menuItem1);
myNativeMenu.addItem(menuItem2);
```

Finally, you can create a new window with the menu and menu items you created displayed under the window's title bar:

```
// create new MenuWindow and pass in a NativeMenu
var myWin:Window = new Window();
myWin.title = "Hello World Window";
myWin.width=280;
var fNativeMenu:FlexNativeMenu = new FlexNativeMenu()
fNativeMenu.dataProvider = myNativeMenu.items;
myWin.menu = fNativeMenu;
myWin.open();
```

LISTING 10.2   NativeMenu Added to a NativeWindow

```
<?xml version="1.0" encoding="utf-8"?>
mx:WindowedApplication xmlns:mx="http://www.adobe.com/2006/mxml"
➥creationComplete="init()" layout="absolute">
    <mx:Script>
    <![CDATA[
    import mx.controls.FlexNativeMenu;
    import mx.core.Window;
    private function init():void{
        // create main menu
        var myNativeMenu:NativeMenu = new NativeMenu();
        // create a couple of menu items
        var menuItem1:NativeMenuItem = new NativeMenuItem("Hello AIR World");
        var menuItem2:NativeMenuItem = new NativeMenuItem("Buy Now");
        // add the menu items
        myNativeMenu.addItem(menuItem1);
        myNativeMenu.addItem(menuItem2);
        // create new MenuWindow and pass in a NativeMenu
        var myWin:Window = new Window();
        myWin.title = "Hello World Window";
        myWin.width=280;
        var fNativeMenu:FlexNativeMenu = new FlexNativeMenu()
        fNativeMenu.dataProvider = myNativeMenu.items;
        myWin.menu = fNativeMenu;
        myWin.open();
    }
    ]]>
    </mx:Script>
</mx:WindowedApplication>
```

10

Context Menus

Context Menus are the menu type that you have already seen within Adobe® Flash® (formerly Macromedia Flash) applications and are sometimes referred to as the right-click or command-click menus. Adding this functionality to an Adobe AIR application is easy and is shown in Listing 10.3, with the resulting Adobe AIR application shown in Figure 10.3.

FIGURE 10.3   Adobe AIR example—`NativeMenu` added as a Context Menu.

LISTING 10.3   `NativeMenu` Added as a Context Menu

```
<?xml version="1.0" encoding="utf-8"?>
mx:WindowedApplication xmlns:mx=http://www.adobe.com/2006/mxml
➥creationComplete="init()" layout="absolute">
    <mx:Script>
    <![CDATA[
    private function init():void{
        // create main menu
        var myNativeMenu:NativeMenu = new NativeMenu();
        // create a couple of menu items
        var menuItem1:NativeMenuItem = new NativeMenuItem("Hello AIR World");
        var menuItem2:NativeMenuItem = new NativeMenuItem("Buy Now");
        // add the menu items
        myNativeMenu.addItem(menuItem1);
        myNativeMenu.addItem(menuItem2);
        // create new MenuWindow and pass in a NativeMenu
        var myApplication:WindowedApplication = this;
        this.title = "Hello World Window";
        this.contextMenu = myNativeMenu;
    }
    ]]>
    </mx:Script>
</mx:WindowedApplication>
```

Dock and System Tray Menus

Dock and System Tray menus are new to Adobe AIR since the alpha Apollo (former code name of the alpha release of Adobe AIR) was first introduced and are another powerful example of the capabilities of the Adobe AIR runtime's interaction with the native OS. These icon menus are similar to the Context menus and are either assigned to an application icon in the Mac OS X Dock or to the Windows system tray area in the Windows OS. Coding for this capability is also straightforward, as shown in Listing 10.4. The code is demonstrated in Figure 10.4 and is similar to what you have seen before except for this code block. In this example we leverage the property `supportsSystemTrayIcon` to programmatically load an image as the system tray icon only on a Windows OS:

```
//Load an icon image for system tray, if supported (for Windows OS only)
if(NativeApplication.supportsSystemTrayIcon){
    // assign the main menu to the systemTrayIconMenu property
➥(for Windows OS only)
    this.systemTrayIconMenu = fNativeMenu;
    // define the icon image
    var sysTrayImageURL:String = "app:/icons/AIRApp_16.png";
    // instantiate a Loader object
    var loader:Loader = new Loader();
    // add an event listener
    loader.contentLoaderInfo.addEventListener
➥(Event.COMPLETE,iconLoaded,false,0,true);
    // load the icon image
    loader.load(new URLRequest(sysTrayImageURL));
}
```

FIGURE 10.4   Adobe AIR example—Dock and System Tray Icon Menu.

LISTING 10.4   Dock and System Tray Icon Menu

```
<?xml version="1.0" encoding="utf-8"?>
mx:WindowedApplication xmlns:mx="http://www.adobe.com/2006/mxml"
➥creationComplete="init()" layout="absolute">
    <mx:Script>
    <![CDATA[
        import mx.controls.FlexNativeMenu;

        private function init():void
```

10

```
        {
            // create main menu
            var myNativeMenu:NativeMenu = new NativeMenu();

            // create a couple of menu items
            var menuItem1:NativeMenuItem = new NativeMenuItem("Hello AIR World");
            var menuItem2:NativeMenuItem = new NativeMenuItem("Buy Now");

            // add the menu items
            myNativeMenu.addItem(menuItem1);
            myNativeMenu.addItem(menuItem2);

            var fNativeMenu:FlexNativeMenu = new FlexNativeMenu()
            fNativeMenu.dataProvider = myNativeMenu.items;

            this.dockIconMenu = fNativeMenu;
            this.systemTrayIconMenu = fNativeMenu;

            var sysTrayImageURL:String;
            if( NativeApplication.supportsDockIcon )
            {
                sysTrayImageURL = "app:/icons/AIRApp_128.png";
            } else {
                sysTrayImageURL = "app:/icons/AIRApp_16.png";
            }

            var loader:Loader = new Loader();
            loader.contentLoaderInfo.addEventListener( Event.COMPLETE,
➥iconLoaded, false, 0, true );
            loader.load(new URLRequest( sysTrayImageURL ));
        }

    //Show the system tray icon by setting an image
    private function iconLoaded(event:Event):void
    {
        this.nativeApplication.icon.bitmaps =
➥[event.target.content.bitmapData];
    }
    ]]>
    </mx:Script>
</mx:WindowedApplication>
```

Pop-Up Menus

Pop-Up Menus are similar to Context Menus, as shown in the code in Listing 10.5. The main difference is in the triggering of the Pop-Up Menus. Pop-Up Menus are triggered by calling the *display* method of the `NativeMenu` object defined in the Adobe AIR application, whereas Context Menus add the `NativeMenu` object to the application's `contextMenu` property. Additionally, a Pop-Up Menu display generally waits for a user-initiated, developer-defined event (a `click` or `mouseUp` event, for example), whereas the Context Menu waits for a specific, user-initiated right-click or command-click event. Figure 10.5 shows the resulting Adobe AIR application. The new code block for this example is:

```
// create new MenuWindow and pass in a NativeMenu
var myApplication:WindowedApplication = this;
// sets the AIR application Title
this.title = "Hello World Window";
// displays the main menu
myNativeMenu.display(stage, event.stageX, event.stageY);
```

FIGURE 10.5   Adobe AIR example—NativeMenu Added as a Pop-Up Menu.

LISTING 10.5   NativeMenu Added as a Pop-Up Menu

```
<?xml version="1.0" encoding="utf-8"?>
<mx:WindowedApplication xmlns:mx="http://www.adobe.com/2006/mxml"
➥layout="absolute">
    <mx:Script>
    <![CDATA[
    private function init(event:MouseEvent):void{
        // create main menu
        var myNativeMenu:NativeMenu = new NativeMenu();
        // create a couple of menu items
        var menuItem1:NativeMenuItem = new NativeMenuItem("Hello AIR World");
        var menuItem2:NativeMenuItem = new NativeMenuItem("Buy Now");
        // add the menu items
        myNativeMenu.addItem(menuItem1);
        myNativeMenu.addItem(menuItem2);
        // create new MenuWindow and pass in a NativeMenu
```

```
        var myApplication:WindowedApplication = this;
        this.title = "Hello World Window";
        myNativeMenu.display(stage, event.stageX, event.stageY);
    }
    ]]>
    </mx:Script>
    <mx:PopUpButton x="67" y="10" label="Click Me" mouseUp="init(event)"/>
</mx:WindowedApplication>
```

Flex Menus

Flex Menus are displayed by the Adobe AIR runtime rather than the native OS and, there-fore, are not characterized as Native. Additionally, the Native Menus require system chrome, and the Flex Menus do not. The main benefit of using the Adobe Flex menu component is that you can program the menus in Adobe's XML-based markup language (MXML, originally from Macromedia) with the Adobe Flex-bags tags, and as shown in Listing 10.6, the amount of code you, as the developer, write will generally be less. Figure 10.6 shows the corresponding Adobe AIR application.

FIGURE 10.6   Adobe AIR example—Adobe Flex-Based Menu.

LISTING 10.6   Flex-Based Menu

```
<?xml version="1.0" encoding="utf-8"?>
<mx:WindowedApplication xmlns:mx="http://www.adobe.com/2006/mxml"
▸menu="{myNativeMenu}" title="Hello World Window" layout="absolute">
    <!— Menu definition for application —>
    <mx:XML id="appMenu" format="e4x">
        <menubar>
            <menu label="Hello AIR World">
                <menuitem label="Hello AIR World"/>
                <menuitem label="Buy Now"/>
            </menu>
        </menubar>
    </mx:XML>
```

```
<!— Menu components —>
<mx:FlexNativeMenu id="myNativeMenu" dataProvider="{appMenu}"
labelField="@label" keyEquivalentField="@key" showRoot="false"/>


</mx:WindowedApplication>
```

The Hierarchical Nature of Adobe AIR Menus

Menus are hierarchical in nature and depend on the `NativeMenu` and `NativeMenuItem` classes. A `NativeMenu` contains one or more child `NativeMenuItem[s]`, and a `NativeMenuItem` can include one or more submenus starting the usage of additional child `NativeMenu` objects nested deeper in the overall menu structure. Listing 10.7 is the MXML-based code for a deeply nested menu. Figure 10.7 depicts the deeply nested menu example.

FIGURE 10.7   Adobe AIR example—deeply nested hierarchical menu.

LISTING 10.7   Deeply Nested Hierarchical Menu

```
<?xml version="1.0" encoding="utf-8"?>
<mx:WindowedApplication xmlns:mx="http://www.adobe.com/2006/mxml"
➡menu="{myNativeMenu}" title="Hello World Window" layout="absolute">
    <!— Menu definition for application —>
    <mx:XML id="appMenu" format="e4x">
        <menubar>
            <menu label="Hello AIR World">
                <menuitem label="Hello AIR World"/>
                <menu label="Buy Now">
                    <menuitem label="Vendors">
                        <menuitem label="Sams"/>
                        <menuitem label="Amazon"/>
                    </menuitem>
                </menu>
            </menu>
        </menubar>
    </mx:XML>
```

10

```
<!— Menu components —>
<mx:FlexNativeMenu id="myNativeMenu" dataProvider="{appMenu}"
labelField="@label" keyEquivalentField="@key" showRoot="false"/>
</mx:WindowedApplication>
```

Listing 10.8 is the AS3-based code for a deeply nested menu. Note the extra `NativeMenu` objects created to hold the submenu items. Figure 10.8 depicts the deeply nested menu example.

FIGURE 10.8   Adobe AIR example—deeply nested hierarchical menu in AS3.

LISTING 10.8   Deeply Nested Hierarchical Menu—AS3

```
<?xml version="1.0" encoding="utf-8"?>
<mx:WindowedApplication xmlns:mx=http://www.adobe.com/2006/mxml
➥creationComplete="init()" layout="absolute">
    <mx:Script>
    <![CDATA[
    private function init():void{
        // create main menu
        var myNativeMenu:NativeMenu = new NativeMenu();
        // create a couple of menu items
        var menuItem1:NativeMenuItem = new NativeMenuItem("Hello AIR World");
        var menuItem2:NativeMenuItem = new NativeMenuItem("Buy Now");
        // add the menu items
        myNativeMenu.addItem(menuItem1);
        myNativeMenu.addItem(menuItem2);
        // create submenu
        var mySubNativeMenu:NativeMenu = new NativeMenu();
        // create a submenu item
        var menuSubItem1:NativeMenuItem = new NativeMenuItem("Vendors");
        // add the submenu items
        mySubNativeMenu.addItem(menuSubItem1);
        menuItem2.submenu = mySubNativeMenu;
        // create submenu
        var mySubNativeMenu2:NativeMenu = new NativeMenu();
```

```
        // create a couple of submenu items
        var menuSubItem2:NativeMenuItem = new NativeMenuItem("Sams");
        var menuSubItem3:NativeMenuItem = new NativeMenuItem("Amazon");
        // add the submenu items
        mySubNativeMenu2.addItem(menuSubItem2);
        mySubNativeMenu2.addItem(menuSubItem3);
        menuSubItem1.submenu = mySubNativeMenu2;

        // create new MenuWindow and pass in a NativeMenu
        var myApplication:WindowedApplication = this;
        this.title = "Hello World Window in AS 3";
        this.contextMenu = myNativeMenu;
    }
    ]]>
    </mx:Script>
</mx:WindowedApplication>
```

A Few More Details for Adobe AIR Menus

As with any menu system, the ability to use shortcut keys in lieu of the mouse is an important, must-have feature, and this too is also available for Adobe AIR applications. A keyboard shortcut can be assigned by setting the menu's `keyEquivalent` property. The coding is straight-forward, as in the previous examples, and nearly identical. After you have your main menu, submenus, and their menu items defined, use the `keyEquivalent` property of the menu item as shown in the following:

```
menuSubItem2.keyEquivalent = "s";
menuSubItem3.keyEquivalent = "a";
```

Adding an event listener with the supporting handler function completes the steps:

```
// add the event listener - doCommand is the handler
mySubNativeMenu2.addEventListener(Event.SELECT, doCommand);
// handler function shows an alert of which menu item was selected
private function doCommand(event:Event): void {
    Alert.show(event.target.label + " clicked from the " +event.currentTarget.par-
ent.items[0].label + " menu");
}
```

10

NOTE

Key equivalents can only be used to select commands in Application or Windows Menus.

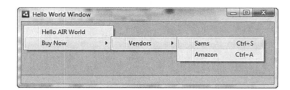

FIGURE 10.9   Adobe AIR example—`keyEquivalent` property in AS3.

Listing 10.9 is the code in ActionScript 3 to leverage the `keyEquivalent` property. Figure 10.9 shows the resulting Adobe AIR application.

LISTING 10.9   `keyEquivalent` Property in AS3

```
<?xml version="1.0" encoding="utf-8"?>
<mx:WindowedApplication xmlns:mx="http://www.adobe.com/2006/mxml"
➥creationComplete="init()" layout="absolute">
    <mx:Script>
    <![CDATA[
    import mx.core.Window;
    import mx.controls.Alert;
    private function init():void{
        // create main menu
        var myNativeMenu:NativeMenu = new NativeMenu();
        // create a couple of menu items
        var menuItem1:NativeMenuItem = new NativeMenuItem("Hello AIR World");
        var menuItem2:NativeMenuItem = new NativeMenuItem("Buy Now");
        // add the menu items
        myNativeMenu.addItem(menuItem1);
        myNativeMenu.addItem(menuItem2);
        // create submenu
        var mySubNativeMenu:NativeMenu = new NativeMenu();
        // create a submenu item
        var menuSubItem1:NativeMenuItem = new NativeMenuItem("Vendors");
        // add the submenu items
        mySubNativeMenu.addItem(menuSubItem1);
        menuItem2.submenu = mySubNativeMenu;
        // create a submenu
        var mySubNativeMenu2:NativeMenu = new NativeMenu();
        // create a couple of submenu items
        var menuSubItem2:NativeMenuItem = new NativeMenuItem("Sams");
        var menuSubItem3:NativeMenuItem = new NativeMenuItem("Amazon");
        // add the submenu items
        mySubNativeMenu2.addItem(menuSubItem2);
        mySubNativeMenu2.addItem(menuSubItem3);
        menuSubItem1.submenu = mySubNativeMenu2;
```

```
        menuSubItem2.keyEquivalent = "s";
        menuSubItem3.keyEquivalent = "a";
        mySubNativeMenu2.addEventListener(Event.SELECT, doCommand);

        // create new MenuWindow and pass in a NativeMenu
        var myApplication:WindowedApplication = this;
        this.title = "Hello World Window";
        this.contextMenu = myNativeMenu;
    }
    private function doCommand(event:Event): void {
        Alert.show(event.target.label + " clicked from the "
+event.currentTarget.parent.items[0].label + " menu");
    }
    ]]>
    </mx:Script>
</mx:WindowedApplication>
```

Responding to menu events is a concept that has not been discussed much to this point. Menu items dispatch a select event when they are selected by the user. The Adobe AIR example shown in Listing 10.9 uses an event handler, doCommand, for the two submenu items. An event listener monitors the Event.SELECT in the addEventListener property for the two submenu items. Select events also bubble up through the menu hierarchy. Each parent menu in the chain might also dispatch a select event. The target property of the event object is the NativeMenuItem object of the selected command, and the currentTarget property is the NativeMenu object of the current menu. See Figure 10.10 to see the resulting menu label, *Vendors*, seen when selecting either vendor.

FIGURE 10.10   Adobe AIR example—bubble up the currentTarget property.

Summary

Native Menus with the Adobe AIR Native Menu API are a powerful feature that you can leverage during development of your Adobe AIR applications. As mentioned, Adobe AIR supports the following types of menus: Application Menus, Window Menus, Context Menus, Dock and System Tray Menus, Pop-Up Menus, and Flex Menus. This ability to add your own menus and enhance the existing OS native windows for your application gives you an opportunity to make your applications as rich and professionally attractive as

10

possible. Compared with competing products used for desktop development, the workflow for the Adobe AIR developer is much improved when creating Native Menus. Additionally, Native Menus further differentiate Adobe AIR applications from competing web-based applications. Trying to create OS-affecting menus (Dock or System tray icons, for example) is not possible, and creating OS-looking menus to work within the constraints of the browser is awkward and subject to browser differences in both their implementation and final appearance.

CHAPTER 11

Adding User Notifications

What are user notifications as they relate to an Adobe® AIR™ application? User notifications are visual alerts sent from an Adobe AIR application through the operating system that can be informational (such as your hard drive is getting a bit full) or critical (such as your hard drive is out of space). A full-featured desktop application should be able to communicate informational and critical alerts to the user to be considered a complete success. You have no doubt seen applications that fail to warn you that the next action you take will wipe out all the data you just spent 20 minutes entering. Your Adobe AIR application can avoid this common user frustration by leveraging notifications— bouncing the Mac OS X Dock icon, system tray icon ToolTips on Windows, StatusBar notifications, Taskbar high-lighting, and toastlike messages (a message similar to a new email alert from Microsoft Outlook that rises up from the lower right of the desktop, pauses for a moment so you notice it, and then lowers back out of sight).

In this chapter, you see examples of these different types of notifications. As alluded to earlier, some are Mac OS X– or Windows–only features, but you learn how to code your Adobe AIR applications for flexible deployment on either operating system (OS), taking full advantage of the notifications available.

Bounce the Mac OS X Dock Icon—NativeWindow Class

The NativeWindow class, as described in Table 11.1, is an important class for Adobe AIR applications and has the notifyUser()method related to user notifications.

TABLE 11.1   NativeWindow Class

Package	Class	Description
flash.display	NativeWindow	The NativeWindow class provides an interface for creating and controlling native desktop windows.

Use the NativeWindow notifyUser()method to communicate visually with the end user, for example, bouncing the docked icon on OS X. You can also bounce the Dock icon by calling the NativeApplication.nativeApplication.icon.bounce() method. Setting the bounce() priority parameter to informational bounces the icon once. Setting it to critical bounces the icon until the user interacts with the application. Constants for the priority parameter are defined in the NotificationType class. You can also examine a property to determine if the OS can handle Dock icons—the property supportsDockIcon of the NativeApplication class is useful for this purpose. The code for bouncing the Dock icon is shown in Listing 11.1.

LISTING 11.1   Bouncing Dock Icons Code Example

```
<?xml version="1.0" encoding="utf-8"?>
<mx:WindowedApplication xmlns:mx="http://www.adobe.com/2006/mxml" title="AIR™
➥User Notifications - Bounce Example" applicationComplete="init()"
➥layout="absolute">
    <mx:Script>
    <![CDATA[
        import flash.desktop.DockIcon;
        import flash.desktop.NotificationType;
        import flash.desktop.NativeApplication;
    private function init():void {
        if (NativeApplication.supportsDockIcon) {
            trace("supports dock icon"); // Mac OS X
            var dockIcon:DockIcon = NativeApplication.nativeApplication.icon as
➥DockIcon;
            dockIcon.bounce(NotificationType.CRITICAL);
        }
    }
    ]]>
    </mx:Script>
</mx:WindowedApplication>
```

Toast Messages—NativeApplication Class

The NativeApplication class (shown in Table 11.2) is also important when creating user notification features, known as "toast" messages.

TABLE 11.2   NativeApplication Class

Package	Class	Description
flash.desktop	NativeApplication	The NativeApplication class provides application information, application-wide functions, and dispatches application-level events.

Use the NativeApplication events, userIdle (User_Idle constant), and userPresent (User_Present constant) to implement "toast-style" window messages that rise up from the lower right of the screen, pause briefly, and then lower back down out of sight. Listing 11.2 shows the basic code to begin building a "toast-style" feature for an Adobe AIR application. Figures 11.1 and 11.2 show the result of this code.

FIGURE 11.1   USER_IDLE alert triggered.

FIGURE 11.2   USER_PRESENT alert triggered.

LISTING 11.2   The NativeApplication Class, USER_IDLE/USER_PRESENT Events

```
<?xml version="1.0" encoding="utf-8"?>
<mx:WindowedApplication xmlns:mx=http://www.adobe.com/2006/mxml
➥applicationComplete="init()" title="AIR User Notifications
➥Example 1" layout="absolute">
    <mx:Script>
    <![CDATA[
    import flash.desktop.NativeApplication;
    import mx.controls.Alert;
    private const IDLETIME:int = 5; //seconds
```

```
    private function init():void {
        //Detect user presence
        NativeApplication.nativeApplication.idleThreshold = IDLETIME;
        NativeApplication.nativeApplication.addEventListener(Event.USER_IDLE,
➥onIdle);
        NativeApplication.nativeApplication.addEventListener
➥(Event.USER_PRESENT, onPresence);
    }
    private function onIdle(event:Event):void {
        Alert.show("I'm idle...", "I am idle");
    }
    private function onPresence(event:Event):void {
        Alert.show("I have a presence...", "My presence is noted");
    }
    ]]>
    </mx:Script>
</mx:WindowedApplication>
```

Taking this basic example to the next level, a "toastlike" feature is beginning to take form in Listing 11.3. Figure 11.3 shows the Adobe AIR application. In the code, you see that both the USER_IDLE and USER_PRESENT events are leveraged. The USER_IDLE is triggered after 5 seconds of idle time (idleThreshold), and the first pop-up message (in this example, an Adobe® Flex™-based TitleWindow—see the Flex Tip for more information) appears. Mouse or keyboard activity by the user triggers the USER_PRESENT event, and the subsequent code uses the Timer class to close the pop-up window. If there is not any activity, the toast message remains displayed. This is one fundamental difference between a toastlike message and a ToolTip message—the toast-type message is not tied to just the idleThreshold. The idleThreshold is the number of seconds that must elapse without keyboard or mouse activity before a presenceChange event is dispatched. The default idleThreshold is 300 seconds.

FIGURE 11.3   Adobe AIR application—it's toast.

LISTING 11.3   It's Simply Toast Code

```
The Main App of Macromedia Extensible Markup Language (MXML):
<?xml version="1.0" encoding="utf-8"?>
<mx:WindowedApplication xmlns:mx=http://www.adobe.com/2006/mxml
➥applicationComplete="init()" layout="absolute" backgroundColor="white"
➥headerHeight="0" cornerRadius="0" statusBarBackgroundColor="white">
    <mx:Script>
```

```
    <![CDATA[
    import mx.containers.TitleWindow;
    import flash.desktop.NativeApplication;
    import mx.managers.PopUpManager;
    import mx.controls.Alert;
    import flash.utils.Timer;
    import flash.events.TimerEvent;
    [Bindable] private var winwidth:Number = Capabilities.screenResolutionX/1.5;
    [Bindable] private var winheight:Number = Capabilities.screenResolutionY/1.5;
    [Bindable] private var aryText:Array = [{text:'Hello Air World'},
➥{text:'I hope you enjoy this chapter'},{text:'Mike G'}];

    private var count:int = 0;
    private var popup:ToastWindow;
    private const IDLETIME:int = 5; //seconds
    private function setDefaultWindowSize():void {
        setDefaultWindowSize();
        this.bounds = new Rectangle(100, 100, Capabilities.screenResolutionX/8,
➥Capabilities.screenResolutionY/8);
    }
    private function init():void {
        //Detect user presence
        NativeApplication.nativeApplication.idleThreshold = IDLETIME;
        NativeApplication.nativeApplication.addEventListener(Event.USER_IDLE,
➥onIdle);
        NativeApplication.nativeApplication.addEventListener(Event.USER_PRESENT,
➥onPresence);
    }
    private function onIdle(event:Event):void {
        //Alert.show("I'm idle...", "I am idle");
        createNewWindow();
        count++;
    }
    private function onPresence(event:Event):void {
        //Alert.show("I have a presence...", "My presence is noted");
        popup.startTimer();
    }
    private function createNewWindow():void {
        // create popup window, position to appear like a toast window
        popup=ToastWindow(PopUpManager.createPopUp(this, ToastWindow , false));
        popup.x = 12;
        popup.y = 12;
        popup.alpha = 0.4;
        // protect array from out of bounds error
        if (count > 2) {
            // close the toast
            this.close();
```

```
        }
        //
        popup.txt.text = aryText[count].text;
    }
    ]]>
    </mx:Script>
</mx:WindowedApplication>
```

The TitleWindow code used in this example:

```
<?xml version="1.0" encoding="utf-8"?>
<mx:TitleWindow xmlns:mx="http://www.adobe.com/2006/mxml" creationComplete="init()"
➥x="168" y="86" height="100" width="100" cornerRadius="0" layout="absolute"
➥headerHeight="0" backgroundColor="white" borderColor="white"
➥dropShadowEnabled="false">
    <mx:Script>
    <![CDATA[
    import mx.managers.PopUpManager;
        private var myTimer:Timer = new Timer(1500, 0);
        private function init():void {
            myTimer.addEventListener("timer", onTimer);
    }
    private function onTimer(event:TimerEvent):void {
        remove();
    }
    public function startTimer():void {
        // start the 1.5 second timer
        myTimer.start();
    }
    private function remove():void {
        PopUpManager.removePopUp(this);
    }
    ]]>
    </mx:Script>
    <mx:Text id="txt" text="AIR World" color="navy" width="63" height="68"
➥y="10" x="7" fontSize="9"/>
</mx:TitleWindow>
```

The XML-based Adobe AIR application Descriptor is modified, as shown in Listing 11.4. The modifications in the application Descriptor might vary depending on your approach to creating the toast messages. For instance in this code, the application is positioned and sized to appear in the lower right of the desktop (on Windows, in the system tray area) and resizing, minimizing, and maximizing the application are not allowed.

LISTING 11.4   Adobe AIR Toast Application Descriptor Snippet

```
    <initialWindow>
        <!-- The main SWF or HTML file of the application. Required. -->
        <!-- Note: In Flex Builder, the SWF reference is set automatically. -->
```

```
        <content>[This value will be overwritten by Adobe Flex Builder in the
➥output app.xml]</content>

        <!-- The title of the main window. Optional. -->
        <!-- <title></title> -->

        <!-- The type of system chrome to use (either "standard" or "none").
➥Optional. Default standard. -->
        <systemChrome>none</systemChrome>

        <!-- Whether the window is transparent. Only applicable when systemChrome
➥is false. Optional. Default false. -->
        <transparent>true</transparent>

        <!-- Whether the window is initially visible. Optional. Default false. -->
        <visible>false</visible>

        <!-- Whether the user can minimize the window. Optional. Default true. -->
        <minimizable>false</minimizable>

        <!-- Whether the user can maximize the window. Optional. Default true. -->
        <maximizable>false</maximizable>

        <!-- Whether the user can resize the window. Optional. Default true. -->
        <resizable>false</resizable>

        <!-- The window's initial width. Optional. -->
        <width>100</width>

        <!-- The window's initial height. Optional. -->
        <height>100</height>

        <!-- The window's initial x position. Optional. -->
        <x>860</x>

        <!-- The window's initial y position. Optional. -->
        <y>650</y>

        <!-- The window's minimum size, specified as a width/height pair,
➥such as "400 200". Optional. -->
        <!-- <minSize></minSize> -->

        <!-- The window's initial maximum size, specified as a width/height
➥pair, such as "1600 1200". Optional. -->
        <!-- <maxSize></maxSize> -->
    </initialWindow>
```

FLEX TIP

Creating a pop-up window, or in Adobe Flex, a `TitleWindow`, is easy. Note that the `TitleWindow` in this case is an MXML-based file named `ToastWindow.mxml`:

```
import mx.containers.TitleWindow;

import mx.managers.PopUpManager;

private var popup:ToastWindow;

// create popup window, position to appear like a toast window

popup=ToastWindow(PopUpManager.createPopUp(this, ToastWindow , false));

popup.x = 12;

popup.y = 12;

popup.alpha = 0.4;

popup.txt.text = aryText[count].text;
```

StatusBar Notifications—NativeWindow Class

Another user notification type includes `statusBar` notifications. Status bar messages, such as the one shown in Listing 11.5, are a nice addition to any Adobe AIR application. Giving the user feedback and suggestions are a way of providing baked-in customer service and should always be a part of your development efforts. In Listing 11.5, the users are informed that they would experience the application better by changing their screen resolution. Instead of leaving this information in the status bar perpetually, by invoking the `Timer` class, you can display the information briefly without being a pest to your end users.

LISTING 11.5   Adobe AIR Application `statusBar` Screen Resolution Notification

```
<?xml version="1.0" encoding="utf-8"?>
<mx:WindowedApplication xmlns:mx="http://www.adobe.com/2006/mxml" xmlns="*"
title="AIR™ User Notifications - statusBar Example"
➥applicationComplete="initApp()" layout="absolute">
    <mx:Script>
    <![CDATA[
    import flash.system.Capabilities;
    private var myTimer:Timer = new Timer(5000, 1);
    private var blnResolutionPassed:Boolean = true;
        private var xResolution:Number = flash.system.Capabilities.screenResolutionX;
        private var yResolution:Number = flash.system.Capabilities.screenResolutionY;
        private function initApp():void {
         myTimer.addEventListener("timer", onTimer);
        //Alert.show("width: " + xResolution + " height: " + yResolution);
        if (xResolution < 1600 && yResolution < 1200) {
            // start the 5 second timer
            myTimer.start();
```

```
            var message:String = 'This App looks best at a 1600 x 1200 or
➥higher screen resolution ...';
            this.status = message;
            blnResolutionPassed = false;
        }
    }
    private function onTimer(event:TimerEvent):void {
        this.status = '';
    }
    ]]>
    </mx:Script>
</mx:WindowedApplication>
```

Figure 11.4 shows a statusBar notification that alerts the users about their screen resolution.

FIGURE 11.4   Adobe AIR application—user notification in the statusBar.

Taskbar Highlighting—NativeWindow Class

Highlighting the application in the taskbar on Windows is another type of user notification within the realm of Adobe AIR development. The NativeWindow class and the notifyUser method code are very easy and are shown in Listing 11.6. Listing 11.7 combines the taskbar highlighting and the icon in the system tray features.

LISTING 11.6   Adobe AIR Application TaskBar Highlighting

```
// highlight the taskBar
 this.nativeWindow.notifyUser(NotificationType.INFORMATIONAL);
```

LISTING 11.7   Adobe AIR Application TaskBar Highlighting and Sys Tray Icon

```
<?xml version="1.0" encoding="utf-8"?>
<mx:WindowedApplication xmlns:mx="http://www.adobe.com/2006/mxml" title="AIR™
➥User Notifications - taskBar Example" applicationComplete="init()"
➥layout="absolute">
```

```
<mx:Script>
<![CDATA[
import mx.events.FlexNativeMenuEvent;
import mx.controls.FlexNativeMenu;
import flash.display.NativeMenu;
import flash.display.NativeMenuItem;
import flash.events.Event;
import flash.desktop.DockIcon;
import flash.desktop.NotificationType;
import flash.desktop.NativeApplication;
private function init():void {
    // highlight the taskBar
    this.nativeWindow.notifyUser(NotificationType.INFORMATIONAL);
    // create main menu
    var myNativeMenu:NativeMenu = new NativeMenu();
    // create a couple of menu items
    var menuItem1:NativeMenuItem = new NativeMenuItem("Close");
    // add the menu items
    myNativeMenu.addItem(menuItem1);
    var fNativeMenu:FlexNativeMenu = new FlexNativeMenu()
    fNativeMenu.dataProvider = myNativeMenu.items;
    if (NativeApplication.supportsDockIcon) {
        var dockIcon:DockIcon = NativeApplication.nativeApplication.icon as
➥DockIcon;
        dockIcon.bounce(NotificationType.CRITICAL);
        trace("supports dock icon"); // Mac OS X
        this.dockIconMenu = fNativeMenu;
        this.dockIconMenu.addEventListener(FlexNativeMenuEvent.
➥ITEM_CLICK, doCommand);
    }
    //Load an icon image for system tray, if supported
    if(NativeApplication.supportsSystemTrayIcon){
        trace("supports system tray icon"); // Windows
        this.systemTrayIconMenu = fNativeMenu;
        this.systemTrayIconMenu.addEventListener(FlexNativeMenuEvent.
➥ITEM_CLICK, doCommand);
        var sysTrayImageURL:String = "app:/assets/icons/AIRApp_16.png";
        var loader:Loader = new Loader();
                                loader.contentLoaderInfo.addEventListener
➥(Event.COMPLETE,iconLoaded,false,0,true);
        loader.load(new URLRequest(sysTrayImageURL));
    }
}
private function doCommand(event:Event):void {
    this.close();
```

```
    }
    //Show the system tray icon by setting an image
    private function iconLoaded(event:Event):void{
        this.nativeApplication.icon.bitmaps = [event.target.content.bitmapData];
    }
    ]]>
    </mx:Script>
</mx:WindowedApplication>
```

Figure 11.5 shows the resulting Adobe AIR application utilizing the `notifyUser()` method of the `NativeWindow` class and the informational `NotificationType` class.

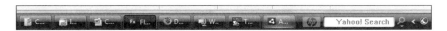

FIGURE 11.5   Adobe AIR application—user notification in highlighted taskbar.

System Tray Icon ToolTips—**NativeWindow** Class

To wrap up this topic, system tray icon ToolTips are another Adobe AIR application user notification type. The tricky detail you need to remember when working with this notification strategy is an instance of the `SystemTrayIcon` class cannot be created. Instead, you should create a variable of type `Object` to hold the `NativeApplication`. `nativeApplication.icon`, as depicted in Listing 11.8. The resulting Adobe AIR application that shows the system tray icon ToolTip is shown in Figure 11.6.

FIGURE 11.6   Adobe AIR application—user notification in SysTray icon ToolTip.

LISTING 11.8   Adobe AIR Application—User Notification in System Tray Icon ToolTip

```
<?xml version="1.0" encoding="utf-8"?>
<mx:WindowedApplication xmlns:mx="http://www.adobe.com/2006/mxml" title="AIR™
➥User Notifications - Icon toolTip Example" applicationComplete="init()"
➥layout="absolute">
    <mx:Script>
    <![CDATA[
        import flash.desktop.SystemTrayIcon;
        import flash.desktop.NotificationType;
        import flash.desktop.NativeApplication;
    private function init():void {
        if(NativeApplication.supportsSystemTrayIcon){
```

```
            trace("supports system tray icon"); // Windows
            var sysTrayImageURL:String = "app:/assets/icons/AIRApp_16.png";
            var loader:Loader = new Loader();
            loader.contentLoaderInfo.addEventListener
➡(Event.COMPLETE,iconLoaded,false,0,true);
            loader.load(new URLRequest(sysTrayImageURL));
        }
    }
    //Show the system tray icon by setting an image
    private function iconLoaded(event:Event):void{
        this.nativeApplication.icon.bitmaps = [event.target.content.bitmapData];
        var systray:Object = this.nativeApplication.icon;
        systray.tooltip = "Hello AIR World";
    }
    ]]>
    </mx:Script>
</mx:WindowedApplication>
```

Summary

Adobe AIR applications leverage user notifications to keep the end user informed while minimizing the actual level of user involvement to gain that information. A good design is one that does not interfere with the main goal of the desktop application while maintaining informational and critical notifications to the user on a need-to-know basis. Bouncing the Dock icon and displaying status bar messages, taskbar highlighting, and system tray icon ToolTips are nice ways to keep the user informed. Toast messages are a prime example of the latest best practice for alerting a user to this need-to-know information. Displayed above other windows, they should not steal the keyboard or mouse focus of the running Adobe AIR application. In addition, they should expire automatically so that the user doesn't have to close them, but they should remain ready to be read when the user is away from the computer.

CHAPTER 12

Working with Local Databases

If you've done any software development before picking up this book, chances are you have worked with a database. To the uninitiated, a database is a facility for collecting, organizing, and supplying information in an efficient manner. Database design and implementation can vary widely depending on the focus. As with most things in life, it's hard to do *everything* well, so there are databases that focus more on optimizing data storage than retrieval and vice versa. However, in the context of the Adobe® AIR™ platform, we're fortunate in that we won't be facing all the same challenges, at least in terms of scale, as larger server-side database systems.

Why? For one, databases in Adobe AIR are local, as in they exist on the user's system rather than some far off remote system. This way we do not have to deal with thousands or potentially hundreds of thousands or more clients, the way traditional n-tier systems operate. This doesn't mean we should abandon all the best practices the industry and communities have stitched together over the years, but operating locally does allow us to be more creative from a design perspective when needed.

Secondly, we have significant opportunity with respect to application responsiveness because we can now push larger datasets down to the client. Data can be sifted through and sorted directly on the user's machine, which offloads the server infrastructure—not to mention a huge reduction in data transmission over the wire. Add in the fact that Adobe AIR clients can also operate offline on these local databases, and you add a whole new dimension to the application landscape.

In this chapter we investigate what the Adobe AIR platform has to offer in terms of database functionality. After we've stepped through the mechanics, we also touch on some best practices and common challenges you might face in the real world.

About SQLite in Adobe AIR

Adobe AIR includes a SQL-based relational database engine called SQLite. Database instances are created and run locally, enabling your Adobe AIR applications to leverage their functionality even if you don't have a network connection available.

An Adobe AIR application can access one or many separate databases, each of which is represented as an individual file on the user's system. These database files can be created at will and stored anywhere the application has write-access to, just like creating any other `File` object. Using the `app-storage:URL` scheme as a common database location might be considered a best practice:

```
app-storage:/databases/orders.db
```

SQLite is an ACID-compliant (Atomicity, Consistency, Isolation, Durability) relational database. It is self-contained and cross-platform and requires no configuration. If you've worked with any server-based database solutions, you will be happy to learn that many of the same features are available to you in SQLite's tiny package. In fact, it implements most of the SQL-92 that is an established standard for the SQL database query language.

The SQLite library is linked directly into the Adobe AIR platform. This avoids any cross-process communication, delivering optimal performance.

> **NOTE**
>
> For more information on SQLite, you can visit their website:
>
> http://www.sqlite.org/about.html

Here are some feature highlights of the SQLite engine:

- ▶ Transactions are atomic, consistent, isolated, and durable (ACID) even after system crashes and power failures.
- ▶ Zero-configuration and serverless in operation.
- ▶ Implements most of SQL-92 language standard.
- ▶ A complete database is stored in a single, cross-platform disk file.
- ▶ Supports terabyte-sized databases and gigabyte-sized strings and blobs.
- ▶ Small code footprint: less than 250KiB fully configured or less than 150KiB with optional features omitted.
- ▶ Faster than popular client/server database engines for most common operations.

▶ Simple, easy to use application programming interface (API).

▶ Self-contained with no external dependencies.

▶ Operates across platforms, that is, Linux, Mac OS X, Windows, and others.

Why Use a Local SQL Database?

Having a local database engine is a huge deal. It opens so many doors with respect to the types of Adobe AIR applications you can build. Most important, it can be used to dramatically improve the user experience.

Data-oriented applications are clearly the biggest winner. Typically these applications pull a large volume of data over the wire onto the local machine. Traditionally, in the browser world, much of this happens repeatedly as the user moves from one page to another. Even a simply page refresh requires another round-trip to the server. Now with local storage, it's conceivable to pull down these large record sets, store them in a database, and perform operations on that data locally. You have all the benefits of a relational database, such as indexes and, of course, the SQL language itself. Having access to all this functionality from ActionScript, you can sort, create, read, update, and delete to your heart's content.

> **NOTE**
>
> With the release of version 2.6 of Adobe LiveCycle Data Services (LCDS), Adobe AIR and LCDS can operate together to automatically sync data sets between the server and local database instances. If the client is disconnected from the network, data is cached in the database and automatically re-syncs with the data service when network connectivity is restored.
>
> For more information on Adobe LCDS 2.6 (or later), visit http://www.adobe.com/products/livecycle/dataservices/.
>
> Adobe's Christophe Coenraets has published a great example on his blog: http://coenraets.org/blog/2008/05/insync-automatic-offline-data-synchronization-in-air-using-lcds-26/.

Creating Database Tables

This section covers the basics of creating a database and then a basic schema within that database.

First, you need to create a `SQLConnection` instance (see Table 12.1). You can do this by calling its `open()` method to open it in synchronous execution mode, or its `openAsync()` method to open it in asynchronous execution mode. We start with examples using synchronous operations.

TABLE 12.1   ActionScript Classes Introduced

Package	Class	Description
flash.data	SQLConnection	Used for the creation of connections to local SQL database files.

By passing a `File` instance that refers to a nonexistent file, the `open()` or `openAsync()` method creates a database file at that file location and opens a connection. As for the file itself, you're not restricted to any specific naming scheme or extension.

Listing 12.1 outlines a simple example of the database creation process in a synchronous fashion—"synchronous" meaning that, until the database connection is established, code execution is on hold. Considering the connection happens virtually instantaneously in this simple example, there isn't much of a need to go the asynchronous route.

LISTING 12.1   Establishing a Synchronous Database Connection

```
<?xml version="1.0" encoding="utf-8"?>
<mx:WindowedApplication
    xmlns:mx="http://www.adobe.com/2006/mxml"
    layout="vertical"
    creationComplete="init()">

    <mx:Script>
        <![CDATA[

        private var conn:SQLConnection;
        private var db:File;

        private function init():void
        {
         db = File.applicationStorageDirectory.resolvePath( "contacts.db" );
         conn = new SQLConnection();
         conn.open( db );
        }

        ]]>
    </mx:Script>
</mx:WindowedApplication>
```

Listing 12.2 demonstrates the same example, but it uses an asynchronous approach. In this instance, the connection is initiated, and code execution continues in the code block. The `SQLConnection` then dispatches an `OPEN` event when the connection has finally been established. We need to listen for that event so that we know when the database can be accessed:

```
conn.addEventListener( SQLEvent.OPEN, onConnectionOpen );
```

For more in-depth information on the synchronous and asynchronous operations see the subsection, "Synchronous Versus Asynchronous Database Operations."

LISTING 12.2   Establishing an Asynchronous Database Connection

```
<?xml version="1.0" encoding="utf-8"?>
<mx:WindowedApplication
    xmlns:mx="http://www.adobe.com/2006/mxml"
    layout="vertical"
    creationComplete="init()">

    <mx:Script>
        <![CDATA[

        private var conn:SQLConnection;
        private var db:File;

        private function init():void
        {
            db = File.applicationStorageDirectory.resolvePath( "contacts.db" );
            conn = new SQLConnection();
            conn.addEventListener( SQLEvent.OPEN, onConnectionOpen );
            conn.openAsync( db );
        }

        private function onConnectionOpen( event:SQLEvent ):void
        {
            trace( "SQLConnection is open" );
        }

        ]]>
    </mx:Script>
</mx:WindowedApplication>
```

NOTE

By calling the open() or openAsync() method with null for the reference parameter, you'll create a new in-memory database instead of a database file on the disk. When the application is closed down, the data in this database will not be persisted.

Working with Database Tables

In Adobe AIR, any SQL statement supported by the embedded SQLite engine can be executed from ActionScript. Although this includes creating, reading, updating, and deleting data, you can also *create*, *alter*, and *update* database tables. In many cases you will find yourself creating databases from scratch at application runtime, but you always have the option of distributing a premade or even prepopulated database, too.

Let's start with how to create database tables. You can use the CREATE TABLE statement for this task. Table 12.2 shows ActionScript classes. Listing 12.3 outlines the creation of a single table after the application has started up and the initial database connection has been made.

TABLE 12.2   ActionScript Classes Introduced

Package	Class	Description
flash.data	SQLStatement	Used to execute a SQL statement against a SQL database through an open SQLConnection.

NOTE

Extensive coverage on how to write queries in SQL is beyond the scope of this book. However, an enormous amount of books and content on the web provide in-depth detail. The Adobe Flex Builder 3 help documentation covers a significant portion.

LISTING 12.3   Example of Creating an Initial Table Structure

```
<?xml version="1.0" encoding="utf-8"?>
<mx:WindowedApplication
   xmlns:mx="http://www.adobe.com/2006/mxml"
   layout="vertical"
   creationComplete="init()">

   <mx:Script>
     <![CDATA[

     private var conn:SQLConnection;
     private var db:File;

     private function init():void
     {
      db = File.applicationStorageDirectory.resolvePath( "contacts.db" );
      conn = new SQLConnection();
      conn.open( db );
```

```
      initializeDatabase();
   }

   private function initializeDatabase():void
   {
    var stmt:SQLStatement = new SQLStatement();
    stmt.sqlConnection = conn;

    var sql:String =
    "CREATE TABLE IF NOT EXISTS contacts (" +
    " contactId INTEGER PRIMARY KEY AUTOINCREMENT," +
    " name TEXT," +
    " address1 TEXT," +
    " address2 TEXT," +
    " city TEXT," +
    " province TEXT," +
    " country TEXT," +
    " postalCode TEXT" +
    " )";
    stmt.text = sql;

    try
    {
          stmt.execute();
    }
    catch( error:SQLError )
    {
    trace( "Error message: " + error.message );
    }
   }
   ]]>
   </mx:Script>
</mx:WindowedApplication>
```

In our `initializeDatabase()`function, we are creating a `SQLStatement` object. The `text` property of this object will contain our SQL statement to be executed against our database that was initialized in the `init()` function:

```
stmt.text = sql;
```

We've housed our database connection variable outside of the `init()` function because it's best to reuse a preexisting connection when possible. After we've assigned the connection instance to the property of our SQLStatement, we can execute SQL queries against our database:

```
stmt.execute();
```

We're using the IF NOT EXISTS portion of the statement after CREATE TABLE to avoid destroying data the next time the application starts up. In larger databases, where initialization scripts might be considerably longer, a more elegant approach would be to query the structure of the database itself to see if it has already been initialized. Perhaps even easier than that, establish a flag that is changed after the first run of the application to indicate the initialization process has already been completed.

Working with Database Data

Now that we're able to create database tables, we start thinking about inserting and retrieving some data. We're halfway there already, actually. From a code perspective, the essence of data manipulation isn't all that different from our previous example of creating a database table. It boils down to our SQLStatement. Rather than using CREATE TABLE, we migrate over to using INSERT, SELECT, UPDATE, and DELETE.

Inserting Data

You can insert records into a database table using an INSERT SQL statement. Table 12.3 shows the ActionScript classes. Listing 12.4 takes our previous table creation example and extends that by inserting a default record into the table.

TABLE 12.3   ActionScript Classes Introduced

Package	Class	Description
flash.data	SQLResult	Provides access to data returned in response to the execution of a SQL statement.

LISTING 12.4   Inserting a Record into a Database Table

```
<?xml version="1.0" encoding="utf-8"?>
<mx:WindowedApplication
    xmlns:mx="http://www.adobe.com/2006/mxml"
    layout="vertical"
    creationComplete="init()">

    <mx:Script>
        <![CDATA[

        private var conn:SQLConnection;
        private var db:File;

        private function init():void
        {
         db = File.applicationStorageDirectory.resolvePath( "contacts.db" );
         conn = new SQLConnection();
```

```
conn.open( db );
initializeDatabase();
insertRecord();
selectDefaultRecord();
}

private function initializeDatabase():void
{
 var stmt:SQLStatement = new SQLStatement();
 stmt.sqlConnection = conn;

 var sql:String =
         "CREATE TABLE IF NOT EXISTS contacts (" +
         " contactId INTEGER PRIMARY KEY AUTOINCREMENT," +
         " name TEXT," +
         " address1 TEXT," +
         " address2 TEXT," +
         " city TEXT," +
         " province TEXT," +
         " country TEXT," +
         " postalCode TEXT" +
         ")";

 stmt.text = sql;

 try
 {
         stmt.execute();
 }
 catch( error:SQLError )
 {
         trace( "Error message: " + error.message );
 }
}

private function insertRecord():void
{
 var stmt:SQLStatement = new SQLStatement();
 stmt.sqlConnection = conn;

 var sql:String =
         "INSERT INTO contacts (" +
         " name, " +
         " address1, " +
         " address2, " +
         " city, " +
```

12

```
            " province, " +
            " country, " +
            " postalCode" +
            ")" +
            "VALUES (" +
            " 'Joe Smith'," +
            " '123 Main Street'," +
            " 'Apt 1'," +
            " 'Los Angeles'," +
            " 'CA'," +
            " 'US'," +
            " '90002'" +
            ")";

  stmt.text = sql;

  try
  {
        stmt.execute();
  }
  catch( error:SQLError )
  {
        trace( "Error message: " + error.message );
  }
}

private function selectDefaultRecord():void
{
 var stmt:SQLStatement = new SQLStatement();
 stmt.sqlConnection = conn;

 var sql:String =
        "SELECT * FROM contacts";

  stmt.text = sql;

  try
  {
        stmt.execute();
  }
catch( error:SQLError )
  {
        trace( "Error message: " + error.message );
  }

  var result:SQLResult = stmt.getResult();
```

```
    trace( "First row retrieved: \nName: " + result.data[0].name +
      "\nAddress: " + result.data[0].address1 );
  }


  ]]>
</mx:Script>
</mx:WindowedApplication>
```

In addition to creating a table at startup, we're now inserting a new record into that same table. The ActionScript code required for the operation is virtually identical to the table creation process, aside from the `SQLStatement` itself. Just as with any other relational database, we're using an `INSERT` statement to populate our record. We follow up by selecting back all the records in the database in the `selectDefaultRecord()`method.

At the tail end of `selectDefaultRecord()` you can see we're using another new class, `SQLResult`. We're creating an instance of `SQLResult` and then calling `getResult()` on the `SQLStatement` to populate our result object:

```
var result:SQLResult = stmt.getResult();
```

Accessing the `data` property of our SQLResult gives us an array of objects that represent the results of our query. Each object within the array has properties that correspond to the column names in the database tables—unless, of course, you have specified column aliases within your SQL SELECT statement. In our query results from our contact database, we can now trace out items in the record set:

```
trace( result.data[0].name );
```

Retrieving the Primary Key of an Inserted Row

Sometimes after you insert a row of data into a table, you might want to add rows in a related table. In that case, you need a database-generated primary key or row identifier value for this new row. You then insert the primary key value as a foreign key in the related table.

The primary key of the last inserted row can be retrieved via the `SQLResult` object. In Listing 12.5, we've now augmented the `selectDefaultRecord()` by adding a trailing trace statement that outputs the primary key value of the last inserted row. This is done by accessing `lastInsertRowID` on the `SQLResult` object.

LISTING 12.5   Retrieving an Auto-Incremented Primary Key

```
private function selectDefaultRecord():void
{
   var stmt:SQLStatement = new SQLStatement();
   stmt.sqlConnection = conn;
```

```
  var sql:String =
    "SELECT * FROM contacts";

  stmt.text = sql;

  try
  {
    stmt.execute();
  }
  catch( error:SQLError )
  {
    trace( "Error message: " + error.message );
  }

  var result:SQLResult = stmt.getResult();
  trace( "First row retrieved: \nName: " + result.data[0].name +
    "\nAddress: " + result.data[0].address1 );

  trace( "Last primary key: " + result.lastInsertRowID );
}
```

If the table is defined with multiple primary key columns (a composite key) or with a single primary key column whose affinity is not INTEGER, the database generates a row identifier value for the row. That generated value is the value of the lastInsertRowID property.

The value assigned to lastInsertedRowID is always the most recently inserted record. Be aware, however, in cases where you are using triggers in response to an INSERT:. If that trigger causes another INSERT to fire at another junction, the lastInsertedRowID will not reflect the original INSERT.

If you want to have a defined primary key column where the value is available after an INSERT command through the SQLResult.lastInsertRowID property, the column must be defined as an INTEGER PRIMARY KEY column.

Handling Database Query Results

Retrieving data from a database involves using a SQLStatement in tangent with a SELECT SQL statement. We've touched on handling query results briefly in Listing 12.4 but let's take a deeper look at this topic. Listing 12.6 highlights a method using SQLResult to store results from a query from our contact database:

```
var result:SQLResult = stmt.getResult();
```

LISTING 12.6   Reading Data from a Table

```
private function selectDefaultRecord():void
{
```

```
        var stmt:SQLStatement = new SQLStatement();
        stmt.sqlConnection = conn;
                var sql:String =
                "SELECT * FROM contacts";
                stmt.text = sql;
                try
        {
                stmt.execute();
        }
        catch( error:SQLError )
        {
                trace( "Error message: " + error.message );
        }

        var result:SQLResult = stmt.getResult();
        trace( "First row retrieved: \nName: " + result.data[0].name +
          "\nAddress: " + result.data[0].address1 );
}
```

The challenge here is that the objects being returned inside `result.data` are not typed.
They're generic ActionScript objects, not ideal for most applications. Let's say for instance
that we have a contact manager application sitting on top of this database. Then more
than likely we can expect to have some form of value object that represents a contact (see
Listing 12.7).

LISTING 12.7   Example of a Contact Value Object

```
package org.stacyyoung.contactmanager.domain
{
   import mx.collections.ArrayCollection;

   /**
   * Value object for the Contact entity.
   */
   [Bindable]
   public class Contact
   {
       public var contactId:Number = 0;
       public var name:String;
       public var address:String;
       public var email:String;

       public function Contact()
       {
```

```
        }
    }
}
```

You can have your database query results automatically mapped to specific ActionScript classes by specifying the associated class in the `itemClass` property of the `SQLStatement`. Each result object is cast to an instance of the class you've specified:

```
var statement:SQLStatement = new SQLStatement();
statement.sqlConnection = conn;
statement.text = "SELECT contactId, name, address, email FROM contacts;
statement.itemClass = Contact;
```

There are some prerequisites, however. First, your class must have a matching property for each of the column names coming back in your result set. (Having additional properties above and beyond is fine.) The second requirement is that each class must not expect parameters to be passed into its constructor.

Synchronous Versus Asynchronous Database Operations

When executing SQL statements against a database in synchronous mode, your application waits for the query to finish before moving on to the next line of code. That next line of code is typically there to deal with the query results accordingly. With asynchronous database operations, however, the SQL statement is added to the execution queue of the database, and your application moves on immediately. When results are eventually returned from the database, a callback function is invoked. In many cases, the logic contained in the callback function would closely mimic that of the synchronous version, just in a different location.

There are advantages and disadvantages of both approaches. Depending on the situation, at times you might not have a choice to use one over the other.

Writing Synchronous Database Operations

The main advantage of synchronous operations is simplicity in code. All the logic having to do with a particular query and its subsequent result can reside nice and neat in a single location. This can make debugging easier and your code more readable for teammates. This becomes apparent to you when it's time to chain multiple queries together, particularly if all the operations must participate in a database transaction.

The disadvantage of the synchronous approach is that your application code stops running while each database operation is executing against the database. In cases where queries are returning in a matter of milliseconds, this delay isn't noticeable. When queries start taking a number of seconds, things can really add up and make your application seem sluggish. It's always a judgment call, but personally I'd opt for synchronous wherever applicable. Listing 12.8 demonstrates a synchronous operation.

LISTING 12.8   Synchronous Database Operation

```
<?xml version="1.0" encoding="utf-8"?>
<mx:WindowedApplication
    xmlns:mx="http://www.adobe.com/2006/mxml"
    layout="vertical"
    creationComplete="init()">

    <mx:Script>
       <![CDATA[
       private var conn:SQLConnection;
       private var db:File;

       private function init():void {
        db = File.applicationStorageDirectory.resolvePath( "contacts.db" );
        conn = new SQLConnection();
        conn.open( db );
        initializeDatabase();
       }

       private function initializeDatabase():void {
        var stmt:SQLStatement = new SQLStatement();
        stmt.sqlConnection = conn;

        var sql:String =
        "CREATE TABLE IF NOT EXISTS contacts (" +
        " contactId INTEGER PRIMARY KEY AUTOINCREMENT," +
        " name TEXT," +
        " address1 TEXT," +
        " address2 TEXT," +
        " city TEXT," +
        " province TEXT," +
        " country TEXT," +
        " postalCode TEXT" +
        " )";

        stmt.text = sql;

        try {
          stmt.execute();
        }
        catch( error:SQLError ){
           trace( "Error message: " + error.message );
        }
       }
       ]]>
```

```
</mx:Script>
</mx:WindowedApplication>
```

Writing Asynchronous Database Operations

The main advantage of using the asynchronous execution mode for SQL statements is that you can make additional calls to the same database while waiting for the first query to complete. This is in addition, of course, to not having a database query "hang" the execution of code for your entire application as with synchronous operations. Listing 12.9 outlines the asynchronous version of Listing 12.8 for contrast.

LISTING 12.9 Asynchronous Database Operation

```
<?xml version="1.0" encoding="utf-8"?>
<mx:WindowedApplication
    xmlns:mx="http://www.adobe.com/2006/mxml"
    layout="vertical"
    creationComplete="init()">

    <mx:Script>
        <![CDATA[

        private var conn:SQLConnection;
        private var db:File;

        private function init():void
        {
         db = File.applicationStorageDirectory.resolvePath( "contacts.db" );
         conn = new SQLConnection();
         conn.addEventListener( SQLEvent.OPEN, onDatabaseOpen );
         conn.openAsync( db );
        }

        private function onDatabaseOpen( event:SQLEvent ):void
        {
         var stmt:SQLStatement = new SQLStatement();
         stmt.sqlConnection = conn;
         stmt.addEventListener( SQLEvent.RESULT, onDatabaseResult );

         var sql:String =
         "CREATE TABLE IF NOT EXISTS contacts (" +
         " contactId INTEGER PRIMARY KEY AUTOINCREMENT," +
         " name TEXT," +
         " address1 TEXT," +
         " address2 TEXT," +
```

```
         " city TEXT," +
         " province TEXT," +
         " country TEXT," +
         " postalCode TEXT" +
         " )";

         stmt.text = sql;
         stmt.execute();
      }

      private function onDatabaseResult( event:SQLEvent ):void
      {
         trace("Table created successfully");
      }
      ]]>
   </mx:Script>
</mx:WindowedApplication>
```

When executing multiple statements in asynchronous mode, one thing you can't do is change the value of a SQL statement while it's being executed. You can circumvent this limitation by using individual SQL statements for each operation on the database (see Listing 12.10).

LISTING 12.10   Executing Multiple Statements Against a Database in Asynchronous Mode

```
// Database has been opened using openAsync()
var statement1:SQLStatement = new SQLStatement();
statement1.sqlConnection = conn;
statement1.text = "SELECT * FROM TABLE A";
statement1.addEventListener( SQLEvent.RESULT, onStatement1Result );
statement1.execute(); // Added to the SQL connection execution queue

var statement2:SQLStatement = new SQLStatement();
statement2.sqlConnection = conn; // Using the same connection
statement2.text = "SELECT * FROM TABLE B";
statement2.addEventListener( SQLEvent.RESULT, onStatement2Result );
statement2.execute(); // Added to the execution queue
```

In Listing 12.10, both SQL statements are added to the execution queue and are run in the order they were called. With the database being opened in asynchronous mode, however, you cannot depend on the order that the results will come back—that is, it's possible the result for statement2 might return before statement1, depending on their respective query execution times.

Another aspect of asynchronous mode to consider is that, if you need one statement parameterize by the result of another statement, your only option is to execute the second statement from the result handler of the first SQL statement, in essence "chaining" the calls together. Unless the queries involved are long running, it might serve you better to use synchronous mode when opening the database.

Working with Encrypted Databases

As of Adobe AIR 1.5, you have the ability to encrypt local SQLite databases. The same approach is taken in creating a regular database, with the exception of an additional parameters passed in to open() method of the SQLConnection instance. This key must be supplied in the form of a ByteArray with a length of sixteen.

As a developer, you have complete control over the key management aspects when creating encrypted databases. That means you can generate the ByteArray key however you like. Any 16-byte value will work. A typical approach might be to generate a hash value of one or more input parameters, such as username and password of the user. This way your application is only capable of reading the database associated with the current user.

> **NOTE**
>
> Although some might opt for using an MD5 algorithm, it's recommended that you use a stronger option, such as SHA-256. This algorithm is available in the as3corelib project available on Google Code:
>
> http://code.google.com/p/as3corelib/
>
> You can also find the compiled as3corelib library in the sample source code for Chapter 12 of this book.

In the sample application shown in Listing 12.11, a new encrypted database is created each time you press the Create Database button at runtime. Although not the most practical example, it does show all the moving parts in creating the ByteArray key and ensuing database instance. Note the use of UIDUtil.createUID() in the createDatabase() function to generate the filename for the database. This generates a brand new database file each time the button is pressed. The reason for this is that if the stringToHash value were to be changed and the application re-executed, a runtime exception would be generated. This is because an encrypted database with the same file but a different encryption key already existed. You can, however, re-encrypt the same database any number of times provided you supply the *same* key.

LISTING 12.11   Creating an Encrypted Database

```
<?xml version="1.0" encoding="utf-8"?>
<mx:WindowedApplication
```

```
      xmlns:mx="http://www.adobe.com/2006/mxml"
      layout="vertical"
      verticalAlign="middle" horizontalAlign="center"
      title="Create Encrypted Database">

      <mx:Script>
         <![CDATA[
         import mx.utils.UIDUtil;
         import com.adobe.crypto.SHA256;

         private var stringToHash:String = "usernameAndPassword";

         private function createEncryptedDatabase():void
         {
            var str:String = SHA256.hash( stringToHash );
            var key:ByteArray = getKey( str );
            createDatabase( key );
         }

         private function createDatabase( key:ByteArray ):void
         {
            var db:File = File.applicationStorageDirectory.resolvePath
➥( UIDUtil.createUID() + ".db" );
            output.text += "Database filename: " + db.name + "\n";
            var conn:SQLConnection = new SQLConnection();
            conn.open( db, SQLMode.CREATE, false, 1024, key );
         }

         private function getKey( passCode:String ):ByteArray
         {
            var key:ByteArray = new ByteArray();
            var j:int = 0;
            for( var i:int=0; i < 16; i++ )
            {
               j = (hexToInt(passCode.charCodeAt(i))*15) +
➥hexToInt(passCode.charCodeAt(i+1));
               key.writeByte(j&0x00FF);
            }
            return key;
         }

         private function hexToInt(hex:Number):int
         {
            return parseInt("0x" + hex);
```

```
    }
    ]]>
  </mx:Script>

  <mx:Button label="Create Database" click="createEncryptedDatabase()" />
  <mx:TextArea id="output" width="100%" height="100%" />
</mx:WindowedApplication>
```

If you need to change the encryption key on a database, this can be accomplished by using the reencrypt() method on SQLConnection (see Listing 12.12).

LISTING 12.12   Re-encrypting a Database with a New Key

```
private function createDatabase( key:ByteArray ):void
{
   var db:File = File.applicationStorageDirectory.resolvePath(
"EncryptedDatabase.db" );
   var conn:SQLConnection = new SQLConnection();
   if( db.exists )
   {
      conn.open( db, SQLMode.UPDATE, false, 1024, key );
      conn.reencrypt( newkey );
   } else {
      conn.open( db, SQLMode.CREATE, false, 1024, key );
   }
}
```

To re-encrypt an existing database, you first need to open the SQLConnection in UPDATE mode with the original key. At this point the reencrypt() method can be called and the new key applied (see Listing 12.12).

You should keep in mind a few things when using encrypted databases in Adobe AIR:

▶ Encrypted databases cannot be unencrypted.

▶ Databases created without encryption cannot be encrypted later.

▶ Re-encryption works only on databases that are encrypted upon creation.

▶ There is a performance hit at runtime when accessing data from an encrypted database.

▶ Data read from an encrypted database exists as unencrypted data in memory.

Adobe AIR SQLite Tool

Christophe Coenraets, a technology evangelist with Adobe Systems, wrote an invaluable free tool for anyone wanting to manage SQLite databases. It can also serve as a great debugging tool when developing your own Adobe AIR applications. You can download the latest version from his blog:

```
http://coenraets.org/blog/2008/02/sqlite-admin-for-air-10/
```

You can examine the structure of an existing database, execute any SQL statements, or even create new databases. You can use this SQLite tool to look at the structure of a database, create a new database, open an existing one, or execute a SQL statement. This is useful while developing your Adobe AIR applications because there is no way to visualize the data in your SQLite databases at runtime—aside from adding verbose debug statements, of course! I think you will find it much easier to have Christophe's application running alongside your Adobe AIR application. Figure 12.1 shows this Adobe AIR-based SQLite tool at start-up.

FIGURE 12.1   Startup screen.

Because the tool leverages its own SQLite database to store query information, the user interface offers a handy feature of saving a history of SQL statements that have been executed (Figure 12.2). Again, this is great for debugging when you're monitoring values being pushed in and out of a project's database.

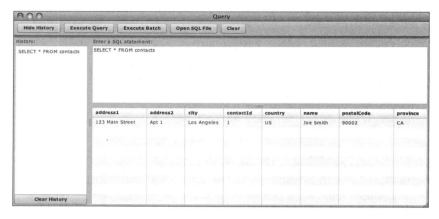

FIGURE 12.2   Coenraets Query editor.

When creating databases in Adobe AIR applications, it's considered a best practice to use the `applicationStorageDirectory` relative path when writing out the database file. To open the database from SQLite manager (Figure 12.3), you need to locate this file.

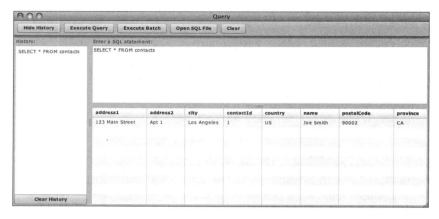

FIGURE 12.3   Examining the structure of a database table.

▶ On Mac OS:

```
/Users/{ username }/Library/Preferences/ { applicationID.publisherID
}/Local Store/
```

▶ On Windows:

```
{ local drive }/Documents and Settings/{ username }/Application Data/ {
applicationID.publisherID }/Local Store/
```

Summary

The inclusion of SQLite in Adobe AIR makes for one of the biggest features for this platform in comparison to traditional web-based applications. Data-centric applications in particular take a dramatic step forward in terms of a better user experience. No longer must your application repeatedly download large chunks of data just to do it again on the next page refresh. Now these large data sets can be stored locally and even periodically synchronized with a server when the user is online. This can drive snappy reporting and data mining applications that were once only possible on traditional native desktop applications.

Now, as of Adobe AIR 1.5, you can even encrypt your local SQLite databases for that extra level of privacy and security!

CHAPTER 13

Understanding Networking and Local Connections

Building Adobe® AIR™ applications that run on the desktop but that also combine the power of server-side operations is another important capability for the Adobe AIR runtime. Combining the proximity that only desktop applications provide with the powerful capabilities of remote server interactions, Adobe AIR applications can provide a one-two punch to other competing technologies with

▶ Remoting

▶ HTTP communication

▶ Web services

▶ Messaging

▶ Local connections

Remoting, with technologies such as ASP.NET, ColdFusion, J2EE, and PHP, via Flash Remoting, Adobe® Flex™'s HTTPService and WebService communication, or Live Cycle Data Services and now with Blaze DS, is the way Adobe AIR applications with a server-side tendency will be built. Although a separate topic in itself, local connections are an important capability in communication between an existing Shockwave Flash (SWF) file and the Adobe AIR application. This communication can be within a single SWF file, between multiple SWF files, between content (SWF or HTML) in Adobe AIR applications, or between content (SWF or HTML) in an Adobe AIR application and SWF content running in a browser. Using local connections, you could create a unified experience between a web-based and an Adobe AIR version of an application. For example, a user could launch the Adobe AIR application from a website and still access data in the browser-based version—courtesy of the local connection object.

This chapter introduces you to three important Adobe Flex tags—the `<mx:RemoteObject/>` tag, the `<mx:HTTPService/>` tag, and the `<mx:WebService/>` tag—as well as Blaze DS for messaging and local connections for inter/intracommunication between Adobe AIR applications and browser-based SWF or HTML content. Each of these techniques can bring the powerful server-side infrastructure investment in the enterprise to the rich desktop capabilities of an Adobe AIR application.

Remoting with Flash Remoting and ColdFusion

From day one, ColdFusion and Adobe Flex have been brothers as far as Flash Remoting is concerned. Adobe AIR applications built with Adobe Flex have this same relationship. Figures 13.1 and 13.2 demonstrate the close relationship between Adobe Flex-based Adobe AIR projects and ColdFusion in Adobe Flex Builder 3. The remoting package and class are shown in Table 13.1.

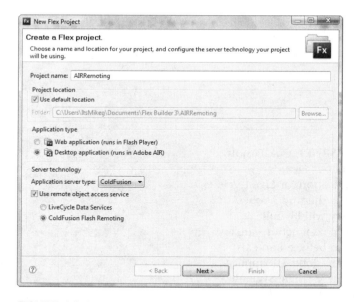

FIGURE 13.1   Creating an Adobe AIR project with ColdFusion Flash Remoting—Create a Flex Project dialog.

TABLE 13.1   `RemoteObject` Class

Package	Class	Description
mx.rpc.remoting.mxml	RemoteObject	The `RemoteObject` class gives you access to classes on a remote application server.

FIGURE 13.2   Creating an Adobe AIR project with ColdFusion Flash Remoting— configure ColdFusion Server.

A sample Adobe AIR application originally written for the former Apollo Alpha (the code name for what is now Adobe AIR) combines the desktop capabilities of Adobe AIR with a server-side ColdFusion component (CFC) to gain real-time air flight information. The Adobe AIR application communicates with the CFC via the Adobe Flex-based <mx:RemoteObject/> tag shown in the sample code in Listing 13.1.

LISTING 13.1   Adobe Flex Tag Using ColdFusion Flash Remoting

```
<mx:RemoteObject id="roFlight"
    destination="ColdFusion"
    endpoint="http://localhost/flex2gateway/"
    source="AIRRemoting-debug.info.airination.cfcs.flight"
    showBusyCursor="true">
    <mx:method name="getFlightDetails" result="getFlightDetailsHandler(event)"
➥fault="ro FaultHandler(event)"/></mx:RemoteObject>
```

NOTE

Flash Remoting, since Adobe Flex 2, is a binary format called AMF3. It is inherently better performing than the other RPC types, HTTPService and WebService. Given the choice, you should always opt for remoting when performance matters.

So how does this all work? In the sample application, the Adobe Flex `TextInput` control accepts a flight number (for example, COA1444 is a Continental Airlines flight), and in this application, a default flight number is supplied. When trying out this code on your own, feel free to enter any other flight number you wish to monitor. Clicking the Search button triggers the `callRemoting()` function that, in turn, triggers the `RemoteObject` service, roFlight to communicate with the server-side function `getFlightDetails()` in the ColdFusion Component (CFC):

```
private function callRemoting():void {
    this.status = "Searching for Flight " + tiFlight.text + "...";
    roFlight.getFlightDetails(tiFlight.text);
}
```

The `getFlightDetails()` function communicates with a third-party website that monitors air flight traffic through a ColdFusion tag, `CFHTTP`, but because this is not a ColdFusion book, there is no need to focus our attention here. Suffice to say, the CFC function returns real-time data about the flight number that the Adobe AIR application transmits via Flash remoting and the `<mx:RemoteObject>` tag you saw previously. After the result is tunneled back (recall the binary format is called AMF3) to the application, a result handler function, `getFlightDetailsHandler()`, passes the data to an Adobe Flex HTML control. Because the data is HTML, the control displays a nicely formatted display of the flight data:

```
private function getFlightDetailsHandler(event:ResultEvent):void {
    //Alert.show(ObjectUtil.toString(event.result));
    this.status = "Flight Info: " + tiFlight.text + "...";
    html.htmlLoader.loadString(event.result as String);
}
```

Listing 13.2 shows the complete Adobe AIR application leveraging ColdFusion Flash Remoting to communicate with the `flight.cfc`. The CFC code is also shown after the Macromedia Extensible Markup Language (MXML) in the listing.

LISTING 13.2   Adobe AIR Application Using ColdFusion Flash Remoting

```
The main application's MXML code:
<?xml version="1.0" encoding="utf-8"?>
<mx:WindowedApplication xmlns:mx="http://www.adobe.com/2006/mxml" title="AIR
➥Remoting Example" layout="absolute" backgroundColor="navy" height="395">
    <mx:RemoteObject id="roFlight"
        destination="ColdFusion"
        endpoint="http://localhost/flex2gateway/"
        source="AIRRemoting-debug.info.airination.cfcs.flight"
        showBusyCursor="true">
        <mx:method name="getFlightDetails" result="getFlightDetailsHandler(event)
➥"fault="roFaultHandler(event)"/>
    </mx:RemoteObject>
    <mx:TraceTarget/>
    <mx:Script>
```

```
<![CDATA[
import mx.rpc.events.ResultEvent;
import mx.rpc.events.FaultEvent;
import flash.events.Event;
import mx.controls.Alert;
import mx.utils.ObjectUtil;
private function callRemoting():void {
    this.status = "Searching for Flight " + tiFlight.text + "...";
    roFlight.getFlightDetails(tiFlight.text);
}
private function getFlightDetailsHandler(event:ResultEvent):void {
    //Alert.show(ObjectUtil.toString(event.result));
    this.status = "Flight Info: " + tiFlight.text + "...";
    html.htmlLoader.loadString(event.result as String);
}
private function roFaultHandler(event:FaultEvent):void {
    Alert.show(ObjectUtil.toString(event.fault));
}
]]>
</mx:Script>
<mx:HBox>
    <mx:Label text="Flight Number" toolTip="enter a flight number in this
➡format - COA1444" color="white" y="57" x="33" fontFamily="verdana"/>
    <mx:TextInput id="tiFlight" text="COA1444" y="57" x="123"/>
</mx:HBox>
<mx:Button x="90" y="38" label="Search" click="callRemoting()"/>
<mx:HTML id="html" y="87" width="100%" height="100%" scaleX=".7" scaleY=".7"/>
</mx:WindowedApplication>
```

Calling the `RemoteObject` class in ActionScript 3 is also possible, so you are not limited to the `<mx:RemoteObject/>` MXML tag. The following code snippet shows the `callRemoting()` function defined in ActionScript code:

```
private function callRemoting():void {
    this.status = "Searching for Flight " + tiFlight.text + "...";
    roFlight = new RemoteObject();
    roFlight.destination = "ColdFusion";
    roFlight.source = "AIRRemoting-debug.info.airination.cfcs.flight";
    roFlight.getFlightDetails.addEventListener("result", getFlightDetailsHandler);
    roFlight.getFlightDetails.addEventListener("fault", roFaultHandler);
    roFlight.getFlightDetails(tiFlight.text);
}
```

Here is the entire code for the same application with the RemoteObject called in ActionScript 3:

```
<?xml version="1.0" encoding="utf-8"?>
<mx:WindowedApplication xmlns:mx="http://www.adobe.com/2006/mxml" title="AIR
➡Remoting Example in AS3" layout="absolute" backgroundColor="navy" height="395">
```

```
<mx:TraceTarget/>
<mx:Script>
<![CDATA[
import mx.rpc.events.ResultEvent;
import mx.rpc.events.FaultEvent;
import flash.events.Event;
import mx.controls.Alert;
import mx.utils.ObjectUtil;
import mx.rpc.remoting.RemoteObject;
private var roFlight:RemoteObject;
private function callRemoting():void {
    this.status = "Searching for Flight " + tiFlight.text + "...";
    roFlight = new RemoteObject();
    roFlight.destination = "ColdFusion";
    roFlight.source = "AIRRemoting-debug.info.airination.cfcs.flight";
    roFlight.getFlightDetails.addEventListener("result",
➥getFlightDetailsHandler);
    roFlight.getFlightDetails.addEventListener("fault", roFaultHandler);
    roFlight.getFlightDetails(tiFlight.text);
}
private function getFlightDetailsHandler(event:ResultEvent):void {
    //Alert.show(ObjectUtil.toString(event.result));
    this.status = "Flight Info: " + tiFlight.text + "...";
    html.htmlLoader.loadString(event.result as String);
}
private function roFaultHandler(event:FaultEvent):void {
    Alert.show(ObjectUtil.toString(event.fault));
}
]]>
</mx:Script>
<mx:HBox>
    <mx:Label text="Flight Number" toolTip="enter a flight number in this format
➥COA1444" color="white" y="57" x="33" fontFamily="verdana"/>
    <mx:TextInput id="tiFlight" text="COA1444" y="57" x="123"/>
</mx:HBox>
<mx:Button x="90" y="38" label="Search" click="callRemoting()"/>
<mx:HTML id="html" y="87" width="100%" height="100%" scaleX=".7" scaleY=".7"/>
</mx:WindowedApplication>
```

CAUTION

The cffunction tag's access attribute must be set to remote for Flash Remoting to
have access to a particular function (method).

The CFC that the Adobe AIR application communicates with is as follows:

```
<cfcomponent displayname="flight" hint="This component contains the functions that
➥handles the Flex data requirements" output="false">
    <cffunction name="getFlightDetails" displayname="getFlightDetails" hint="This
➥function cfhttp's a page and scrapes out the data for a flight's details"
➥access="remote" output="false" returntype="String">
        <cfargument name="flightnumber" type="string" required="true">
            <cfsetting enableCFoutputOnly="yes" showDebugOutput="no">
            <cftry>
                <cfhttp url="http://flightaware.com/live/flight/#arguments.
➥flightnumber#" method="GET" resolveurl="Yes"/>
                <cfcatch type="Any">
                    <cfscript>
                        data = "GoFly couldn't find Flight " & arguments.flightnumber &
➥" just yet.";
                    </cfscript>
                    <cfthrow message="getFlightDetails Error: #cfcatch.message#
#cfcatch.detail#">
                    <cflog log="getFlightDetails" application="false"
➥text="#cfcatch.message# #cfcatch.detail#">
                </cfcatch>
            </cftry>
            <!—- two second delay to allow cfhttp to complete --->
            <cfset createObject("java", "java.lang.Thread").sleep(JavaCast
➥("int", 2000))>
            <cftry>
                <cfscript>
                    searchforstart = '<div id="bodyHeader">';
                    searchforend = '<td style="border: solid 5px ##ED8000;"
➥colspan="2" class="midAd">';
                    charsbefore = #Find(searchforstart,  cfhttp.fileContent ,  1)#;
                    tmpdisplaythis = #RemoveChars(cfhttp.fileContent, 1,
➥(charsbefore-1))#;
                    charsafter = #Find(searchforend,  tmpdisplaythis ,  1)#;
                    data = #RemoveChars(tmpdisplaythis, charsafter,
➥len(tmpdisplaythis) - len(charsafter))#;
                    data = "<div align='left'>" & data & "</div>";
                    //DBwrite = writeFlightDetails(data, flightnumber);
                </cfscript>
            <cfcatch type="Any">
                <cfscript>
                    data = "GoFly couldn't find Flight " &
➥arguments.flightnumber & " just yet.";
                </cfscript>
                <cfthrow message="getFlightDetails Error: #cfcatch.message#
➥#cfcatch.detail#">
```

```
                <cflog log="getFlightDetails" application="false"
text="#cfcatch.message# #cfcatch.detail#">
            </cfcatch>
            </cftry>

        <cfreturn data/>
    </cffunction>
</cfcomponent>
```

Figure 13.3 shows the Adobe AIR application in action.

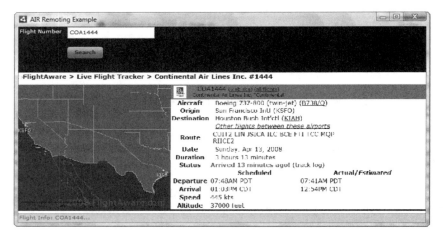

FIGURE 13.3   Adobe AIR application with ColdFusion Flash Remoting.

Adding the Adobe Flex tag `<mx:TraceTarget/>` gives you valuable insight into the Flash Remoting data transferred to and from the CFC. Listing 13.3 shows the Flex Output Console.

TIP

The `<mx:TraceTarget/>` tag is activated during Adobe Flex debugging and has no impact during the routine operation of your Adobe AIR application.

LISTING 13.3   Adobe Flex Output Console Using `<mx:TraceTarget/>`

```
[SWF] AIRRemoting.swf - 1,117,900 bytes after decompression
'367B3B28-2396-DA49-C60E-490AF960DAE5' producer set destination to 'ColdFusion'.
'null' channel endpoint set to http://localhost/flex2gateway/
'367B3B28-2396-DA49-C60E-490AF960DAE5' producer sending message
'6FDA6261-D5E4-8F6C-88CA-490B0543A184'
```

```
'null' pinging endpoint.
'null' channel is connected.
'null' channel sending message:
(mx.messaging.messages::RemotingMessage)#0
  body = (Array)#1
    [0] "COA1444"
  clientId = (null)
  destination = "ColdFusion"
  headers = (Object)#2
  messageId = "6FDA6261-D5E4-8F6C-88CA-490B0543A184"
  operation = "getFlightDetails"
  source = "AIRRemoting-debug.info.airination.cfcs.flight"
  timestamp = 0
  timeToLive = 0
'367B3B28-2396-DA49-C60E-490AF960DAE5' producer connected.
'367B3B28-2396-DA49-C60E-490AF960DAE5' producer acknowledge of
➥'6FDA6261-D5E4-8F6C-88CA-490B0543A184'.
```

Figure 13.4 shows an Adobe Flex debugging session for the RemoteObject call and provides useful information.

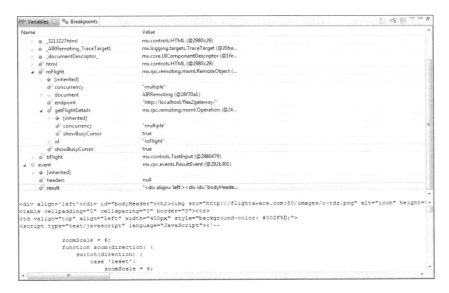

FIGURE 13.4   Adobe AIR application debugging session.

You might also want to invest in a third-party tool such as ServiceCapture if you need any introspection of the data transferred remotely. There are times when annoyances, such as case-sensitivity, that such tools can highlight can save you hours of frustration.

You can also use `RemoteObject` components with other server-side languages such as PHP and .NET objects in conjunction with third-party software, such as the open source projects AMFPHP, SabreAMF, and Midnight Coders' WebORB. Exploring these other remoting server-side languages is left for the reader.

Using an Adobe Flex `HTTPService`

The Adobe Flex `<mx:HTTPService/>` tag is another method that you can use to communicate between an Adobe AIR application and some server-side functionality that you want to leverage. To highlight the differences in coding when using the `<mx:HTTPService/>` tag versus the `<mx:RemoteObject/>` tag, we use the same Adobe AIR application that you saw in the previous section—our "AIR in Flight" sample application. The following code snippet shows using the `<mx:HTTPService/>` tag. Note the `resultFormat` property; ECMAScript For XML (e4x) makes working with XML type of data much easier than in earlier versions of Flex (1.0 and 1.5).

```
<mx:HTTPService id="httpFlight" resultFormat="e4x"
    result="getFlightDetailsHandler(event)"
    fault="httpFaultHandler(event)"
    showBusyCursor="true"/>
```

The flight number is again entered in the Adobe Flex `TextInput` control, the Search button is clicked, and the `callRemoting()` function is called. Note that the `url` property of the `HTTPService` (id property is `httpFlight`) points to the CFC, the method—`getFlightDetails()`—and appends the flight number to the CFC argument, `flightnumber`. The next line, `httpFlight.send()`, actually sends or posts the http request defined in the `url`:

```
private function callRemoting():void {
    this.status = "Searching for Flight " + tiFlight.text + "...";
    httpFlight.url = "http://localhost/AIRRemoting-debug/info/airination/
➥cfcs/flight.cfc?method=getFlightDetails&flightnumber=" + tiFlight.text;
    httpFlight.send();
}
```

When the data is returned from the ColdFusion server, an event handler, `getFlightDetailsHandler()`, is waiting to process the result. Because of the e4x data format, working with the result is much easier than in prior versions of Flex. In this example, the data needs a bit of parsing, so a custom function, `parseXMLtoHTML()`, gets the job done. Finally, the parsed data is pumped into an Adobe Flex HTML control just as in the previous example:

```
private function getFlightDetailsHandler(event:ResultEvent):void {
    xmlFlightInfo = event.result as XML;
    //Alert.show(ObjectUtil.toString(xmlFlightInfo.toXMLString()));
    this.status = "Flight Info: " + tiFlight.text + "...";
```

```
    var myHTML:String = parseXMLtoHTML(xmlFlightInfo);
    html.data = myHTML;
}
private function parseXMLtoHTML(inXML:XML):String {
    var safeString:String = inXML;
    if (safeString.indexOf("&amp;")>=0) {
        safeString = safeString.split("&amp;").join("&");
    }
    if (safeString.indexOf("&lt;")>=0) {
        safeString = safeString.split("&lt;").join("<");
    }
    if (safeString.indexOf("&gt;")>=0) {
        safeString = safeString.split("&gt;").join(">");
    }
    if (safeString.indexOf("&quot;")>=0) {
        safeString = safeString.split("&quot;").join("\"");
    }
    if (safeString.indexOf("&apos;")>=0) {
        safeString = safeString.split("&apos;").join("'");
    }
    return (safeString);
}
```

Listing 13.4 shows the complete Adobe AIR application leveraging the <mx:HTTPService/> tag to communicate with the flight.cfc. The CFC code is not shown again, as no changes from the previous listing are needed.

LISTING 13.4   Using the Adobe Flex HTTPService to Display Flight Information

```
<?xml version="1.0" encoding="utf-8"?>
<mx:WindowedApplication xmlns:mx="http://www.adobe.com/2006/mxml" title="
➥AIR HTTPService Example" layout="absolute" backgroundColor="navy" height="395">
    <mx:HTTPService id="httpFlight" resultFormat="e4x"
        result="getFlightDetailsHandler(event)" fault="httpFaultHandler(event)"
        showBusyCursor="true"/>
    <mx:TraceTarget/>
    <mx:Script>
    <![CDATA[
    import mx.utils.StringUtil;
    import mx.rpc.events.ResultEvent;
    import mx.rpc.events.FaultEvent;
    import flash.events.Event;
    import mx.controls.Alert;
    import mx.utils.ObjectUtil;
    import mx.collections.ArrayCollection;
    [Bindable] private var xmlFlightInfo:XML;
    private function callRemoting():void {
        this.status = "Searching for Flight " + tiFlight.text + "...";
```

```
        httpFlight.url = "http://localhost/AIRRemoting-debug/info/airination/
➥cfcs/flight.cfc?method=getFlightDetails&flightnumber=" + tiFlight.text;
        httpFlight.send();
    }
    private function getFlightDetailsHandler(event:ResultEvent):void {
        xmlFlightInfo = event.result as XML;
        //Alert.show(ObjectUtil.toString(xmlFlightInfo.toXMLString()));
        this.status = "Flight Info: " + tiFlight.text + "...";
        var myHTML:String = parseXMLtoHTML(xmlFlightInfo);
        html.data = myHTML;
    }
    private function parseXMLtoHTML(inXML:XML):String {
        var safeString:String = inXML;
        if (safeString.indexOf("&amp;")>=0) {
            safeString = safeString.split("&amp;").join("&");
        }
        if (safeString.indexOf("&lt;")>=0) {
            safeString = safeString.split("&lt;").join("<");
        }
        if (safeString.indexOf("&gt;")>=0) {
            safeString = safeString.split("&gt;").join(">");
        }
        if (safeString.indexOf("&quot;")>=0) {
            safeString = safeString.split("&quot;").join("\"");
        }
        if (safeString.indexOf("&apos;")>=0) {
            safeString = safeString.split("&apos;").join("'");
        }
        return (safeString);
    }
    private function httpFaultHandler(event:FaultEvent):void {
        Alert.show(ObjectUtil.toString(event.fault));
    }
    ]]>
    </mx:Script>
    <mx:HBox>
        <mx:Label text="Flight Number" toolTip="enter a flight number in this
➥format - COA1444" color="white" y="57" x="33" fontFamily="verdana"/>
        <mx:TextInput id="tiFlight" text="COA1444" y="57" x="123"/>
    </mx:HBox>
    <mx:Button x="90" y="38" label="Search" click="callRemoting()"/>
    <mx:HTML id="html" y="87" width="100%" height="100%" scaleX=".7" scaleY=".7"/>
</mx:WindowedApplication>
```

Figure 13.5 shows the resulting Adobe AIR application.

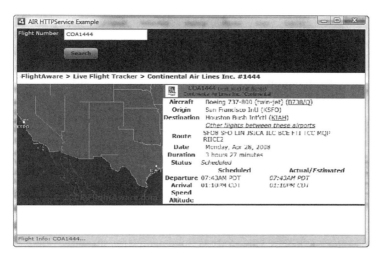

FIGURE 13.5   Adobe AIR application—AIR in Flight with the HTTPService tag.

Using an Adobe Flex `WebService`

The Adobe Flex `<mx:WebService/>` tag is another method that you can use to communicate between an Adobe AIR application and some server-side goodness. Once again, to highlight the differences between using this tag and the other two you have seen, the AIR in Flight application is retooled. Using the `<mx:WebService/>` tag is even easier than the `<mx:HTTPService/>` tag and is shown in this code snippet:

```
<mx:WebService id="wsFlight" wsdl="http://localhost/AIRRemoting-
➥debug/info/airination/cfcs/flight.cfc?wsdl" showBusyCursor="true">
    <mx:operation name="getFlightDetails" result="getFlightDetailsHandler
➥(event)" fault="wsFaultHandler(event)"/>
</mx:WebService>
```

As in the previous examples, the flight number is passed in via the Adobe Flex `TextInput` control during the Search button click event. The click event triggers the `callRemoting()` function, and this time the code looks similar to the remoting technique. The `getFlightDetails()` CFC function is passed the flight number. Once again, there are no changes required in the CFC (not shown for brevity):

```
private function callRemoting():void {
    this.status = "Searching for Flight " + tiFlight.text + "...";
    wsFlight.getFlightDetails(tiFlight.text);
}
```

The handler function, getFlightDetailsHandler(), for the data returned via the web service is shown. In this case, you see a property of the web service: WSFlight called lastResult. This property contains the data returned and is cast as a String. Finally, the data is pushed into the HTML control just as in the previous examples:

```
private function getFlightDetailsHandler(event:ResultEvent):void {
    txtFlightInfo = wsFlight.getFlightDetails.lastResult as String;
    //Alert.show(ObjectUtil.toString(xmlFlightInfo.toXMLString()));
    this.status = "Flight Info: " + tiFlight.text + "...";
    html.data = txtFlightInfo;
}
```

Listing 13.5 shows the complete Adobe AIR application leveraging the <mx:WebService/> tag to communicate with the flight.cfc. The CFC code is once again not shown, as no changes from the previous listing are needed.

LISTING 13.5   Using the Adobe Flex WebService to Display Flight Information

```
<?xml version="1.0" encoding="utf-8"?>
<mx:WindowedApplication xmlns:mx="http://www.adobe.com/2006/mxml" title="AIR
➥WebService Example" layout="absolute" backgroundColor="navy" height="395">
    <mx:WebService id="wsFlight" wsdl="http://localhost/AIRRemoting-
➥debug/info/airination/cfcs/flight.cfc?wsdl" showBusyCursor="true">
        <mx:operation name="getFlightDetails" result="getFlightDetailsHandler
➥(event)" fault="wsFaultHandler(event)"/>
    </mx:WebService>
    <mx:TraceTarget/>
    <mx:Script>
    <![CDATA[
    import mx.utils.StringUtil;
    import mx.rpc.events.ResultEvent;
    import mx.rpc.events.FaultEvent;
    import flash.events.Event;
    import mx.controls.Alert;
    import mx.utils.ObjectUtil;
    import mx.collections.ArrayCollection;
    [Bindable] private var txtFlightInfo:String;
    private function callRemoting():void {
        this.status = "Searching for Flight " + tiFlight.text + "...";
        wsFlight.getFlightDetails(tiFlight.text);
    }
    private function getFlightDetailsHandler(event:ResultEvent):void {
        txtFlightInfo = wsFlight.getFlightDetails.lastResult as String;
```

```
        //Alert.show(ObjectUtil.toString(xmlFlightInfo.toXMLString()));
        this.status = "Flight Info: " + tiFlight.text + "...";
        html.data = txtFlightInfo;
    }
    private function wsFaultHandler(event:FaultEvent):void {
        Alert.show(ObjectUtil.toString(event.fault));
    }
    ]]>
    </mx:Script>
    <mx:HBox>
        <mx:Label text="Flight Number" toolTip="enter a flight number in this
➥format - COA1444" color="white" y="57" x="33" fontFamily="verdana"/>
        <mx:TextInput id="tiFlight" text="COA1444" y="57" x="123"/>
    </mx:HBox>
    <mx:Button x="90" y="38" label="Search" click="callRemoting()"/>
    <mx:HTML id="html" y="87" width="100%" height="100%" scaleX=".7" scaleY=".7"/>
</mx:WindowedApplication>
```

Figure 13.6 shows the resulting Adobe AIR application.

FIGURE 13.6   Adobe AIR application—AIR in Flight with the `WebService` tag.

Messaging with BlazeDS

BlazeDS is a Java-based remoting and messaging server technology that facilitates the connection between front-end client applications—such as Adobe Flex, Adobe AIR, and AJAX—and back-end systems. It's both free and open source. As for Mac users, the only supported platforms at this time include Windows, Linux, or Solaris. However, a number of users have been able to get it up and running. Refer to the online installation guide and the user comments that follow for more detailed information:

http://opensource.adobe.com/wiki/display/blazeds/Installation+Guide

The remoting gateway in BlazeDS provides a foundation for performing Remote Procedure Call (RPC) type connections to server applications using a fast and efficient binary protocol called Action Message Format (AMF). The AMF protocol has a considerable advantage over Web Services or JavaScript Object Notation (JSON). Not only does it offer lower latency over the wire, but also both server and client pre- and postprocessing overhead is significantly reduced.

> **NOTE**
>
> James Ward of Adobe has a fantastic protocol explorer-type tool in which you can benchmark various ways of loading data into a Rich Internet/Desktop application. You can find it at www.jamesward.org/wordpress/2007/04/30/ajax-and-flex-data-loading-benchmarks/.

Installing BlazeDS

In this section we look at setting up BlazeDS using an available turnkey solution. You are free to download either the latest binary distribution or even the source code, but both of these methods are beyond the scope of this book. Refer to the Adobe open source website for more specific information:

http://opensource.adobe.com/wiki/display/blazeds/BlazeDS

Follow these steps to download and install the BlazeDS turnkey build:

1. Download the turnkey bits from the Adobe open source website:
   http://opensource.adobe.com/wiki/display/blazeds/Release+Builds.

2. Unzip the contents into a location easily accessible via command line.

3. Start the sample database by navigating to

   `{ BlazeDS root }/sampledb`

   Then run `./startdb.sh` or double-click `startdb.bat` on Windows.

4. Now that the sample database has been started, open a new command prompt and navigate to

   `{ BlazeDS root }/tomcat/bin`

   Then run `./catalina.sh run`. Or on Windows, double-click `catalina.bat` or run `catalina run` from the command prompt.

5. To verify BlazeDS is running, open a web browser and navigate to http://localhost:8400/samples/.

> **NOTE**
>
> The installation instructions for BlazeDS assume you have a properly configured Java environment on your machine, including having JAVA_HOME set and the JRE bin directory added to your system path. See Chapter 2, "Setting Up the Development Environment," for more information

Figure 13.7 shows the default Samples page after the installation is complete.

FIGURE 13.7   Default Samples page after installation.

Creating an Adobe AIR Messaging Application

Let's take a look on how to leverage the BlazeDS messaging features in an Adobe AIR application. All pertinent classes introduced in this section are listed in Table 13.2.

TABLE 13.2   ActionScript Classes Introduced

Package	Class	Description
mx.messaging.messages	AsyncMessage	Base class for asynchronous messages.
mx.messaging.messages	IMessage	Interface for constructing message objects.
mx.messaging	Consumer	Used to subscribe to messaging destination. Dispatches MessageEvent when messages are received from the server destination.
mx.messaging	Producer	Used to send messages to a destination. Dispatches MessageAckEvent when a message is transmitted and processed successfully.

The sample application for this topic is called AIRChat. As you might have guessed, it's a chat client running in Adobe AIR. Chat applications are a common usecase for messaging in Adobe® Flash® or Adobe Flex, but there are some unique differences when using Adobe AIR.

In the context of AIRChat, every client instance is both a subscriber and a producer to a messaging destination. Chat messages need to be both pushed out to the destination (Producer) and retrieved from the destination (Consumer) when messages from other clients arrive.

Figure 13.8 depicts how AIRChat clients communicate with each other via BlazeDS.

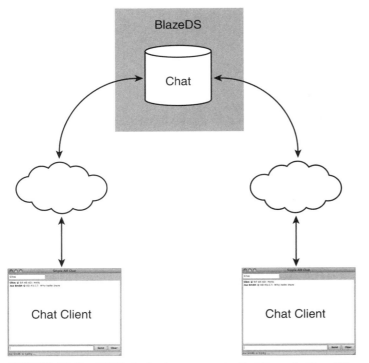

FIGURE 13.8   AIRChat clients communicating through BlazeDS.

For the chat application to successfully push and pull messages from our previously configured destination, be sure BlazeDS is running as outlined in the previous section, "Installing BlazeDS." In addition, you need to set a compile parameter to coincide with your environment to properly compile this application after checking it out of the repository:

1. Right-click the project in Adobe Flex Builder and select Properties.
2. Click Flex Compiler in the left menu.
3. Under Additional Compiler Arguments, change the path inside the double quotes to match the install path of your BlazeDS server: { path to your BlazeDS folder }/tomcat/webapps/blazeds/WEB-INF/flex/services-config.xml.
4. Click Apply.

5. Open that same `services-config.xml` file with a text editor and change the following entry to match the address of your server or local machine and save:

```
<channel-definition id="my-amf" class="mx.messaging.channels.AMFChannel">
    <endpoint url="http://{ your server address }:8400/blazeds/messagebroker/
➥amf" class="flex.messaging.endpoints.AMFEndpoint"/>
    </channel-definition>
```

6. In that same directory, open `messaging-config.xml` and add the following destination right before the closing `</services>` tag and save:

```
<destination id="chat">
    <channels>
        <channel ref="my-amf"/>
    </channels>
    </destination>
```

7. Restart BlazeDS.

When the AIRChat project is compiled, these XML configuration files are used to determine where the Adobe AIR application can locate the messaging destinations referenced in the source code. In a traditional Adobe Flex scenario, the compiled application typically resides on the server that explains the use of environment variables in these configuration files. With Adobe AIR however, we're dealing with an independent entity living off the server and on the user's desktop. For the sake of simplicity, this is why we've hard-coded the server address. In a production application, one might deliver a properties file in the Adobe AIR package indicating the location of any messaging servers and possibly even channel information.

Now, with BlazeDS up and running with the aforementioned changes, you can compile and run the chat application from Adobe Flex Builder. To simulate multiple clients, you can create and install an Adobe AIR file and run that along side the instance launched from Adobe Flex Builder running the Adobe AIR Debug Launcher (ADL). Listing 13.6 outlines the source for the AIRChat application.

LISTING 13.6   AIRChat Messaging Example

```xml
<?xml version="1.0" encoding="utf-8"?>
<mx:WindowedApplication
    xmlns:mx="http://www.adobe.com/2006/mxml"
    layout="vertical"
    horizontalAlign="left"
    verticalAlign="middle"
    paddingBottom="5" paddingLeft="5" paddingRight="5" paddingTop="5"
    applicationComplete="init()"
    status="{ statusMessage }">

    <mx:Script>
        <![CDATA[
        import mx.collections.ArrayCollection;
```

13

```
import mx.utils.UIDUtil;
import mx.formatters.DateFormatter;
import mx.messaging.messages.AsyncMessage;
import mx.messaging.messages.IMessage;

[Bindable]
private var clientsTyping:ArrayCollection = new ArrayCollection();
[Bindable]
private var statusMessage:String = "";

private var idleTime:Number = 9000;
private var lastCount:Number = 0;
private var timer:Timer = new Timer( 2000 );
private var clientId:String;

private function init():void
{
   username.setFocus();
   username.setSelection( 0, username.length );

   timer.addEventListener( TimerEvent.TIMER, onTick );
   timer.start();

   clientId = UIDUtil.createUID();
   consumer.subscribe( clientId );
}

private function onTick( event:TimerEvent ):void
{
    purgeClients();
    updateStatus();
}

/**
* Cycle through all chat peers and remove any
* old entries. i.e. are no longer broadcasting
* 'typing' messages
*/
private function purgeClients():void
{
    var now:Date = new Date();
    var ms:Number = now.time;

    for( var i:int=0; i < clientsTyping.length; i++ )
    {
       var clientMs:Number = (clientsTyping[i].timestamp as Date).time;
```

```
            if( ms - clientMs > idleTime )
            {
                clientsTyping.removeItemAt(i);
                i—;
            }
        }
}


/**
* Update the status bar to reflect which users
* are currently typing a chat message
*/
private function updateStatus():void
{
   if( clientsTyping.length )
   {
     var status:String = "";

     for( var i:int=0; i < clientsTyping.length; i++ )
     {
        status += clientsTyping[i].username;
        if( clientsTyping.length > 1 && i < clientsTyping.length-1 )
           status += ", ";
     }

     if( clientsTyping.length > 1 )
     {
        statusMessage = status + " are typing ...";
     }
     else
     {
        statusMessage = status + " is typing ...";
     }
   }
   else
   {
     statusMessage = "";
   }
}

/**
* Broadcast a message signaling the user
* is currently typing
*/
private function broadcastType():void
{
```

```
            var msg:IMessage = new AsyncMessage();
            msg.body.username = username.text;
            msg.body.typing = 1;
            msg.body.clientId = clientId;
            producer.send( msg );

            var now:Date = new Date();
            lastCount = now.time;
        }

        /**
        * Send chat messages
        */
        private function send():void
        {
            var msg:IMessage = new AsyncMessage();
            msg.body.message = "<b>" + username.text + "</b>" + " @ " + getTime() +
➥": " + messageInput.text;
            producer.send( msg );
            messageInput.text = "";
        }

        private function getTime():String
        {
            var now:Date = new Date();
            var formatter:DateFormatter = new DateFormatter();
            formatter.formatString = "LL:NN:SS";
            return formatter.format( now );
        }

        private function setScroll():void
        {
            chatlog.verticalScrollPosition = chatlog.maxVerticalScrollPosition + 10;
        }

        /**
        * Broadcast a message every 2 secs while the
        * user is typing.
        */
        private function onType():void
        {
            var now:Number = (new Date()).time;
            if( now - lastCount > 2000 || lastCount == 0 )
            {
            broadcastType();
            }
```

```
      }

      private function onMessage( event:IMessage ):void
      {
         if( event.body.message != null )
         {
            chatlog.htmlText += event.body.message + "\n";
            callLater( setScroll );
         }
         else
         {
            for( var i:int=0; i < clientsTyping.length; i++ )
            {
               if( clientsTyping[i].clientId == event.body.clientId )
               {
                  clientsTyping[i].timestamp = new Date();
                  return;
               }
            }

            var user:Object = {};
            user.clientId = event.body.clientId;
            user.username = event.body.username;
            user.timestamp = new Date();

            clientsTyping.addItem( user );
         }
      }
      ]]>
   </mx:Script>

   <mx:Consumer id="consumer" destination="chat" message="onMessage(
➥event.message )" />
   <mx:Producer id="producer" destination="chat" />

   <mx:TextInput
      id="username"
      text="Anonymous"
      enter="messageInput.setFocus()"
      tabIndex="1" />
   <mx:TextArea
      id="chatlog"
      height="100%" width="100%"
      editable="false"
      focusEnabled="false" />
```

```
<mx:HBox width="100%" horizontalGap="5" paddingLeft="0" paddingRight="0">
    <mx:TextInput
        id="messageInput"
        width="100%"
        enter="send()"
        tabIndex="2"
        change="onType()" />
    <mx:Button label="Send" click="send()" focusEnabled="false" />
    <mx:Button label="Clear" click="chatlog.text=''" focusEnabled="false" />
</mx:HBox>

</mx:WindowedApplication>
```

Let's take a look at the init() function that is being invoked when the applicationComplete event is fired. This is where the connection is made between the client Adobe AIR application and the messaging destination on the server:

```
clientId = UIDUtil.createUID();
consumer.subscribe( clientId );
```

Calling subscribe() tells the server that we want to receive all messages coming into the destination. After the script block, you can find a MXML tag that's specifying the specific destination we will be subscribing to, as well as our callback function, onMessage(), to be invoked whenever a server message arrives:

```
<mx:Consumer id="consumer" destination="chat" message="onMessage(
➥event.message )" />
```

> **NOTE**
>
> Although the Consumer and Producer are instantiated via MXML tags in our sample application, they can also be created in ActionScript. Refer to the Adobe Flex API documentation for more detail.

AIRChat can receive two types of messages: first, a message object containing a chat message from another client or second, a message indicating that a user is "typing." Looking at the onMessage() callback function, we can see how each type is handled:

```
if( event.body.message != null )
{
    chatlog.htmlText += event.body.message + "\n";
    callLater( setScroll );
}
```

An `AsyncMessage` typed as an `IMessage` contains a header and body attribute. In this example we're passing the text of each chat message as an attribute of the body called `message`. If that value is not null, then we know the asynchronous message we've just received from the server is chat text from another client. In this case we append this value to our `TextArea` control, which is acting as our chat history.

If the body of our `AsyncMessage` does not exist, then we process the message as a `type` event. In this case the event is indicating that another user subscribed to our chat destination is in the midst of typing a chat message. This information is stored in a local `ArrayCollection` with a timestamp. If the client in question, identified by a unique UID, already exists in the collection, this means we've previously received an "is typing" message. In this case the timestamp is updated to reflect the fact that the user is apparently still typing:

```
for( var i:int=0; i < clientsTyping.length; i++ )
{
   if( clientsTyping[i].clientId == event.body.clientId )
   {
      clientsTyping[i].timestamp = new Date();
      return;
   }
}
```

Meanwhile a timer constantly running in the background periodically examines the collection of "typing users" and concatenates a single string value with all the users' names and sets the status bar via binding. This is what causes "Joe Smith is typing..." to show up in the status bar of the native window:

```
<mx:WindowedApplication
   xmlns:mx="http://www.adobe.com/2006/mxml"
   layout="vertical"
   horizontalAlign="left"
   verticalAlign="middle"
   paddingBottom="5" paddingLeft="5" paddingRight="5" paddingTop="5"
   applicationComplete="init()"
   status="{ statusMessage }">
```

At the same time, old entries are being pruned from the collection by examining the associated timestamp and checking to see if the last "is typing" is beyond the configured `idleTime` variable; that is, after n seconds of no new messages are recieved from a client, it's assumed they are idle and no longer typing.

When a chat message is sent, either by the user hitting the Enter key or clicking the Send button, the `send()` method is invoked. (Figure 13.9 shows the chat client in action.) This function creates a new `AsyncMessage` and specifies a `message` element to the body containing the user's name, timestamp, and chat text from the `TextInput` control:

```
var msg:IMessage = new AsyncMessage();
msg.body.message = "<b>" + username.text + "</b>" + " @ " + getTime() + ": " +
messageInput.text;
producer.send( msg );
messageInput.text = "";
```

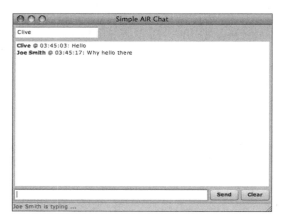

FIGURE 13.9   The AIRChat client operating with BlazeDS messaging.

It's worth noting that most of the code in the AIRChat example is centered around the user interface behavior and not so much on the messaging. This is a *good* thing. The fact that a complex messaging architecture can be wired together in seconds is truly groundbreaking.

Messaging under BlazeDS is yet another powerful tool for elevating your Adobe AIR applications to the next level. That the server component is free and open source is an incredible bonus. Be sure to dive into the sample applications documented with the turnkey install for BlazeDS. We've really only scratched the surface in this chapter.

Adobe AIR Applications and Local Connections

Another winning capability for Adobe AIR applications is their capability to work with `LocalConnection` objects to communicate with a single SWF file, between multiple SWF files, between content (SWF or HTML) in Adobe AIR applications, or between content (SWF or HTML) in an Adobe AIR application and SWF content running in a browser. The `LocalConnection` package and class are shown in Table 13.3.

TABLE 13.3   LocalConnection Class

Package	Class	Description
flash.net	LocalConnection	The LocalConnection class lets you create a LocalConnection object that can invoke a method in another LocalConnection object.

Intercommunication between your Adobe AIR application and the rest of what makes up your rich desktop experience is what `LocalConnection` objects were created to handle. Suppose you have an Adobe AIR application and you want to drag and drop some images into your Adobe AIR application and have them magically appear in, for example, a browser; this is local connection in play. In the following example, the Adobe AIR application is the sender, and the Adobe Flex application is the receiver. (Although the Adobe Flex application communicates back to the Adobe AIR application, too.) See Listing 13.7 for the code for this hybrid application. You will note that the sender, the Adobe AIR application, contains a `LocalConnection` object and a call to the `send()` method. The Adobe Flex application contains another `LocalConnection` object and a call to the `connect()` method, and because it communicates back to the Adobe AIR application, it also utilizes the `send()` method. Your use of the `send()` and the `connect()` methods depends on whether the files are in the same domain, in different domains with predictable domain names, or in different domains with unpredictable or dynamic domain names.

In the following simple example, you can see how easy it is to communicate from an Adobe AIR application and an Adobe Flex SWF loaded in a browser. The first step is to import the LocalConnection class:

```
import flash.net.LocalConnection;
```

Next, you create a target URL, create two `LocalConnection` objects—one for outgoing data and one for incoming data—define a `String` to be passed as the `LocalConnection` objects simple data, and a timer:

```
[Bindable] private var targetURL:String =
"http://localhost/FlexLocalConnection/bin-debug/FlexSimpleLocalConnection.html";
public var outLC:LocalConnection = new LocalConnection();
public var inLC:LocalConnection = new LocalConnection();
public var myString:String = "Hello AIR World!";
private var timer:Timer;
```

The Adobe AIR application's `applicationComplete` event triggers the `initApp()` function. The message, `myString` ("Hello AIR World"), is added to an Adobe Flex `Text` control, and an `openBrowser()` function is called. An event listener is created to listen to the `outLC` `LocalConnection`, and the `onStatus` handler function monitors the connection. Note that the `Timer` class is used to delay the outLC send method so the receiving browser can be launched in the `openBrowser()` function. The `openBrowser()` function opens an Adobe Flex-based SWF located on a website:

```
public function initApp():void{
    openBrowser();
    outLC.addEventListener(StatusEvent.STATUS, onStatus);
```

```
    inLC.allowDomain('*');
    inLC.client = this;
    try {
        inLC.connect("myString");
    } catch (error:ArgumentError) {
        Alert.show("Connection Failure");
    }
    timer = new Timer(1000, 0);
    timer.addEventListener("timer", timerHandler);
    timer.start();
}
private function onStatus(event:StatusEvent):void {
    if(event.level != "error"){
        trace("Woot! I am connected to another SWF.");
    }
}
public function timerHandler(event:TimerEvent):void {
    outLC.send("localhost:lcon", "updateText", outLC.domain);
}
public function updateText(s:String):void {
    trace("Woot! I updated the Text control.");
}
private function openBrowser():void{
    var url:String = targetURL;
    var urlRequest:URLRequest = new URLRequest(url);
    navigateToURL(urlRequest);
}
```

This Adobe Flex application includes code that mirrors that of the Adobe AIR application, so the LocalConnection objects exist in its SWF, too. You see the event listener for the outLC LocalConnection and the event handler onStatus function that, when the LocalConnection receives the data from the Adobe AIR application, updates the Adobe Flex Text control with the data, "Hello AIR World!" (see Figure 13.10).

```
public function init():void{
    outLC.addEventListener(StatusEvent.STATUS, onStatus);
    inLC.allowDomain('*');
    inLC.client = this;
    try {
        inLC.connect("lcon");
    } catch (error:ArgumentError) {
        Alert.show("Connection failed, already in use", "Error");
    }
}
private function onStatus(event:StatusEvent):void {
    if(event.level != "error"){
```

```
        txtReceived.text = myString;
    }
}
public function updateText(s:String):void {
    outLCDomain = s;
    outLC.send(outLCDomain + ":myString", "updateText", "OK");
    timer = new Timer(1000, 0);
    timer.addEventListener("timer", timerHandler);
    timer.start();
}
public function timerHandler(event:TimerEvent):void {
    outLC.send(outLCDomain + ":myString", "updateText", "OK");
}
```

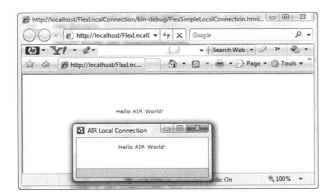

FIGURE 13.10   Adobe Flex Text control with the data "Hello AIR World!"

The next example expands on the previous simple code by adding drag-and-drop functionality. Running the code, you can drag and drop an image into the Adobe AIR application, and the image appears in the Adobe Flex-based SWF loaded in a browser. The drag-and-drop code is as follows:

```
private function onDragIn(event:NativeDragEvent):void{
  NativeDragManager.acceptDragDrop(this);
}
private function onDrop(event:NativeDragEvent):void{
  var dropfiles:Array =
event.clipboard.getData(ClipboardFormats.FILE_LIST_FORMAT)as Array;
  for each (var file:File in dropfiles){
    switch (file.extension.toLowerCase()){
      case "png" :
        addImage(file.nativePath);
        break;
```

```
      case "jpg" :
        addImage(file.nativePath);
        break;
      case "jpeg" :
        addImage(file.nativePath);
        break;
      case "gif" :
        addImage(file.nativePath);
        break;
      default:
        Alert.show("Unmapped Extension");
      }
    }
}
```

The addImage() function creates a new Image and places it in the operating system's nativePath. The handler sendJPEG function converts the BitmapData to a ByteArray data type and sends the ByteArray through the outLC LocalConnection object:

```
private function addImage(nativePath:String):void{
    var i:Image = new Image();
    i.visible = false;
    i.addEventListener(FlexEvent.UPDATE_COMPLETE,sendJPEG);
    if(Capabilities.os.search("Mac") >= 0){
        i.source = "file://" + nativePath;
    } else {
        i.source = nativePath;
    }
    this.addChild(i);
}
private function sendJPEG(event:FlexEvent):void{
    try{
        var img:Image = event.target as Image;
        bitmapData = new BitmapData(img.width, img.height);
        bitmapData.draw(img);
        var bitmap:Bitmap = new Bitmap(bitmapData);
        var jpg:JPEGEncoder = new JPEGEncoder();
        var ba:ByteArray = jpg.encode(bitmapData);
        outLC.send("localhost:lcon", "receiveImage", ba);
        imgDropped.load(ba);
        } catch(e:Error){
    }
}
```

On the Adobe Flex-based SWF side, the browser receives the ByteArray data via the LocalConnection object and uses it in the source property of the waiting Adobe Flex Image control. Finally, the respond() function is called, and the outLC LocalConnection sends the message back to the Adobe AIR application, which triggers an `Alert` to "Check your browser."

```
public function receiveImage(ba:ByteArray):void {
    img.source = ba;
    respond();
}
private function respond():void {
    outLC.send(outLCDomain + ":airimage", "getResponse", 'Check your browser');
}
```

The complete code listing for this example is shown in Listing 13.7 and includes the Adobe AIR application code as well as the Adobe Flex application code.

LISTING 13.7   Adobe AIR Application and Local Connection Usage

The Adobe AIR application code is as follows:

```
<?xml version="1.0" encoding="utf-8"?>
<mx:WindowedApplication xmlns:mx="http://www.adobe.com/2006/mxml" title="AIR Local
Connection Example" layout="absolute" applicationComplete="initApp()"
horizontalScrollPolicy="off" verticalScrollPolicy="off" width="321" height="357"
backgroundColor="#FFFFFF">
    <mx:Script>
    <![CDATA[
    import mx.events.FlexEvent;
    import mx.graphics.codec.JPEGEncoder;
    import mx.controls.Alert;
    import flash.net.LocalConnection;
    import flash.events.StatusEvent;
    import mx.controls.Image;
    import flash.filesystem.File;
    [Bindable] private var targetURL:String = "http://localhost/FlexLocalConnection/bin-
debug/FlexLocalConnection.html";
    [Bindable] private var blnConnected:Boolean = true;
    [Bindable] private var blnBrowser:Boolean = false;
    [Bindable][Embed(source="assets/jpgs/leprichaun.jpg")] private var fleximage: Class;
    [Bindable][Embed(source="assets/jpgs/AIRApp_16.jpg")] private var airimage: Class;
    public var outLC:LocalConnection = new LocalConnection();
    public var inLC:LocalConnection = new LocalConnection();
    private var timer:Timer;
    private var statusBarTimer:Timer;
    private var bitmapData:BitmapData;
    public function initApp():void{
        browserLaunched();
        outLC.addEventListener(StatusEvent.STATUS, onStatus);
        inLC = new LocalConnection();
```

```
        inLC.allowDomain('*');
        inLC.client = this;
        try {
            inLC.connect("airimage");
        } catch (error:ArgumentError) {
            Alert.show("Connection Failure");
        }
        timer = new Timer(1000, 0);
        timer.addEventListener("timer", timerHandler);
        timer.start();
        this.addEventListener(NativeDragEvent.NATIVE_DRAG_ENTER,onDragIn);
        this.addEventListener(NativeDragEvent.NATIVE_DRAG_DROP,onDrop);
        this.statusBar.addEventListener(MouseEvent.CLICK, openBrowser);
    }
    private function browserLaunched():void {
        if (blnBrowser) {
            lbl.text = "Browser is launched";
            setUI(true);
        } else {
            lbl.text = "Browser is not launched";
            setUI(false);
        }
    }
    public function timerHandler(event:TimerEvent):void {
        outLC.send("localhost:lcon", "testCon", outLC.domain);
    }
    public function testCon(s:String):void {
        blnConnected = true;
    }
    public function getResponse(s:String):void {
        //Alert.show(s,"Success");
        this.status = s;
        if (this.status == 'exit') {
            blnBrowser = false;
            browserLaunched();
        }
    }
    private function onStatus(event:StatusEvent):void {
        if(event.level == "error"){
            blnConnected = false;
        } else{
            blnConnected = true;
        }
    }
    private function onDragIn(event:NativeDragEvent):void{
      NativeDragManager.acceptDragDrop(this);
```

```
    }
    private function onDrop(event:NativeDragEvent):void{
       var dropfiles:Array = event.clipboard.getData(ClipboardFormats.FILE_LIST_
➥ FORMAT) as Array;
       for each (var file:File in dropfiles){
          switch (file.extension.toLowerCase()){
             case "png" :
               addImage(file.nativePath);
               break;
             case "jpg" :
               addImage(file.nativePath);
               break;
             case "jpeg" :
               addImage(file.nativePath);
               break;
             case "gif" :
               addImage(file.nativePath);
               break;
             default:
               Alert.show("Unmapped Extension");
             }
          }
       }
    private function addImage(nativePath:String):void{
       var i:Image = new Image();
       i.visible = false;
       i.addEventListener(FlexEvent.UPDATE_COMPLETE,sendJPEG);
       if(Capabilities.os.search("Mac") >= 0){
          i.source = "file://" + nativePath;
       } else {
          i.source = nativePath;
       }
       this.addChild(i);
    }
    private function sendJPEG(event:FlexEvent):void{
       try{
       var img:Image = event.target as Image;
       bitmapData = new BitmapData(img.width, img.height);
       bitmapData.draw(img);
       var bitmap:Bitmap = new Bitmap(bitmapData);
       var jpg:JPEGEncoder = new JPEGEncoder();
       var ba:ByteArray = jpg.encode(bitmapData);
       outLC.send("localhost:lcon", "receiveImage", ba);
       imgDropped.load(ba);
       } catch(e:Error){
```

```
            }
        }

    private function setUI(bln:Boolean):Boolean{
        if(bln){
            received.source = fleximage;
            message.text = "Drop an image in the dropzone below:";
            this.status = message.text;
        } else {
            received.source = airimage;
            message.text = "Open your browser by clicking on the statusBar"
            this.status = message.text;
            statusBarTimer = new Timer(3000, 1);
            statusBarTimer.addEventListener("timer", statusBarTimerHandler);
            statusBarTimer.start();
        }
        return bln;
    }
    private function statusBarTimerHandler(event:TimerEvent):void {
        this.status = "Click here: " + targetURL ;
    }
    private function openBrowser(event:Event):void{
        var url:String = targetURL;
        var urlRequest:URLRequest = new URLRequest(url);
        navigateToURL(urlRequest);
        blnBrowser = true;
        browserLaunched();
    }
    ]]>
    </mx:Script>
    <mx:Label id="lbl" x="100.5" y="61"/>
    <mx:Image id="received" x="247.5" y="61" width="16" height="18"
➥ source="{airimage}"/>
    <mx:Text id="message" x="22" y="10" width="275" textAlign="center"
➥ color="#000000" fontWeight="bold"/>
    <mx:HBox id="dropzone" x="22" y="91" width="275" height="218"
➥ borderStyle="solid" borderThickness="3" borderColor="#150B75">
        <mx:SWFLoader id="imgDropped"/>
    </mx:HBox>

</mx:WindowedApplication>
```

The Adobe Flex code for this example features accepting the ByteArray data from the
Adobe AIR application's LocalConnection object to display the image that was dropped
onto the Adobe AIR application, in the Flex-based SWF file's browser instance:

```
<?xml version="1.0" encoding="utf-8"?>
<mx:Application xmlns:mx="http://www.adobe.com/2006/mxml" layout="absolute"
➥ creationComplete="init()">
    <mx:Script>
        <![CDATA[
                import flash.net.LocalConnection;
                import mx.controls.Alert;
                private var inLC:LocalConnection = new LocalConnection();;
                private var outLC:LocalConnection = new LocalConnection();;
                private var outLCDomain:String;
                private var timer:Timer;
                 [Bindable][Embed(source="assets/jpgs/leprichaun.jpg")] private
➥ var fleximage:Class;
                [Bindable][Embed(source="assets/jpgs/AIRApp_16.jpg")] private
➥ var airimage:Class;
        public function init():void{
            outLC.addEventListener(StatusEvent.STATUS, onStatus);
            inLC.allowDomain('*');
            inLC.client = this;
            try {
                inLC.connect("lcon");
            } catch (error:ArgumentError) {
                Alert.show("Connection failed, already in use", "Error");
            }
        }
        private function onStatus(event:StatusEvent):void {
            if(event.level == "error"){
                received.source = fleximage;
            } else{
                received.source = airimage;
            }
        }
        public function testCon(s:String):void{
            outLCDomain = s;
            outLC.send(outLCDomain + ":airimage", "testCon", "OK");
            timer = new Timer(1000, 0);
            timer.addEventListener("timer", timerHandler);
            timer.start();
        }
        public function timerHandler(event:TimerEvent):void {
            outLC.send(outLCDomain + ":airimage", "testCon", "OK");
        }
        public function receiveImage(ba:ByteArray):void {
            img.source = ba;
            respond();
        }
        private function respond():void {
```

13

```
            outLC.send(outLCDomain + ":airimage", "getResponse",
➥ 'Check your browser');
        }
        private function closeMyWindow():void {
            outLC.send(outLCDomain + ':airimage', 'getResponse', 'exit');
                var urlString:String = "javascript:self.close()";
                var request:URLRequest = new URLRequest(urlString);
                navigateToURL(request, "_self");
        }
        ]]>
    </mx:Script>
    <mx:Canvas horizontalCenter="0" verticalCenter="0" backgroundColor="#FFFFFF"
➥ width="100%" height="100%">
        <mx:Image id="img" x="163" y="40"/>
        <mx:Label text="Connected to the AIR Application" x="74" y="14"
➥ color="#000000"/>
        <mx:Image id="received" x="268" y="14" width="16"
➥ height="16"source="{fleximage}"/>
        <mx:Button x="150" y="343" label="Close" click="closeMyWindow()"/>
    </mx:Canvas>
</mx:Application>
```

Figure 13.11 shows an image that is dropped onto the Adobe AIR application in this example.

FIGURE 13.11   Adobe AIR application—drag and drop an image.

Figure 13.12 shows that the same image magically appears in the browser courtesy of the LocalConnection.

FIGURE 13.12   Adobe Flex application—local connection to Adobe AIR image.

A nice feature of ActionScript 3–created `LocalConnection` objects is that they can communicate with `LocalConnection` objects created in ActionScript 1.0 or 2.0. This makes communication with older versions of Flash SWF files possible. The reverse is also true—the earlier version of Flash SWF files can communicate from AS 1.0 or AS 2.0 to AS 3.

Summary

Remoting, messaging, and local connections combine the power of server-side operations and are another important capability for the Adobe AIR runtime. By combining a desktop application with the powerful capabilities of a server, Adobe AIR applications can provide full-featured coverage over other competing technologies. Remoting, with technologies such as ASP.NET, ColdFusion, J2EE, and PHP, via Flash Remoting or Live Cycle Data Services and now with Blaze DS, is the way Adobe AIR applications can be fashioned. Local connections is an important capability in communication within a single SWF file, between multiple SWF files, between content in Adobe AIR applications, or between content in an Adobe AIR application and some SWF content running in a browser.

# CHAPTER 14

Working with Adobe Flex AIR Components

In addition to the traditional set of user interface controls included in Adobe® Flex™, Adobe® AIR™ includes a new set of components specifically designed to interact with the user's file system. The advantage to you, the developer, is that you now have a new set of tools to aid in rapid application development.

The Adobe Flex AIR components are made up of components you might already be familiar with such as `CombBox`, `List`, `Tree`, and the `DataGrid` control. Where they differ from their Adobe Flex-only counterparts is a suite of Adobe AIR-only methods and behaviors you can leverage to build your applications. If you need to offer your users controls that enable them to select, move, or even delete items off the file system, these components are your starting point.

FileSystemComboBox Component

The first component we explore is the `FileSystemComboBox` component. It's a `ComboBox` with the added intelligence to display directory information. It's primarily used for navigation purposes. Microsoft Window users might not recognize this user interface idiom, but it's used often on Apple's Mac OS X operating system.

The example in Listing 14.1 sets the default directory of the `FileSystemComboBox` control to the user's document directory. At that point, opening the `ComboBox` reveals the folder hierarchy above the current location, which allows the user to navigate upward through the directory structure.

LISTING 14.1   Using the FileSystemComboBox Component

```
<?xml version="1.0" encoding="utf-8"?>
<mx:WindowedApplication
    xmlns:mx="http://www.adobe.com/2006/mxml"
    layout="horizontal" verticalAlign="top"
    title="FileSystemComboBox Component"
    initialize="init()">

    <mx:Script>
    <![CDATA[
        import mx.binding.utils.BindingUtils;

        private function init():void
        {
            fileSystemCombo.directory = File.documentsDirectory;
            BindingUtils.bindProperty( fileSystemPath, "text", fileSystemCombo,
["directory","nativePath"] );
        }
    ]]>
    </mx:Script>

    <mx:FileSystemComboBox id="fileSystemCombo" width="100%" />
    <mx:VBox width="100%">
        <mx:Label text="Current Directory:" fontWeight="bold" />
        <mx:TextArea id="fileSystemPath" width="100%" height="40" />
    </mx:VBox>
</mx:WindowedApplication>
```

An interesting thing to point out in Listing 14.1 is the use of `BindingUtils`. This class is an alternative means of establishing binding between properties of objects (as opposed to using the more common curly braces approach { }). The `bindProperty` method is saying, "Whenever the value of `nativePath` changes on the directory property of `fileSystemCombo`, change the text property on our `TextArea` to match." The square brackets indicate a "property chain" allowing you to specify a property nested inside a complex object. If we had been attempting to bind the "text" property of two `TextArea`s, the method call would be somewhat simpler:

```
BindingUtils.bindProperty( fileSystemPath, "text", anotherTextArea, "text" );
```

Figure 14.1 shows the `FileSystemComboBox` example in action. Thanks to our use of `BindingUtils`, the `TextArea` will now update to reflect the selected directory.

One thing is painfully obvious in the `FileSystemComboBox` example in Listing 14.1. The component is not very useful on its own because there is no mechanism to navigate downward or any indication as to the contents of the selected directory.

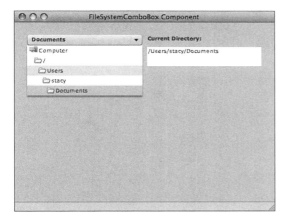

FIGURE 14.1   The FileSystemComboBox component.

FileSystemList Component

Listing 14.2 incorporates the FileSystemList component to accommodate the shortcomings in the previous example in Listing 14.1. The FileSystemList is essentially a directory browser. By setting the directory property on this control, the component populates itself with an ArrayCollection of File objects for the given location on the file system. Using the FileSystemList, we can now display the directory contents to the users based on their selection via the FileSystemComboBox or via the FileSystemList.

LISTING 14.2   Using the FileSystemList Component

```
<?xml version="1.0" encoding="utf-8"?>
<mx:WindowedApplication
   xmlns:mx="http://www.adobe.com/2006/mxml"
   layout="vertical" horizontalAlign="left"
   title="FileSystemList Component">

   <mx:Script>
     <![CDATA[
        import mx.events.FileEvent;

        [Bindable]
        private var directory:File = File.documentsDirectory;

        private function onDirectoryChange( event:FileEvent ):void
        {
           if( event.target == fileSystemList )
           {
              callLater( function():void{ directory = fileSystemList.directory } );
```

```
            }
            else
            {
                directory = event.file;
            }
        }

    ]]>
    </mx:Script>

    <mx:HBox>
        <mx:Button label="Up"
            click="fileSystemList.navigateUp()"
            enabled="{ fileSystemList.canNavigateUp }" />
        <mx:Button label="Down"
            click="fileSystemList.navigateDown()"
            enabled="{ fileSystemList.canNavigateDown }" />
        <mx:FileSystemComboBox
            id="fileSystemCombo"
            width="100%"
            directory="{ directory }"
            directoryChange="onDirectoryChange( event )" />
    </mx:HBox>

    <mx:FileSystemList
        id="fileSystemList"
        width="100%"
        directory="{ directory }"
        directoryChange="onDirectoryChange( event )" />
</mx:WindowedApplication>
```

Listing 14.2 leverages the data-binding features in Adobe Flex to drive the `directory` property of both the `FileSystemComboBox` and the `FileSystemList` controls. This way, we can strive toward componentizing this application by having to change only the working directory in one spot. When the `directory` variable changes, so do all controls bound to that variable. Figure 14.2 shows our example in action.

Coordinating the selected directory for both the `FileSystemComboBox` and the `FileSystemList` can be a bit tricky. In our example, we've leveraged the data-binding features within Adobe Flex to drive both controls. Both controls invoke the `onDirectoryChange` function when the user changes their value by interacting with the component.

You can run into trouble with this approach. When a directory change has been made within the `FileSystemList`, the value of its directory property is temporarily `null`. This is because the control is busy enumerating all the `File` objects in the newly selected directory.

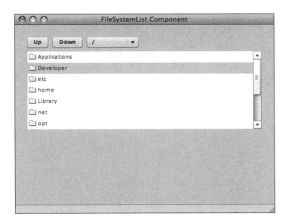

FIGURE 14.2   Incorporating the `FileSystemList` component.

Listing 14.2 gets around this by using the `CallLater` function. In short, this tells Adobe Flex to, "Run this function after all other processing has completed," which includes the work involved in enumerating all the new `File` objects to be displayed within the `FileSystemList` control based on the users' selection.

FileSystemTree Component

The `FileSystemTree` component can allow your users to navigate much more quickly by supplying the ability to "jump around" the system's directory structure. This is made possible by exposing the folder hierarchy as a "tree" with branches the users can open and dive into without losing their place. This type of control is the cornerstone of both Microsoft Windows Explorer and the Mac OS Finder application. Listing 14.3 outlines how we can combine the `FileSystemTree` component with the `FileSystemList` to mimic the behavior of major operating systems.

LISTING 14.3   Creating File System Explorer Functionality Using the `FileSystemTree` Component

```
<?xml version="1.0" encoding="utf-8"?>
<mx:WindowedApplication
    xmlns:mx="http://www.adobe.com/2006/mxml"
    layout="horizontal"
    title="FileSystemTree Component">

    <mx:Script>
      <![CDATA[
          import mx.events.ListEvent;

          [Bindable]
```

```
        private var directory:File = File.documentsDirectory;

        private function onChange( event:ListEvent ):void
        {
           var item:File = event.itemRenderer.data as File;
           if( item.isDirectory )
           {
              fileSystemList.directory = item;
           }
           else if( item != null )
           {
              fileSystemList.directory = item.parent;
           }
        }
     ]]>
   </mx:Script>

      <mx:FileSystemTree
         id="fileSystemTree"
         directory="{ directory }"
         width="100%" height="100%"
         showHidden="false"
         change="onChange( event )" />

      <mx:FileSystemList
     id="fileSystemList"
     width="100%" height="100%"
     showHidden="true"
     directory="{ directory }" />
</mx:WindowedApplication>
```

The onChange event handler has some interesting logic. Because the FileSystemTree
shows both files and directories, we need to include some basic logic to react accordingly
to the users' selection. For instance, if they select an item that is a directory, show the
directory listing. If they select a file, however, show the directory listing of the parent of
the selected file. This provides the users with context by displaying the contents of the
directory of where the selected file resides. Figure 14.3 outlines just such an example.

Another added benefit of these new Adobe Flex AIR components extending their traditional Adobe Flex counterparts is that they also inherit all the same capabilities, such as
drag and drop. Because each item represented in both the tree and the list are instances of
the File object, you can move, copy, or even delete files and directories. You would
accomplish this by conducting file operations in the drag-and-drop event-handler functions.

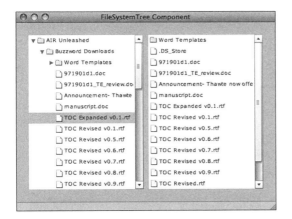

FIGURE 14.3   File system explorer example using the `FileSystemTree` and
`FileSystemList` components.

FileSystemDataGrid Component

The `FileSystemDataGrid` is useful when you need to relay more detailed information back
to the user. Whereas the `FileSystemList` shows only the directory and filenames, the data
grid can offer as many columns of information as the directory listing can provide (see
Listing 14.4). Another added bonus, of course, is that all the columns can be sorted by
clicking on the column header!

LISTING 14.4   File System Explorer Example Using the `FileSystemDataGrid` Component

```
<?xml version="1.0" encoding="utf-8"?>
<mx:WindowedApplication
    xmlns:mx="http://www.adobe.com/2006/mxml"
    layout="horizontal"
    title="FileSystemDataGrid Component">

    <mx:Style source="styles.css" />

    <mx:Script>
        <![CDATA[
            import mx.events.ListEvent;

            [Bindable]
            private var directory:File = File.documentsDirectory;
```

```
        private function onChange( event:ListEvent ):void
        {
            var item:File = event.itemRenderer.data as File;
            if( item.isDirectory )
            {
                fileSystemDataGrid.directory = item;
            }
            else if( item != null )
            {
                fileSystemDataGrid.directory = item.parent;
            }
        }
    ]]>
  </mx:Script>

  <mx:FileSystemTree
     id="fileSystemTree"
     directory="{ directory }"
     width="250" height="100%"
     showHidden="false"
     change="onChange( event )" />

  <mx:FileSystemDataGrid
     id="fileSystemDataGrid"
     directory="{ directory }"
     width="100%" height="100%" />
</mx:WindowedApplication>
```

The approach in Listing 14.4 is almost identical to the FileSystemList sample application in Listing 14.3. The same data-binding technique and event-handler approach are used. We gain the sortable and expandable column functionality for free—just by using the FileSystemDataGrid control. Figure 14.4 shows the final product.

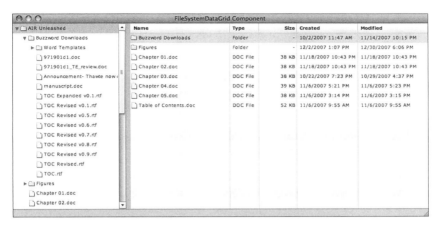

FIGURE 14.4   Using the `FileSystemDataGrid` component to show additional directory details.

Summary

This chapter added more tools to your development arsenal by exploring the Adobe Flex AIR components. Although the concepts of these controls are not new, their awareness of the underlying file system is definitely groundbreaking.

As with all user interface components in the Adobe Flex software development kit (SDK), these new controls can be styled and skinned until your heart's content. Or make them your own by extending their base functionality to incorporate new features and behaviors. Whatever the case may be, development of rich desktop applications just got a whole lot quicker.

PART III

Securing Adobe AIR Applications

IN THIS PART

CHAPTER 15

Understanding Security Sandboxes

In Adobe® AIR™, permissions are granted to files according to their origin. They are then assigned into logical security groupings called sandboxes.

A sandbox can be thought of as a virtual environment that isolates and restricts how files interact with the local system, the network, and each other. Restricting how a file can interact helps keep your computer and files safer.

In this chapter we dive into how to work within the confines of sandboxes when loading content remotely. We discuss how to selectively expose functions from the application sandbox. We also investigate how to more safely load Adobe® Flex™ modules into the application sandbox.

Security Sandboxes in Adobe AIR

The Adobe AIR platform uses a security model referred to as sandboxing. A sandbox is a runtime container that dictates the level of access for assets contained within that given sandbox. For example, assets distributed with your Adobe AIR application exist in the application sandbox by default. The application sandbox provides unrestricted access to the Adobe AIR APIs. This means any Adobe® Flash®, Adobe Flex, or JavaScript code in your application can read, write, or delete resources from the user's local machine.

A number of sandbox types exist, all of which, aside from the aforementioned application sandbox, stem from the Flash Player security architecture. One such example would be remote sandboxes. If your application loads an external resource, such as an image or a Flash SWF file at runtime, those assets are loaded into their own remote sandbox. This type of sandbox is domain-based, meaning assets are grouped by their originating domain. For example:

- ▶ For http://www.foo1.com/file.swf, the sandbox is www.foo1.com.

- ▶ For http://foo.bar.com/file.swf, the sandbox is foo.bar.com

Those assets would not have access to the parent application. In other words, executable code loaded from a remote domain could not "reach" into the application sandbox and run code. This is as designed to prevent cross-site scripting attacks. Without this in place, there's nothing to stop a rogue script from leveraging the Adobe AIR API to inflict serious damage to the user's local machine.

The particular type of sandbox applied to a resource can vary based on a number of factors. Table 15.1 outlines all the sandbox categories applicable to the Adobe AIR platform.

TABLE 15.1   Sandbox Types in Adobe AIR

Sandbox	Description
application	All assets distributed inside an Adobe AIR application reside in this type of sandbox. Access to Adobe AIR APIs is completely unrestricted. This sandbox type is unique to the Adobe AIR platform.
remote	Any asset loaded from an Internet site is placed into a domain-based sandbox; that is, each domain has its own sandbox within the parent Adobe AIR application. This sandbox originates from the Flash Player security model.
local-trusted	This is a sandbox containing assets that have been explicitly trusted by the user. This is done either via the Flash Settings Manager or by a Flash Player trust configuration file added to the local system. Files assigned to this sandbox can work with data both remote and local data. This sandbox originates from the Flash Player security model.
local-with-networking	Flash SWF files compiled with a specific local networking flag reside in this sandbox. These assets can communicate over a network but cannot read any data off the local system. One additional caveat is that each remote site must explicitly allow access from a Flash client via a cross domain policy. This is an XML file hosted on the target server that dictates which clients may access server assets based on their originating domain. This sandbox originates from the Flash Player security model.

TABLE 15.1   Continued

Sandbox	Description
local-with-filesystem	Flash SWF files compiled without the networking flag can read data from the local file system or network paths but cannot communicate over a network.
	In Adobe AIR this also includes JavaScript files not packaged within an application or explicitly trusted by the user.
	This sandbox originates from the Flash Player security model.

NOTE

With the exception of the application sandbox, the security model in Adobe AIR is based on the security model for the Adobe Flash Player. For more information on cross-domain policy files usage, visit Adobe's website: www.adobe.com/devnet/flashplayer/articles/cross_domain_policy.html

When an Adobe AIR application is installed, all assets are installed into an application directory. All these resources automatically reside in the application sandbox at runtime.

These assets can be referenced via code as follows:

```
app:/images/foo.jpg
```

In many instances, Adobe AIR applications only use this specific set of files. Considering the dynamic nature of the Adobe AIR platform there are of course cases in which data or perhaps even additional functionality is loaded from a remote source. These loaded resources reside outside of the application sandbox. We explore the proper precautions in these cases later in this chapter.

The FileStream class is a perfect example of a restricted API within Adobe AIR. Exposing this type of direct file system access to a remote SWF with unknown origins would be cause for alarm, to say the least. An easy way to remember what is and isn't possible for remote sandboxed files is to think of them as operating in traditional fashion—inside a web browser.

The ActionScript APIs published by Adobe highlight items that pertain only to content loaded within the application sandbox. You notice the small Adobe AIR logo symbols beside classes, methods, properties, and events in the ActionScript documentation (ASDocs), signifying that they pertain to projects compiled with the Adobe AIR libraries.

For HTML content loaded via the HTMLLoader object, all Adobe AIR JavaScript APIs (those that are available via the window.runtime property or via the air object when using the AIRAliases.js file) are available to content in the application security sandbox—in other words, only HTML content packaged in your Adobe AIR application. Any remote content loaded into the HTMLLoader control is contained within a remote sandbox and requires a sandbox bridge to leverage any functionality in the parent application. In a remote

15

sandbox, HTML content does not have access to the `window.runtime` property, so this content cannot access the Adobe AIR APIs.

> **NOTE**
>
> Security sandboxing applies regardless of the file type loaded into your application. Hypertext Markup Language (HTML) files have the same security privileges/restrictions as loaded Shockwave Flash (SWF) files.

The Application Sandbox

When an application is installed, all the files that are included in the Adobe AIR installer file are installed into an application directory on the user's computer. These files are assigned to the application sandbox when the application is run. This means that they have full security privileges, including interaction with the local file system.

To protect Adobe AIR applications from accidental leakage of privileged information or control, the following restrictions are placed on content in the application security sandbox:

▶ Code in the application security sandbox cannot allow cross-scripting to other sandboxes by calling the `Security.allowDomain()` method. Calling this method from the application security sandbox has no effect.

▶ Importing nonapplication content into the application sandbox by setting the `LoaderContext.securityDomain` or the `LoaderContext.applicationDomain` property is prevented.

Some packages that contain application programming interfaces (APIs) available only to content in the application sandbox are as follows:

▶ `flash.desktop`—Such as `Clipboard`, `NativeApplication`, `NativeDragManager`, `NativeWindow`, and so on

▶ `flash.data package`—Such as `EncryptedLocalStore`, `SQLConnection`, `SQLMode`, and so on

▶ `flash.filesystem`—Such as `FileStream`, `FileMode`, and `File`

Using Sandbox Bridges

It's crucial that the privileges given to files on the application sandbox not be shared with other sandboxes by default. However there are times when you'll want to expose specific functionality to external content loaded from a remote domain. To accomplish this situation, the Adobe AIR platform provides a sandbox bridge mechanism.

A sandbox bridge acts as a restricted pathway between content residing in the application sandbox and nonapplication content. In other words, content can be loaded from a remote source and be provided a specific set of properties and methods to retrieve data from the parent application. This gives developers the increased flexibility of integrating third-party content without compromising the user's environment—if, of course, proper decisions are made when determining just what functionality should be exposed.

Listing 15.1 is a straightforward example of loading an external flash file (SWF) and providing it with a fixed set of methods for accessing user information from the parent application. Whereas the host Adobe AIR application has full access to the Adobe AIR APIs, including file I/O and local databases and such, the remote content is restricted to the functionality provided via parentSandboxBridge. In this example, we're demonstrating an application loading in an outside application responsible for generating target advertising to our user. The information being exposed is just enough to tailor the ad content while maintaining a level of privacy for the user.

CAUTION

The sample application demonstrated in this chapter is exactly that, a sample. Take every precaution when exposing any user information to content that is not under your direct control. At the very least, the users should have to opt-in to having any of their information shared with third parties.

LISTING 15.1   Providing a Limited API to Content Loaded in a Remote Sandbox

```
<?xml version="1.0" encoding="utf-8"?>
<mx:WindowedApplication
   xmlns:mx="http://www.adobe.com/2006/mxml"
   layout="horizontal"
   paddingLeft="5" paddingRight="5" paddingBottom="5"
   title="Sandbox  Bridge Example"
   creationComplete="init()">

   <mx:Script>
     <![CDATA[

     private var userVO:Object;
     private var userAPI:UserAPI;
     private var loader:Loader;
     [Bindable]
     private var content:String;

     private function init():void
     {
        userVO = new Object();
        userVO.name = "Joe Smith";
        userVO.address = "123 Main Street";
        userVO.zip = "50345";
```

```
        userVO.phone = "555-4256";
        userVO.gender = "M";
        userVO.email = "joe.smith@domain.com";

        userAPI = new UserAPI( userVO );

        var request:URLRequest =
                new URLRequest( "http://oconnick.googlepages.com/ad.swf" );

        loader = new Loader();
        loader.contentLoaderInfo.parentSandboxBridge = userAPI;
        loader.contentLoaderInfo.addEventListener( Event.COMPLETE, onComplete );
        loader.load( request );

        content = "This application exposes a limited API for external " +
                "advertising SWFs to retrieve target ads for the user.";
    }

    private function onComplete( event:Event ):void
    {
        var loaderInfo:LoaderInfo = event.target as LoaderInfo;
        ad.addChild( loaderInfo.content );
    }

    ]]>
</mx:Script>

<mx:VBox
    id="appContainer"
    width="100%" height="100%">

    <mx:TabNavigator width="100%" height="100%">
        <mx:VBox label="Tab 1">
            <mx:Text text="{ content }" width="100%" />
        </mx:VBox>
        <mx:VBox label="Tab 2" />
        <mx:VBox label="Tab 3" />
    </mx:TabNavigator>
</mx:VBox>

<mx:VBox
    id="adContainer"
    width="200" height="100%"
    backgroundColor="#FFFFFF"
    borderColor="#999999"
    borderThickness="1"
```

```
      borderStyle="solid">

      <mx:Label text="Ad Space:" />
      <mx:UIComponent id="ad" width="100%" height="100%" />
   </mx:VBox>

</mx:WindowedApplication>
```

What we've done is created a `UserAPI` class that, upon instantiation, is populated with a user value object. Although the user value object contains the full spectrum of data about the user, we're using the `UserAPI` class to selectively expose a subset of that same data. A reference to the `UserAPI` class is then set as the `parentSandboxBridge` on the `contentLoaderInfo` property belonging to the Loader instance that will be loading our external content.

Listing 15.2 outlines our external application that is loaded into the parent application at runtime. In Listing 15.1 we're passing in the location of our external SWF:

```
var request:URLRequest =
   new URLRequest( "http://oconnick.googlepages.com/ad.swf" );
```

When the parent application is launched, this external SWF is loaded into a remote sandbox and is assigned a sandbox bridge—an instance of our `UserAPI`. Note that in Listing 15.2 we've included a private property called `user`. Inside the constructor function, `ad()`, we're assigning the `parentSandboxBridge` to this variable to maintain a reference to the sandbox bridge. After it is assigned, we can invoke any methods or reference any properties exposed via the bridge:

```
adMessage.text = "Hello " + user.getName() + ",\n";
```

LISTING 15.2 External Application Loaded into the Parent Application at Runtime

```
/**
 * This application is designed to run in a remote sandbox
 * within a parent application. When loaded at runtime, user
 * information will be supplied by the parent application
 * which will be used to generate target ads.
 */

package
{
   import flash.display.Sprite;
   import flash.text.TextField;
   import flash.text.TextFieldAutoSize;

   public class ad extends Sprite
   {
      private var user:Object;
      private var adMessage:TextField;
```

```
      public function ad():void
      {
         user = loaderInfo.parentSandboxBridge;

         adMessage = new TextField();
         adMessage.width = 190;
         adMessage.text = "Hello " + user.getName() + ",\n";

         if( user.getGender() == "F" )
         {
            adMessage.appendText( "Women's running shoes on sale" );
         }
         else
         {
            adMessage.appendText( "Men's running shoes on sale" );
         }
         addChild( adMessage );
      }
   }
}
```

Listing 15.3 outlines the UserAPI class. By using a reference of this class as the sandbox bridge, externally loaded content can only access members defined in this class.

LISTING 15.3   The UserAPI Used as the Sandbox Bridge

```
/**
 * This class is used to expose limited information
 * about the user to external SWFs being loaded
 * into the parent application.
 */
package
{
   public class UserAPI
   {
      public var userVO:Object;

      public function UserAPI( user:Object )
      {
         userVO = user;
      }

      public function getName():String
      {
         return userVO.name;
      }
```

```
    public function getGender():String
    {
        return userVO.gender;
    }

    public function getEmail():String
    {
        return userVO.email;
    }
  }
}
```

Methods you define within the sandbox bridge can invoke any of the available Adobe AIR APIs. But use caution: Treat the bridge as a firewall to the user's desktop and construct your functions accordingly. For example, exposing methods that accept file paths or SQL statements could be fatal in the wrong hands. With great power comes great responsibility.

Summary

Although the application of specifying security sandboxes could be viewed as an added inconvenience for developers, it's important to understand the consequences of the alternatives. If you are distributing trusted applications signed with you or your company's digital certificate, your users are relying on you to provide a more secure environment for them to do their jobs. Any lapse in security from a design perspective puts both you and your users at risk. If it is essential that you integrate remote content into your application, be sure to be prudent when evaluating what information you want to expose.

15

CHAPTER 16

Using the Encrypted Local Store

The encrypted local store is a facility to more securely persist data on the user's machine using AES-CBC 128-bit encryption. Every user has his own dedicated store for every Adobe® AIR™ application installed on the local machine (see Figure 16.1). Thankfully all the underlying machinery to make this happen is obfuscated for you, the developer. If you've worked with reading and writing cookies in the browser world, you will see this isn't all that different.

> **NOTE**
>
> The encrypted local store should not be confused with local shared objects. Although local shared objects offer similar functionality with regard to storing data on the client, encryption facilities are not automatically provided for you.

Feature highlights include the following:

▶ When debugging an Adobe AIR application using the AIR Debug Launcher (ADL), a different encrypted local store is created. In other words, any items contained in the store of an installed version of the application are not available during debug sessions.

▶ Uninstalling an Adobe AIR application will *not* remove any data contained in an encrypted local store. When you uninstall an Adobe AIR application, the uninstaller does not delete data stored in the encrypted local store.

▶ Data in the encrypted store is located in a subdirectory of the application data directory.

▶ The maximum capacity is 10MB. This value is fixed.

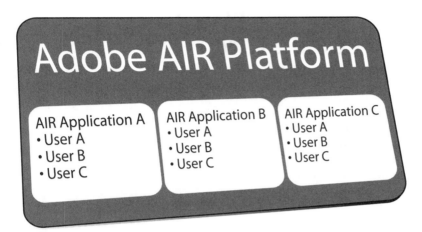

FIGURE 16.1   Encrypted storage by application and user.

Adobe AIR leverages the Data Protection API (DPAPI) on Windows and the Keychain on Mac OS to link encrypted stores to applications and users.

The local store data resides within a subdirectory of the user's application data directory. The naming convention used for each application is a concatenation of the application name and application ID.

On Mac OS X, find the data here:

```
/Users/{ user name }/Library/Application Support/Adobe/AIR/ELS/
```

On Windows, find the data here:

```
C:\Documents and Settings\{ user name }\Application Data\Adobe\AIR\ELS
```

API Reference

Let's explore the new classes made available with the introduction of Adobe AIR. We follow that with a breakdown of the methods used in this chapter and sample application. See Table 16.1.

TABLE 16.1   New ActionScript Classes Introduced

Package	Class	Description
flash.data	EncryptedLocalStore	Provides methods for setting and getting objects in the encrypted local data store for an Adobe AIR application

Storing Data

Let's take a look at what's involved in storing data. The first step is to create a ByteArray:

```
var uBytes:ByteArray = new ByteArray();
```

Next, we use the writeUTFBytes method on the ByteArray to store text from a TextInput field:

```
uBytes.writeUTFBytes( username.text );
```

Lastly, we use the static method setItem() of the EncryptedLocalStore class to store the ByteArray.

```
EncryptedLocalStore.setItem( "username", uBytes );
```

For additional security, a third parameter is available on the setItem() method called stronglyBound. Setting this argument to true causes the encrypted local store to bind the stored item to the calling Adobe AIR application's digital signature as well as the applications publisher ID:

```
EncryptedLocalStore.setItem( "username", uBytes, true );
```

This helps prevent an attacker from accessing the encrypted data if the publisher ID alone is compromised.

Reading Data

After data has been stored, how is it retrieved? First use the getItem() method specifying the same key we used to store the data (username):

```
var uBytes:ByteArray = EncryptedLocalStore.getItem( "username" );
```

Now we need to read the bytes out of the array into our String variable:

```
var uString:String = uBytes.readUTFBytes( uBytes.length );
```

Removing Data

Keep in mind that it's up to you, the developer, to remove data from the local store. Even after uninstalling the application, any data in the store remains on the system.

Here's how we can programmatically remove an item by key:

```
EncryptedLocalStore.removeItem("username");
```

If you need to do a complete wipe of *all* the data in an application store, use the `reset` method:

```
EncryptedLocalStore.reset();
```

Sample Application—Storing Login Credentials

Many Adobe AIR applications are a mash-up of desktop functionality intertwined with web services and content. It's not much of a stretch to suggest there will be applications that demand additional authentication on startup.

Instant messaging is a great example. Although the service itself is not overly secure, many people would rather not have their client automatically log in. Perhaps the machine is used by multiple people or is in a public place. Others, on the other hand, are the sole operators of the machine and another login prompt is just a pain.

To accommodate both scenarios, we could opt to store the person's username and password on the local machine and automatically populate the fields on his next startup.

Storing credentials in a file or local database is not a very secure option unless you implement an encryption/decryption scheme yourself. An alternative is to simply use the built-in facilities in Adobe AIR to store and retrieve data more securely.

Figure 16.2 displays the login screen to our sample application. We've got a typical login form with an added option of persisting the user's information. If the user checks that option, the form fields will be prepopulated on his next visit.

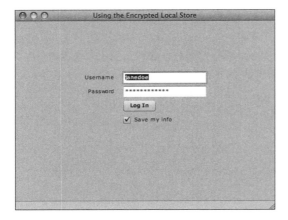

FIGURE 16.2   Persisting user login information.

Take a look at the code in Listing 16.1. When the login button is clicked, the onLogin() function is called. This function checks to see if the check box is selected; if so, the username and password are converted to byte arrays and passed into EncryptedLocalStore.setItem() calls. The setItem() method requires a key, used to retrieve the information later, and the byte array containing the data you want to store.

LISTING 16.1   Persisting User Login Information

```
<mx:WindowedApplication
    xmlns:mx="http://www.adobe.com/2006/mxml"
    layout="absolute"
    title="Using the Encrypted Local Store"
    creationComplete="onLoad()"
    applicationComplete="onInit()">

    <mx:Script>
        <![CDATA[

        import mx.events.FlexEvent;
        import mx.controls.Alert;

        private function onInit( event:Event=null ):void
        {
            username.setFocus();
            callLater( username.setSelection, [ 0,username.length ] );
        }

        private function onLoad():void
        {
            var uBytes:ByteArray = EncryptedLocalStore.getItem( "username" );

            if( uBytes != null )
            {
                var uString:String = uBytes.readUTFBytes( uBytes.length );
                var pBytes:ByteArray = EncryptedLocalStore.getItem( "password" );
                var pString:String = pBytes.readUTFBytes( pBytes.length );

                username.text = uString;
                password.text = pString;
            }
        }

        private function onLogin():void
        {
            if( saveUserInfo.selected )
            {
```

16

```
                var uBytes:ByteArray = new ByteArray();
                uBytes.writeUTFBytes( username.text );

                var pBytes:ByteArray = new ByteArray();
                pBytes.writeUTFBytes( password.text );

                EncryptedLocalStore.setItem( "username", uBytes );
                EncryptedLocalStore.setItem( "password", pBytes );

                Alert.show(
                    "Re-open this application to see your login credentials " +
                    "retrieved from the encrypted local store and populated in the " +
                    "login form.", "Your Credentials Have Been Saved",
                    mx.controls.Alert.OK , null, onClose );
            }
            else
            {
                EncryptedLocalStore.removeItem( "username" );
                EncryptedLocalStore.removeItem( "password" );

                Alert.show(
                    "You have chosen not to save your login credentials. You will " +
                    "need to re-enter your credentials the next time this " +
                    "application is launched.", "Your Credentials Have NOT Been
                    ➥Saved",
                    mx.controls.Alert.OK , null, onClose );
            }


        }

        private function onClose( event:Event ):void
        {
            NativeApplication.nativeApplication.exit();
        }

        ]]>
</mx:Script>

<mx:Form
    horizontalCenter="0" verticalCenter="-25"
    defaultButton="{ buttonLogin }">

    <mx:FormItem label="Username">
```

```
            <mx:TextInput id="username" />
        </mx:FormItem>
        <mx:FormItem label="Password">
            <mx:TextInput id="password" displayAsPassword="true" />
        </mx:FormItem>
        <mx:FormItem id="formitem4">
            <mx:Button id="buttonLogin" label="Log In" click="onLogin()" />
        </mx:FormItem>
        <mx:FormItem id="formitem3">
            <mx:CheckBox id="saveUserInfo" label="Save my info" selected="true" />
        </mx:FormItem>

    </mx:Form>

</mx:WindowedApplication>
```

The `onLoad()` function is executed when the application first initializes. This happens when we attempt to load the username and password values from the encrypted local store. If the results are null, the form remains unpopulated, as we know it's either the user's first visit or he chose not to persist his credentials.

Adobe Flex Quick Tip

There is a series of events fired from all Adobe® Flex™ application components throughout their startup processes. All the component events, in order, are *preinitialize, initialize, creationComplete, updateComplete*.

You will notice two events defined in the WindowedApplication tag in Listing 16.1: `creationComplete` and `applicationComplete`. We're listening for the `creationComplete` event to know when all of our components (and their children) are instantiated. At this point it's safer for us to access to encrypted local store and check for existing data.

The `applicationComplete` event is the last event to be fired long after all the components of the application have initialized. We're taking advantage of that fact to set focus to the first username field and highlight its contents. If you were to attempt this in the `creationComplete` function immediately after setting the text content of that same field, the text length will not yet be reflected.

Lastly, the `callLater()` method queues the `setSelection` function (highlighting the contents of the text input field) until the next screen refresh. This ensures the text value change has completed and we can now highlight its contents.

Summary

Whether to persist user data is always a judgment call. Many factors need to be taken into account. Most importantly, what is the nature of the data in question, and does storing it locally truly contribute to an improved user experience?

The login sample application in this chapter tackles one of the most common use cases when it comes to adding a dash of convenience for users: saving the users' login information, or at least the usernames, so they are not required to reenter every time they need to access the application.

User credentials are the most sensitive information of all. If an unscrupulous attacker compromises a user's identity and password, the attacker can access any *other* data or perform any action according to the victim's access level. So you should take that into account before implementing any variation of this behavior in your application. At the very least, leverage the Encrypted Local Store to protect your users' data.

For applications providing access to sensitive data, be sure to sign your application with a purchased certificate and leverage the `stronglyBound` attribute when using the encrypted local store.

PART IV

Deploying Adobe AIR Applications

IN THIS PART

# CHAPTER 17

Distributing Adobe AIR Applications

In this chapter you learn about installing an Adobe® AIR™ application in a one-off approach, installing Adobe AIR applications seamlessly from a web page, and digitally signing an Adobe AIR installation file (.air). You will see that there is plenty of flexibility in distributing your Adobe AIR applications in a customized experience and that you can do so in a manner, with the digital code-signing, that helps your end users feel comfortable.

Efficient distribution of your Adobe AIR applications is a matter that should not be overlooked or done without due consideration. Is your application a one-off .air file that will never be modified or supported? This is probably the exception and not the rule. How many users will receive your application distribution? Will there be ongoing versions of your application that need to be deployed—if so, how frequently do they need to be deployed? These questions and others should be carefully considered and answered. The answers to your questions might simply point to creating a link on your web server that a user can access to download the .air file (see the following caution). If this is the case, you need to include a link to the Adobe AIR runtime found on the Adobe website: http://get.adobe.com/air/. It is practical and prudent to clearly indicate that the Adobe AIR runtime is required to run your Adobe AIR application. Another type of distribution includes what has been coined as a badge install or a seamless install. This seamless install can determine if the end user already has the Adobe AIR runtime and, if not, prompt the user through dialogs to install it. Distribution through such sites as www.O2Apps.com and the Adobe AIR Marketplace are also viable channels. Distribution by media such as a CD-ROM or DVD is also possible if the cost of distribution is not a concern. Emailing the `.air` file is also possible.

CAUTION

You will need to add a new `mime` type to your web server's configuration, so it will know what an Adobe `.air` file is. According to Adobe, you should add the `mime` type `application/vnd.adobe.air-install-package` (associated with the `.air` extension). For the Apache HTTP Server, adding the following to your httpd conf file works well:

    AddType application/vnd.adobe.air-install-package .air.

See Figures 17.1–17.4 to see before (`mime` type is added) and after screenshots of the Microsoft Internet Explorer browser experiences.

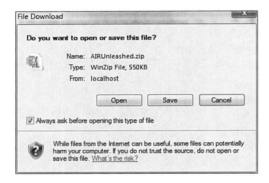

FIGURE 17.1   Browser "sees" a Zip archive instead of Adobe AIR.

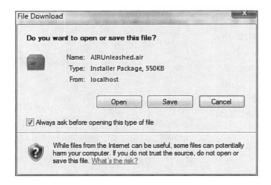

FIGURE 17.2   Browser "sees" an Adobe AIR file.

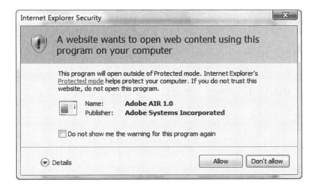

FIGURE 17.3   Windows Vista launches a warning.

FIGURE 17.4   Adobe AIR installation dialog begins.

17

TIP

The Adobe AIR runtime can be widely distributed by your organization by following the guidelines found here: www.adobe.com/products/air/runtime_distribution1.html.

Installing an Adobe AIR Application—The One-Off Approach

After users have your Adobe AIR application's `.air` file staring at them from a website link or on their PCs, they need to understand an important requirement. It is your job to let them know this requirement. They should understand that they need adequate administrative-type privileges on their PC or Mac to be able to install the Adobe AIR runtime or an Adobe AIR application, as the nature and power of this type of application requires elevated privileges to the native OS over the typical web application they are familiar with. These elevated privileges could, in the wrong hands, be dangerous to their OS. Part of the distribution process is to educate and comfort your users into accepting the risks because of the great benefits the Adobe AIR runtime and your Adobe AIR application provides them. After the user has been informed, the installation process is as follows:

1. Obtain and install the Adobe AIR runtime from Adobe.

2. Obtain the .air file from your website.

3. Double-click the .air file to launch the installation process (see Figure 17.5).

FIGURE 17.5   Launching the **.air** file.

4. The installation process begins, as shown in Figure 17.6.

   A dialog prompts the end user regarding whether they are sure they want to install the Adobe AIR application, as shown in Figure 17.7. The end user has the option to cancel or install the application. Security-related information is shown to the end user, including the Adobe AIR application's code-signing credentials. In the example shown in Figure 17.7, Adobe has signed this application.

FIGURE 17.6   Getting ready to install the application.

5. In the dialog, you can leave the default settings selected and then click the Continue button. You can now choose your installation preferences by clicking (to add or remove the check marks) the Add Shortcut Icon to My Desktop and the Start Application After Installation check boxes, as shown in Figure 17.8.

   After the Continue button is clicked, the Adobe AIR application completes the installation process, as shown in Figure 17.9.

   If the end user checks the Start Application After Installation in the dialog shown in Figure 17.8, as was done in this example, the Adobe AIR application automatically starts at the conclusion of the installation, as shown in Figure 17.10.

FIGURE 17.7   Are You Sure You Want to Install This Application to Your Computer? dialog.

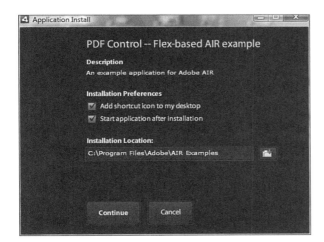

FIGURE 17.8   Continuing to install the application.

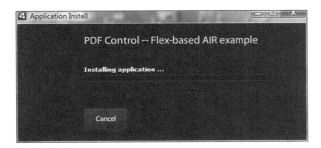

FIGURE 17.9   Installing the application.

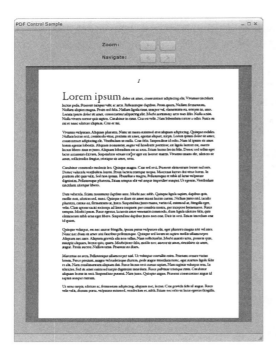

FIGURE 17.10   Running the application by default.

In Windows, for this example, Adobe AIR automatically does the following: installs a desktop shortcut, installs a shortcut in the Programs listing, and installs the Adobe AIR application in the location that the end user selected or in a default location that you provided in the installation package.

Figure 17.11 depicts a desktop shortcut for the application. (You as the developer can choose the shortcut icon you want to use for your Adobe AIR application, but the end users have control over whether it is actually placed on their desktop.)

FIGURE 17.11   Desktop shortcut.

Figure 17.12 shows the Start Menu shortcut created automatically during the Adobe AIR installation.

Figure 17.13 shows the location where the application was installed—in this case it was in the Program Files directory. (You as the developer can choose the default location for where the application is installed, but the end user can override this during the installation.)

FIGURE 17.12   Start menu shortcut.

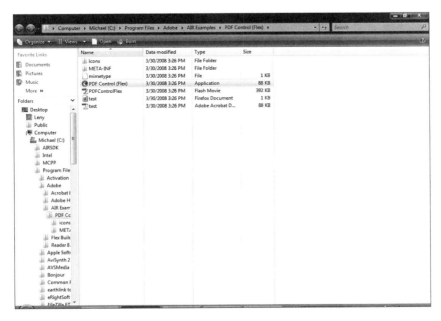

FIGURE 17.13   Installs into the Program Files.

During the Adobe AIR application installation, an entry for the application in the Add/Remove Programs Control Panel is created, as shown in Figure 17.14.

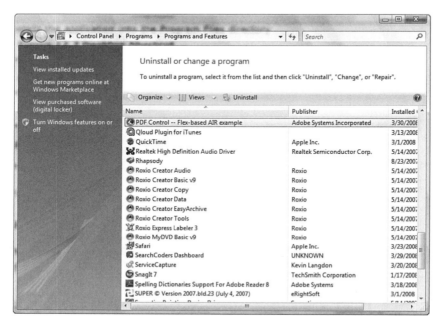

FIGURE 17.14   Add/Remove Programs Control Panel.

NOTE

On the Mac OS, the application is added to the Applications directory.

If the application is already installed and is the same version, the installer gives the user the choice of opening the existing version of the application, uninstalling the application, or canceling. The installer identifies the application using the application ID and publisher ID found in the `.air` file. The developer can see both of these ID properties in the code, as follows:

```
var appID:String = this.applicationID;
var pubID:String = nativeApplication.publisherID;
```

Figure 17.15 shows this scenario.

If the application is already installed and this installation is an updated version, the installer gives the user the choice of opening the existing version of the application, installing (replacing) the application with the updated version, or canceling. As noted previously, the installer identifies the application using the application ID and publisher ID found in the `.air` file. Figure 17.16 depicts this situation. It is important to note that it is the developer's responsibility to ensure that an updated `.air` file is, in fact, an improved version of the Adobe AIR application and not a retrograde.

FIGURE 17.15   Application previously installed—same version.

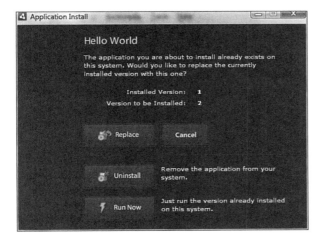

FIGURE 17.16   Application previously installed—updated version.

6. When the installation is complete, the end user should click the Finish button.

On a Windows OS, double-click the application's icon (which is either installed on the desktop or in a folder) or select the application from the Start menu.

On the Mac OS, double-click the application in the folder in which it was installed. The default installation directory is the /Applications directory.

Installing Adobe AIR Applications Seamlessly

The badge install or seamless install method is a nice alternative to the one-off style of installation, previously discussed. The seamless install feature lets you embed a special Shockwave Flash (SWF) file in a web page that lets the user install an Adobe AIR application from the browser. If the runtime is not installed, and the user allows it, the seamless install feature installs the runtime and then begins the Adobe AIR application installation dialog. The seamless install feature allows users to install the Adobe AIR application directly from their browser, or if the users desire, the .air file can be saved to their PC and run manually at a later time (like a one-off type of installation). Included in the Adobe AIR software development kit (SDK) is a badge.fla file (shown in Figure 17.17), and in the Adobe® Flex™ SDK is a badge.swf file as well as other supporting files (shown in Figure 17.18), which lets you easily build your custom Adobe AIR application distribution, leveraging this seamless install feature.

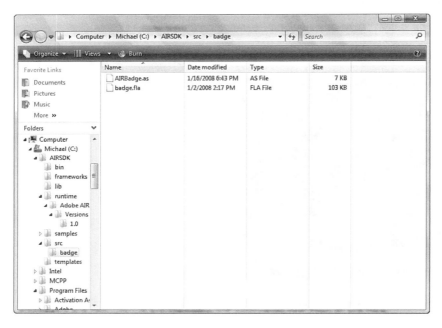

FIGURE 17.17   Badge.fla in the Adobe AIR SDK.

As mentioned, the seamless badge.swf can install the runtime and your Adobe AIR applications from a link on a web page. Everything you need to build a custom, seamless distribution is supplied—the badge.fla or badge.swf files (and its source code) are provided to you and can easily be deployed on your website. To do so, add the files (badge.swf, default_badge.html, and AC_RunActiveContent.js) provided in the Adobe AIR SDK or the Adobe Flex SDK (see Figure 17.18) to your web server. The resulting web page is shown in Figure 17.19. Clicking on the Install Now link launches the installer, as shown in Figure 17.20. If the Adobe AIR runtime is missing on the user's PC, the user is prompted to install the runtime and then, seamlessly, the application installation dialog is displayed.

To modify the seamless installation web page, open the default_badge.html page in a text editor and modify it as described in the following paragraphs.

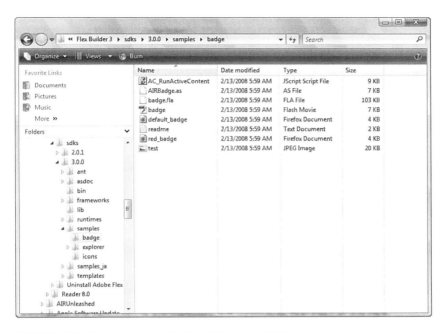

FIGURE 17.18   Badge.swf in the Adobe Flex SDK.

FIGURE 17.19   Web page utilizing the Badge.swf.

Open the default_badge.html file with your code editor of choice (see Listing 17.1), look in the AC_FL_RunContent() JavaScript function, and adjust the FlashVars parameters for the customization you want based on those shown in Table 17.1.

There is a minimum size for the badge.swf—a 217 pixels width by 180 pixels height. You can adjust the values of the width and height parameters found in the AC_FL_RunContent() function to suit your user-interface requirements.

Renaming the default_badge.html and adjusting its code to suit your needs is also possible.

FIGURE 17.20   Seamless installation utilizing the Badge.swf.

TABLE 17.1   FlashVars Parameters That Can Be Customized

Parameter	Description
appname	The name of the application, displayed by the SWF file when the runtime is not installed.
appurl (Required)	The URL of the .air file to be downloaded. You must use an absolute, not relative, URL.
airversion (Required)	For the 1.0 version of the runtime, set this to 1.0.
imageurl	The URL of the image (optional) to display in the badge.
buttoncolor	The color of the download button (specified as a hex value, such as FFCC00).
messagecolor	The color of the text message displayed below the button when the runtime is not installed (specified as a hex value, such as FFCC00).

LISTING 17.1   default_badge.html

```
<html xmlns="http://www.w3.org/1999/xhtml" xml:lang="en" lang="en">
<head>
<meta http-equiv="Content-Type" content="text/html; charset=iso-8859-1" />
<title>Adobe AIR Application Installer Page</title>
```

```
<style type="text/css">
<!--
#AIRDownloadMessageTable {
    width: 217px;
    height: 180px;
    border: 1px solid #999;
    font-family: Verdana, Arial, Helvetica, sans-serif;
    font-size: 14px;
}
#AIRDownloadMessageRuntime {
    font-size: 12px;
    color: #333;
}
-->
</style>
<script language="JavaScript" type="text/javascript">
<!--
// -------------------------------------------------------------
// Globals
// Major version of Flash required
var requiredMajorVersion = 9;
// Minor version of Flash required
var requiredMinorVersion = 0;
// Minor version of Flash required
var requiredRevision = 115;         // This is Flash Player 9 Update 3
// -------------------------------------------------------------
// -->
</script>
</head>
<body bgcolor="#ffffff">
<script src="AC_RunActiveContent.js" type="text/javascript"></script>
<script language="JavaScript" type="text/javascript">
<!--
// Version check based upon the values entered above in "Globals"
var hasRequestedVersion = DetectFlashVer(requiredMajorVersion,
➥requiredMinorVersion, requiredRevision);
// Check to see if the version meets the requirements for playback
if (hasRequestedVersion) {
    // if we've detected an acceptable version
    // embed the Flash Content SWF when all tests are passed
    AC_FL_RunContent(
 'codebase','http://fpdownload.macromedia.com/pub/shockwave/cabs/
➥flash/swflash.cab',
        'width','217',
        'height','180',
```

```
            'id','badge',
            'align','middle',
            'src','badge',
            'quality','high',
            'bgcolor','#FFFFFF',
            'name','badge',
            'allowscriptaccess','all',
            'pluginspage','http://www.macromedia.com/go/getflashplayer',
'flashvars','appname=My%20Application&appurl=http://yourdomain/yourwebapp/AIRUnleashed.
➥air&airversion=1.0&imageurl=test.jpg',    'movie','badge' ); // appurl should be an
➥absolute URL } else {  // Flash Player is too old or we can't detect the plugin
    document.write('<table id="AIRDownloadMessageTable"><tr><td>Download
➥<a href="AIRUnleashed.air">My Application</a> now.<br /><br /><span
➥id="AIRDownloadMessageRuntime">This application requires the <a href="');
    var platform = 'unknown';
    if (typeof(window.navigator.platform) != undefined)
    {
        platform = window.navigator.platform.toLowerCase();
        if (platform.indexOf('win') != -1)
            platform = 'win';
        else if (platform.indexOf('mac') != -1)
            platform = 'mac';
    }
    if (platform == 'win')
    document.write('http://airdownload.adobe.com/air/win/download/1.0/
➥AdobeAIRInstaller.exe');
    else if (platform == 'mac')
document.write('http://airdownload.adobe.com/air/mac/download/
➥1.0/AdobeAIR.dmg');
    else
    document.write('http://www.adobe.com/go/getair/');
    document.write('">Adobe&#174; AIR&#8482;
➥runtime</a>.</span></td></tr></table>');
}
// -->
</script>
<noscript>
<table id="AIRDownloadMessageTable">
<tr>
    <td>
    Download <a href="AIRUnleashed.air">My Application</a> now.<br /><br /><span
➥id="AIRDownloadMessageRuntime">This application requires
➥Adobe&#174; AIR&#8482; to be installed for
➥<a href="http://airdownload.adobe.com/air/mac/download/1.0/AdobeAIR.dmg">
➥Mac OS</a> or <a href="http://airdownload.adobe.com/air/win/download/1.0/
```

```
➥AdobeAIRInstaller.exe">Windows</a>.</span>
    </td>
</tr>
</table>
</noscript>
</body>
</html>
```

Additionally, you can edit and recompile the `badge.swf` file using Flash CS3 to redesign the user interface of the `badge.fla` file. An example of a more complex `badge.swf` seamless installer is shown in Figure 17.21.

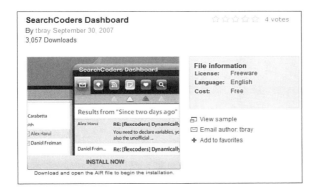

FIGURE 17.21   Customized `badge.swf`.

The inner workings of the seamless installer might seem a bit complex but is described here to help you understand the main features. Basically, the seamless installer, via the Adobe supplied `air.swf`, is equipped with these methods that provide the seamless features: (1) to determine if the Adobe AIR runtime is installed (`getStatus`), (2) to determine the current version of an Adobe AIR application (`getApplicationVersion`), (3) to perform the installation (`installApplication`), or (4) to launch the application (`launchApplication`). These methods are available because the `AIRBridge.as` file, utilized in the `badge.swf`, contains an `AIRBadge()` constructor function that loads the `air.swf` file hosted at http://airdownload.adobe.com/air/browserapi/air.swf. This `air.swf` file includes the code (the methods) for using the seamless installation features.

The `air.swf` can determine if the Adobe AIR runtime is installed by calling the `getStatus()` method, as shown here:

```
var Status:String = airSWF.getStatus();
```

The status returns a string—"available" (the runtime is not installed but can be installed), "unavailable" (the runtime cannot be installed), or "installed" (the runtime is already installed).

> **CAUTION**
>
> The getStatus() method throws an error if the required version of Flash Player (version 9 upgrade 3) is not installed in the browser.

The air.swf can also determine if an Adobe AIR application (with a matching application ID and matching publisher ID) is already installed by calling the getApplicationVersion() method, as in the following:

```
var appID:String = "com.example.air.myTestApplication";
var pubID:String = "02D88EEED35F84C264A183921344EEA353A629FD.1";
var version:String = airSWF.getApplicationVersion(appID, pubID, versionDetectCall-
  back);
function versionDetectCallback(version:String):void {
    if (version==null) {
        trace("This version, ", version, " is not installed.");
        // Take appropriate actions. For instance, present the user with
        // an option to install the application.
    } else {
        trace("Version ", version, " installed.");
        // Take appropriate actions. For instance, enable the
        // user interface to launch the application
        // or upgrade the application.
    }
}
```

Figure 17.22 depicts the case where the Adobe AIR application is already installed on the user's PC.

FIGURE 17.22   Dialog for an existing Adobe AIR application.

The air.swf seamless installation can perform the installation of an Adobe AIR application by calling the installApplication() method, as in the following code:

```
var url:String = "http://www.example.com/myApplication.air";
var runtimeVersion:String = "1.0.M6";
var arguments:Array = ["launchFromBrowser"]; // Optional
airSWF.installApplication(url, runtimeVersion, arguments);
```

CAUTION

The installApplication() method can only operate when called in the event handler for a user event, such as a mouse click.

To use this browser invocation feature (allowing it to be launched from the browser), the application descriptor file of the target application (for example, myApplication-app.xml) must include the following setting:

```
<allowBrowserInvocation>true</allowBrowserInvocation>
```

Another important method found in the air.swf application programming interface (API) is the launchApplication() method. This method can launch an Adobe AIR application from the browser, as in the following code:

```
var appID:String = "com.example.air.myTestApplication";
var pubID:String = "02D88EEED35F84C264A183921344EEA353A629FD.1";
var arguments:Array = ["launchFromBrowser"]; // Optional
airSWF.launchApplication(appID, pubID, arguments);
```

Calling this method causes the Adobe AIR runtime to launch the specified application (if it is installed and browser invocation is allowed, via the allowBrowserInvocation setting in the application descriptor file, discussed previously).

If the allowBrowserInvocation element is set to false in the application descriptor file, calling the launchApplication() method has no effect.

17

NOTE

An interesting blog post takes the seamless installation feature to the next level. Read more about this at www.rogue-development.com/blog/2008/03/interacting-with-air-app-from-browser.html.

Digitally Signing an Adobe AIR File

An important topic is digitally signing your Adobe AIR application. It is so important to more securely distributing Adobe AIR applications that you cannot complete the .air file creation without signing your application. This is true whether you use Adobe Flex Builder 3, the Dreamweaver CS3 Adobe AIR extension, the Flash CS3 Adobe AIR upgrade, or the Adobe AIR SDK command line tool to compile your .air file. Additionally, digitally signing your .air files with a certificate issued by a recognized certificate authority (also known as a CA) provides an extra level of assurance to your users. This certificate identifies you as the signer or publisher. The Adobe AIR installation dialog displays the publisher name during the installation steps when the Adobe AIR application has been signed with a certificate that is trusted, or which chains to a certificate that is trusted on the installation computer. Figure 17.23 shows the publisher as "Adobe Systems Incorporated" and would help put the end users' mind at ease so they would be more likely to continue with the remaining steps of the Adobe AIR installation.

FIGURE 17.23   Dialogs for Adobe as the Adobe AIR publisher.

Figure 17.24 depicts the case where the Adobe AIR 1.0 runtime is missing and shows that it is required as the check box is selected and cannot be changed.

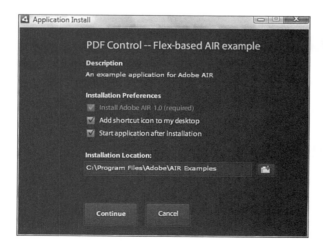

FIGURE 17.24   Dialog for install of Adobe AIR runtime.

Figure 17.25 demonstrates that Adobe published this Adobe AIR application and even includes a license agreement. Once again, this would help an end user to be more likely to trust and install this Adobe AIR application.

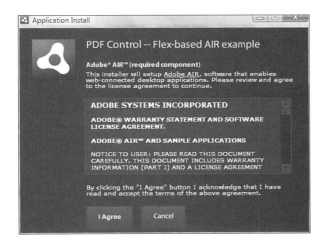

FIGURE 17.25   Dialogs for Adobe AIR runtime license.

Otherwise, the publisher name is displayed as "Unknown"—as shown in Figure 17.26.

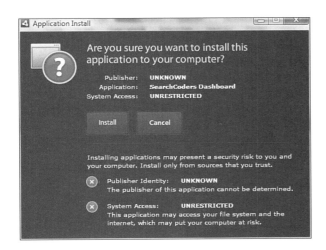

FIGURE 17.26   Dialogs for an unsigned Adobe AIR application.

When an Adobe AIR file is signed, a digital signature is included in the installation file. The signature includes a digest of the package (signature.xml), which is used to verify that the Adobe AIR file has not been altered since it was signed, and it includes information about the signing certificate, which is used to verify the publisher's identity. See the signature.xml file shown in Listing 17.2.

LISTING 17.2   The Contents of the signature.xml File

```
<signatures>
  <Signature xmlns="http://www.w3.org/2000/09/xmldsig#" Id="PackageSignature">
    <SignedInfo>
      <CanonicalizationMethod Algorithm="http://www.w3.org/TR/2001/
➥REC-xml-c14n-20010315"/>
      <SignatureMethod Algorithm="http://www.w3.org/TR/xmldsig-core#rsa-sha1"/>
      <Reference URI="#PackageContents">
        <Transforms>
          <Transform Algorithm="http://www.w3.org/TR/2001/REC-xml-c14n-20010315"/>
        </Transforms>
        <DigestMethod Algorithm="http://www.w3.org/2001/04/xmlenc#sha256"/>
        <DigestValue>8xgmkk9GjJu7XNQ7L2NIzDXWqnYtGfr7ej784CA137s=</DigestValue>
      </Reference>
    </SignedInfo>
    <SignatureValue>DH+ZscIkbEvDsKdjIRZs11ktQnUhVOui+
➥Aj3SygaAEIQrz5dKvgLwtt7m7OFvQzlQ+Yf20zeu/Fx
m7bpTj2mRePweNn+MqbT6x/GbXSftXfH8wHejAPTjMxONLy5eAR31E0j4OlRs8htTkc02hr1sQL1
BPopDPgYubboXRhTeu/tsGI6NHtR/ehEy57IZGxlTt1lLOqQSp31FiIZTe3ancy1GhrJDabVEqsv
LDIhzYvkxq5iYuyyiiMLyBvJS03ATNeqzIBGgcdUuRgdbz19q3kLvQLMWEcjKw7ZSYU9r9sbD4/r
rh56jSI1f+KY0043ppkpSUnjaSmjvVTbH/W12w==</SignatureValue>
    <KeyInfo>
      <X509Data>
        <X509Certificate>
➥MIIDmTCCAoGgAwIBAgIaN2MwODBlZDQ6MTE5MDliMjQ5MDc6LTgwMDAwDQYJKoZIhvcNAQEFBQAw
dzELMAkGA1UEBhMCVVMxHTAbBgNVBAoTFFUgU2F3IEl0IEVudGVycHJpc2VzMSowKAYDVQQLEyFB
SVIgRGV2ZWxvcG1lbnQgU2VjdXJpdHkgU2VydmljZXMxHTAbBgNVBAMTFFUgU2F3IEl0IEVudGVy
cHJpc2VzMB4XDTA4MDQwMTExMTQ0OVoXDTEzMDQwMTExMTQ0OVowdzELMAkGA1UEBhMCVVMxHTAb
BgNVBAoTFFUgU2F3IEl0IEVudGVycHJpc2VzMSowKAYDVQQLEyFBSVIgRGV2ZWxvcG1lbnQgU2Vj
dXJpdHkgU2VydmljZXMxHTAbBgNVBAMTFFUgU2F3IEl0IEVudGVycHJpc2VzMIIBIjANBgkqhkiG
9w0BAQEFAAOCAQ8AMIIBCgKCAQEAkxdJWuAi3B/leozma0ZA0pld1/VA8lcwwdLLunE5Ko1jc0I
Ccfuz/424mjF9U5cgN1Qs0kQdW1ldGyrFMdhmYkZ9O38UrWvc2K6/tI/QVCEB1pAqQP2FobmKtcv
mbHSpP0sU+l205tKZpBcqDXuYF7o3vo66s8Aj+eKTv7GcP6rSrdiC3Ni80SiClpnD7VucFj39mYb
+hI5XRW3xpadkqEy3rFmtQcfNNAUddSmgt1txe9+h62MqPgHHvlVL1n6FCcGlqdcHf73Zw7f8FUu
exGaI0NHq5jwQ8gpyLDdK35V6WMjVpckjC08by9YgFrgZS3mGOctf4TDmj82k3hfJwIDAQABoxcw
FTATBgNVHSUEDDAKBggrBgEFBQcDAzANBgkqhkiG9w0BAQUFAAOCAQEAVwQwJ9Qu6mLsWyEjY2HQ
8vA6aBz7IEHu3KME1y/blE5jtdZAu7yNrBA73ra+hNzroQhkL/abHg1J2efkKBCYYW5Kt308K9bL
IAu7RHf+6LLfd6v3h684uQ7BX4VLF5lpmGML0j6vWLpYxMaAMhg7w7fRGOLHaH5Lzr6P3R+tIr4c
ShOoeLal0m/DJeb2tVN0BG8YTCSJ/g47C5aXfQyJFBolkqOs9Za6TD7fVjDV8xM8zHNXZjgv3P3J
+R418mUZob8egYTPUl9nuOBsmkeG8oJt0Jnf4+P4C13pZiraxeYiZMJbhGEPtu0bC7sgmGI7zs96
AhMI6rxwUZq8InVgZQ==</X509Certificate>
```

```
      </X509Data>
    </KeyInfo>
    <Object>
      <Manifest Id="PackageContents">
        <Reference URI="mimetype"><DigestMethod Algorithm=
"http://www.w3.org/2001/04/xmlenc#sha256"></DigestMethod><DigestValue>0/oCb84THK-
MagtI0Dy0KogEu92TegdesqRr/clXct1c=</DigestValue></Reference><Reference URI="META-
INF/AIR/application.xml"><DigestMethod
Algorithm="http://www.w3.org/2001/04/xmlenc#sha256"></DigestMethod><DigestValue>eUN
ZcvhLJjKpeeSz4wilTuf90g2aNANpXTaoQge7HDQ=</DigestValue></Reference><Reference
URI="AIRUpdatingApps.swf"><DigestMethod
Algorithm="http://www.w3.org/2001/04/xmlenc#sha256"></DigestMethod><DigestValue>ktF
P/f4PROPIK7dxp8zppYhV5XuuaEkz5hB7N5CjYdE=</DigestValue></Reference>
      </Manifest>
    </Object>
  </Signature>
</signatures>
```

If an Adobe .air file is signed with a certificate that is not a trusted root certificate or is a self-signed certificate, the end user sees the publisher as "Unknown" in the introductory installation dialog. During the install, this is evident—as shown in Figure 17.26, the Publisher is shown as "Unknown" and the Publisher Identity is also shown as "Unknown."

As part of the process of packaging an Adobe .air file, the Adobe AIR Developer Tool (ADT) generates an unique publisher ID. This is an ID that is based on the certificate used to package the .air file. If you reuse the same certificate for multiple Adobe AIR applications, they will have this same publisher ID. This unique publisher ID is also used to identify the Adobe AIR application during Local Connection communication. You can retrieve the publisher ID of an installed application by reading the NativeApplication. nativeApplication.publisherID property, as in the following code:

```
var pubID:String = nativeApplication.publisherID;
```

To sign Adobe AIR files, you can use any of the following types of certificate (marked for code signing) from VeriSign: Microsoft Authenticode Digital ID or Sun Java Signing Digital ID; from Thawte you can use the following: Adobe AIR Developer Certificate, Apple Developer Certificate, JavaSoft Developer Certificate, or Microsoft Authenticode Certificate.

When you sign an .air file, the packaging tool queries the server of a time stamp authority to obtain an independently verifiable date and time of signing. The time stamp (you must be connected to the Internet to get to the Geotrust time stamp server) obtained is embedded in the .air file. The capability for an Adobe AIR application to be installed revolves around the combination of the time stamp and the certificate's expiration date. As long as the signing certificate is valid at the time of signing, the .air file can be installed perpetually. On the other hand, if no time stamp is obtained during the signed .air file creation, it ceases to be installable when the certificate expires or is revoked. To

17

allow applications to be packaged when the time stamp service is unavailable, you can turn time stamping off, but it is recommended that all publically distributed .air files include a time stamp.

To obtain a certificate, you should visit either VeriSign or Thawte. There are distinct instructions for obtaining instructions based on several factors, including the browser that you use to obtain the certificate. For more information, you can do a search for "AIR Code-Signing Certificates." You can generate a self-signed certificate using the Adobe AIR Development Tool (ADT) used to package the .air installation files. You can also export and sign the .air files using Adobe Flex Builder, Dreamweaver, and the Adobe AIR update for Flash CS3.

If you are using Adobe Flex Builder to package and sign your .air files, during the "Export a Release Build" step, you can browse to the location of your CA-provided certificate or to the location of your self-signed certificate. You need to enter the password that is associated with either certificate and decide whether you want to include a Timestamp.

Figure 17.27 shows the Certificate Wizard built in to Adobe Flex Builder.

FIGURE 17.27   Certificate Wizard for Adobe AIR applications.

If you are using Dreamweaver CS3 with the Adobe AIR Extension to package and sign your .air file, you can either browse to the location of your CA-provided certificate or as shown in Figure 17.28, create a self-signed certificate to add to the .air file you are packaging.

Figure 17.29 shows the resulting dialog after the self-signed certificate is created with Dreamweaver CS3 with the Adobe AIR Extension. You can see that the location of the certificate is shown in the dialog.

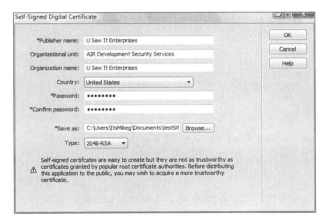

FIGURE 17.28   Self-signed digital certificate creation using Dreamweaver CS3 with the Adobe AIR Extension.

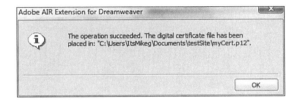

FIGURE 17.29   Self-signed digital certificate created successfully with Dreamweaver CS3 with the Adobe AIR Extension.

Figure 17.30 shows the selection of the self-signed certificate with the `Timestamp` feature selected immediately before the `.air` file is created using Dreamweaver CS3 with the Adobe AIR Extension.

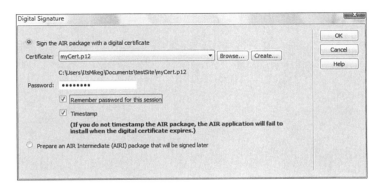

FIGURE 17.30   Self-signed digital signature and `Timestamp` selected prior to the creation of the `Adobe` `.air` file using Dreamweaver CS3 with the Adobe AIR Extension.

Figure 17.31 shows the progress dialog during the creation of the Adobe `.air` file.

FIGURE 17.31   Creating the Adobe `.air` file with Dreamweaver CS3 with the Adobe AIR extension.

Figure 17.32 shows the confirmation dialog that the Adobe `.air` file was created successfully and the location where it has been stored.

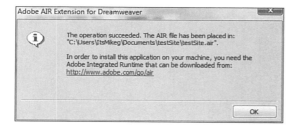

FIGURE 17.32   Adobe `.air` file created successfully with Dreamweaver CS3 with the Adobe AIR extension.

Figure 17.33 shows the HTML-based Adobe AIR application that was created with Dreamweaver CS3, packaged with Dreamweaver CS3 with the Adobe AIR extension, and then installed as a one-off type of installation.

FIGURE 17.33   Hello World Adobe AIR application created with Dreamweaver CS3 and packaged with Dreamweaver CS3 with the Adobe AIR extension.

Summary

Adobe AIR applications can be distributed as a single Adobe AIR installation file (.air), which contains the application code and all assets necessary to run the application. You can distribute this file through any of the typical means, such as by download from a website, by email, or by physical media, such as a CD-ROM or DVD. Users can install the application by double-clicking the .air file. You can alternatively use the badge or seamless install feature, which lets users install your Adobe AIR application (and the Adobe AIR runtime, if needed) by clicking a single link on a customizable web page.

Digitally signing your .air installation files with a certificate issued by a recognized CA provides assurance to your users that the application they are installing has not been accidentally or intentionally altered and identifies you as the signer or publisher. This ensures a better user experience in providing a higher level of security comfort to the end user.

# CHAPTER 18

Updating Adobe AIR Applications

One of the elegant convenience features of deployed Adobe® AIR™ applications is their capability to seamlessly update (by a detection-and-notification capability—the end user still has the power to say no to any updates) the version and features as soon as new updates are available. The capability for the deployed Adobe AIR application to "poll" or employ "pull technology" allows this to be driven by the desktop application. This resembles the "old school" client/server paradigm, where the server maintains the latest and greatest version of the application, and the client simply utilizes the latest deployed server application. This auto-update feature eliminates the painful distribution process that a system administrator, desktop-to-desktop upgrade method entails. Of course, the traditional method of updating an application is still perfectly valid. Users can update an Adobe AIR application by double-clicking on a new Adobe AIR file on their computer or from a browser (using the seamless install feature) that is developer-supplied in an email, on their website, on a mailed CD-ROM or DVD, or in an Adobe AIR library such as found on the Adobe AIR Marketplace or a third-party site such as www.O2Apps.com. Whether push or pull technology is used, the Adobe AIR installer application manages the update, alerting the user if they are updating an already existing application.

Meet the Updater Class

The new class that makes all the magic happen is the Updater class (an Adobe AIR class), shown in Table 18.1.

Use the update() method to kick off the installation dialog for an upgrade to your Adobe AIR application. As can be seen in the application programming interface (API), the update() method requires that a reference to the Adobe AIR file (File class) and the version (String class) be passed when calling it. After this method is called, the currently running Adobe AIR application closes, and a new Adobe AIR installer dialog opens. The user is then prompted to update the application, uninstall the currently installed application, run the currently installed version, or cancel the installation process. The snippet of code in Listing 18.1 briefly outlines the type of code you would write to accomplish this. (You must instantiate an Updater object and call the update() method on it as this method is not static.)

TABLE 18.1   Updater API

Package	Class	Description
flash.desktop	Updater	The Updater class includes a single public method (outside of the constructor), update(), which updates the running version of an Adobe AIR application to an updated version of the application contained in the specified Adobe AIR file.

LISTING 18.1   Adobe AIR Using the Updater Class

```
import flash.fileSystem.File;
import flash.desktop.Updater;
// instantiate the Updater object
var myUpdater:Updater = new Updater();
// instantiate a file reference to the .air file
var myAIRFile:File = File.applicationStore.resolvePath("AIRUnleashed.air");
// initialize the version variable as a String
var myVersion:String = "2.01";
// call the update method passing in the air file and the version variable
myUpdater.update(myAIRFile, myVersion);
```

TIP

If you try to run the update() method directly from the Adobe AIR Debug Launcher or ADL, as you do when testing your application in Adobe® Flex™ Builder or from a command prompt, you will see this error: "Error: This method is not supported if application is launched from ADL. at flash.desktop::Updater/update()."

The end user would see the dialog shown in Figure 18.1 during the upgrade process. Note that if the updated Adobe AIR application requires an updated Adobe AIR runtime, this step would also be handled during the installation process—again under the complete free will of your end user. Because a user can skip the upgrade of the Adobe AIR runtime or might not have adequate administrative permissions, it is your responsibility to write code to handle the unexpected actions of your users to prevent possible endless loops of the installation process from occurring.

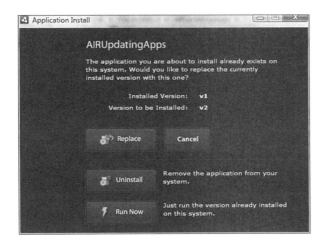

FIGURE 18.1   Adobe AIR application update dialog.

After the Adobe AIR application has been updated, running the same `.air` file again detects that nothing has changed, so your user sees the dialog shown in Figure 18.2.

FIGURE 18.2   Adobe AIR application run now or uninstall dialog.

Step-by-Step Instructions to Updating an Adobe AIR Application

When updating your Adobe AIR applications, follow these general steps:

1. Determine the update version of your application (the new version you will be updating to, which is also used in step 4).

   For instance, in the sample code shown in Listing 18.2, the version you want to update to is `AIRUpdatingApps_v4`.

2. Provide instructions or a delivery mechanism for delivering the new version of the Adobe AIR application to the user's computer.

   For instance, a copy of the Adobe AIR file (in this example, `AIRUpdatingApps_v4.air`) is downloaded to the desktop and is shown in Figure 18.3.

This is an example of what happens if the wrong version is supplied. Additional error-handling code is shown in Listing 18.2 (use the `exists()` method from the `File` class) that handles the `.air` file mismatch.

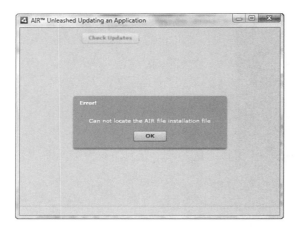

FIGURE 18.3   Adobe AIR application—wrong Adobe AIR file downloaded.

LISTING 18.2   Adobe AIR Application—Updating an Application

```
<mx:WindowedApplication xmlns:mx="http://www.adobe.com/2006/mxml" title="AIR™
Unleashed Updating an Application" layout="absolute">
    <mx:Script>
    <![CDATA[
        import mx.controls.Alert;
        import mx.utils.ObjectUtil;
        private function testVersion():Object {
            var appID:String = this.applicationID;
            var pubID:String = nativeApplication.publisherID;
            var appDescriptor:XML = NativeApplication.nativeApplication.applica
              tionDescriptor;
            var ns:Namespace = appDescriptor.namespace();
            var appVersion:String = appDescriptor.ns::version;
            var objAppInfo:Object = new Object();
            objAppInfo.appID = appID;
            objAppInfo.pubID = pubID;
            objAppInfo.version = appVersion;
            return objAppInfo;
        }
        private function check4Updates():void {
            var myUpdate:Updater = new Updater();
            var airFile:File =
File.desktopDirectory.resolvePath("AIRUpdatingApps_v4.air");
            //Alert.show(ObjectUtil.toString(airFile));
```

```
            var myVersion:String = "v4";
            var objTestAppVersion:Object = testVersion();
            if (objTestAppVersion.version != myVersion) {
                if (airFile.exists) {
                    try {
                        myUpdate.update(airFile, myVersion);
                    } catch (e:TypeError){
                        trace(e.message);
                    }
                } else {
                    Alert.show("Cannot locate the AIR file installation file",
"Error!");
                }
            } else {
                Alert.show("AIR App is version " + objTestAppVersion.version,
"Success");
            }
        }
    ]]>
    </mx:Script>
    <mx:Button x="119" y="10" label="Check Updates" click="check4Updates()"/>
</mx:WindowedApplication>
```

3. Instantiate the Updater class.

4. Call the update() method of the Updater class, passing in a File object that corresponds to the new Adobe AIR file and the version number in a String (from the previous step 1). See Figure 18.4 to show the resulting installation dialog.

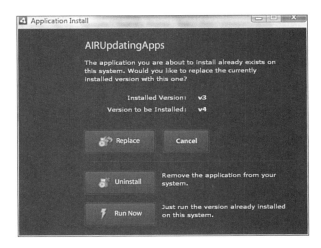

FIGURE 18.4 Adobe AIR application—upgrade dialog.

5. Call the "installation successful" function that you placed in your Adobe AIR application (in Listing 18.2, see the `testVersion()` function) to ensure that the Adobe
   AIR application detects that the version has been updated. This ensures that your
   user does not get caught in an endless loop installation scenario.

6. The Adobe AIR runtime shuts down your Adobe AIR application, installs the new
   version, and then restarts the application, as shown in Figure 18.5.

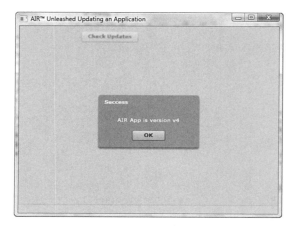

FIGURE 18.5   Adobe AIR application—upgrade success.

Update Adobe AIR Applications via a Remote Server

Another method for updating an Adobe AIR application is via remote server monitoring of
an Internet-accessible .air file to detect changes in the XML-based Descriptor file. As
changes in the Descriptor file's version are detected, email notifications or, even better,
your Adobe AIR application can monitor for changes to the .air file on a remote server
through a monitoring method that you bake into your Adobe AIR application. The
method is remotely alerted that an updated .air file is available, and the user can receive
an alert from the running Adobe AIR application that an upgrade is available.

> **NOTE**
>
> Examples of this type of automatic updating are springing up all over the Internet. To
> read more about this exciting topic, feel free to browse the following URLs:
>
> http://blog.simb.net/2007/08/09/auto-updating-your-air-applications/
>
> http://blog.everythingflex.com/2007/03/20/apollo-self-updating-applications/
>
> http://www.rogue-development.com/blog/2008/03/interacting-with-air-app-from-
> browser.html
>
> http://www.O2Apps.com

Of course, this chapter would not be complete unless you see a code example for this type of remote server monitoring for a deployed Adobe AIR application. Listing 18.3 shows such an example. The `applicationComplete` event runs each time the application starts and triggers the function that contacts the remote server that checks the version information for the latest and greatest `.air` file by some server-side technology. If a more proactive and frequent check is required, simply add a `Timer`-based function that does the polling of the remote server more frequently (see the following tip about the Adobe Flex 3 `Timer`).

LISTING 18.3   Check For Remote Updates

```
<mx:WindowedApplication xmlns:mx=http://www.adobe.com/2006/mxmlapplicationCom-
plete="checkForRemoteUpdates()" title="AIR™ Unleashed Updating an Application"
layout="absolute">
    <mx:HTTPService id="myService"
➥url="http://209.41.164.34/airtraining/gofly/getVersion.cfm" result="getVersionHan-
➥dler(event)" fault="errorHandler(event)"/>

    <mx:Script>
        <![CDATA[
        import mx.controls.Alert;
        import mx.utils.ObjectUtil;
        import mx.rpc.events.*;
        private var objRemoteAIRInfo:Object = new Object;
        private function checkForRemoteUpdates():void {
            myService.send();
        }
        private function getVersionHandler(event:ResultEvent):void {
            var version:String = event.result as String;
            onLoad(version);
        }
        private function errorHandler(event:FaultEvent):void {
            // dump error message
            Alert.show(ObjectUtil.toString(event.fault) + '\n\n'
➥+event.fault.faultDetail);
        }
        private function onLoad(version:String):void {
            var remoteVersion:String = version;
            testVersion();
            var objTestAppVersion:Object = testVersion();
            if (objTestAppVersion.version != remoteVersion) {
                Alert.show("An updated version is available...", "Notice");
                /* add code to create a link to the .air file */
            } else {
                Alert.show("You already have the latest version...", "Notice");
            }
```

```
        }
        private function testVersion():Object {
            var appID:String = this.applicationID;
            var pubID:String = nativeApplication.publisherID;
            var appDescriptor:XML = NativeApplication.nativeApplication.applica
➥tionDescriptor;
            var ns:Namespace = appDescriptor.namespace();
            var appVersion:String = appDescriptor.ns::version;
            var objAppInfo:Object = new Object();
            objAppInfo.appID = appID;
            objAppInfo.pubID = pubID;
            objAppInfo.version = appVersion;
            return objAppInfo;
        }
        ]]>
    </mx:Script>
</mx:WindowedApplication>
```

TIP

The Adobe Flex 3 `Timer` class is a great "poor man's" polling tool. The `Timer` class is the interface to timers, which let you run code on a specified time interval. A code example follows:

```
    private function TimerExample() {
        var myTimer:Timer = new Timer(60000, 0); //poll every min.
        myTimer.addEventListener("timer", myTimerHandler);
        myTimer.start();
    }
    private function myTimerHandler (event:TimerEvent):void {
        trace("myTimerHandler: " + event);
            checkForRemoteUpdates();
    }
```

Summary

Updating Adobe AIR applications is an exciting, feature-differentiating topic from competing products. The ability to code your Adobe AIR applications in such a way as to automatically monitor for updates of the .air file gives you a great "icing on the cake" feature for your deployed applications. An Adobe AIR application, through the update API, minimizes any versioning differences that a similar web-based application would already be immune from. Additionally, as you have seen, the desktop features and offline capability are superior to a web-based application. When your users ask you how often you update your Adobe AIR applications and how they will deploy the updates throughout their enterprise, you can just smile and say, "That's not an issue, it's a feature."

18

PART V

Architecting Adobe AIR Applications

IN THIS PART

# CHAPTER 19

Introduction to Frameworks and Design Patterns

In previous chapters, we have gradually increased our knowledge of how to build Adobe® AIR™ applications using Adobe® Flex™. We have done so using the various components available within Adobe Flex, such as `Buttons`, `Lists`, `DataGrids`, `TextInput` controls, and much more. Furthermore, because we are learning about Adobe AIR, we have additional capabilities available to us, such as working with native windows, local file access, desktop interactivity, and, again, much more. Understanding all these various components and how to use the specialized application programming interfaces (API) for Adobe AIR is the easy part. Throughout the previous chapters, you've seen small examples that quickly demonstrate how to put these components and APIs to use.

However, in a real-world scenario, you will not be building small examples; you will be developing real applications using Adobe AIR that will be used by various end users to perform various tasks, which might range from applying for a mortgage to listening to music. Such applications can grow quickly in size and complexity, resulting in an application with thousands of lines of code, many sections and subsections, and probably requiring an entire development team to create.

To make the job of the development team easier to create such applications, we require a way to bring structure to our application code base, to make it so that any developer who joins the project can jump right in and contribute. Furthermore, we must make the application easy to maintain, allowing the development team to easily enhance existing features or add new features with every release.

The structure we are looking for can be easily provided by an architecture framework. Thus, this chapter explores what an architecture framework brings to the Adobe AIR development process and takes a look at one architecture framework in particular in great detail.

What Is a Framework?

Before you can understand how a framework can help bring structure to your Adobe AIR application code base, you must first understand what a framework is. This is important because the term framework is broadly used in software development and it means different things to different people.

Libraries

Sometimes when people talk about a framework, they are simply talking about a software library. Such libraries don't actually provide any structure and are nothing more than a set of reusable APIs used to perform some common tasks.

> **NOTE**
>
> For those coming from a Java development background, a perfect example of a framework library is the Java Collections Framework, which is merely a collection of APIs to work with a list of objects. Refer to the following URL for more details: http://java.sun.com/j2se/1.3/docs/guide/collections/overview.html.

Application Framework

An application framework is something you are probably already familiar with because you have been using one up to this point in the book—Adobe Flex. The definition of an application framework is a software structure composed of a set of class libraries that allows you to build applications for a particular platform. Or simply put, it is a framework that provides low-level APIs that can be reused across various applications, thus facilitating the developer's task and allowing him to focus specifically on solving the business problem at hand.

As just mentioned, Adobe Flex is a perfect example of an application framework that allows a developer to create applications for two different platforms: web-based applications that run in the Adobe® Flash® Player and desktop applications that are run using Adobe AIR.

Another example—this one coming from the Java world—is the Spring Framework (www.springframework.org/). Spring is an application framework that allows you to develop structured applications that run in the Java Virtual Machine (JVM).

Architecture Framework

Architecture frameworks are completely different. They do not provide a collection of APIs that you can use; instead, they define a structure or a foundation upon which you build your application. For example, if you were a home builder, the architecture framework is the concrete and the metal beams that hold the house in place.

In essence, the architecture framework is the starting point for your application.

How an Architecture Framework Helps Adobe AIR Development

When building Adobe AIR applications, you will find yourself writing many lines of code. You will write code for the custom components you've created, for the interaction with various services, and, quite possibly, for adding some lovely visual effects. Your Adobe AIR application is sure to be elegant and functional, but your application code base will probably lack some structure.

Although you have probably done your best to follow object-oriented programming practices, you probably still could use some help. You are probably asking yourself how to properly maintain application state, how to cleanly look up various remote services, or even how to make the code less intertwined than it already is. Furthermore, working in a team environment, without good structure within the code base itself, can lead to unnecessary code duplication, lack of cohesion, or, worse yet, spaghetti code. This is because the various developers on the team don't know where to find or place certain pieces of code. These problems only compound themselves as the Adobe AIR application gets bigger, more elaborate, and more complex.

This is where an architectural framework can help because it is like a template, consisting of known patterns that a developer can recognize and follow.

Design Patterns

As just mentioned, an architectural framework is composed of known patterns or, more precisely, design patterns. But what is a design pattern? A design pattern is a documented common solution to a recurring problem in a specific context. Think about it: How many times have you found yourself working on a project, have been faced with a problem, and have remembered that you had this same problem before in a previous project and, thus, have already formulated a solution?

To gain a quick understanding of a design pattern, let's take one of the simplest ones, the *Transfer Object* pattern. This one emanated from the J2EE world where Entity Beans were used to represent persistent data in a database and how to interact with the data they represented. However, the transferring of data between tiers, most notably between the presentation and business tiers, became heavy using Entity Beans. Therefore, a simple solution was devised to use Plain Old Java Objects (POJO) to carry the data in a lightweight and efficient manner between tiers.

## 19

Therefore, with experience gathered by working on various software development projects over the years, software engineers have documented several design patterns that are still used today and quite common. The best part is that these design patterns are so generic that they can be applied to almost any software development project regardless of the programming language used or the intended delivery platform. So they are perfect for use in Adobe AIR application development.

> **TIP**
>
> The term *design patterns* in software development was popularized back in the 1990s by a group of software engineers known as the Gang of Four in a book titled Design Patterns: Elements of Reusable Object-Oriented Software (ISBN: 0-20-163361-2). We also recommend reading *Core J2EE Patterns: Best Practices and Design Strategies* (ISBN: 0-13-142246-4), which contains an in-depth knowledge of design patterns in use today in Java Enterprise applications.

Where to Apply Design Patterns in Adobe AIR

So, the question is what recurring problems are you most likely to face during development on an Adobe AIR application? Several issues must be dealt with; the following sections take a look at these one by one, and then we take a look at an architectural framework that will help us solve these problems.

Managing State

Unlike web applications, where the HTTP request/response protocol used is stateless; Adobe AIR applications that run on the desktop can maintain their own state. This is one of the advantages of a stateful client as it does not require retrieving the same data from the server over and over again, thus helping reduce network chatter.

Also when talking about *state*, we are basically talking about the data itself, also referred to as the *model*. The state can be anything, from the list of roles a user has, to the items in a shopping cart, or to a list of products being displayed. So, what we need is a place to hold this data so that it is available to the entire application. This is necessary because, in some cases, the same data might be rendered differently depending on which part of the Adobe AIR application is making use of it.

Handling User Gestures

It goes without saying that an Adobe AIR application contains a visual interface—also known as the *view*—with which the user interacts. Depending on this interaction, we execute some business logic. Typically, this interaction consists of clicking a button or selecting an item in a list. In some cases, these user gestures also require the application to trigger some action to occur, like sending/retrieving data to/from a server or simply performing a calculation and updating the view.

The actions triggered by these user gestures need to be grouped into logical business units that can be executed when needed, can also be chained together with other actions when required, and must also be easy to maintain from a development standpoint.

Interacting with Services

It goes without saying that an Adobe AIR application on its own is not as useful as an Adobe AIR application that communicates with remote services in the cloud (meaning via a network, most likely the Internet). Two issues arise when we add this type of functionality to our Adobe AIR application.

First, how do we provide an abstract approach to retrieving references to different services? Remember, an Adobe AIR application can interact with web services, execute a method on a remote object, or invoke a classic HTTP GET/POST. Second, how can we obfuscate the complexity of calling such various remote business services?

> **NOTE**
>
> When talking about executing a method on a remote object, we typically refer to performing a method call on a Java or ColdFusion class using the ActionScript Messaging Format (AMF) protocol. However, if you are developing on the PHP and .NET platforms and want to have this capability as well, we recommended you look into AMFPHP (www.amfphp.org/) and WebORB (www.themidnightcoders.com/weborb/dotnet/), respectively.

Transferring Data

As with any application, the data itself is the most important part. The user will use the application to view, manipulate, and possibly store the data for future use. The data in question can be a simple structure, meaning a single object, or a complex structure made up of several objects. So, how do we effectively encapsulate and allow for the easy transfer of this data between tiers?

Reducing Tight Coupling

With all the previously mentioned problems that the architectural framework must deal with, they must all directly resolve one common problem as well, which is tight coupling. Tight coupling refers to pieces of software code that are so dependent or intertwined with each other that it is difficult to separate from each other. When such is the case, the extensibility and maintainability of the application suffer. Therefore, we are looking for the architectural framework to provide a structure such that our application code is loosely coupled—allowing parts of the application code to easily be discarded and replaced with new parts in an effortless manner.

Introducing Cairngorm

Up to this point, we have discussed what an architecture framework is and what problems it will help us address during our Adobe AIR application development. In this section, we take a look at Cairngorm, a lightweight model-view-controller (MVC) architectural framework written in ActionScript that we will put into practice to help us solve the issues we brought up earlier in this chapter.

Before we get into the details about Cairngorm, let's talk about how it came about. Soon after the release of Adobe Flex 1.0 in March 2004, developers were already planning to use

Adobe Flex to build complex user interfaces to either replace existing ones or for use in brand-new applications. So during the early stages of development, several developers were already beginning to ask themselves the same questions we have already raised earlier in this chapter: how to interact with various types of services, how to handle user gestures in large-scale applications, how to properly separate business logic within the application from the view components, and how to effectively manage state. And so, two gentlemen by the names of Steven Webster and Alistair McLeod contributed to the Adobe Flex community an open source MVC microarchitecture framework known as Cairngorm.

NOTE

At the time of the first Cairngorm release, both Steven Webster and Alistair McLeod worked for iteration::two. Since then, the company was acquired by Adobe and, thus, Cairngorm is now maintained by Adobe, which is where Steven and Alistair work.

Because of the authors' background in creating Flash MX and Java applications, they put their design experiences into Cairngorm, thus making it an easy-to-use framework built with familiar concepts to many developers. Since that time, Cairngorm has seen several other releases and continues to be used in many Adobe Flex applications and now in Adobe AIR applications. We will now take a look at the two main reasons Cairngorm has been so successful.

TIP

The version of Cairngorm we are using as of this writing is version 2.2.1. The binary distribution and relevant documentation can be found at the following site: http://labs. adobe.com/wiki/index.php/Cairngorm. Although the website only mentions Adobe Flex 2.x, the binary distribution can be used with Adobe Flex 3.0.

Another good reference for the Cairngorm framework can be found at the following site: www.cairngormdocs.org. It contains a diagram explaining the various parts of the framework and how they interact as well as an online version of the Cairngorm API reference.

NOTE

Many people wonder where the name *Cairngorm* came from. Both Steven Webster and Alistair McLeod are from Scotland, which contains a mountain named *Cairn Gorm*.

Microarchitecture

The first reason for Cairngorm's success is the fact that it is not only an architecture for building rich Internet applications (RIA) in Adobe Flex and Adobe AIR, but it is also a microarchitecture. By microarchitecture, we mean a small architectural framework that doesn't get in the way of your own application logic.

If you look at the documentation of Cairngorm, you will notice it is composed of only a few interfaces and classes. These interfaces and classes put into action the design patterns that Cairngorm is made up of, and it does so in a lightweight manner. We say that it is lightweight because in practice an application will make use of only three interfaces, the `ICommand`, `IModelLocator`, and `IValueObject`, and each of those only contain one function that needs implementation or none at all. The other interfaces are already implemented by Cairngorm itself in concrete classes that actually realize the remainder of the design patterns. And those concrete classes, which we take a look at shortly, are lightweight as well, as they too only contain a few functions that an application will make use of.

Familiar Concepts

The second reason for Cairngorm's success is because it is built on familiar concepts, which have been in practice for many years in various programming languages and platforms. The original authors of Cairngorm worked primarily on applications that used Java on the server-side, where using design patterns to solve problems is common. Thus, those tried, tested, and true design patterns found their way into Cairngorm to solve similar problems that arose during development of RIAs.

One of those familiar concepts is the model-view-controller (MVC) philosophy. This concept promotes decoupling such that the view is separated from the business logic, allowing each piece to easily be modified without affecting the other. This sort of concept is crucial to building easily maintainable Adobe AIR applications that can be quickly modified due to ever-changing business requirements.

Working Parts of Cairngorm

With the Cairngorm framework being a microarchitecture framework, it contains few parts. However, every part within the framework is important, and each part plays a significant role in solving the problems we will deal with as we create more complex Adobe AIR applications.

So now, let's walk through the various design patterns that the framework employs and see how they are implemented in detail to gain a better understanding of the advantages that Cairngorm brings to the table.

Value Object

How to properly deal with services is one of the issues that must be dealt with properly when building Adobe AIR applications. When dealing with services, we are essentially talking about the transfer of data to and from an Adobe AIR application. Therefore, the first pattern we explore is the Value Object pattern (also known as the Data Transfer Object pattern or simply the Transfer Object pattern), which we briefly mentioned when first introducing design patterns earlier in this chapter.

When the first J2EE applications were being built in an n-tier configuration, the presentation tier typically used remote calls to Entity Beans in the business tier to retrieve data. Although this was the correct way to do things, it was inefficient when dealing with large object graphs or when dealing with retrieval of different pieces of data because it required many remote calls, thus decreasing application performance. Thus, the Value Object pattern employs the developer to use a POJO to transfer the data from one tier to another because it is the most lightweight manner to do so.

This, then, becomes a perfect pattern to use when building Adobe AIR applications because Adobe AIR applications are remote clients residing on an end user's computer and are communicating with one or several services over a network.

Therefore, in Cairngorm, you will see this pattern defined as a simple ActionScript interface with no body, as seen in the following code segment:

```
package com.adobe.cairngorm.vo
{
    public interface IValueObject
    {
    }
}
```

There are no methods to implement because the class that will implement this interface contains no business logic whatsoever and is used simply for the transfer of specific domain data. It is basically a marker interface that, when used, provides greater readability into the code itself by identifying which classes are, indeed, transfer objects:

```
public class Person implements IValueObject
{
    public var firstName:String;
    public var lastName:String;
    public var age:int;
    public var phoneNumbers:ArrayCollection;
}
```

As you can see from the sample implementation, the Person class is a transfer object used to move data to and from an Adobe AIR application regarding a person. It is, in fact, a complex object because it also contains a list of phone numbers associated with a person. As a result, we can retrieve various pieces of information regarding a complex domain object without requiring multiple remote calls.

ModelLocator

As mentioned earlier in this chapter, one of the issues we will deal with when building larger applications is how to properly maintain state information. By *state*, we mean where to properly maintain the model data that is used across the Adobe AIR application. One of the advantages of using RIAs is that you can retrieve all the data required by the application and hold it for the life span of the application and use it in different contexts without having to retrieve it over and over again from the server. This also does away with the various methods developers have employed over the years to build web applications to maintain application state. Such methods include using server-side sessions, HTTP request/response, and local browser cookies.

So, how do you properly maintain state throughout an Adobe AIR application? The solution to this is to use the Singleton pattern. The Singleton pattern states that you should allow only one instance of any particular class to exist within a virtual machine (the ActionScript Virtual Machine [AVM] in the case of Adobe AIR applications). Therefore, if only one instance of a particular class exists during runtime, you can use this class to hold all relevant information required application-wide. In Cairngorm, this is represented by the ModelLocator interface.

Like the Value Object, the ModelLocator interface is simply a marker interface that you implement in the concrete model class so that the class itself can be easily identified as being the ModelLocator used in the Adobe AIR application. The interface definition is as follows:

```
package com.adobe.cairngorm.model
{
    public interface IModelLocator
    {
    }
}
```

Thus, when implementing the ModelLocator in a sample application such as a contact manager, it should look similar to the following (some code was omitted for brevity):

```
[Bindable]
public class ContactModel implements IModelLocator
{
    public var contacts:ArrayCollection;
    public var selectedContact:Person;
    public var viewIndex:int = 0;

    // the single class instance variable
    private static var _instance:ContactModel = null;

    public static function getInstance():ContactModel
    {
        if( _instance == null )
        {
            _instance = new ContactModel();
        }
        return _instance;
    }
}
```

As you can see, the ContactModel is a container class where different pieces of model data reside, such as the list of contacts, the currently selected contact, and the index of the current view being displayed to the end user. Thus, other classes or views within the application can access the data in the following simple fashion:

```
var contacts:ArrayCollection = ContactModel.getInstance().contacts;
```

With this global structure, we now have an easy way to access our data from the various views and other classes throughout the application. Finally, it allows the classes that implement various pieces of business logic to easily update any data as needed.

19

> **TIP**
>
> In some applications, we have noticed that our single implementation of the `ModelLocator` class grew to be quite large. Depending on the size of an application, then, it is not uncommon to find several implementations of the `ModelLocator` interface. As an example in an online store, you might have `ProductModel` and `ShoppingCartModel` classes. The purpose of this is to provide greater code clarity.

FrontController and Commands

We mentioned earlier that Cairngorm is an MVC framework and so far, we have looked at how to handle the model portion (the *M* in MVC) with the Value Object and ModelLocator patterns. Cairngorm does not deal with the view portion because it is already handled very well by the Adobe Flex framework. Cairngorm does deal with the last portion, the controller, by implementing two design patterns known as the *Front Controller* and *Service to Worker*.

To start, we take a look at the Front Controller pattern, which states that every presentation tier request should go through a central access point for handling. For an Adobe AIR application, this means that every user request (or gesture) should go through some central concrete class before the invocation of any business logic. Without this, the execution of business logic would be scattered throughout the Adobe AIR application code base and tightly coupled to the view code, thus making the application difficult to maintain with every development cycle.

The second design pattern Cairngorm makes use of to handle user gestures is the Service to Worker pattern, which simply states that some class should do the request handling and perform any business logic before returning control back to the view. Basically, some class should perform all the *work* related to a request before the user can execute another action. By performing all necessary work in a worker class, this further decouples the view from any business logic, which is one of our goals.

Now, let's see how this is all implemented in Cairngorm, as both concepts are tied together.

A user gesture refers to the user performing some action or generating an event. However, unlike component events, which identify when a user interacts with a component (clicks a button or selects an item in a list), we are now talking about application events. Application events are specific features that the user wants to execute. Some examples of application events are loading a contact, deleting a contact, and updating a contact. Cairngorm contains a concrete class called simply enough, `CairngormEvent`. Therefore, your own application events should extend this class, as follows:

```
public class LoadContactEvent extends CairngormEvent
{
    public static const LOAD_CONTACT:String = "LOAD_CONTACT";
    public var contactId:int;

    public function LoadContactEvent()
```

```
    {
        super( LOAD_CONTACT );
    }
}
```

You can see that the `LoadContactEvent` class extends the `CairngormEvent` class, passing the associated event name (which is declared as a constant) to the superconstructor and declaring a variable to hold the identifier for the contact we want to load. Finally, in any view in the application, this event can be dispatched by using the following code:

```
var event:LoadContactEvent = new LoadContactEvent();
event.contactId = 55;
event.dispatch();
```

As you can see, this is quite simple, but who listens for the event? This brings us to the next class, Cairngorm's `FrontController`, akin to the design pattern of the same name. The `FrontController` class is the central point through which all Cairngorm events are routed and is the one that will respond to the event and then have some other class execute the related work. So now another question is raised, who does the work? Cairngorm handles this by having the `FrontController` call a command class, which is responsible for executing business logic and then returning control back to the view. So, the `FrontController` class allows us to make this one-to-one link between an application event and the command that will perform the work requested by the user. Furthermore, the command can perform any variety of actions, but one thing is for certain, it will manipulate the model in some way and cause some view to be updated. After this is done, the control is returned to the view, so the user can execute the next gesture and the cycle repeats itself.

Now, let's find out what this all looks like from a code perspective. First, we create our own class that extends Cairngorm's `FrontController`:

```
public class ContactManagerController extends FrontController
{
    public function ContactManagerController()
    {
    }
}
```

To perform the one-to-one link between event and command, we use the `addCommand()` function in the class' constructor, as follows:

```
addCommand( LoadContactEvent.LOAD_CONTACT, LoadContactCmd );
```

That part was easy; now, let's see what is involved in creating the related command class. The Cairngorm framework defines an `ICommand` interface, which defines only one function called `execute()`. Creating the command class to load the contact can be done without much difficulty:

```
public class LoadContactCmd implements ICommand
{
    public function execute( event:CairngormEvent ):void
```

```
    {
    // ... do work here ...
    }
}
```

As you can see, the `execute()` function takes a single parameter, the reference to the `CairngormEvent`, which caused the execution of this command class; in this case a reference to the `LoadContactEvent` instance was dispatched by the view. Although omitted here, the actual work to be done by the command is to manipulate the model in some way. This work can either be done by the command itself or can be the result of executing a remote service call.

Therefore, by making use of two design patterns, the Front Controller and Service to Worker, Cairngorm has given us a way to handle user gestures in a centralized fashion using the `FrontController` class and has decoupled the actual business logic from the view by putting all the work inside segregated command classes.

ServiceLocator

When building Adobe AIR applications, the application is likely to use one or many types of remote services. These can range from calling a remote object, to performing an HTTP POST/GET, to calling a web service. One of the problems of an application dealing with multiple services is that the declaration of these remote services is likely to be spread out throughout the application, leading to what is referred to as "spaghetti code" in software development. This is especially true when multiple developers are working on the same project.

Cairngorm's solution to this problem is to make use of another well-known pattern, the *ServiceLocator* pattern. The ServiceLocator pattern states that accessing different types of services should be transparent and uniform. Therefore, the framework contains a concrete class of the same name with several functions to allow the application to easily retrieve access to a diverse set of remote services. Table 19.1 briefly describes the most common functions.

TABLE 19.1   List of the Most Common ServiceLocator Functions Used to Access Various Remote Services

Function	Description
getRemoteObject()	Returns a `RemoteObject` class, allowing access to a remote Java class or ColdFusion component. With third-party software, access to PHP and .NET classes is also possible
getHTTPService()	Returns an `HTTPService` class, allowing access to a server-side technology, including PHP pages, ColdFusion Pages, JavaServer Pages (JSPs), Java servlets, Ruby on Rails, and Microsoft ASP pages
getWebService()	Returns a `WebService` class, allowing access to a web service that implements the WSDL 1.1 specification via a uniform resource locator (URL)

> **NOTE**
>
> The `ServiceLocator` class also defines `getProducer()` and `getConsumer()` functions used to interact with Java Messaging Service (JMS) queues and topics. Furthermore, it defines a `getDataService()` function, which returns a `DataService` instance for advanced data service operations. Please refer to the Live Cycle Data Services (LCDS) documentation for more details on Data Services.

In conclusion, the `ServiceLocator` within Cairngorm provides a clean and standardized method for accessing a variety of services throughout the Adobe AIR application.

Business Delegate

You were just introduced to the `ServiceLocator` class, which helped to resolve one issue when dealing with remote services; however, one issue remains: how to obfuscate the remote calls. This is needed so that when a client, such as an Adobe AIR application, calls various remote services, when and if those remote services change their implementation, you can ensure that only small changes will be required within the Adobe AIR application. We are basically introducing an extra layer between the business code invoking the remote service and the call to the service.

To solve this final problem, Cairngorm recommends the use of the Business Delegate pattern. The Business Delegate pattern simply states that communication with remote services should be hidden from clients. A typical business delegate in an Adobe AIR application looks similar to the following:

```
public class ContactManagerDelegate
{
    private service:Object;

    public function ContactManagerDelegate()
    {
        service = ServiceLocator.getInstance().getRemoteObject("contactManager");
    }

    public function loadContact( contactId:int ):void
    {
        service.load( contactId );
    }
}
```

As you can see, little coding is involved. The `ContactManagerDelegate` class is used to encapsulate all remote calls to a service named `"contactManager"` and defines a function called `loadContact()` that will be used by some business logic within the Adobe AIR application to retrieve all data regarding a particular contact. In a real-world scenario, this delegate is likely to declare other functions for other related operations, such as creating, updating, and deleting a contact. Using this technique, if the signature of any remote function changes, the only modifications required are in this class. In addition, you should notice that the delegate makes use of the ServiceLocator to retrieve an instance of the remote service we want to call.

So using a business delegate essentially provides a contract for the Adobe AIR application to invoke remote services while hiding any complexity.

Now that we have delved into the Cairngorm framework in detail, refer to Figure 19.1 to see a visual representation of how the pieces in the framework interact with each other.

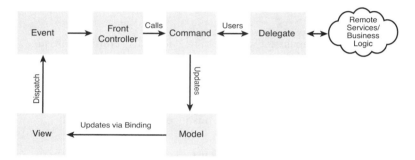

FIGURE 19.1   Illustration of the various parts within Cairngorm framework and how they interact.

Summary

Earlier in this book, we learned how to build Adobe AIR applications, but in this chapter, we learned how to architect them. The reason for learning how to properly architect an Adobe AIR application is to better manage the application as it grows in complexity. To do this, we made use of an architectural framework known as Cairngorm to provide a proper development foundation upon which an Adobe AIR application can be built.

The reason for doing this is to provide a means of easily handling several recurring issues that would only become more problematic as an application grows in size and scope. To deal with these recurring problems, Cairngorm employs the use of several well-known design patterns, which have solved similar problems in other software languages and platforms. These problems deal with three main areas of Adobe AIR application development: handling user gestures, maintaining application state, and invocation of services. For user gestures, we used the Front Controller and Service to Worker design patterns to decouple the view from the application business logic. To properly maintain application state, we introduced the ModelLocator pattern to centralize the access of data. Finally, the Value Object, Service Locator, and Business Delegate patterns were used to obfuscate the interaction of remote services and to simplify the transfer of complex object graphs.

By applying the proper architecture to Adobe AIR application development, working with large-scale applications is easier, and the code base becomes more familiar to the entire development team.

CHAPTER **20**

Building Adobe AIR Applications Using the Cairngorm Microarchitecture

In the previous chapter, you learned about architectural frameworks and how they apply to Adobe® AIR™ application development. You saw that using an architectural framework from the beginning of development of an Adobe AIR application provides a good foundation and, thus, helps as the application grows in size and complexity.

The preceding chapter also took a look at one framework in particular, the Cairngorm microarchitecture framework. You learned about how it came about, what problems it solves, and how it solves them to help properly maintain an Adobe AIR application in today's business world of ever-changing business requirements.

In this chapter, we actually apply Cairngorm in practice on a small application that helps us understand all the basics about Cairngorm and, therefore, makes it easier later on to use the framework to add new features to an Adobe AIR application. We build an electronic shopping cart application step-by-step. We see how to set up both a basic view that displays the items in the cart and another view that allows the user to add a new item to the cart, and, finally, we learn how to retrieve information required by the application by performing a remote call to a Java service.

> **NOTE**
>
> The sample application we build in this chapter also contains a small Java server-side component (two classes, in fact, named: `Product.java` and `ProductClient.java`) that we do not take a look at here because it is beyond the scope of this book.

Defining the Model and Value Objects

The reason we create applications revolves around the display and manipulation of data, so we start creating our eCart application by looking at the domain objects we need to work with. Being a small application, there are only two domain objects we create and then we set up our own ModelLocator class to hold data needed application-wide.

Product.as

Because we are building a mini shopping cart application, where the end user will purchase a certain amount of units of a certain product, defining the product is a good place to start.

Listing 20.1 shows the actual code for the Product ActionScript class that is defined in a file called Product.as.

LISTING 20.1   The Product Class

```
package ecart.domain
{
  import com.adobe.cairngorm.vo.IValueObject;

  [RemoteClass(alias="ecart.Product")]
  public class Product implements IValueObject
  {
    public var name:String;
    public var price:Number;

    public function Product()
    {
    }
  }
}
```

As you can see, the Product class is quite simple. First, because we are using the Cairngorm framework and because the Product class is a value object, we must make it implement the IValueObject interface. As mentioned in the previous chapter, the IValueObject interface does not force us to implement any functions, it is simply there to remind us of the purpose of this class. From a development standpoint, it is easy for any developer looking at this class for the first time to recognize what it is used for. Second, the class declares two properties to represent the name and price of a product. And, finally, we must pay attention to the following metadata that is placed before the class declaration:

```
[RemoteClass(alias="ecart.Product")]
```

This metadata information is basically stating that the ActionScript Product class maps directly to the fully qualified class named ecart.Product. In this application, the Product class maps to the Java class named ecart.Product on the server side.

> **CAUTION**
>
> When using Java on the server side, for the `Product` class to be properly mapped to its equivalent Java class, the Java class must conform to the JavaBeans specification. This means that the Java class must declare a public, no-arguments constructor, must declare a `get()` and `set()` method for each property, and, finally, must implement the `java.io.Serializable` interface.

> **NOTE**
>
> Although in our sample application we are using Java on the server side, we could have easily used ColdFusion, Ruby, or PHP. If that were the case, the `RemoteClass` metadata tag would serve the exact same purpose of mapping the ActionScript class to a class in any of those languages.

CartItem.as

The next value object we need to create is the one that will represent an item in the shopping cart. So without further ado, let's take a look at the conveniently named `CartItem` class, as shown in Listing 20.2.

LISTING 20.2   The `CartItem` Class

```
package ecart.domain
{
  import com.adobe.cairngorm.vo.IValueObject;

  public class CartItem implements IValueObject
  {
    public var product:Product;
    public var quantity:int;

    public function get cost():Number
    {
      return product.price * quantity;
    }

    public function CartItem()
    {
    }
  }
}
```

As you can see, this class is similar to the `Product` class we just created a step earlier. This class extends the `IValueObject` interface once again for the same reasons as the `Product` class does and, it declares two public properties, `product` and `quantity`, to hold the product being purchased and the amount of units of that product that is being purchased, respectively. You will also notice it declares a third, read-only property called cost. This is used to calculate the actual amount that will be charged for purchasing a certain amount of units of the set product.

Finally, you will notice, unlike the Product class, the CartItem class does not define any special metadata information because it will not be used for any data transfer to/from the server. It is for use within Adobe AIR only.

CartModel.as

Now that our value objects are defined, we need to create the class that will hold our global application state. Thus, we need to create a class where we can store various pieces of information that will be accessible from anywhere in our application, by the commands that need to manipulate the data and the views that will display the data.

Listing 20.3 shows the CartModel class, which implements Cairngorm's IModelLocator interface. (Some code has been omitted for brevity.) The details are explained in the paragraphs following Listing 20.3.

LISTING 20.3   The CartModel Class Holding Global Application Data

```
package ecart.model
{
  ...
  [Bindable]
  public class CartModel implements IModelLocator
  {
    public static const VIEW_LIST:int = 0;
    public static const VIEW_ADD:int = 1;

    public var viewIndex:int = VIEW_LIST;
    public var products:ArrayCollection;
    public var cartItems:ArrayCollection = new ArrayCollection();
    public var grandTotal:Number;

    private static var _instance:CartModel = null;

    public static function getInstance():CartModel
    {
      if( _instance == null )
      {
        _instance = new CartModel();
      }

      return _instance;
    }

    public function CartModel()
```

```
        {
        }
    }
}
```

The first thing you should notice is that the `CartModel` class uses the Singleton pattern to ensure only one instance of this class exists at runtime. Using this technique ensures only one version of the various pieces of data is available for use at runtime. Thus, the static variable `_instance` holds the only instance of the class.

> **NOTE**
>
> In Listing 20.3, you might notice that only one single instance of the `CartModel` class will ever exist; however, the scope of the class' constructor is public. When employing the Singleton pattern in most software languages, like Java, the constructor will have private scope; however, because we are developing in ActionScript 3.0, the language specification does not allow for private constructors. Regardless of this fact, various solutions have been created to solve this problem; we recommend reading the solutions proposed at the following URL: http://en.wikipedia.org/wiki/Singleton_pattern.

Next, the class declares several public variables used to hold the actual application data. The `products` variable holds the list of products, the `cartItems` variable holds the items in the cart, and the `grandTotal` variable holds the total amount to be owed based on the items in the shopping cart.

You will also notice a variable called `viewIndex`, which is of type `integer`, that is used by the application to determine which view in the main `viewstack` is being displayed at any one time. The `viewIndex` variable can have only one of two values defined by the `VIEW_LIST` and `VIEW_ADD` constants, with `VIEW_LIST` being the default. You will see exactly how all these variables are used later in this chapter.

Finally, you will observe that the class defines the `[Bindable]` metadata tag, thus making all the variables in the `CartModel` class bindable.

> **TIP**
>
> If you want only certain variables to be bindable within the `CartModel` class, you can remove the class level metadata tag and place it only on the variables that you want to be bindable. For example, to make the `products` variable bindable, you would write the following:
>
> `[Bindable] public var products:ArrayCollection;`

Creating the `ServiceLocator` and Delegate

Now that we have created all the classes that relate to the data we want to work with, it's time to code the portion of the shopping cart application that will communicate with a remote Java service. For this sample shopping cart application, the only remote call we need is a call to retrieve the list of services. Now this might sound simplistic, but it is enough to demonstrate how to use the Cairngorm framework to your advantage when working with remote services so that when you are faced with a real-world scenario, you will easily know how to configure an Adobe AIR application to connect to many remote services.

First let's set up Cairngorm's ServiceLocator and then write our delegate class that will be used from a command object later in this chapter.

ServiceLocator

To centralize the list of remote services an Adobe AIR application will communicate with, we need to make use of Cairngorm's ServiceLocator class. To do this, we will create an MXML component called Services (that will be located in a file called Services.mxml) that will extend Cairngorm's ServiceLocator class.

We will use an MXML file to declare our services rather than a custom ActionScript class to save on coding statements. Listing 20.4 looks at the Services.mxml file, and some of the details are explained in the following paragraphs.

LISTING 20.4   The ServiceLocator Defining a Single Remote Java Class to Communicate With

```
<business:ServiceLocator
  xmlns:mx="http://www.adobe.com/2006/mxml"
  xmlns:business="com.adobe.cairngorm.business.*">

  <mx:RemoteObject
    id="productClient"
    destination="productClient"
    showBusyCursor="true">
  </mx:RemoteObject>

</business:ServiceLocator>
```

The MXML file defines a root tag called ServiceLocator, which can be found in the business namespace (it is the same as a package definition in ActionScript), and a single child element, which is the actual service with which we want to communicate. This remote service is defined by the RemoteObject tag and its several properties. First, the id property gives the RemoteObject we are defining an instance name of productClient. Then, the destination property defines which remote object it will actually communicate with (for this project, it is a Java class named ecart.ProductClient), and, finally, the showBusyCursor property is set to true so that the user has a visual reference that something is going on while the remote call is being made.

TIP

To have a full understanding of how to set up a Java server with which an Adobe AIR application can communicate, check out Adobe's open source BlazeDS technology at the following URL: http://opensource.adobe.com/wiki/display/blazeds/BlazeDS.

This is all that is needed to initialize Cairngorm's `ServiceLocator`. Of course, if we had more services to configure, we would only have to add another child `RemoteObject` element or perhaps even a `WebService` or an `HTTPService` element.

NOTE

To understand how to configure and use various service tags in Adobe AIR, read the "Data Access and Interconnectivity" chapter of the Adobe® Flex™ software development kit (SDK) documentation located at the following URL: http://livedocs.adobe.com/flex/3/html/index.html.

Once again, simplicity is the key; there isn't much going on in the `Service.mxml` file, but it is enough to provide us with a centralized method of retrieving a reference to one or several remote services. The following section covers how to use the `ServiceLocator`.

NOTE

You can also configure the `ServiceLocator` with a child `DataService` tag to make use of the advanced Data Management Services provided in Adobe's Live Cycle Data Services ES product. For more information on this product, please visit the following website: www.adobe.com/products/livecycle/dataservices/.

ProductDelegate.as

Now that we have a centralized way of accessing remote services, we need to create our business delegate that will be used as an access point to a particular service. So, we will create a `ProductDelegate` class, as shown in Listing 20.5, that will be used to interact with the `ecart.ProductClient` Java class on the server side.

LISTING 20.5   The Business Delegate as Defined in the `ProductDelegate.as` File

```
package ecart.business
{
  ...
  public class ProductDelegate
  {
```

20

```
    private var service:Object;
    private var responder:IResponder;

    public function ProductDelegate( responder:IResponder )
    {
      service = ServiceLocator.getInstance().getRemoteObject( "productClient" );
      this.responder = responder;
    }

    public function getProducts():void
    {
      var call:AsyncToken = service.loadAllProducts();
      call.addResponder( responder );
    }
  }
}
```

Our business delegate class defines two properties, a constructor and one business function that is used elsewhere in the Adobe AIR application. First, let's review the service and responder properties. The service property is of type Object and is used to reference the actual service with which we will be communicating. The service property is of type Object for two reasons: because it can represent any number of possible service types (RemoteObject, WebService, HTTPService) and because it is actually representing the remote object and its methods. However, we do not know at design time what those methods are.

Next, the ProductDelegate constructor does two things. First, it receives a reference to the RemoteObject that it will need to call by using the ServiceLocator and assigning it to the service property. Here is where we see for the first time different parts of the Cairngorm framework interacting with each other. Second, it is caching the responder reference it is receiving as a parameter so that it can be used later by the functions within the class.

Finally, the delegate declares one function called getProducts() that uses the service property to initiate the remote call to the loadAllProducts() method on the remote Java class. By performing this call, an AsyncToken object is returned that can then be used to specify the class that will handle the result of the remote method call (be it either successful or not). The responder property holds the reference to the class or, as we will see next, the command class that will do this handling.

Creating Commands, Events, and the FrontController

Up to this point, we have taken care of creating the portion of the Adobe AIR application using the Cairngorm framework that will represent the data and handle remote data communications. The data is represented using value objects, and the CartModel class stores the data for global access. As for remote communications, we used the

`Service.mxml` file to configure Cairngorm's `ServiceLocator` and build the `ProductDelegate` class to handle the retrieval of some data.

Now that we have this data to work with, it is time to build the classes that will use this data. As we learned in the previous chapter, the Cairngorm framework specifies that data manipulation should be done in command classes so that this logic is decoupled from the views. This makes it easy to handle user gestures and add new features; it also makes maintaining the code base more straightforward for everyone on the development team.

To accomplish this, we need to create an event and command for every feature in the shopping cart application, and the whole thing will be held together by a single `FrontController` class. There are four features in this shopping cart application: loading products, preparing to add an item to the cart, canceling the addition of an item, and, finally, actually adding an item to the cart.

LoadProductsEvent.as

One of the first things to do is create the event and command class to fulfill the loading of the list products a user can purchase in the shopping cart application. Listing 20.6 creates the `LoadProductEvent` event class, and this code is explained in the paragraphs following the listing.

LISTING 20.6   The LoadProductsEvent.as File

```
package ecart.commands
{
  ...
  public class LoadProductsEvent extends CairngormEvent
  {
    public static const LOAD_PRODUCTS:String = "LOAD_PRODUCTS";

    public function LoadProductsEvent()
    {
      super( LOAD_PRODUCTS );
    }
  }
}
```

As mentioned previously, simplicity is the key and this is because Cairngorm is a microarchitecture framework. The framework doesn't get in the way—it doesn't hinder the developer from having to write loads of plumbing code. So, in this case, the event class simply extends the `CairngormEvent` class defined within the framework. Then, the constructor calls the base class constructor and passes it the event name, which is defined by the public constant `LOAD_PRODUCTS`.

That's all there is to it, folks. The rest of the event classes in this Adobe AIR application are the same with one exception, the `AddItemEvent` class. The `AddItemEvent` class also

20

defines a property that holds the actual item we want to add to the cart; the property is defined as follows:

```
public var item:CartItem;
```

So, basically, in an event class, you can define as many properties as is necessary so that the corresponding command can do its work. We will see later in this chapter how this is used when we examine the `AddItemCmd.as` command class.

TIP

The `CairngormEvent` class actually defines a `data` property that can be used to hold event data as it gets passed to the command. However, because it is of type `Object`, we recommend you declare your own property with the exact data type for better code clarity.

LoadProductsCmd.as

Now that we have built the event class for loading products, it is time to build the corresponding command class. Of all the command classes in our shopping cart application, this is the most complex one because it deals with remote service communication.

This command class also demonstrates how several pieces of our application come together. Listing 20.7 shows the code for the command class and how it makes use of the `ProductDelegate` and `CartModel` classes, which we have already created.

LISTING 20.7   The Most Complex Command Class in Our Application, the `LoadProductsCmd` Class Deals with Retrieving Remote Data

```
package ecart.commands
{
  ...
  public class LoadProductsCmd implements ICommand, IResponder
  {
    public function execute( event:CairngormEvent ):void
    {
      var delegate:ProductDelegate = new ProductDelegate( this );
      delegate.getProducts();
    }

    public function result( data:Object ):void
    {
      var event:ResultEvent = data as ResultEvent;
      var model:CartModel = CartModel.getInstance();
      model.products = event.result as ArrayCollection;
    }

    public function fault( info:Object ):void
    {
      var event:FaultEvent = info as FaultEvent;
```

```
    Alert.show( "Unable to load products: "
            + event.fault.faultString, "Error" );
    }
  }
}
```

There are two parts to examine here, based on the fact that the command implements two interfaces. The first interface implemented is `ICommand`, which is part of the Cairngorm framework. The interface defines a single function called `execute()`, which is called by the framework when the command is, like the function name says, executed. The `execute()` function is where you see `ProductDelegate` being used to call a remote Java class to load the list of products. Furthermore, the delegate's constructor takes a single parameter, which is a reference (`this`) to the command class itself; the reason for this is to be able to handle the results returned by the remote call.

That brings us to the second interface implemented, `IResponder`. This interface defines two functions, `result()` and `fault()`, which are called after the remote request is completed based on whether the request was successful or failed. Let's examine the failed case first. A remote request can fail due to one of two reasons, either the call could not be made, in which case Adobe AIR itself returns the error details, or the request was sent, but an error was returned by the remote class. In either case, the generic object returned is cast to a `FaultEvent` object, and the error details obtained from the `fault.faulString` property are displayed using the `Alert` component.

However, when the remote request is successful, the `result()` function is called and the generic object returned in this case is cast to an object of type `ResultEvent`. Should the remote method that was called return some kind of data, the result property of the `ResultEvent` object contains the data. In this case, the result returned is a list of `Product` objects, so the result is cast to an `ArrayCollection` and assigned to the `products` property of the `CartModel` class.

Before we started examining the `LoadProductsCmd` class, we mentioned it is the most complex—and now, you understand why. It makes use of several classes we built up to this point, the delegate, and the model, and it also demonstrates how to handle the response returned from a remote call.

PrepAddCartCmd.as

From a complex command class, we now take a look at a command class at the opposite end of the spectrum. The `PrepAddCartCmd` command is used to do one simple thing: to switch the view to display a form the user can use to add a new item to the shopping cart. So without further ado, let's take a look at the code for the command (see Listing 20.8).

LISTING 20.8   The Simple `PrepAddCartCmd` Command

```
package ecart.commands
{
  ...
```

20

```
public class PrepAddCartCmd implements ICommand
{

  public function execute( event:CairngormEvent ):void
  {
     CartModel.getInstance().viewIndex = CartModel.VIEW_ADD;
  }
 }
}
```

As you can see, this command class is far simpler. Because it does not make any remote calls, it implements only one interface, the ICommand. And because of this, the class contains only the execute() function, which is required. Within the execute() function, we set the viewIndex property on the CartModel to a new value. A little later in the chapter, you will see how this affects the view.

Although we did not show it, the PrepAddCartCmd has a corresponding event class called PrepAddCartEvent, which is exactly the same as the LoadProductsEvent event class (shown in Listing 20.6).

CancelAddCmd.as

As we keep moving to the next class, we will be creating, you might have observed that all the classes up to this point are autonomous. This means that the classes are loosely coupled from each other because of how they are employed by the Cairngorm framework. So in the future, when changes are required to a specific feature, we will easily be able to update the appropriate command class and complete the work.

Now let's implement the command for canceling the add item action, as shown in Listing 20.9.

LISTING 20.9   The CancelAddCmd.as File

```
package ecart.commands
{
  ...
  public class CancelAddCmd implements ICommand
  {
    public function execute( event:CairngormEvent ):void
    {
       CartModel.getInstance().viewIndex = CartModel.VIEW_LIST;
    }
  }
}
```

If you think the CancelAddCmd command looks similar to the PrepAddCartCmd command, you are entirely correct. The only difference is the value of the viewIndex property is set to the value specified by the VIEW_LIST constant in the CartModel class. By setting it to a value of CartModel.VIEW_LIST, we are essentially returning the user back to the default view where the list of shopping cart items is displayed.

AddItemCmd.as

The final command we are going to build is the one for adding an item to the shopping cart. For this command, unlike the others, we are going to build it one piece at a time.

Like all other commands, this command has a corresponding `AddItemEvent` event. We previously said that all event classes are the same (see Listing 20.6); however, the `AddItemEvent` class defines an additional property named `item`, which is the item to add to the shopping cart. The property is defined as follows:

```
public var item:CartItem;
```

So in the `AddItemCmd` class, the first thing we need to do is take the item from the event, and add it to the list of items in the shopping cart, like so:

```
var evt:AddItemEvent = event as AddItemEvent;
...
model.cartItems.addItem( evt.item );
```

As you can see, before we can add the item to the cart, we have to cast the `event` object, which is of type `CairngormEvent`, to the specific `AddItemEvent` type, which contains the extra `item` property. Then, the item is added to the list of items defined by the `cartItems` property on the `CartModel` class (see Listing 20.3).

Next, we need to calculate the total amount to be purchased based on the items in the shopping cart. To do this, we simply need to loop through all the items in the cart and add each item's cost value to the `grandTotal` property on the `CartModel` class.

```
for( var i:int = 0; i < model.cartItems.length; i++ )
{
  item = model.cartItems.getItemAt( i ) as CartItem;
  model.grandTotal += item.cost;
}
```

Finally, the last action we want to perform in the command is to return the user to the main view, so we do this by changing the value of the `viewIndex` property on the `CartModel` class, like so:

```
model.viewIndex = CartModel.VIEW_LIST;
```

Now that we have gone thru the class piece by piece, Listing 20.10 below shows the entire code for the class.

LISTING 20.10   The Full Code for the `AddItemCmd` Command Used for Adding an Item to the Shopping Cart

```
package ecart.commands
{
  ...
  public class AddItemCmd implements ICommand
  {
    public function execute( event:CairngormEvent ):void
    {
      var evt:AddItemEvent = event as AddItemEvent;
```

```
    var model:CartModel = CartModel.getInstance();
    var item:CartItem;

    model.cartItems.addItem( evt.item );
    model.grandTotal = 0;

    for( var i:int = 0; i < model.cartItems.length; i++ )
    {
      item = model.cartItems.getItemAt( i ) as CartItem;
      model.grandTotal += item.cost;
    }

    model.viewIndex = CartModel.VIEW_LIST;
    }
  }
}
```

CartController.as

Now that we have built all the commands and events within the shopping cart application, it is time to code the controller class that is going to make the link between each event and its corresponding command class.

Creating the controller is easy because the FrontController class within the Cairngorm framework has all the plumbing that is required to make the link between events and commands. So in creating the CartController class, we are simply subclassing Cairngorm's FrontController class and using the addCommand() method as many times as needed to make the connection between all the events we created and the corresponding command classes that perform the actual work, as shown in Listing 20.11.

LISTING 20.11   The CartController Class

```
package ecart.business
{
  public class CartController extends FrontController
  {
    public function CartController()
    {
      super();

      addCommand( PrepAddCartEvent.PREP_ADD, PrepAddCartCmd );
      addCommand( CancelAddEvent.CANCEL_ADD, CancelAddCmd );
      addCommand( LoadProductsEvent.LOAD_PRODUCTS, LoadProductsCmd );
      addCommand( AddItemEvent.ADD_ITEM, AddItemCmd );
    }
  }
}
```

Building the Views

So far in this chapter, we built all the classes and components (the commands, events, `Services.mxml`, and so on) that do all the heavy lifting; now, it is time to build the visual portion of the Adobe AIR application. After all, what is an Adobe AIR application without an interface?

The interface for the shopping cart application is in three parts: the main application window and two subviews. Of the two subviews, one view displays the list of items in the cart, and the other view allows the end user to add an item to the cart.

So without further ado, let's start coding!

ecart.mxml

The starting point for any Adobe AIR application is an MXML component whose root tag is `WindowedApplication`. Within this main application file, we will declare a `ViewStack` with the two subviews, and we will also initialize two of the classes we built previously in this chapter, the `CartController` and the `Services` component. If we don't initialize those two parts, when events are dispatched, nothing will be listening for them, and when we attempt a remote call, we will get an error.

To easily understand what the main application file is doing, Listing 20.12 shows the code and the following paragraphs explain it in detail.

LISTING 20.12   The Starting Point for the Shopping Cart Application, the `ecart.mxml` File

```
<?xml version="1.0" encoding="utf-8"?>
<mx:WindowedApplication xmlns:mx="http://www.adobe.com/2006/mxml"
  xmlns:vw="ecart.views.*"
  xmlns:business="ecart.business.*"
  layout="vertical"
  backgroundGradientAlphas="[1.0, 1.0]"
  backgroundGradientColors="[#9EDEFF, #1E648D]"
  creationComplete="initApp()">

  <mx:Script>
  <![CDATA[
    import ecart.commands.LoadProductsEvent;
    import ecart.model.CartModel;

    private function initApp():void
    {
      var event:LoadProductsEvent = new LoadProductsEvent();
      event.dispatch();
    }
  ]]>
  </mx:Script>
```

```
<business:CartController id="controller"/>
<business:Services id="services"/>

<mx:ViewStack width="100%" height="100%"
  selectedIndex="{CartModel.getInstance().viewIndex}">

  <vw:CartView width="100%" height="100%"/>
  <vw:AddItemView width="100%" height="100%"/>
</mx:ViewStack>

</mx:WindowedApplication>
```

To begin, the root tag `WindowedApplication` defines that this is the main file for the Adobe AIR application we are building. It sets some style information and declares two namespaces, `vw` and `business`, that are used to locate the views, controller, and services components in their respective packages. It also declares that when the `creationComplete` event fires, that it should execute the `initApp()` function defined in the `Script` block. This is done so that after the application is completely created, we can retrieve the list of products from our remote service. Therefore, in the `initApp()` function, we create an instance of the `LoadProductsEvent` event and dispatch it.

The middle portion declares the `CartController` and `Services` component, so that they are initialized by Adobe AIR upon application startup. Finally, the last portion defines a `ViewStack` component that contains the two subviews, `CartView` and `AddItemView`, which we will build in a moment. Notice also that the `selectedIndex` property of the `ViewStack` is binded (with the curly braces) to the `viewIndex` property of the `CartModel` class; if you recall, the various commands set the value of this property such that one of the two subviews is displayed.

> **NOTE**
>
> One of the reasons we can achieve loosely coupled components and classes is because of the binding mechanism available to us via the Adobe Flex framework. As demonstrated in this section, we can easily affect the value of some property (`selectedIndex`) on a component by binding it to a property (`viewIndex`) on our global model and have a class that is unknown to the view change the global property, thus altering the view.

CartView.mxml

Now it is time to look at the view that displays the list of items in the shopping cart. This is the main view the user will be looking at when the application starts. It is actually quite simple from a visual standpoint, but it has quite a few lines of code.

The view (shown in Figure 20.1) is composed of a main grid that shows the list of items, a button to allow the user to add a new item, and a label at the bottom of the grid displaying the grand total to be purchased. (Being a sample application, it actually does not contain any functionality to perform the actual purchase.)

FIGURE 20.1   The list of items in the shopping cart and the total amount to be purchased.

Now that we've briefly described what the view does and seen what it looks like, let's get into the details. (Some code is omitted for brevity in Listing 20.13.)

LISTING 20.13   The `CartView.mxml` Component Used to Display the List of Items in the Shopping Cart

```
<mx:VBox xmlns:mx="http://www.adobe.com/2006/mxml">
  <mx:Script>
  <![CDATA[
  ...
  [Bindable] private var model:CartModel = CartModel.getInstance();

  private function doPrepForAdd():void
  {
    var event:PrepAddCartEvent = new PrepAddCartEvent();
    event.dispatch();
  }
  ...
  private function displayProductName( item:Object, column:DataGridColumn ):String
  {
    return (item as CartItem).product.name;
  }

  private function displayGrandTotal( value:Number ):String
  {
    return ( isNaN(value) )
```

20

```
                ? "0"
                : numberFormatter.format( value );
        }
    ]]>
    </mx:Script>

    <mx:NumberFormatter id="numberFormatter" precision="2"/>

    <mx:Label fontSize="14"
            fontWeight="bold"
            text="eCart Store"/>

    <mx:Button id="addBtn" label="Add Item to Cart" click="doPrepForAdd()"/>

    <mx:DataGrid width="100%"
        resizableColumns="false"
        sortableColumns="false"
        dataProvider="{model.cartItems}">
        <mx:columns>
            <mx:DataGridColumn headerText="Product" labelFunction="displayProductName"/>
            <mx:DataGridColumn headerText="Quantity" dataField="quantity" width="65"/>
            <mx:DataGridColumn headerText="Unit Price" labelFunction="displayUnitPrice"
➥width="80"/>
            <mx:DataGridColumn headerText="Total" labelFunction="displayCost"
width="80"/>
        </mx:columns>
    </mx:DataGrid>

    <mx:HBox width="100%" horizontalAlign="right">
        <mx:Label id="totalLbl"
            fontSize="14"
            fontWeight="bold"
            color="#8D2130"
            text="Grand Total: ${displayGrandTotal(model.grandTotal)}"/>
    </mx:HBox>
</mx:VBox>
```

To begin, let's look at what the button to add an item does. It simply fires an instance of the PrepAddCartEvent event, which, in turn, calls the corresponding command to switch the ViewStack to now display the AddItemView view (refer to Listing 20.12).

Next, the DataGrid defines several columns for displaying information on the items in the cart, such as the product name, quantity, unit price, and total cost. The data is held in the cartItems property of the CartModel class and is bound to the dataProvider property of the grid. Thus, when items are added to the list, the grid is automatically refreshed.

Finally, the Label control, named totalLbl, displays the total purchase price, which is held in the grandTotal property defined in the CartModel class. You will notice that before the grandTotal value is displayed, it is passed the displayGrandTotal function (defined in the Script block) so that the value is properly formatted before it is displayed in the Label control.

AddItemView.mxml

Now we come to the final piece of the puzzle, the AddItemView subview. This subview (as seen in Figure 20.2) is basically a form containing two form elements that compose a shopping cart item, the product and quantity. It also contains two buttons: one to add the item to the cart and the other to cancel and return us to the CartView subview.

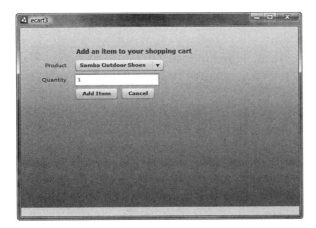

FIGURE 20.2   The AddItemView view, allowing the user to add an item to the shopping cart.

So, let's take a look at the form in question, and then we will focus on several aspects that are important to us. (Some code is omitted for brevity in Listing 20.14.)

LISTING 20.14   The Complete List of the AddItemView Component

```
<mx:Form xmlns:mx="http://www.adobe.com/2006/mxml"
  show="resetView()">

<mx:Script>
<![CDATA[

...
```

```
  private function resetView():void
  {
    products.selectedIndex = 0;
    quantity.text = "";
  }

  private function doCancel():void
  {
    var event:CancelAddEvent = new CancelAddEvent();
    event.dispatch();
  }

  private function doAdd():void
  {
    var item:CartItem = new CartItem();
    item.product = products.selectedItem as Product;
    item.quantity = int( quantity.text );

    var event:AddItemEvent = new AddItemEvent();
    event.item = item;
    event.dispatch();
  }
  ]]>
</mx:Script>

<mx:FormHeading fontWeight="bold" fontSize="12">
  <mx:label>Add an item to your shopping cart</mx:label>
</mx:FormHeading>
<mx:FormItem label="Product">
  <mx:ComboBox id="products" labelField="name"
    dataProvider="{CartModel.getInstance().products}"/>
</mx:FormItem>
<mx:FormItem label="Quantity">
  <mx:TextInput id="quantity" restrict="0-9"/>
</mx:FormItem>
<mx:FormItem direction="horizontal">
  <mx:Button label="Add Item" click="doAdd()"/>
  <mx:Button label="Cancel" click="doCancel()"/>
</mx:FormItem>
</mx:Form>
```

First, let's look at the products combo box, which is used to display the list of products we can purchase. Notice that, once again, we are using data binding to populate the combo box dataProvider property from the products property of the CartModel class, demonstrating once again the concept of loose coupling, which is advocated by the Cairngorm framework. Another way to look at this is that the view has no idea how the list of products is going to be retrieved—it simply knows that it can find it on the `products` property of the `CartModel` class.

Next up are the two buttons used to cancel the action of adding an item or to actually add an item to the shopping cart. When the button labeled *Cancel* is clicked, the `doCancel()` function is called, which, in turn, creates an instance of the `CancelAddEvent` class and fires it off. When the button labeled *Add Item* is clicked, the `doAdd()` function is called. In the `doAdd()` function, two steps are executed: First, a `CartItem` object is created with appropriate values and, second, an instance of the `AddItemEvent` class is created and the `CartItem` object is passed to it before it is dispatched. In the case of both buttons, after the event is fired, the corresponding command classes are executed and appropriate logic is performed (see Listings 20.9 and 20.10 for details).

One final thing to observe is that every time this form is shown, the `resetView()` function is called, such that the two form fields are set to their default values so that the user can begin entering the desired data.

> **TIP**
>
> You might have noticed throughout this chapter that depending on the class or component that was being built, we applied a certain naming convention to the name of the class or component. This is a simple case of helping code readability, and although it is not necessary, it is recommended. Therefore, events, commands, views, and models are suffixed with the words *Event*, *Cmd*, *View*, and *Model*, respectively.

Summary

Lots of keystrokes have been spent in this chapter writing the code for the electronic shopping cart application. But those keystrokes have been spent wisely. By using the Cairngorm microarchitecture framework, we have built this Adobe AIR application out of individual classes and components that are unaware of each other.

We have seen that the view components make use of only the model and by referring to it, they can display data in any fashion. The command classes, on the other hand, know of this model as well, and by manipulating it, they can affect changes in the views. The two (views and commands) are indirectly connected together by way of a `FrontController` that responds to application events fired by the views, which, in turn, executes the appropriate command. Finally, an abstract remote communication layer consisting of a delegate and `ServiceLocator` was built to simplify the interaction of server-side calls from the commands.

This loosely coupled model-view-controller framework that is at the heart of Cairngorm is what allows developers to easily build and maintain Adobe AIR applications of varying size and scope.

20

PART VI

Agile Development with Adobe AIR

IN THIS PART

CHAPTER 21

Creating a Build Process

In today's world of short development life cycles, automation is the key. The first step in the automation process is the build tool you will use to compile and package your application and execute the very important unit tests that will help maintain your application's quality at a high level.

> **NOTE**
>
> Writing and executing unit tests for Adobe® AIR™ applications built with Adobe® Flex™ is actually a whole topic in itself, so we will cover that in depth in the next chapter.

Build tools are nothing new; they have been around for quite a while. One of the most popular back in the day was *make*, the UNIX build tool used by C/C++ developers to compile their applications. *Make*, however, had its limitations and, thus, a gentleman named James Duncan Davidson created an open source build tool called Ant, which has since found a home over at the Apache Foundation and become very popular with developers worldwide.

The reason for Ant's success is twofold: portability and extensibility. Unlike *make*, Ant is Java-based and, thus, portable across operating systems. And also unlike *make*, Ant can be extended—thus, developers have been adding new capabilities to fit various needs and adapt to new technologies such as Adobe Flex and Adobe AIR.

Based on these capabilities, Apache Ant is the perfect build tool to use for Adobe AIR applications. This chapter shows you everything you need to know about Apache Ant to build, run, and export your Adobe AIR application by creating a sample build script from scratch and showing you all the little details.

Installing Apache Ant

Before you can actually get to the point of using Ant to compile, build, and export your Adobe AIR application, you have to do some setup work, so the following sections detail how to get started.

> **CAUTION**
>
> Make sure you have JDK version 1.4.2 or higher installed before proceeding.

Downloading and Configuring Apache Ant

To use Apache Ant, the first thing you need to do is get it. So fire up your favorite web browser and follow these steps:

1. Go to the Apache Ant website: http://ant.apache.org/.
2. From the menu on the left side, click on Binary Distributions.
3. Under the Current Release of Ant heading, select the archive to download based on your operating system, and save it to a location of your choice on your computer (see Figure 21.1).
4. Create a folder called **opt** from the root of your hard drive (for example, C:\opt).
5. Extract the contents of the archive to the opt folder.
6. Create a new environment variable called ANT_HOME that points to the location where you installed Ant (for example, C:\opt\apache-ant-1.6.5).
7. Add Apache Ant's bin folder to your command path (for example, C:\opt\ apache-ant-1.6.5\bin).

Downloading and Installing Adobe Flex Ant Tasks

Now that you have Apache Ant installed, you need to download a custom extension built by Adobe. This custom extension contains customized Ant tasks that will be used to compile your Adobe Flex source code. Follow these steps:

1. Go to this website: http://labs.adobe.com/wiki/index.php/Flex_Ant_Tasks.
2. Scroll down to the section called Installation and download the Adobe Flex Ant Tasks Zip file and save it to a location of your choice on your computer.
3. Extract from the archive the flexTasks.jar file and copy it to Apache Ant's lib folder (for example, C:\opt\apache-ant-1.6.5\lib).

Now that we have downloaded and configured both Apache Ant and the Adobe Flex Ant tasks, we are ready to get started and actually write our build script.

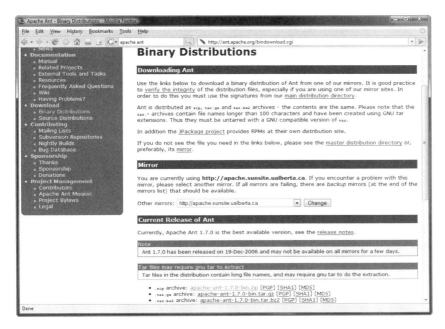

FIGURE 21.1   A view of the Apache Ant Binary Distributions page. Notice the download links at the bottom.

> **NOTE**
>
> The Adobe Flex Ant tasks are not necessary if the main source content for Adobe AIR application is HTML-based.

Creating Your Project's `build.xml`

The way Apache Ant works is by reading an Extensible Markup Language (XML) build file that contains all the instructions required to execute various tasks related to a project. In the case of an Adobe AIR project, the main task is compiling the Adobe Flex source code. Other tasks include running the application, exporting the application, and much more. So let's get started.

Begin by creating the `build.xml` in the root folder of your project and filling it up with the following skeleton that we will complete as we go along.

```
<project name="myproject" basedir="." default="build">

    <!— init target —>
    <target name="init">
        <property name="CONFIG_FOLDER" value="${basedir}/config"/>
        <property name="BUILD_FOLDER" value="${basedir}/build"/>
```

```
    <property name="FLEX_HOME" value="C:/Program Files/Adobe/Flex Builder 3
➡Plug-in/sdks/3.0.0"/>
        <property name="ADL" value="${FLEX_HOME}/bin/adl.exe"/>
        <property name="ADT" value="${FLEX_HOME}/lib/adt.jar"/>

        <taskdef resource="flexTasks.tasks" classpath="d:/opt/apache-ant-1.6.5/lib"/>
    </target>

    <!— target to compile our flex source code —>
    <target name="build" depends="init">
    </target>

    <!— execute the application —>
    <target name="runapp" depends="init">
    </target>

    <!— package the application for distribution —>
    <target name="export" depends="init">
    </target>
</project>
```

As you can see, we have a good base to start with. We have defined the project's working directory and the default target—the build target—which is the one that will be executed the most.

Next, the init target is the primary target, which all the other targets depend upon because of the setup work that is performed. It has two parts: first setting up properties that will be needed (refer to Table 21.1), and second loading Adobe Flex Ant task definitions from the flexTasks.jar, which we downloaded earlier.

Now that we have performed the initial setup work, we are ready to start the real work.

TABLE 21.1   Description of Ant Build Properties

Property	Value/Description
FLEX_HOME	Points to the location of the Adobe Flex 3 software development kit (SDK)
CONFIG_FOLDER	Points to the location of your project's configuration folder; this folder should contain your Adobe AIR application's descriptor file and the certificate used to sign your Adobe AIR application
BUILD_FOLDER	Points to the location of your project's build folder where the application .air distribution file will be created
ADL	Points to the location of the adl.exe, which will be used to execute your Adobe AIR application
ADT	Point to the location of the adt.exe, which will be used to create the .air distribution file

Compiling Your Adobe AIR Application

The most important part of delivering an application is taking all that source code and compiling it into a distributable application that can be executed and used by an end user. For an Adobe AIR application, this means taking the ActionScript classes (`.as`) and MXML component files (`.mxml`) and compiling them using the Adobe Flex compiler, thus resulting in a binary Shockwave Flash (SWF) file that will be executed by Adobe AIR.

> **NOTE**
>
> Although not covered in this book, Adobe AIR applications can also be created using traditional web technologies such as Hypertext Markup Language (HTML), JavaScript, and Asynchronous JavaScript and XML (AJAX). In that case, compiling is not required and this step can be omitted from your project's Ant build script.

Compiler Background Information

The Adobe Flex 3 compiler is actually located in your SDK's lib folder in the `mxmlc.jar` file.

That is because the Adobe Flex 3 compiler is actually written in Java and distributed in a Java Archive (JAR) file, which makes it a great fit for working with Ant.

The compiler needs a single entry point to compile your Adobe AIR application, be it either an ActionScript class or an MXML component file—the latter is almost always the case. After obtaining this information, the compiler links in all dependent files and generates the resulting binary SWF file.

> **NOTE**
>
> Actually, MXML component files are converted into ActionScript classes prior to the compilation process. To see the ActionScript classes generated, refer to the Adobe Flex 3 SDK documentation and the `keep-generated-actionscript` compiler option.

There are various ways to execute and use the compiler on your projects. One method is to have it execute automatically during the development process, which is possible by using Adobe Flex Builder. You can also execute it via the command line by using the `mxmlc` executable located in the Adobe Flex SDK's bin folder. The `mxmlc` executable is there to facilitate the execution of the compiler without having to write out a long command-line statement and without having to set up a classpath.

> **NOTE**
>
> When using Adobe Flex Builder, the compiler is executed after every file save operation. Thus, for performance reasons, the compiler is executed by Adobe Flex Builder using the `incremental` option set to `true`.

Writing the build Target

Now let's get to the real meat by writing the build target, which will be used to compile the source code for our Adobe AIR application. Basically what we want to do is twofold: First create the build folder where we will place the binary SWF file that will be generated, and second, actually run the compiler on our Adobe AIR application's main file called myapp.mxml. Here is the actual code for the target:

```
<!— target to compile our flex source code —>
<target name="build" depends="init">
   <mkdir dir="${BUILD_FOLDER}"/>

   <mxmlc file="${basedir}/src/myapp.mxml"
      output="${BUILD_FOLDER}/myapp.swf">

      <load-config filename="${FLEX_HOME}/frameworks/air-config.xml"/>
      <source-path path-element="${FLEX_HOME}/frameworks"/>
      <compiler.library-path dir="${FLEX_HOME}/frameworks" append="true">
         <include name="libs" />
         <include name="../bundles/{locale}" />
      </compiler.library-path>
   </mxmlc>
</target>
```

Now let's review what the build task is actually doing for us. Creating the build folder is the easy part by using the <mkdir /> task and using the previously set BUILD_FOLDER property. Next, we actually run the compiler using the <mxmlc /> task. Remember, this task is not part of the standard set that comes with Ant; it is available to us because we imported the Adobe Flex Ant tasks, as explained earlier.

As you can see from the previous example, we need to specify various options when using the mxmlc task, allowing us to control the generated SWF file. One way to specify the compiler options is to put them in a compiler config file and then reference it, as we do in the example using the load-config option. (The air-config.xml file is the default one supplied with the Adobe Flex 3 SDK.) Then, you can override or specify additional options directly by using the mxmlc task, as we are doing here for some options.

The file and output options specify the file to compile and the name of the resulting binary SWF file and its location. Next, the source-path element allows us to add the SDK's frameworks folder to the compiler's source path. You add as many folders as you need here depending on if you have spread your source code in different folders. Finally, the library-path option allows us to specify additional folders where the compiler can look to find Shockwave Component (SWC) files to link in required ActionScript classes by your Adobe AIR application. It also allows the compiler to locate any resource bundles that are required to be included as well. (Typically, these are text files with a .properties extension containing name-value pair entries.)

> **NOTE**
>
> SWC files are redistributable archives containing ActionScript classes and other files that can be used in any Adobe AIR application. These can be generated by yourself to support your many applications or can be acquired from a third-party author.
>
> For a complete list of `mxmlc` compiler options, please refer to the Adobe Flex 3 "Developer's Guide."

Running Your Adobe AIR Application

Now that we have actually compiled our Adobe AIR application, we will want to take it out for a test drive. To do this during the development cycle, we don't actually need Adobe AIR to be installed; we can simply use the Adobe AIR Debug Launcher (ADL).

For developers using Adobe Flex Builder, a simple icon click allows them to launch an Adobe AIR application with the ADL. To do this in our Ant build script, we will need a couple of lines of code, but it is not that much more complicated. So let's get right to it:

```
<target name="runapp" depends="init">
   <copy file="${CONFIG_FOLDER}/myapp-app.xml"
      tofile="${BUILD_FOLDER}/myapp-app.xml"/>

   <exec executable="${ADL}">
      <arg value="${BUILD_FOLDER}/myapp-app.xml"/>
   </exec>
</target>
```

As you can see, that is pretty easy! We execute the Adobe AIR Debug Launcher via the ADT command (referenced in the build script by the $ADL property) by simply using Ant's exec task. The ADT command takes one mandatory parameter, the Adobe AIR application descriptor file, to launch the application. You will notice, of course, before the launch of the application, we copied the application descriptor file to the build folder from the config folder. This is required because the ADT command requires the application descriptor file to be in the same folder as the compiled Adobe AIR application's main file, in this case the `myapp.swf` file.

> **NOTE**
>
> For details on the optional parameters for the Adobe AIR Debug Launcher, please refer to the Adobe AIR documentation.

Exporting Your Adobe AIR Application

Now, we get to the final part of the Ant build script: the export. Exporting your Adobe AIR application (that's what Adobe Flex Builder calls it) can be looked upon as the packaging of the application. Basically, you now need to take the new toy you just created, put it in a box with some accessories and perhaps a manual, and make it available for public consumption. I guess that is the best anecdote for what you need to do. Basically, this boils down to creating a distributable archive that will normally be downloaded from a website and will, in turn, launch the installation of your Adobe AIR application on an end user's computer.

The actual distributable archive will have an .air extension, which allows Adobe AIR to recognize it and launch the installation process on an end user's computer.

TIP

Although the typical method of distribution for an Adobe AIR application is to download it from a website, it can also be put on a CD or use any other means of delivery. It is up to you to decide how your end users will be able to get access to it.

So let's first show the export target and then we will explain the details:

```
<target name="export" depends="init">
    <java jar="${ADT}" fork="true" failonerror="true">
        <arg value="-package"/>
        <arg value="-storetype"/>
        <arg value="PKCS12"/>
        <arg value="-keystore"/>
        <arg value="${CONFIG_FOLDER}/certFile.pfx"/>
        <arg value="-storepass"/>
        <arg value="mypassword"/>
        <arg value="${BUILD_FOLDER}/myapp.air"/>
        <arg value="${CONFIG_FOLDER}/myapp-app.xml"/>
        <arg value="-C"/>
        <arg value="${BUILD_FOLDER}"/>
        <arg value="myapp.swf"/>
    </java>
</target>
```

To create the distributable archive, we are making use of the Adobe AIR Developer Tool (ADT). Like the Adobe Flex Compiler, the ADT is Java-based and is thus found within the adt.jar (referenced here by the $ADT property) in the Adobe Flex 3 SDK's lib folder. Unlike the Adobe Flex Compiler, however, there is no convenient Ant task that is provided to us, so we have to use Ant's java task to execute the ADT.

As you can see, the ADT command takes several parameters, from the input and output files to the signing information. Table 21.2 describes all the parameters. The storetype, keystore, and storepass parameters are required because all .air archives must be signed with a digital certificate. You can either use code-signed certificates from the VeriSign or Thawte certificate authorities or use a self-signed certificate.

TABLE 21.2   ADT Parameter Descriptions for Exporting

Parameter	Value/Description
-package	None
-storetype	The type of certificate; either PKCS12 or 1024-RSA
-keystore	The location of the certificate itself (with a .pfx extension)
-storepass	The password associated with the certificate
output file	The name of the .air distributable archive to create
app descriptor	The location and name of the Adobe AIR application descriptor file
-C	The working folder to use
input files/folders	The name of the SWF file to include

The working folder (specified with the –C parameter) is where the ADT command will create the .air distributable archive. After the last parameter, you can continue to specify additional files and/or folders (such as assets, third-party SWC files, or data files) to be included in the archive.

NOTE

Like the Adobe Flex 3 compiler, the Adobe AIR Developer Tool has a utility command (conveniently named adt) located in the SDK's bin folder that allows you to run it via the command line with the same parameters as just described.

Creating a Self-Signed Certificate for Testing

At times, you might find yourself needing to test the creation of your .air distributable file. And, during these times, you might not have the final certificate available. In this case, you can create a self-signed certificate and use that during the export process for testing.

The ADT not only allows you to create your application's .air archive, but also allows you to create a self-signed certificate for testing purposes. So, for our example, we will create another optional target in our Ant build file that we can use to create a certificate in our application's config folder. Here is the target code:

```
<target name="createcert" depends="init">
   <java jar="${ADT}" fork="true" failonerror="true">
      <arg value="-certificate"/>
      <arg value="-cn"/>
      <arg value="SelfSign"/>
      <arg value="-ou"/>
      <arg value="Testing"/>
      <arg value="-o"/>
      <arg value="Example, Co"/>
```

```
        <arg value="-c"/>
        <arg value="US"/>
        <arg value="2048-RSA"/>
        <arg value="${CONFIG_FOLDER}/certFile.pfx"/>
        <arg value="mypassword"/>
    </java>
</target>
```

The way we execute the ADT command is exactly as we did before to export our application. The only difference here is that the parameters we pass to the ADT command are completely different, so they are explained in Table 21.3.

TABLE 21.3   ADT Parameter Descriptions for Creating a Self-Signed Certificate

Parameter	Value/Description
-certificate	None
-cn	The certificate name
-ou	The organizational unit to which the certificate belongs
-o	The organization to which the certificate belongs; can be the same as the organizational unit
-c	The country in which the organization operates
key-type	The certificate key type
pfx-file	The location and name of the certificate file to create
password	The password to associate with the certificate

Project's Final `build.xml`

After all that hard work, we now have a complete Ant build script for our Adobe AIR application. The Ant build script contains the three major operations to be performed: build, run, and export. It also contains an optional target for creating a self-signed certificate for development testing purposes.

Listing 21.1 shows the complete Ant script.

LISTING 21.1   Full Listing of `build.xml`

```
<project name="myproject" basedir="." default="build">


    <target name="init">
        <property name="CONFIG_FOLDER" value="${basedir}/config"/>
        <property name="BUILD_FOLDER" value="${basedir}/build"/>
        <property name="FLEX_HOME" value="C:/Program Files/Adobe/Flex Builder 3
Plug-in/sdks/3.0.0"/>
```

```xml
        <property name="ADL" value="${FLEX_HOME}/bin/adl.exe"/>
        <property name="ADT" value="${FLEX_HOME}/lib/adt.jar"/>

        <taskdef resource="flexTasks.tasks" classpath="d:/opt/apache-ant-1.6.5/lib"/>
    </target>

    <target name="build" depends="init">
        <mkdir dir="${BUILD_FOLDER}"/>

        <mxmlc file="${basedir}/src/myapp.mxml"
            output="${BUILD_FOLDER}/myapp.swf">

            <load-config filename="${FLEX_HOME}/frameworks/air-config.xml"/>
            <source-path path-element="${FLEX_HOME}/frameworks"/>
            <compiler.library-path dir="${FLEX_HOME}/frameworks" append="true">
                <include name="libs" />
                <include name="../bundles/{locale}" />
            </compiler.library-path>
        </mxmlc>
    </target>

    <target name="runapp" depends="init">
        <copy file="${CONFIG_FOLDER}/myapp-app.xml"
            tofile="${BUILD_FOLDER}/myapp-app.xml"/>

        <exec executable="${ADL}">
            <arg value="${BUILD_FOLDER}/myapp-app.xml"/>
        </exec>
    </target>

    <target name="export" depends="init">
        <java jar="${ADT}" fork="true" failonerror="true">
            <arg value="-package"/>
            <arg value="-storetype"/>
            <arg value="PKCS12"/>
            <arg value="-keystore"/>
            <arg value="${CONFIG_FOLDER}/certFile.pfx"/>
            <arg value="-storepass"/>
            <arg value="mypassword"/>
            <arg value="${BUILD_FOLDER}/myapp.air"/>
            <arg value="${CONFIG_FOLDER}/myapp-app.xml"/>
            <arg value="-C"/>
            <arg value="${BUILD_FOLDER}"/>
            <arg value="myapp.swf"/>
        </java>
    </target>
```

```
<target name="createcert" depends="init">
  <java jar="${ADT}" fork="true" failonerror="true">
    <arg value="-certificate"/>
    <arg value="-cn"/>
    <arg value="SelfSign"/>
    <arg value="-ou"/>
    <arg value="Testing"/>
    <arg value="-o"/>
    <arg value="Example, Co"/>
    <arg value="-c"/>
    <arg value="US"/>
    <arg value="2048-RSA"/>
    <arg value="${CONFIG_FOLDER}/certFile.pfx"/>
    <arg value="mypassword"/>
  </java>
</target>
</project>
```

Running Your `build.xml`

Now that we have our build script, what do we do? Run it, of course! So open up a console window, switch to the project directory (`D:\dev\myapp` for this example), and let's get cracking!

Compiling

As you can see, we launched Ant from the command line and it found our `build.xml` file and ran the default `build` target (see Figure 21.2). The `init` target was actually executed first as it is a dependency of the `build` target. After the `mxmlc` compiler is run, it uses the Adobe AIR compiler configuration file we specified and creates the resulting SWF file also showing the size.

Running

Now, we launch Ant and pass it a parameter, the target that we want to execute, in this case the `runapp` target. Ant, in turn, launches the ADL, which runs our Adobe AIR application; the main window is shown in Figure 21.3. You can notice that the build script hasn't yet completed—this is because the ADL is running our Adobe AIR application, so after we close the application, the Ant build script completes and, as a result, the command prompt is displayed.

Exporting

As before, we launch the Ant build script specifying the target to run, this time the `export` target. Pretty simple: The ADT is executed and it generates the `.air` distributable archive, and the full path and filename are displayed (see Figure 21.4).

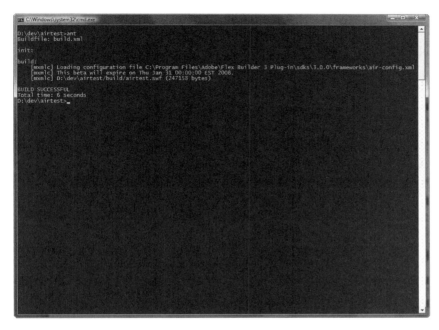

FIGURE 21.2   Using our Apache Ant build script to compile our Adobe AIR application.

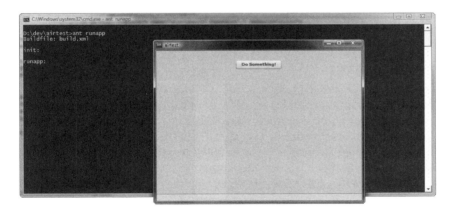

FIGURE 21.3   Enjoying the fruits of our labor, running our Adobe AIR application.

FIGURE 21.4   Final step, creating the `.air` distributable archive.

Anatomy of an `.air` Distributable Archive

One common characteristic among developers is curiosity. We all want to know how things work. And, thus, you are probably wondering what magic materials are in that `.air` archive? Actually, not much. The `.air` archive is, in reality, just a compressed archive file, much like a Zip file. So, in Windows, for example, you can use WinZip to open up and look at the contents of the `.air` archive. Based on our sample Ant build script, the contents will look like so:

```
/myapp.swf
/mimetype
/META-INF/signatures.xml
/META-INF/AIR/application.xml
```

As you can see, the compiled `myapp.swf` file is in the root folder as well as a file named `mimetype`, which, as its name implies, contains mimetype information for this archive. If we had included more files/folders in the archive, they would be included at the root level. Finally, the META-INF subfolder contains two XML files: The `signatures.xml` file contains certificate information we used to sign the archive, and the `application.xml` file is basically the renamed application descriptor file.

Summary

In this chapter, we have taken our Adobe AIR application and made it part of a bigger world. It is now part of our automated build process using the Apache Ant build tool. Using Apache Ant, we have successfully executed the three main tasks of any build cycle, which are to compile, run, and export our Adobe AIR application. We have done so using a familiar, proven, and flexible build tool, which also allows us to integrate with our server-side build process, resulting in a single build process for both our client-side and server-side code.

Finally, the work we have just accomplished is the basis for our next topic of discussion in the automation process: unit testing, which is covered in detail in the next chapter.

# CHAPTER 22

Incorporating Unit Testing

With short release cycles, it is important not to compromise your application's quality because even the smallest of changes can cause a critical bug.

Thus, with small development cycles, quick testing is the key. The Agile software development process states that you should break down an application into the smallest possible pieces and associate a test to each of them. So every piece of code is referred to as a unit, and every unit of code has an associated unit test. So, you typically code a little, test a little, and repeat until your work is done. Or the even better approach is to write the unit test first, run it to confirm it fails, and then write the code that will make the test pass.

So, in this chapter, we show you everything you need to know about creating unit tests for your Adobe® AIR™ applications and, more important, how to incorporate those into your Apache Ant build script so you can easily execute the tests and automate the testing process on a nightly basis.

Introducing FlexUnit

Writing unit tests is much like writing the application code itself. The difference with unit tests is that you need a specialized framework to execute them. In the case of Adobe AIR applications written with Adobe® Flex™, the framework used is called FlexUnit. For those of you who come from a Java development background, you are accustomed to using the JUnit framework to run your unit tests, thus you will notice an uncanny resemblance with FlexUnit. This is because the guys who created FlexUnit have a Java development background as well. One main difference is that in its default mode of operation, FlexUnit runs as an Adobe AIR application and displays the test results in a graphical manner. We will see in the second part of this chapter how to run it via Apache Ant and get a better level of integration with the rest of our automation process.

Downloading FlexUnit

As with many things in life, before we get to the real fun stuff, we first need to do some work. In our case, this entails downloading FlexUnit itself. So once again, please fire up your favorite web browser and follow these steps:

1. Go to the FlexUnit website: http://code.google.com/p/as3flexunitlib/.
2. From the top navigation bar, click on Downloads.
3. From the list of files displayed, download the latest version of the FlexUnit archive, and save it to a location of your choice on your computer.
4. Extract the contents of the downloaded archive to a temporary folder (for example: C:\temp).
5. Finally, copy the `flexunit.swc` file located in `C:\temp\flexunit\bin` to the folder where you typically save third-party libraries (for example, `C:\lib`).

TIP

The files you will extract from the FlexUnit archive contain a lot more than simply the Shockwave Component (SWC) binary. It contains the source code, so you can enhance the framework if you need to, and it contains the reference documentation, which is handy from time to time.

Downloading FlexUnit Ant Tasks

The work is not done, however. After we actually write our unit tests, we need to integrate them into our build process via Apache Ant. To do so, we need a special Ant task and a third-party Adobe Flex library created by Adobe consultant Peter Martin, so here is how to get them:

1. Go to the following website: http://weblogs.macromedia.com/pmartin/archives/2006/06/flexunit_ant.cfm.
2. Scroll down to the end of the blog post (see Figure 22.1) and download both the `FlexAntTasks-src.zip` and `FlexUnitOptional-src.zip` files and save them to a location of your choice on your computer.
3. Extract the contents of the `FlexAntTasks-src.zip` to a temporary folder (for example: C:\temp).
4. Copy the `FlexAntTask.jar` file located in C:\temp\FlexAntTasks\dist to the folder where you typically save third-party libraries (for example, `C:\lib`).
5. Extract the contents of the `FlexUnitOptional-src.zip` to a temporary folder (for example: C:\temp).

6. Copy the `FlexUnitOptional.swc` file located in `C:\temp\FlexUnitOptional\dist` to the folder where you typically save third-party libraries (for example, `C:\lib`).

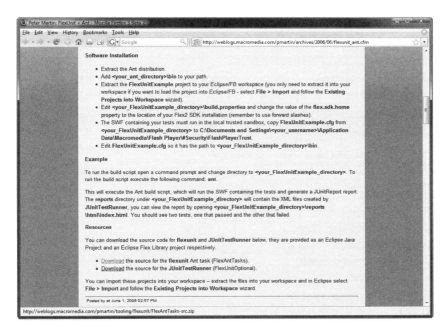

FIGURE 22.1   A view of the download links for `FlexAntTasks` and `FlexUnitOptional` from Peter Martin's blog, an Adobe consultant.

That is basically all you need to get started. If you are using Flex Builder to do your development work, you can add the `flexunit.swc`, `FlexUnitOptional.swc`, and `FlexAntTask.jar` to your project's classpath and start writing your test case, which is what we do next.

Creating a Test Case

Writing a test case is just as simple as writing any ActionScript class. Basically, it is a class that will test the functionality of a class that is used within your application. You do this by passing the various methods of the application's class some sample input data to which you know the output. By knowing the output, you can then write some assertion statements to test that those methods are indeed generating the correct output.

To get started, we will write a test case for our `CartItemImpl` ActionScript class, which is a value object holding the count of many items of a particular product we are purchasing.

The main method we want to test is the read-only cost property, which does a calculation. Here is what that test case will look like:

```
package tests
{
    import ecart.CartItemImpl;
    import ecart.ICartItem;
    import ecart.IProduct;
    import ecart.ProductImpl;

    import flexunit.framework.TestCase;

    public class TestCartItem extends TestCase
    {
        public function TestCartItem() {
        }

        public function testCost():void {
            var product:IProduct = new ProductImpl();
            product.name = "Nike Shoes";
            product.price = 59.99;

            var item:ICartItem = new CartItemImpl();
            item.product = product;
            item.quantity = 2;

            try {
                assertEquals( item.cost, (59.99 * 2) );
            }
            catch( e:Error ) {
                fail( "testCost() failed: " + e );
            }
        }
    }
}
```

As you can see, our test case is very simple. But let's go through all the basics to make sure we understand how things work—before we add some complexity. The first thing you will notice is that our test case extends the TestCase class that is part of the FlexUnit framework—this is mandatory so that the framework will actually execute the test case. Next, you will notice that the test case is composed of a no-arguments constructor and a no-arguments method called testCost().We want to concentrate on the testCost() method.

Within the testCost() method, we are creating some sample data that we need for our test. First, we create a product instance with a fictional name and price. Then, we actually create an instance of a cart item, assign it the product we just created, and specify the quantity of the product that we want to purchase. The next line in the method is the one that concerns us the most. This is where we actually test that the read-only cost property of the cart item class is doing its job. We are making an assertion, comparing that two values are indeed equal; in this case, we are comparing that the value of the cost property is equal to our own calculation. If the values are equal, then the test will be successful and will be recorded as such by the FlexUnit framework; otherwise, it will be recorded as a failed test.

NOTE

In this example, we only used the `assertEquals()` assertion statement. There are, however, several assertion statements available to handle different testing scenarios, most notably `assertTrue()` and `assertNotNull()`. For a complete list, refer to the FlexUnit documentation.

One final thing to note is that the assertion statement is actually wrapped in a `try/catch` block, allowing us to deal with any error that might be thrown and purposely fail the test ourselves. And although our test case here is simple, it is good practice to code it this way to prepare you for dealing with those unexpected errors in more complex testing scenarios.

TIP

In some test cases, you might actually want to catch an error because you are expecting it to be thrown. If this is the case, make the call to fail the test as the last statement in the `try` block, and after you catch the error, simply do nothing. Here is a small example:

```
try {
    ... do something here that will throw an error ...
    fail( "testCost() failed to throw an error" );
}
catch( e:Error ) {
    // all good, do nothing
}
```

Naming Conventions

One thing you might have noticed from the code sample is that there are certain naming conventions you will need to adhere to so that the FlexUnit framework can do its work. First, the name of the test class needs to be prefixed with the word *Test* (must start with an uppercase *T* as per ActionScript class-naming standards). So, if you are writing a test case class for the `CartItem` class, your test class will be called `TestCartItem`. Second, all test method names within the test case class need to be prefixed with the word *test*. So, if you want to test the cost property of the `CartItem` class, the test method name would be `testCost`. (This naming convention for method names is referred to as camel case.)

> **NOTE**
>
> In addition to the naming convention you must adhere to for the method names, you must also remember that they must have public scope. Only test methods with public scope are executed by the FlexUnit framework.

Implementing the `setUp()` and `tearDown()` Methods

In our first test case example, we had only one test method, but the norm is to have several. Because of this, you will likely use the same sample data in the various test methods over and over again. As a good developer, you want to avoid recoding the sample data over and over again, so the FlexUnit framework has a provision for this. The `TestCase` class, which is extended by all test cases, contains two utility methods for exactly this purpose: `setUp()` and `tearDown()`. You can override the `setup()` method in your test case and create all relevant sample test data required by each of the test methods within the test case. You can override the `tearDown()` method as well and use it as a simple means to perform some cleanup.

If we had used the `setUp()` and `tearDown()` methods in our first example, it would look something like this (some code has been omitted for brevity):

```
package tests
{
    ...
    public class TestCartItem extends TestCase
    {
        private var product:IProduct;
        private var item:ICartItem;
        ...
        public override function setUp():void {
            product = new ProductImpl();
            product.name = "Nike Shoes";
            product.price = 59.99;

            item = new CartItemImpl();
            item.product = product;
            item.quantity = 2;
        }

        public override function tearDown():void {
            product = null;
            item = null;
        }

        public function testCost():void {
            try {
                assertEquals( item.cost, (59.99 * 2) );
```

```
        }
        catch( e:Error ) {
            fail( "testCost() failed: " + e );
        }
    }
  }
}
```

As you can now see, we have declared the variables representing our sample data at the class level. Next, we overrode the `setUp()` method to create our sample data, used the sample data in our test method, and, finally, performed some cleanup in the `tearDown()` method, which we overrode as well. The actual cleanup we are doing is to dereference the variables from the actual data to assist the garbage collector in its work.

NOTE

The `setUp()` and `tearDown()` methods are actually executed by the FlexUnit framework before and after every call to a test method within the test case class.

Running Your Test Case

Now that we have written our test case, we obviously want to run it and see it in action. There are two ways to execute a test case or test cases for that matter: by running them as an Adobe AIR application or by executing them via Apache Ant. However, before we get to that, we need to discuss test suites, and then we demonstrate how to execute our test case as an Adobe AIR application; the last section of this chapter shows how to run them via Apache Ant because it involves more work.

Adding Your Test Case to a Test Suite

So far, we have only had one test case class, `TestCartItem`. In a real-life situation, though, you will be writing several test cases and will want all of them to be executed by FlexUnit's test runner. However, we don't want to have to run every test case one-by-one via the test runner; we want to run them all together, like a suite of tests, or better yet, like a test suite. Yes, FlexUnit has the concept of a test suite.

A test suite allows us to take a set of test cases, make them part of a group, and pass them on to FlexUnit's test runner. So, let's make our test case part of a test suite to see what that looks like:

```
package tests
{
    import flexunit.framework.TestSuite;

    public class AllEcartTests {
```

```
        public static function suite():TestSuite {
            var suite:TestSuite = new TestSuite();
            suite.addTestSuite( TestCartItem );
            return suite;
        }
    }
}
```

As you can see, not much is happening; it is a simple class with a single static method returning an instance of a TestSuite. Inside the static method, we create an instance of a TestSuite, add our unit test to it, and then return the instance. The TestSuite instance will then be used by FlexUnit's test runner to execute all the associated test cases, which we take a look at shortly.

One thing that might seem odd is that we are using the addTestSuite() method on the TestSuite class instead of the addTest() method to add our test case to the suite. This is because the addTestSuite() method takes a class as its one sole parameter. So it can either be a TestCase or TestSuite class, and it will take care of instantiating the class appropriately and running all tests contained within. If you use the addTest() method, you must create an instance of your test case class and then pass it to the method itself, so you can save yourself some work by using the addTestSuite() method. After all, one of the most important attributes for being a great developer is speed. This also allows you to subdivide and better manage your test cases by grouping them into various test suites and then adding all the test suites to an über test suite that will be executed by FlexUnit's test runner.

Creating a Visual Test Case Runner

So far, we have created two pieces to this testing puzzle: the test case and the test suite. The final piece is to code the test runner and see the results. Coding the test runner isn't any harder than what we have done so far, so let's get right to it:

```
<mx:WindowedApplication xmlns:mx="http://www.adobe.com/2006/mxml"
    xmlns:flexunit="flexunit.flexui.*"
    creationComplete="initApp()">

    <mx:Script>
    <![CDATA[
        import tests.AllEcartTests;

        private function initApp():void {
            testRunner.test = AllEcartTests.suite();
            testRunner.startTest();
        }
    ]]>
    </mx:Script>
```

```
<flexunit:TestRunnerBase id="testRunner" width="100%" height="100%"/>
```

```
</mx:WindowedApplication>
```

Here, we created a brand-new Adobe AIR application in a file called `EcartTestRunner.mxml`. The application contains only one component, an instance of the `TestRunnerBase` component that is supplied with the FlexUnit's framework; it's the one that will take our test suite and run all the tests contained within it. The actual execution of the tests occurs after the application is created. As you can see from the example, we run the `initApp()` method after the `creationComplete` event is fired and in that method, we pass the test runner the reference to our test suite and then tell it to start running the tests. We end up with something similar to what is shown in Figure 22.2.

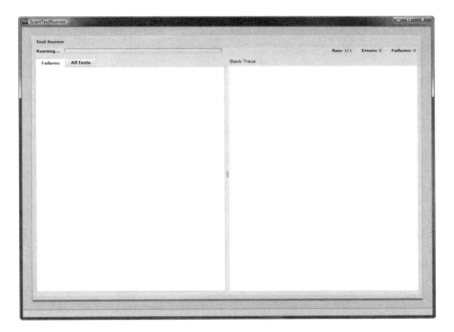

FIGURE 22.2 Using FlexUnit to run our first unit test with successful results.

As you can see, the interface for the visual test runner is simple and to the point. You get an immediate visual queue with the green bar telling you that all tests were successful and the details of how many tests were run (including error and failure counts) in the upper-right corner. The rest of the interface is used to display stack trace information from tests that failed, which doesn't apply in our first run.

Now let's make a quick and simple modification to our test case and see what the results will look like when the test fails. We will modify the assertion statement so that our own manual calculation used for verification is flawed. So, let's multiply the product cost by three instead of by two, like so:

```
try {
    assertEquals( item.cost, (59.99 * 3) );
}
catch( e:Error ) {
    fail( "testCost() failed: " + e );
}
```

When we rerun the Adobe AIR application and the unit test is executed, you will notice the bar at the top is now red, indicating something went wrong and the failure count in the upper-right corner is set to one, as seen in Figure 22.3. Most important, the rest of the interface displays a list of test methods and classes where the failures occurred, and by selecting them one-by-one, the associated stack trace is displayed. The stack trace is actually what you should be looking at to determine what went wrong; in this case, it is telling us that the expected and provided values did not match.

FIGURE 22.3   Our second run of the unit test resulted in a failure. A clear indication is the red status bar and that really long stack trace.

Asynchronous Testing

Now that we have created and run our test case, we need to talk about two special cases that we have not yet dealt with: user interface (UI) and remote testing. Both of these cases are special because they deal with the asynchronous nature of the Adobe Flex framework, used to create our Adobe AIR application. And the initial versions of FlexUnit did not support such testing, but this feature was inevitably added in version 0.85 (the one we are currently using).

In this section, we discuss why it is needed and go through a brief example of how to use it.

Where Asynchronous Testing Comes into Play

Everything we have done so far deals with testing client-side business classes created in ActionScript. This type of testing, because of its nature, is procedural, meaning that all the statements executed in the test case occur one after another. So, it is easy to create some data, pass it to your class, and validate that the computations performed are valid according to the business requirements.

However, there are times when not all of the code executes in such a synchronous fashion. This is because a portion of the Adobe Flex framework is event driven. All the various UI components contain several events that they broadcast to let you know some internal operation was just completed (such as the creation of a control) or when the user performed an action (such as clicking a button). It also occurs whenever a remote call is made to a server (using the `HttpService`, `RemoteService`, or `WebService` classes); the successful or error response is not immediately returned. When such events occur, the flow of control is asynchronous, thus you need to wait for the events to be completed before running the next piece of code within your test case. For this, we need to make use of FlexUnit's `addAsync()` method to handle these asynchronous situations.

Asynchronous Test Example

The best way to understand how this all comes to play in a FlexUnit test case is to view an example.

The shopping cart sample application we have been using so far has a UI portion, obviously, as shown in Figure 22.4. There is no better way to show how to handle asynchronous events in FlexUnit than to build a test case that will use an instance of the UI. We will set some values, click a button, and validate the result of our actions. So, let's write the test case and go through in detail how it all works, as shown in Listing 22.1.

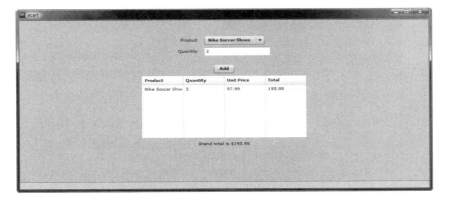

FIGURE 22.4   A view of the sample shopping cart interface.

LISTING 22.1   The Test Case for the CartView UI, Demonstrating How to Handle
Asynchronous Events

```
package tests
{
  import flash.events.MouseEvent;
  import flexunit.framework.TestCase;
  import mx.core.Application;
  import mx.events.FlexEvent;

  public class CartViewTest extends TestCase {

      private var _view:CartView;
      public function CartViewTest() {
      }

      public override function tearDown():void {
          Application.application.removeChild( _view );
          view = null;
      }

      public function testAddItem():void {
          _view = new CartView();
          _view.addEventListener( FlexEvent.CREATION_COMPLETE, addAsync(
➥performAdd, 1000 ) );
          Application.application.addChild( _view );
      }

      private function performAdd( event:FlexEvent, passThrudata:Object ):void {
          _view.quantity.text = "2";
          _view.product.selectedIndex = 1;
          _view.addBtn.dispatchEvent( new MouseEvent( MouseEvent.CLICK ) );
          assertEquals( "Grand total is $119.96", _view.totalLbl.text );
      }
    }
}
```

You will notice our test class has two important methods: testAddItem() and
performAdd(). The testAddItem() is where the testing actually begins and the
performAdd() method is where we actually set some values and do our assertion. Those
two pieces of code are separate and here is why. In the testAddItem() method, we create
an instance of the CartView component that is referenced by the class variable _view, and
add it to the main application canvas. Now you would expect the actual testing code to
follow; however, if we did code it that way, the test would fail because the component
would not have been created yet. It is because the creation of the component happens

asynchronously, so basically we need to wait until it has been created before we perform our testing.

This is why after the component instance is created, we add an event listener to know when the component has been created and added to the application. (Refer to the bolded statement in Listing 22.1.) We are basically saying after the component is created, call the performAdd() method. It is what we refer to as a callback method. However, you will notice that the performAdd() method itself is wrapped by a call to the addAsync() method. This is what you need to do for FlexUnit to handle this asynchronous event. Basically what this line of code is saying is "After the component has been created and added to the application, call the performAdd() method and time out after 1,000 milliseconds if the asynchronous event did not yet complete." The timeout value is the second parameter passed to the addAsync() method (refer to Table 22.1 for a description on all addAsync() parameters) and its value is determined by you, the developer, on a case-by-case basis. In this case, 1,000 milliseconds (one second) is enough, but in the situation where the component you are adding takes longer to create or you are testing a remote call, you might need to increase the timeout value.

TABLE 22.1   addAsync() Method Parameters

Parameter	Value/Description
func	The callback method to be called when the asynchronous event completes
timeout	The maximum amount of time to wait before a timeout occurs (in milliseconds)
passThroughData	An object that can be passed to the callback method that would contain relevant data
failFunc	The method to call if the callback method could not be called

After the component is created, the performAdd() method is called. Then, we set the value in the quantity TextInput field, change the product we want selected, and click the addBtn button. Finally, we make an assertion to make sure the totalLbl label has the correct value after the item is added to the shopping cart. Now, you are probably wondering why the addAsync() method wasn't used when we clicked the addBtn button. This is because clicking a button and the method(s) executed by the button occur synchronously, it does not require time to elapse to know the result of the action.

You will also notice that the performAdd() method declares two parameters, the first one being a reference to the event that called it and the second one being a generic object. The second parameter, the generic object, can actually be set when you make the call to the addAsync() method as a third parameter. This can actually be useful in some testing situations when specific data needs to be used to determine if a test was successful.

Integration with Apache Ant

In Chapter 21, "Creating a Build Process," we showed you how to use a popular build tool like Apache Ant to build, run, and export your Adobe AIR application. Now, we are going to show you how to incorporate the automatic execution of the FlexUnit tests for your Adobe AIR application with Apache Ant. These are very important steps that will culminate in us talking about continuous integration in Chapter 23, "Continuous Integration with Adobe AIR."

Running FlexUnit from Apache Ant

So far, we have used FlexUnit to create and run our unit tests as an Adobe AIR application and examine the results visually. This is all nice and dandy; however, we need to integrate the execution of the unit tests with the work we did in Chapter 21. So, we need to compile our unit tests and then run them via Apache Ant as we have done for the Adobe AIR application itself.

> **NOTE**
>
> Please refer to Listing 21.1 in Chapter 21 for the full Apache Ant build script listing. The next steps will simply be adding to the existing build script.

Modifications for Apache Ant Compatibility

Before we actually get to the fun stuff, we need to modify the `EcartTestRunner.mxml` file, which is the main application file used to execute all the unit tests. Why? The answer is simple: FlexUnit was created before the existence of Adobe AIR and, thus, has no knowledge of Adobe AIR. When FlexUnit is launched from Apache Ant, it attempts to launch an instance of the Adobe® Flash® Player and execute the unit tests. So, we need to make some modifications before we can proceed.

> **NOTE**
>
> As Adobe AIR becomes more and more popular, it is possible that FlexUnit will be modified to support Adobe AIR.

The new version of the `EcartTestRunner.mxml` file is as follows:

```
<mx:Application xmlns:mx="http://www.adobe.com/2006/mxml"
    xmlns:flexunit="flexunit.flexui.*"
    creationComplete="initApp()">

    <mx:Script>
    <![CDATA[
        import flexunit.junit.JUnitTestRunner;
        import tests.AllEcartTests;
```

```
        private var runner:JUnitTestRunner;

        private function initApp():void {
            runner = new JUnitTestRunner();
            runner.run( AllEcartTests.suite(), testComplete );
        }

        private function testComplete():void {
            fscommand( "quit" );
        }
    ]]>
    </mx:Script>
</mx:Application>
```

To begin, the highest-level container is now the Application container.

Next, you will notice the test runner component has been removed and replaced with an instance of the JUnitTestRunner class, referenced by the runner variable.

Next, in the initApp() method, we create an instance of the JUnitTestRunner class and tell it to run our tests by passing it a reference to our test suite and the method to call after all tests have been executed.

Finally, in the testComplete() method, we use a special method to tell the Flash Player to exit and return control to the parent operating system process. (In our case, it will be the Apache Ant build script.)

Compiling the Unit Tests

Now that we got that little update work out of the way, let's get to compiling the unit test that we wrote using FlexUnit. We simply need to add another target called compileunittests to our existing Apache Ant build script, like so:

```
<target name="compileunittests" depends="init">
    <mxmlc file="${basedir}/src/EcartTestRunner.mxml"
        output="${BUILD_FOLDER}/EcartTestRunner.swf">

        <load-config filename="${FLEX_HOME}/frameworks/air-config.xml"/>
        <source-path path-element="${FLEX_HOME}/frameworks"/>
        <source-path path-element="${basedir}/unittest_src"/>
        <compiler.library-path dir="${FLEX_HOME}/frameworks" append="true">
            <include name="libs" />
            <include name="../bundles/{locale}" />
        </compiler.library-path>
        <compiler.library-path dir="${basedir}" append="true">
            <include name="libs" />
        </compiler.library-path>
    </mxmlc>
</target>
```

If you recall in Chapter 21, we had to compile the Adobe AIR application itself and this is basically the same thing with some differences. First, the name of the source and output files is different. Second, we have specified an additional source path element (`${basedir}/unittest_src`), which lets the compiler know where to find our unit test classes. And, finally, we have specified an additional library path so that the compiler can locate the `flexunit.swc` and `flexunitoptional-0.4.swc` files that contain the FlexUnit framework classes.

Running the Unit Tests

The next thing we need to add to our Apache Ant build script is the ability to run our unit tests. So, we will create another target called `runtests`:

```
<target name="runtests" depends="compileunittests,init">
    <flexunit
        swf="${BUILD_FOLDER}/EcartTestRunner.swf"
        toDir="${BUILD_FOLDER}/unittests"
        haltonfailure="false"/>

    <echo message="FlexUnit tests executed successfully!"/>
</target>
```

We execute the unit tests via Apache Ant by running the `flexunit` task, which is located within the `FlexAntTasks-0.4.jar` file we downloaded earlier. Also note that this target depends on our `compileunittests` target we created just a few moments ago. The parameters for the `flexunit` tasks are explained in Table 22.2.

TABLE 22.2   Flexunit Task Parameters

Parameter	Value/Description
swf	The name and location of the SWF file to run that contains the compiled unit tests.
port	The socket port number on which FlexUnit receives test results from the Flash Player. The default is 1024. If you change this value, remember to make the same change in the main MXML test runner file.
toDir	The folder path where the tests results will be stored.
haltonfailure	A boolean value that determines if the execution of the unit tests should stop after the first failure/error. The default is true.
verbose	A boolean value that controls the display of additional information during the execution of the unit tests. The default is false.
timeout	The maximum amount of time to wait for test results (in milliseconds) from the Flash Player before exiting with an error. The default is 60000.

TIP

It is recommended that the `haltonfailure` parameter be set to a value of `false` so that all the unit tests can be executed in one run. This allows you the opportunity to see all errors/failures and correct them in one take.

When we actually run our Ant build script again via the command line, we see the results as depicted in Figure 22.5.

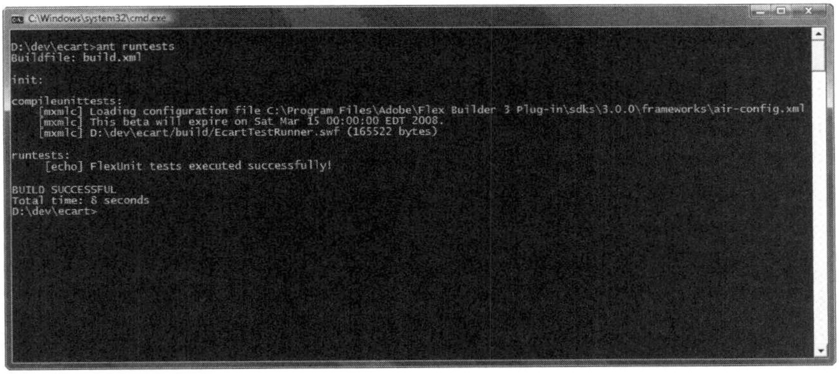

FIGURE 22.5   Compiling and running the FlexUnit tests with Apache Ant.

Unified Reporting with JUnit

So, we have the complete solution, or so you might think. The last question is: How do you view the test results after they have been run with Apache Ant? Well, now that you have run the test at least once, go look in the folder where the test result output was stored. You will notice some Extensible Markup Language (XML) files that contain the results. However, that is not a very eloquent way to view the results.

And so we must perform one last little piece of work. Like JUnit, we must convert the XML data files into a format we can more easily read. And because the generated XML data files are in the same format used by JUnit, we will simply use the `junitreport` task to generate the results in a Hypertext Markup Language (HTML) format. Let's get to work:

```
<target name="runtests" depends="compileunittests,init">
    <!-- run tests -->
    <flexunit
        swf="${BUILD_FOLDER}/EcartTestRunner.swf"
        toDir="${BUILD_FOLDER}/unittests"
        haltonfailure="false"/>
```

```
<echo message="FlexUnit tests executed successfully!"/>

<mkdir dir="${BUILD_FOLDER}/unittest_output"/>

<!— generate report —>
<junitreport todir="${BUILD_FOLDER}/unittest_output">
    <fileset dir="${BUILD_FOLDER}/unittests">
        <include name="TEST-*.xml"/>
    </fileset>

    <report format="frames" todir="${BUILD_FOLDER}/unittest_output"/>
</junitreport>
</target>
```

Here, we added two more steps to our `runtests` target. First, we created the folder where we will store the HTML output. Second, we used the `junitreport` task to take the XML data files returned by FlexUnit and generate the human-readable HTML output, as seen in Figure 22.6.

FIGURE 22.6   Viewing the FlexUnit test results in HTML format.

Summary

In this chapter, we have accomplished the most important work related to any software development project. We have learned how to create unit tests using FlexUnit to test the smallest portions of the business logic contained within our Adobe AIR application. Then as we did in Chapter 21, we used Apache Ant and incorporated the compilation and execution of the unit tests with the rest of our build process.

In doing so, we have increased the likelihood that any coding errors will be discovered and fixed early in the development process, thus increasing the quality of our application. More on this in Chapter 23—don't go anywhere!

22

Continuous Integration with Adobe AIR

Like any good book or movie, everything we have done up to this point is all going to come together now. The entire Part VI, "Agile Development with Adobe AIR," is all about Agile development with Adobe® AIR™. In the previous two chapters, we laid down a very good foundation as we learned about automation and unit testing. But what is it all for?

Well, let's take a look at what we have so far. We created a build script we use to automate the compiling of our Adobe AIR application, and we can also test the various parts of our application. The whole point of completing those two tasks is to increase the quality of our Adobe AIR application as we prepare it for its release into production. The only thing that remains now is to repeatedly perform these tasks on a regular basis to ensure the high-quality release we are looking for.

But there is more to it than that. We also have to take into account that we will be working in a team environment with many developers working on various pieces of the application at the same time. To make sure everything is going smoothly, we need to make sure that something one developer is working on doesn't break the application—and if it does, we need to know about it as early as possible. We already have the tools in place to do this: an automated build and unit tests. We just need to make sure we continuously run these two tools. And we also have to make sure that all developers integrate their individual work into the application as early and as often as possible—hence, the term *continuous integration*.

So as we move along in this chapter, we look at how to run our automated build and unit tests as often as possible using a tool called CruiseControl and delve more deeply into the various parts that constitute continuous integration.

Overview of Continuous Integration

The reason for doing continuous integration is to deliver a high-quality end product. Another reason is that you want to reduce the risk. You want to reduce the number of bugs that will be found within your application. Because, let's face it, no matter how hard we try, no matter what great development methodology we use, there will always be bugs within an application. You just want to make sure they are little ones that do not annoy end users and are easy to find and fix.

This is all very important because in any software development project, you will be working with a group of developers. Each developer will be responsible for a portion of the application and you want to make sure that in the end, it will all work as a whole. The best way to accomplish this is to integrate each others' code early and often. Thus, any issues that arise during development will be found, evaluated, and corrected as early as possible. This is where the benefit is. You don't want to be doing a massive, one-time integration at the very end of the development cycle. Because chances are that problems will arise (always remember Murphy's Law), and not just a few, but many of them, and you will spend far more time at this stage attempting to first find the problems and then correct them. The result of this will be a delayed release and disappointed stakeholders and end users, which is never a good thing.

Some of the keywords in Agile development are *short*, *small*, and *often*—short development cycles, small, concise unit tests, and a release-often approach. And during the development phase, integrate often. This way, when problems arise, be it either bugs or design issues, they will be small and fairly easy to tackle.

Another reason for continuous integration is the physiological impact on a software developer. No one wants to tackle a problem that will take days or even weeks to fix that could have been avoided early on. However, something that will take minutes or hours to resolve is easy to deal with—with much less stress on the mind. It helps keep the development team focused on the end goal and helps keep spirits high.

So now that we understand the reasons behind continuous integration, let's see how we put it all together with what we have already worked on and develop a complete solution.

Version Control System

Everything in software development begins with the code we write. And, thus, it is important that we keep that code in a safe place that is controlled and versioned. Unless you have been working in the smallest of development shops, you are probably already using some version control system.

A version control system is first a repository that holds the code for our Adobe AIR application and any libraries it might use. The files it contains can be either binary or text, but are usually the latter. Second, a version control system also keeps track of changes made to any of the code (or files), which is called versioning. Basically, this allows you to go back in time to see what your application's code base looked like at a certain point and refer to it, if necessary—so nothing is lost.

Several different version control systems are out there; the two most popular ones, however, are the Concurrent Versioning System (CVS) and Subversion (SVN). Both of these version control systems are widely used and contain all the essential features. It doesn't matter which one we use—either one will suit the needs as a repository for the code of our Adobe AIR application. Furthermore, if you are using Eclipse, and most people do, plug-ins exist for both of these version control systems.

NOTE

We recommend you visit the sites for both CVS (http://ximbiot.com/cvs/cvshome) and Subversion (http://subversion.tigris.org) to determine which one is best for you. Both websites contain the necessary information to set up an initial repository to get started.

If you are using something other than Eclipse as a development tool, we recommend you refer to the documentation for your development tool for appropriate plug-ins for CVS and Subversion and guidance on how to use them.

To gain a better understanding of a version control system, the following sections cover the main features that are offered.

Mainline, Checkout, and Commits

All code within a version control system is held by default in what is referred to as the mainline. When developers work on code, they don't modify the code directly in the repository, they first perform what is referred to as a checkout. Basically, they take a copy of the application's code from the repository to their own machines. They now have what is called a working copy. As a developer works on his own local working copy, he makes changes and after the work is completed, the code is resubmitted back to the repository, which is referred to as a commit.

NOTE

Actually, when a commit occurs, you are only sending to the repository the files that have changed—not everything.

Also, after you have committed your changes, you can retrieve all other changes by performing an update.

NOTE

The client for version control systems (like the plug-ins for CVS and Subversion for Eclipse) typically gives you a synchronized view of what is going on. This view basically lets you perform an update and a commit in one take. You are viewing everything coming and going to and from the repository.

Branches and Merging

There are times, however, when you do not want to work on the mainline because the changes that need to be made are far too extensive. In this case, you can create a branch— a copy of the mainline that is independent. After all the changes are completed in the branch, the changes can be recombined with the code in the mainline, which is referred to as merging.

Daily Commits

After introducing repositories and version control systems, let's see how that ties into our continuous integration master plan. Typically, developers will be checking code into the mainline. This should occur as often as possible, hopefully daily. It is understandable that this is sometimes not possible because it might take a day or more to complete the required changes. After all, there is no point in committing partial code when you know it is going to fail.

Committing changes daily, or as often as possible, is one of the main keys to continuous integration because it allows us to catch any problems as early as possible.

But, how can we accomplish this? The answer to that is forthcoming.

Automated Build

Now that we are committing our changes daily, or trying our best to do so, what we want to do is recompile our Adobe AIR application to see that no errors have been introduced from our changes. This is where all that work we did with Apache Ant in a previous chapter comes into play.

Basically, what we want to do is rerun the Ant build script on a daily basis, preferably at the end of the day after all changes by all developers have been committed into the mainline. This way, if an error occurs in the compiling stage, we will know about it the next day and correct it first thing in the morning. This is an excellent way to catch compile errors immediately and make small, quick, and painless fixes.

But who is going to run the Ant build script in the middle of the night? Hold that thought for a moment.

Unit Testing

Because we are recompiling our Adobe AIR application on a nightly basis, why not take it a step further? Compiling our Adobe AIR application nightly will help us catch any syntax errors, build script errors, and much more. What about the application code? What about any logic errors? Well, remember all those FlexUnit tests we wrote in Chapter 22, "Incorporating Unit Testing," to test various portions of the application code? We should definitely be running those on a nightly basis as well.

At this point, if we are recompiling and running the FlexUnit tests on a nightly basis, we will have a pretty good system for detecting errors early and making any corrections easy to do.

But again, who will run all this in the middle of the night? We will solve that mystery shortly.

Automated Deployment

Because we are talking about doing all this nightly stuff, we could also add one item to that nightly list: automated deployments. Wait a minute, Adobe AIR applications are deployed on each end user's computer, so what exactly are we talking about here? It is true that unlike web applications that are deployed to some application server, an Adobe AIR application is deployed to an end user's computer. What we are talking about is taking the distributable archive (the file with the `.air` extension) generated by our Ant build script and deploying it to our test server (sometimes referred to as a staging or development server). This way, we can test the auto-update of the Adobe AIR application and, finally, test the application itself.

Another reason we might want to auto-deploy every night is that our Adobe AIR application might have a server component. There might be a remote object that is called by the application (ColdFusion or Java class) or a web service that gets updated that we will need to eventually test as well. Thus, on a nightly basis, we can deploy the Adobe AIR application and the server-side component as well. Don't forget that server-side deployments are not automatic—they might fail. This is another good reason to auto-deploy every night.

> **NOTE**
>
> Deploying the Adobe AIR application or the server-side component to an application server is beyond the scope of this book. You should refer to the documentation that is provided with your application server to learn how to do this. In many cases, Apache Ant tasks are provided by the vendor to allow easy integration of the deployment into the rest of your build process.

Introducing CruiseControl

So far, we have been talking a lot about doing things during the night: compiling, running unit tests, and perhaps even auto-deploying our application to a test server. But who will do it? Will someone wake up in the middle of the night to do all this work? Probably not.

What we need is a system that will do the continuous integration for us so we just have to wake up in the morning, go into work, and see the results. Several software solutions are available out in the wild for doing continuous integration, and we have chosen to work with CruiseControl. CruiseControl is one of the most recognized continuous integration platforms in the Java community because it is Java-based. This also makes it a good candidate for our Adobe AIR application because the build script we have written is executed by Apache Ant, which, as we have mentioned in a previous chapter, is Java-based as well.

CruiseControl will perform a three-step process for us. First, it will query our repository to see if any code changes have been made since the last run and, if this is the case, it will launch a build. Launching a build is, in effect, the second step, which means executing our Ant build script, thus compiling and running all unit tests. Finally, it will publish a report of the entire build process using a method of our choice (Really Simple Syndication [RSS], Instant Messaging [IM], or email).

So, without further ado, let's get this integration going! In the next few sections, we take care of installing and configuring CruiseControl and then putting it to work.

Downloading CruiseControl

To get started, we need to download CruiseControl. So, follow these five easy steps:

1. Go to the CruiseControl website: http://cruisecontrol.sourceforge.net/.
2. From the left navigation bar, click Download.
3. From the current release section, click Select Distribution (see Figure 23.1).
4. On the next page, download the binary Zip file (as of this writing, `cruisecontrol-bin-2.7.1.zip`) and save it to a temporary location.
5. Extract the contents of the downloaded archive to a folder of your choice (for example, `D:\opt`).

And that's it! Unlike Apache Ant or FlexUnit, there are no third-party extras to download and install, so you are ready to get started using CruiseControl.

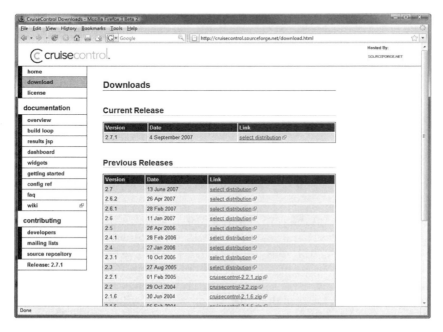

FIGURE 23.1   The CruiseControl download page.

Configuring CruiseControl

We now have one more big piece of work to do before we reach our end goal. We need to configure CruiseControl to tell it to do what we spoke about earlier in this chapter. So now that you have it installed, if you take a look in the root folder, you will notice a file called config.xml. This is the configuration file that tells CruiseControl what to do about every project you want to set up for continuous integration.

Now we need to modify this file for our own purposes. We can do this in one of two ways: Either open the config.xml with your favorite text editor and replace its contents with the configuration we are about to create or rename the existing file (to something like config.xml.orig) and create a new config.xml file with the following:

```
<cruisecontrol>
    <project name="ecart">
        ...
    </project>
</cruisecontrol>
```

As you can see, the CruiseControl configuration file is XML-based with <cruisecontrol> being the root tag. Within the root tag, you can set up as many projects (we can consider them applications) as you want CruiseControl to handle. In this case, we have set up only one project, our eCart project.

The first thing we need to do is tell CruiseControl how to determine if anything has changed so it knows whether it has to launch a build of our Adobe AIR application. In our case, we want to tell it to connect to our remote SVN repository using the following tags:

```
<modificationset>
    <svn RepositoryLocation="https://someurl/svn/trunk/ecart"
        username="someemail@gmail.com"
        password="somepassword"/>
</modificationset>
```

As you can see, it is pretty simple: We pass in the repository location and credential information. The /trunk/ecart path tells it to verify the mainline of the eCart project.

> **NOTE**
>
> CruiseControl has the capability to connect to various repositories (CVS, Visual Source Safe, and so on). You need to simply read the documentation to learn how to configure it for the repository you are currently using.

Next, we need to tell CruiseControl how often to run and, if a modification was made, what to do:

```
<schedule interval="60">
    <ant antscript="D:\opt\apache-ant-1.6.5\bin\ant.bat"
```

```
          buildfile="D:/dev/${project.name}/build.xml"
          target="ccrun"
          uselogger="true"
          usedebug="true"/>
</schedule>
```

Basically, using the `<schedule>` tag, we tell CruiseControl to run every minute and then if
a modification has been found, to run our Apache Ant build script. We need to specify the
location of Apache Ant itself, the Ant build script for our Adobe AIR application, and the
target (ccrun) to execute inside the build script, and we need to turn on logging and
debugging. You are probably thinking back to the Ant build script and don't remember a
target named ccrun. This is because there isn't one until now. It is just a target that
executes all the other targets within the Ant build script that we need. So, here is the code
for the target that you should add to the Ant build script:

```
<target name="ccrun" depends="build,export,runtests">
</target>
```

Now that we have told CruiseControl what to run and when, it is time to tell it what to
do with the results:

```
<log>
    <merge dir="D:/dev/${project.name}/build/unittests" />
</log>
```

The most important results to know about are the results of the FlexUnit tests; basically,
the preceding says to take the results of the FlexUnit tests and merge them with everything else generated for this build run. This way, when we view the status of the project,
we will know which tests were successful and which were not. There is actually a really
nice tool to view the results, but we will get to that in a moment.

The final piece of the puzzle is to publish some information and send out a notification of
the build run. The following shows how we do that:

```
<publishers>
    <onsuccess>
        <artifactspublisher dest="artifacts/${project.name}"
            file="d:/dev/${project.name}/build/${project.name}.air" />
    </onsuccess>

    <email buildresultsurl="http://localhost:8080"
        mailhost="smtp.gmail.com"
        mailport="465"
        usessl="true"
        username="someemail@gmail.com"
        password="somepassword"
        skipusers="true"
        returnaddress="somereturn@host.com">
```

```
        <always address="somerecipient@host.com"/>
    </email>
</publishers>
```

Notice that both instructions are wrapped in <publishers> tags because this is exactly what we are doing—publishing various types of information. First, we take our distributable archive that was generated by our Ant build script and move it to a subfolder of the CruiseControl installation, only upon a successful build. This is necessary so that CruiseControl will be able to link to the actual file. Second, we send out a notification email, regardless of success or failure (because it is not included inside the <onsuccess> tags). To send out the email, we need to specify the Simple Mail Transfer Protocol (SMTP) server information (host, port, whether it is secure, and the credentials), the return address, and the recipient of the email. In this case, we have only one recipient and that recipient will get a build notification email regardless of the results. The buildresultsurl specifies the location of the CruiseControl website we are using; this is used within the email to create a link that the user can use to view the full results of the build run.

One of the great things about CruiseControl is its flexibility. In our example, we sent out an email notification, but we could have easily published something to a server, written to a weblog, or even published to an RSS feed. In addition, you can control what happens depending on the results of the build itself. Needless to say, there are many options, and it is up to you to decide what to do; it might even vary from project to project.

Now that we have configured CruiseControl and explained all the little bits and pieces, Listing 23.1 shows the full look of the build.xml file.

LISTING 23.1   CruiseControl Configuration File Used to Perform Continuous Integration on Our Adobe AIR Application

```
<cruisecontrol>
    <project name="ecart">
        <modificationset>
            <svn RepositoryLocation="https://someurl/svn/trunk/ecart"
                username="someemail@gmail.com"
                password="somepassword"/>
        </modificationset>

        <schedule interval="60">
            <ant antscript="D:\opt\apache-ant-1.6.5\bin\ant.bat"
                buildfile="D:/dev/${project.name}/build.xml"
                target="ccrun"
                uselogger="true"
                usedebug="true"/>
        </schedule>

        <log>
            <merge dir="D:/dev/${project.name}/build/unittests" />
```

```
        </log>

        <publishers>
            <onsuccess>
                <artifactspublisher dest="artifacts/${project.name}"
                    file="d:/dev/${project.name}/build/${project.name}.air" />
            </onsuccess>

            <email buildresultsurl="http://localhost:8080"
                mailhost="smtp.gmail.com"
                mailport="465"
                usessl="true"
                username="someemail@gmail.com"
                password="somepassword"
                skipusers="true"
                returnaddress="someemail@host.com">

                <always address="someemail@host.com"/>
            </email>
        </publishers>
    </project>
</cruisecontrol>
```

TIP

A great reference guide for the CruiseControl configuration file is located at the follow-ing website: http://cruisecontrol.sourceforge.net/main/configxml.html. It can also be found in the docs subfolder of your CruiseControl installation.

Using CruiseControl

Now that we have CruiseControl installed, it's time to take it out for a little spin to see how it runs.

Starting CruiseControl

First, we open a command prompt and navigate to the folder where CruiseControl was installed. In that folder, you will notice a file called cruisecontrol.bat; this is the main executable you must launch to start CruiseControl.

> **NOTE**
>
> The `cruisecontrol.bat` we just referred to applies to people running Microsoft Windows. A shell script is also provided in the root folder that can be used in a UNIX/Linux system (which includes Macs as well).

After you have done this, you will notice some messages appear within the command prompt window; this is normal (refer to Figure 23.2). All the messages up to `BuildQueue started` are related to the initialization of CruiseControl. Because this is the first time we are running CruiseControl, it will also build our Adobe AIR application for the first time, and that portion starts with the message `Project ecart: now building`. Building our Adobe AIR application includes compiling and running all the unit tests.

At the end of the build, you will see that the next build cycle is scheduled in one minute. This doesn't mean that another build will be launched, however. CruiseControl will only launch another build of the application if there were changes committed to the repository, or if it has been forced to do so.

CruiseControl Dashboard

Another, more convenient way to view the build results is to use the CruiseControl Dashboard. The Dashboard is simply a web application that is included with

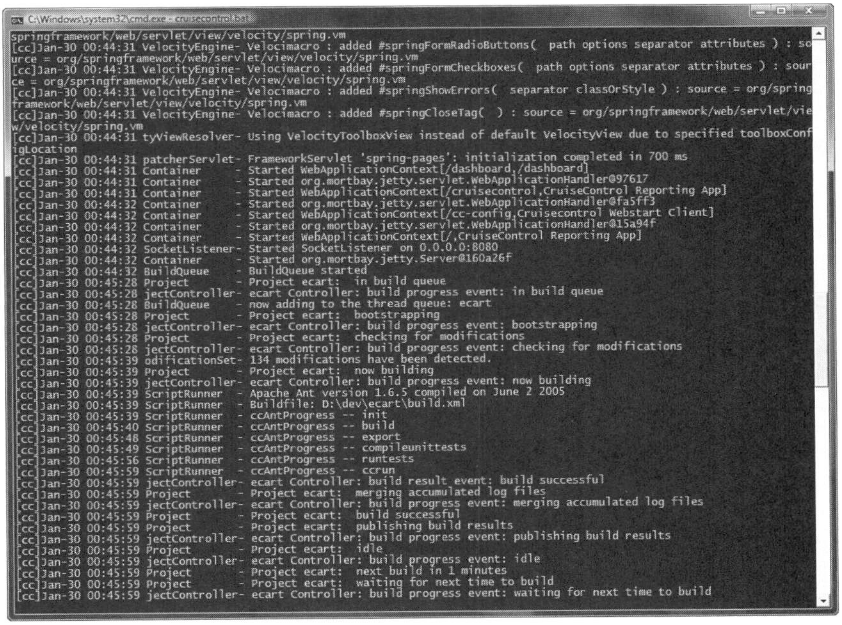

FIGURE 23.2 CruiseControl running for the first time. Initialization is completed and our Adobe AIR application has been built.

CruiseControl that gives everyone the ability to view the build results for every application that is configured for continuous integration and to manage CruiseControl.

So now that CruiseControl is running, fire up your favorite web browser and navigate to the following URL: http://localhost:8080/dashboard. As you can see from Figure 23.3, the main page just has some icons that give you a quick overview of the status of every application CruiseControl is building. You should see a green icon for our eCart Adobe AIR application, meaning it was successfully built.

The Builds tab is actually more useful, presenting the applications in a list with the last build time and quick access to some options. From the Builds tab, drill down on the eCart application, and you are now presented with even more information as seen in Figure 23.4. The Latest Builds panel contains a list of the last n builds, their date and times, and the result—either successful or failed, as indicated by their color and icon. By default the main area contains detailed information about the last build, or if you select one of the builds from the Latest Builds panel, it displays the details of that build. All the

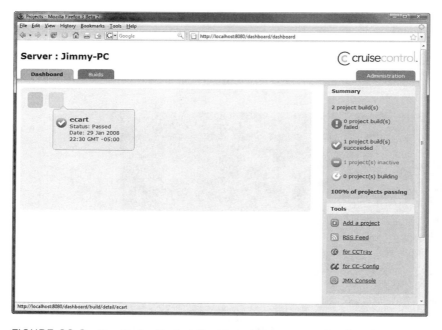

FIGURE 23.3   The CruiseControl Dashboard home page showing that the eCart application was last built successfully.

information is arranged in subtabs for easy access; Table 23.1 explains the contents of each subtab.

One interesting thing to note is that the Artifacts and Tests tabs switch places when the details for a failed build are displayed (see Figure 23.5). This is useful because we can see which FlexUnit tests failed and why at first glance, allowing us to work on the problem immediately.

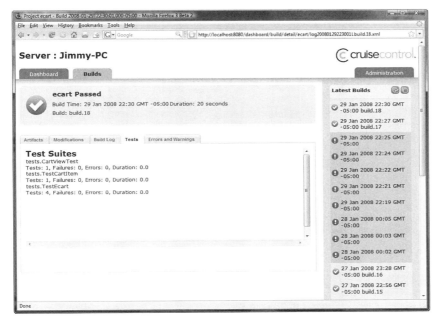

FIGURE 23.4   A detailed view of the last successful build with the Tests subtab selected, showing that all FlexUnit tests passed.

TABLE 23.1   Description of Subtabs Displayed in the Main Area for Every Selected Build

Tab	Description
Artifacts	Contains a link to any artifacts generated by the Ant build script, the distributable archive in our example
Modifications	Lists all files and folders modified since the last build and by whom with descriptions
Build Log	Links to the build log
Tests	Displays the results of all unit tests, the FlexUnit tests in our example
Errors and Warnings	Displays any warning or error message encountered when running the build; this is useful when the build fails

Rebuilding

Now that we have seen a little bit of how CruiseControl works, let's examine one important aspect of continuous integrations: the rebuild. A rebuild occurs in one of two scenarios: The first scenario is when someone commits changes during the day to the repository, and the second scenario is when you force a rebuild using the CruiseControl Dashboard.

FIGURE 23.5   A detailed view of a failed build with the Tests tab now first in order to immediately show which FlexUnit tests failed and with what error message.

The following sections examine both of these scenarios in detail.

Automatic Rebuild   In a real-world scenario, you will be scheduling a build of your Adobe AIR application on a nightly basis, for example at 10:00 p.m. every night. So during the day, developers will commit their changes, and at 10:00 p.m. when CruiseControl launches, it will notice that changes were made in the repository and will launch the Ant build script to compile the application, generate the distributable archive, and run all FlexUnit tests. The next morning, you walk into the office and are eager to know the status of the previous night's build, so you can either read the status emails sent out by CruiseControl or use the Dashboard.

Of course, if nothing was committed to the repository on that day, no build is executed at night.

Forcing a Build   There are times, however, when you won't want to wait until nightfall for a build to be executed. It could be that it is necessary to do an immediate integration test.

You can use the CruiseControl Dashboard to force an immediate build. To do this, follow these steps:

1. Open your favorite web browser and go to the CruiseControl Dashboard website: http://localhost:8080/dashboard.
2. Select the Build tabs.
3. Click the Force Build icon (it looks like a Refresh icon) on the right side of the application you want to rebuild.

After the manual rebuild has been launched, notice that the display now changes to display additional information (see Figure 23.6). The elapsed time and the time remaining are displayed. The time remaining is calculated based on how long it took to build the previous time. Therefore, this value might not be accurate depending on the changes made.

23

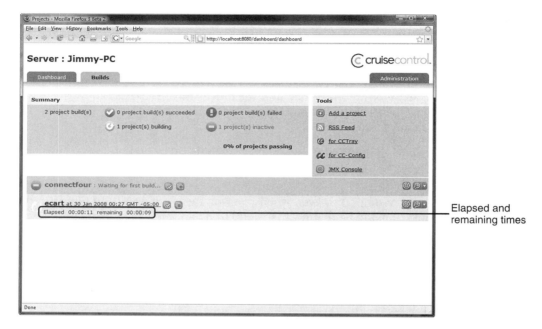

FIGURE 23.6   A build has been forced and is currently under way. The elapsed and remaining times are displayed by CruiseControl.

Summary

This chapter brought together everything we learned in Chapter 21, "Creating a Build Process," and Chapter 22 and put it all together. In choosing to construct state-of-the-art desktop applications using Adobe AIR, we needed to ensure we also delivered a high-quality application. To reach that goal, we decided to use Agile development methodologies that promote short development cycles, small, concise unit tests, and a release-often approach. In doing so, we automated several keys aspects, such as the compiling and distribution of application and, more important, the testing.

In this chapter, we made sure that on a daily basis we were repeating these tasks through a method known as continuous integration. By doing so, we are able to minimize the risk and catch any issues that arise early on in the process and correct them, so as to not affect the quality or delivery date of our Adobe AIR application.

We were also introduced to CruiseControl, a software platform that allows us to easily put our Adobe AIR application into continuous integration on a nightly basis, running all required tasks and reporting the results to us automatically.

PART VII

Real-World Projects

IN THIS PART

Contact Manager with Integrated Yahoo! Maps

This chapter takes a look at a fully functional contact manager application built using Adobe® Flex™ and Adobe® AIR™. We briefly take a look at the application and all its features to see how specific Adobe AIR technology was used to enhance the application, specifically in the domain of offline work.

One of the compelling reasons to use a technology such as Adobe AIR to build an application is that it can offer offline capabilities. If you think about it, most applications today mainly work with data that is held in a remote location that is accessible via a network connection. When that network connection becomes unavailable, the application is useless. Thus by using Adobe AIR's embedded database, we can build an application that is useful offline and then synchronizes the local data with the remote server when the network connection is reestablished.

Our contact manager application makes use of several other features as well, so we take a look at those and finally focus our attention on its offline capabilities.

> **NOTE**
>
> Although we do not take a look at the server-side portion of the application, for those curious, the server-side portion of the contact manager application is written in Java 6, makes use of the Spring Framework and Hibernate, and is deployed on Apache Tomcat 6. The backend database is MySQL 5.

Contact Manager with Integrated Yahoo! Maps Application Overview

Before we delve into the details of how this application works, let's first take a look at its functionality. As you can see from Figure 24.1, when the application first starts up, we are presented with the list of contacts, an embedded map (set to a default location of San Francisco), and two buttons for the basic create/remove contact operation.

FIGURE 24.1   The loaded application displaying the list of contacts.

You should note a few things—first is the embedded map. The embedded map is used when a contact is loaded; it changes to display the location of residence of the contact based on the address information provided. Second, above the contact list is a `TextInput` field that you can use to filter your contact list by name. Finally, below the list of contacts and to the right is a network icon that is used to visually display the current network connectivity status, and as you can see by the ToolTip in Figure 24.1, we are currently connected.

From Figure 24.2, you can see what the application looks like when a specific contact is loaded. The left panel changes to display the full information of the contact, including address, associated phone numbers, and email addresses. The rest of the left panel contains various buttons used to add/remove phone numbers and email addresses, a Save button to save the contact, and a Cancel button to return to the main list. Notice that the map component on the right now displays the geographical region associated with the address information of the contact (in this case, somewhere in New York City).

FIGURE 24.2   After a contact is loaded, the map for the contact's address is displayed on the right.

The main feature of the application is the offline capability. When we run the application, it loads all the contact information from a remote Java server, and all subsequent create/edit/remove operations change the data on the remote server. However, should the network connection falter, because this is an Adobe AIR application, it makes use of an embedded SQLite database to store all information and, thus, allows the user to continue to work with the data. When the network connection is reestablished, all local data stored on the client is synchronized with the server. This is a great feature for not only those times when a network connection is unavailable, but also for times when people who are constantly on the go are not in a location where network connectivity is easily available.

Using Third-Party Components

As you might have noticed from the first two figures of the contact manager, the application makes use of several third-party components. The following sections take a quick look at them.

Cairngorm Microarchitecture Framework

Because this is the Cairngorm Contact Manager, as the name implies, the application makes use of the Cairngorm microarchitecture framework. This framework was detailed in Chapter 19, "Introduction to Frameworks and Design Patterns," and you learned all about the various parts that compose Cairngorm. By using Cairngorm, it was easy to create a structured application that was loosely coupled and, thus, allowed us to perform some modifications to enhance the application functionality. By this, we mean we modified the Business Delegate class called `ContactManagerDelegate` to use the embedded database whenever a network connection was not available. Further details on this are forthcoming.

PromptingTextInput

If you look at Figure 24.1, you notice that above the contact list a `TextInput` component allows the user to filter the list based on name. However, it is not just any regular `TextInput` component because it allows us to specify a faded prompt. This is a `PromptingTextInput` component that is found inside the Flexlib third-party library, which you can find at the following website: http://code.google.com/p/flexlib.

To use the `PromptingTextInput` component in an MXML file, you first have to declare a namespace to reference the component like so:

```
xmlns:fx="flexlib.controls.*"
```

Then, you simply use the `PromptingTextInput` component as you would a regular `TextInput` component, except you specify the extra prompt property:

```
<fx:PromptingTextInput id="criteria" width="100%"
  prompt="Filter contacts"
  change="doFilter()"/>
```

> **TIP**
>
> The Flexlib library actually contains other components that might prove useful in one application or another; you should examine them and use them as needed.

Yahoo! Maps

It is hard not to notice the map embedded within the application when looking at Figure 24.1. Once again, the map component is a third-party component provided by Yahoo! You can find the component and all relevant documentation at the following URL: http://developer.yahoo.com/flash/maps.

To make use of the `YahooMap` component, we actually created our own component called `MapView` that contains one child, the `YahooMap` component itself. We did this so that the `MapView` component could have one property called `mapRequest`, which would cause the `YahooMap` component to retrieve the new map location and display it every time it was set via binding. So, the declaration of the `MapView` component looks like this:

```
<view:MapView id="map"
  width="100%" height="100%"
  mapRequest="{ContactModel.getInstance().mapRequest}"/>
```

The internals of the `MapView` component are quite simple. Because it is an extension of the `Canvas` container, it already contains a lot of the plumbing required to add the `YahooMap`

component as a child. So, we simply need to create an instance of the `YahooMap` component in the overridden `createChildren()` function and add it to our component:

```
_map = new YahooMap( APP_ID, this.width, this.height );
_map.addPanControl();
_map.addZoomWidget();
_map.addTypeWidget();
_map.addEventListener( YahooMapEvent.MAP_INITIALIZE, onInitialize, false, 0,
➥true );
rawChildren.addChild( map );
```

Then, every time the `mapRequest` property of our `MapView` component is updated, we
need to change what is currently being displayed by the map. This is done by writing
some code in the `commitProperties()` function. We basically create a new instance of the
`Address` class, provide it with the address information of the currently loaded contact,
and set it as the center of the map:

```
_addr = new Address( _req.street + " " + _req.city + "," + _req.province + " " +
➥req.postalCode );
_addr.removeEventListener( GeocoderEvent.GEOCODER_SUCCESS, handleGeocodeSuccess );
_addr.addEventListener( GeocoderEvent.GEOCODER_SUCCESS, handleGeocodeSuccess );
_map.setCenterAddress( addr );
```

Online/Offline Synchronization

The part of the Cairngorm Contact Manager application that shines is its capability to
work in an offline mode. This means that even without a network connection to the
server, the application can continue to function and allow the user to synchronize all the
changes made when the network connection is restored.

Embedded Database

For the application to have this offline capability, it must maintain a copy of the data
being edited locally. This is possible using Adobe AIR because every application can read
and write to a local SQLite database. The embedded SQLite database that comes with the
Cairngorm Contact Manager was created in advance and contains the same structure as
the one that resides on the remote server with one difference. All the tables contain two
extra columns called `syncFlag` and `syncAction`, which are used to determine if the data
stored locally requires synchronization with the server when a connection is reestablished
and what type of action should be taken, either a create or update. Therefore, it is easy for
the application to maintain a local copy of the data and perform create/update operations.

Working with the local database should be familiar if you have worked with other relational databases in the past. To work with the contacts in the local database, we created a
class called `ContactDAO` to handle all the data access. First, of course, we must connect to
the local database, and this is handled in the `ContactManager` class, which uses the
`ContactDAO` class. The connection is established as follows:

```
_cn = new SQLConnection();
var dbFile:File = File.applicationDirectory.resolvePath( "contacts.db" );
cn.open( dbFile, SQLMode.UPDATE );
```

After this connection is established, the various methods on the `ContactDAO` class can be used. As you can see from Listing 24.1, the `create()` function uses the connection to create a `SQLStatement` object with the appropriate SQL text, sets the parameters for the statement, and executes the call. After the statement is executed, the primary key for the newly created row is returned. Notice also that the statement differs depending on if the contact we are creating was just loaded remotely from the server or if we are creating the user for local storage. If the contact is being created for local storage (until it is synchronized with the server), this is when the `syncFlag` and `syncAction` columns are set.

LISTING 24.1   The `create()` Function of the `ContactDAO` Data Access Class (Some Code Omitted for Brevity)

```
...
private static const CREATE_CONTACT_FROM_SERVER:String = "...";
private static const CREATE_CONTACT_FROM_LOCAL:String = "...";
...
public function create( contact:Contact, fromServer:Boolean = false ):Number
{
  try
  {
    var sql:String = ( fromServer )
                ?CREATE_CONTACT_FROM_SERVER
                :CREATE_CONTACT_FOR_LOCAL;

    var stmt:SQLStatement = new SQLStatement();
    stmt.sqlConnection = cn;
    stmt.text = sql;

    if( fromServer )
    {
      stmt.parameters[":contactId"] = contact.contactId;
    }
    else
    {
      stmt.parameters[":syncAction"] = Contact.SYNC_ACTION_CREATE;
    }

    stmt.parameters[":name"] = contact.name;
    stmt.parameters[":address1"] = contact.address1;
    stmt.parameters[":address2"] = contact.address2;
    stmt.parameters[":city"] = contact.city;
    stmt.parameters[":province"] = contact.province;
    stmt.parameters[":country"] = contact.country;
    stmt.parameters[":postalCode"] = contact.postalCode;
    stmt.parameters[":syncFlag"] = contact.syncFlag;
    stmt.execute();
```

```
    var s:SQLResult = stmt.getResult();
    var id:Number = s.lastInsertRowID;
    return id;
  }
  catch( e:SQLError )
  {
    trace( "Unable to create contact: " + e );
    throw new ContactError( e.message );
  }

  return 0;
}
```

Handling the Offline Scenario

To make the Cairngorm Contact Manager application handle the offline scenario, you must do several things.

First, you must determine when a network connection is available. To do this, we use the URLMonitor class after the application has been initialized to monitor a particular URL:

```
monitor = new URLMonitor( new URLRequest('http://www.adobe.com') );
monitor.addEventListener( StatusEvent.STATUS, announceStatus );
monitor.start();
```

When the status of the connection changes, the announceStatus() function is called and we update a model variable that can then be used at various places in the application:

```
private function announceStatus( e:StatusEvent ):void {
...
ContactModel.getInstance().connected = monitor.available;
...
}
```

Now that we have a mechanism to know when the application is online/offline, we need to make sure that parts of the code use this status to determine if we should then interact with the local or remote data. Thus, the ContactManagerDelegate class that is used to handle all remote communication with the server contains some extra logic. The loadList(), load(), and update() functions make use of the network status to know to either retrieve or update data locally or remotely:

```
public function loadList():void
{
  if( connected )
  {
    var token:AsyncToken = service.loadList();
    token.addResponder( this.responder );
  }
  else
  {
```

```
    var contacts:ArrayCollection = ContactManager.getInstance().loadList();
    var evt:ResultEvent = new ResultEvent( ResultEvent.RESULT, false, true,
➥contacts );
    responder.result( evt );
  }
}
```

As you can see from the preceding code sample, should the application not be connected, it will make use of the ContactManager class to retrieve the list of contacts from the local SQLite database and then create an instance of the ResultEvent object we need to send back to the command class. This is a great example of how the business delegate pattern obfuscates the data access layer; in this case, we added extra logic to determine which source to use to retrieve data. The best part is the rest of the application remains unchanged, and it is great for the user as well, as seen in Figure 24.3, who can continue to work with the local data.

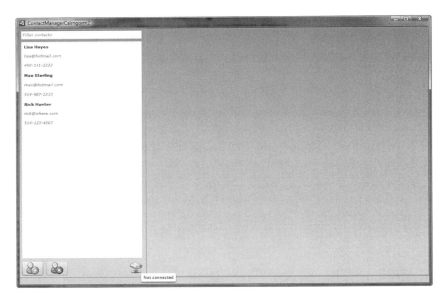

FIGURE 24.3   With no network connection, the application continues to function; notice the disconnect icon under the list of contacts. The map is also not displayed because there is no Internet connection.

On a final note, whenever the status of the network connection changes, the SyncContactsCmd command is called. This command is the one responsible for sending any local changes to the server so that both copies of data can be maintained in sync. It does this first by retrieving from the local database the list of contacts to synchronize (based on the syncFlag column):

```
var unsyncContacts:ArrayCollection = ContactManager.getInstance().loadUnsyncList();
```

Then, if there are any contacts to synchronize, it makes a call to the server, using the business delegate with the list of contacts:

```
if( unsyncContacts.length > 0 )
{
  var delegate:ContactManagerDelegate = new ContactManagerDelegate( this );
  delegate.batchUpdate( unsyncContacts );
  return;
}
```

When the synchronization with the server is completed, the contact list is once again refreshed from the server to maintain the proper list of primary keys for each contact for the next time the synchronization is required.

> **TIP**
>
> The Cairngorm Contact Manager application handles the offline scenario because we developed the application as such. However, you can also use Live Cycle Data Services ES (LCDS) to do this automatically. You can learn about LCDS at the following URL: http://www.adobe.com/products/livecycle/dataservices. Furthermore, Adobe's Flex and AIR evangelist Christopher Coenraets created such an example, which you can read about on his blog by visiting this URL: http://coenraets.org/blog/2008/05/insync-automatic-offline-data-synchronization-in-air-using-lcds-26.

24

Summary

In this chapter we looked at a contact manager application build in Adobe AIR that makes use of third-party components and one of Adobe AIR's main features, the capability to access a local SQLite database. In today's world of cloud computing, it is important for mission-critical applications to be useful even when no network connection is available. Thus, we demonstrated that with some minor changes to an application, we can take advantage of Adobe AIR's capability to access a local database and provide offline functionality for an application. This means that an application can continue to be functional, allowing the users to work with a local copy of the application's data, and, after the network connection is available, all local data changes will be automatically synchronized with the remote server. Therefore, users of any Adobe AIR application with offline capabilities can remain productive anywhere, at anytime.

# CHAPTER 25

Peer-to-Peer Photo Sharing Using Adobe AIR, Bonjour, and Java

Considering this book is part of the Unleashed series by Sams, this chapter is dedicated to pushing beyond the current boundaries of the Adobe® AIR™ platform. With the help of Java, we extend the capabilities of Adobe AIR to include peer-to-peer networking.

Although there are technologies in existence today that can drive communication between Adobe® Flash®, Adobe® Flex™, and Adobe AIR client applications, for the most part they all involve a server-side component to the equation. For example, the Adobe Flash Media Server supports shared remote objects in which any number of clients can push or pull data to and from the server. Changes to these shared objects are then propagated down to other clients, which provide the effect of them being interconnected. One challenge with this model, in terms of cost and scale, is the dependency on a server infrastructure. Of course, there are scenarios in which this architecture is essential, particularly where a server-side application is providing services, security, and functionality around the shared data. However, there are, perhaps, just as many use cases in which direct communication with peers is not only convenient, but also more efficient in terms of scalability.

Instant messaging is a great example. Although an application in the cloud might be required to provide the initial "handshake" between client applications, having the ability to communicate peer-to-peer from that point on relieves the server from the role of data brokering.

A second example, and what this chapter looks at, is the concept of photo sharing utilizing peer-to-peer communication. The sample application in this chapter allows users to browse photos from any client running in the same local network as if the photos were on their local machine. We leverage Java to provide the "network discovery" capabilities.

Application Overview

This chapter starts by taking a bird's-eye view of the overall architecture of the photo-sharing application.

The first challenge of loading and displaying images is easy enough in the context of Adobe AIR, so there are no real design challenges in that respect. However, we need some real magic for our application to be able to discover other Adobe AIR clients running this same application on their local machine.

To tackle the discovery process, we leverage a Java process that runs in parallel to the Adobe AIR application. This Java program uses Apple's proprietary freeware implementation of its Bonjour protocol. It is via this protocol that our clients will be able to broadcast and discover other clients on the network. Of course, there's still the challenge of relaying this event-driven information up to the Adobe AIR application, but let's take one step at a time.

Now assuming the discovery process is feasible, we still need a way to talk to these other clients and exchange information. Thankfully, with the inclusion of Webkit in the Adobe AIR platform, we can simply leverage the HTTP protocol! Oh, but wait, Adobe AIR applications can load HTTP content, but they certainly can't *serve* HTTP content to other clients! Fear not; we will once again leverage Java and include a tiny web server in our application. The word *tiny* might not be the right word to describe this particular web server. Considering the entire web server is only 4 kilobytes in size, let's use the word *mini*!

Understanding the Bonjour Protocol

The Bonjour protocol is Apple Inc.'s implementation of the Zeroconf protocol. Zeroconf, or in its expanded form Zero Configuration Networking, is a protocol for creating local networking groups without having to configure individual clients or set up a server infrastructure.

A perfect example of a common use is for discovering available print servers on a network. Rather than have to find, install, and configure drivers for each and every printer, the Bonjour/Zeroconfig protocol can be used to discover and configure the interoperation between the client and print server automatically. In fact, a number of printer manufacturers today support this protocol (HP, Brother, Epson, and others).

In the context of our sample project, we use the Bonjour protocol to discover other Adobe AIR clients running our photo application. When another client is found on the local network, the IP address is stored locally, and the photo library of the new-found friend is made accessible in the user interface. At this point, the local user can now click on the new photo library and view images as if they were stored locally.

For more information on the Bonjour protocol, see the following website:

www.apple.com/support/bonjour/

For more information on Zeroconf, check out the following URL:

www.zeroconf.org/

Introducing the Mini Web Server

The next step involves retrieving information from remote clients. Because server sockets aren't available in Adobe AIR, we must use our Mini Web Server to fill the gap.

Adding a web server to your Adobe AIR application is not really as dramatic as it sounds. Especially considering the fact that the entire server comes in under 4 kilobytes. For this project, we incorporated the Java Mini Web Server from jibble.org. Each instance of our photo-sharing application is both serving and consuming content over the HTTP protocol. The Mini Web Server hosts content while the built-in HTML control in Adobe AIR renders that same content on another client. See Figure 25.1.

FIGURE 25.1   Peer-to-peer communication between Adobe AIR clients over HTTP.

For more information on the Java Mini Web Server, see the following URL:

www.jibble.org/miniwebserver/

Integrating Adobe AIR and Java via Adobe Flash Socket Connections

To circumvent the lack of server sockets (that is, the ability to "listen" for incoming socket connections) in Adobe AIR, we have a Java process act as a surrogate. The Java process receives incoming events from Bonjour and relays the information up to the Adobe Flex applications residing in the Adobe AIR runtime.

Listing 25.1 outlines the creation of the server socket on the Java side. `RequestThread` is what handles the actual messaging between Java and the ActionScript layer highlighted in Listing 25.2. When the Adobe AIR application is fired up, it makes a socket connection to the Java process. When events need to be "pushed" upstream from Java to Adobe AIR, the `ProgressEvent` fires and invokes the `socketDataEvent`, allowing the Adobe AIR client to process the information:

```
connection.addEventListener( ProgressEvent.SOCKET_DATA, socketDataEvent );
```

Events bubbled up from the Java process might include a newly discovered photo-sharing client on the network or a previous peer that has been lost. With this information, we can manage all the potential photo resources on the network in ActionScript.

LISTING 25.1   Creating the Server Socket in Java

```java
public void run()
{
    System.out.println( "BrokerService.run()" );
    while ( isRunning )
    {
        try
        {
            Socket clientSocket = serverSocket.accept();
            new RequestThread( clientSocket ).start();
        }
        catch ( IOException e )
        {
            e.printStackTrace();
        }
    }
    // close the server socket connection
    try
    {
        this.serverSocket.close();
    }
    catch ( IOException e ) { }
}
```

LISTING 25.2   Establishing the Socket Connection to the Server Socket from ActionScript

```actionscript
public function BrokerConnection( port_number: int )
{
    this._state = 0;
    this._buffer = new ByteArray();
    this._connection = new Socket( HOSTNAME, port_number );
    connection.addEventListener( "connect", socketConnectEvent );
    connection.addEventListener( ProgressEvent.SOCKET_DATA, socketDataEvent );
    connection.addEventListener( "ioError", socketErrorEvent );
}
```

After an event is received on the Adobe AIR client, we pull the information out of the buffer and dispatch a `PacketEvent` along with the data fed up through the socket. See Listing 25.3.

LISTING 25.3   ActionScript Callback Function Invoked in Response to a Bonjour Event

```
private function socketDataEvent( event: ProgressEvent ):void
{
   connection.readBytes( _buffer, 0, _connection.bytesAvailable );
   if ( _buffer.length > 0 )
   {
      var result: MessagePacket = MessagePacket.fromBytes( _buffer );
      if ( result != null )
      {
         dispatchEvent( new PacketEvent( PacketEvent.DATA, result) );
      }
      clearBuffer();
   }
}
```

The last element in the Java-to-ActionScript process revolves around determining what type of Bonjour event is being raised and reacting accordingly. This includes events that reflect the discovery of another client, BROKER_SERVICE_FOUND, or when a previously registered peer connection has been lost, BROKER_SERVICE_LOST. See Listing 25.4.

LISTING 25.4   Handling Various Messages Being Dispatched from the Underlying Bonjour Service

```
private function onPacketDataEvent( e: PacketEvent ):void
{
   trace( "onPacketDataEvent()" );
   var packet: MessagePacket = e.packet;
   if ( packet.packetType == MessagePacket.BROKER_SERVICE_FOUND )
   {
      this.addServer( packet );
      trace("SERVICE_FOUND");
      trace( "serviceName=" + packet.serviceName );
      trace( "serviceType=" + packet.serviceType );
      trace( "serviceDomain=" + packet.serviceDomain );
   } else if ( packet.packetType == MessagePacket.BROKER_SERVICE_RESOLVED ){
      trace("SERVICE_RESOLVED");
      trace( "serviceFullName=" + packet.serviceFullName );
      trace( "serviceHostname=" + packet.serviceHostname );
```

```
      trace( "servicePort=" + packet.servicePort );
      this.updateServerInfo( packet );
   } else if ( packet.packetType == MessagePacket.BROKER_SERVICE_REGISTERED ){
      trace("SERVICE_REGISTERED");
      trace( "serviceName=" + packet.serviceName );
      trace( "serviceType=" + packet.serviceType );
      trace( "serviceDomain=" + packet.serviceDomain );
      trace( "serviceFlags=" + packet.serviceFlags );
   } else if ( packet.packetType == MessagePacket.BROKER_SERVICE_LOST ){
      trace("SERVICE_LOST");
      trace( "serviceName=" + packet.serviceName );
      trace( "serviceType=" + packet.serviceType );
      trace( "serviceDomain=" + packet.serviceDomain );
      trace( "serviceIdentifier=" + packet.serviceIdentifier );
      this.removeServerByName( packet.serviceName );
   }
}
```

With regard to productizing an application of this kind, you definitely have to wrap up the various components (Bonjour service, web server, and Adobe AIR client) into a parent install process and executable. This will most likely have to be in the form of a Java or native program that, in turn, launches subprocesses in sequence, that is, Bonjour Service, Mini Web Server, and, finally, the photo-sharing Adobe AIR application.

Summary

Although having a dependency on another runtime like Java does complicate application deployment, the extended capability of peer-to-peer networking opens the door for an entirely new breed of application. Who knows, perhaps this type of innovation is what we need to drive future versions of the Adobe AIR platform.

CHAPTER 26

Building a Video Distribution System

Video player sample applications based on Adobe® AIR™ are prevalent on the Web. So we're going to throw in a twist to make ours a little more interesting.

In the real world, applications centered around video content have a lot more to them than just the media. In fact, if you've already got the encoded video available to you, integration into the client is perhaps the most straightforward part of the overall project. The more challenging part of the equation is figuring out how to distribute content to users—especially if you intend on securing and eventually monetizing your content.

Although I've been working with rich Internet technologies for years now, ColdFusion (CF) was my first true love in tech. Now you might expect this opinion considering I work for Adobe, but in actuality I was introduced to CF way back in version 2 (it's now at version 8!)—long before my career started at Adobe. My point is that there is nothing out there that can match the breadth of ColdFusion's offering.

What is ColdFusion? Well, there's a language, ColdFusion Markup Language (CFML), and there's a server runtime component. The CF engine itself is a J2EE application that can either be installed as standalone server (using Adobe's JRun) or deployed into a number of Java application servers. The CFML templates and components are eventually compiled down to Java byte code and execute as any Java application would. The best way I've heard ColdFusion described is as a "productivity layer" on top of J2EE. These days, however, it has expanded beyond that with the advent of LiveCycle Data Services.

Adobe LiveCycle Data Services (LCDS) provides real-time data management facilities to drive today's rich clients—both on the web and, of course, within Adobe AIR. Things like syncing data with the server back end or sharing data between clients is a snap. Although BlazeDS does offer a subset of the capabilities found in LCDS, the data management features are LCDS only—and that's where all the magic happens.

This chapter looks at creating a simple, yet powerful video distribution system using Adobe ColdFusion on the back end while leveraging the built-in version of Adobe LiveCycle Data Services—a potent combination right out of the box.

> **NOTE**
>
> For more information on Adobe ColdFusion, check out this URL:
>
> http://www.adobe.com/products/coldfusion/
>
> For more information on Adobe LiveCycle Data Services, visit this website:
>
> http://www.adobe.com/products/livecycle/dataservices/

Application Overview

Starting from a bird's-eye view of the architecture (see Figure 26.1), this section looks at the major components and event process.

First, we have a watch folder event gateway configured to monitor an upload folder on the server. When a new video is uploaded, an event is dispatched to a listener ColdFusion Component (CFC) and supplied the appropriate data containing the event type and path of the video file. The CFC instantiates a new metadata object based on parameters of the uploaded file. A create event is constructed with our metadata object as a property and dispatched to a data management event gateway. Based on a specified LiveCycle Data Service (LCDS) destination in the event object, our metadata object is added to the collection in our data service. This change is then propagated down to all connected Adobe AIR client applications. The metadata objects contain all the necessary information for the clients to connect and download video content.

The data service is responsible for managing the persistence of our collection of video metadata objects. As records are added, modified, or deleted from the collection, LCDS leverages our ColdFusion assembler CFC to direct create, read, update, and delete (CRUD) operations on the database—very cool stuff.

> **NOTE**
>
> Although this example is only relaying location information concerning the video content, there's no reason why this data structure could not be expanded to drive collaboration between users. For instance, the metadata objects could be expanded to include reviewer comments about video content. When comments are added to the data model, they can be immediately distributed across all connected Adobe AIR clients.

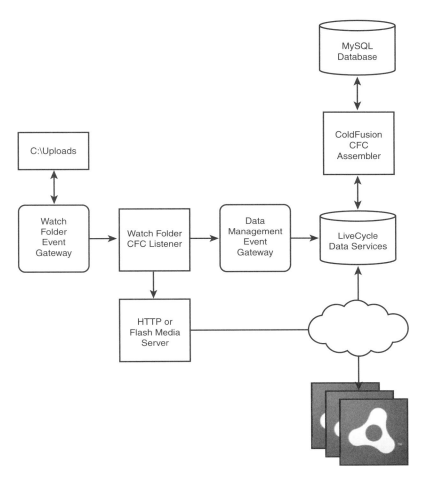

FIGURE 26.1   Video distribution system architecture.

Working with Adobe ColdFusion

This section takes a closer look at the first stage of our video distribution system, namely the watch folder process.

When event gateways are created in the ColdFusion administration console, you can optionally specify configuration files, which, in our case, dictate operational parameters for the process. Listing 26.1 outlines the configuration parameters for our watch folder event gateway. You can see the callback method names are also specified in the configuration file. When a file is added to a directory, `onAdd()` is invoked and is passed a `CFEvent` object containing information about the new file.

NOTE

For information on installing ColdFusion, go to the following website:

http://www.adobe.com/support/documentation/en/coldfusion/

In this chapter, all references to ColdFusion stem from the standalone server installation with LiveCycle Data Services (LCDS). LCDS is available as an option during the ColdFusion install process.

LISTING 26.1   Configuration File for the Watch Folder Event Gateway

```
# The directory you want to watch.  If you are entering a Windows path
# either use forward slashes (C:/mydir) or escape the back slashes (C:\\mydir).
directory=/Applications/ColdFusion8/wwwroot/unleashed/uploads

# Should we watch the directory and all subdirectories too
# Default is no.  Set to 'yes' to do the recursion.
recurse=no

# The interval between checks, in miliseconds
# Default is 60 seconds
interval=15000

# The comma separated list of extensions to match.
# Default is * - all files
extensions=*

# CFC Function for file Change events
# Default is onChange, set to nothing if you don't want to see these events
changeFunction=onChange

# CFC Function for file Add events
# Default is onAdd, set to nothing if you don't want to see these events
addFunction=onAdd

# CFC Function for file Delete events
# Default is onDelete, set to nothing if you don't want to see these events
deleteFunction=onDelete
```

Listing 26.2 outlines the listener ColdFusion Component (CFC) on the receiving end of the watch folder process. When the onAdd() method is invoked, we're creating a new metadata object based on the supplied file information. Second, we're notifying the LiveCycle Data Service destination that a new record has been created along with a reference to our new metadata object. When the data service receives this notification, all connected clients are updated to reflect the addition of our new metadata entry.

LISTING 26.2   CFC Listener for the Event Gateway

```
<cfcomponent hint="Watch Folder Listener">
    <cfset variables.metadataDAO = CreateObject( "component", "metadataDAO") />

    <cffunction name="onAdd">
        <cfargument name="CFEvent" type="struct" required="yes" />
        <cfset var filepath = "" />
        <cfset var name = "" />
        <cfset var result = "" />
        <cfset var metadata = "" />

        <cflock name="SERIALIZE" timeout="90">
            <cfset filepath = CFEvent.data.filename />
            <cfset name = ListLast( filepath, "/" ) />
            <cffile action="move" source="#filepath#"
➥destination="/Applications/ColdFusion8/wwwroot/unleashed/media/#name#" />

            <cfscript>
            metadata = CreateObject("component","metaData").init();
            metadata.setUrl( "http://localhost:8500/unleashed/media/#name#" );
            metadata.setFilename( name );
            variables.metadataDAO.create( metadata );

            createEvent = StructNew();
            createEvent.action = "create";
            createEvent.item = metadata;
            createEvent.destination = "unleashed";
            result = sendGatewayMessage( "UnleashedDataManagement", createEvent );
            </cfscript>
        </cflock>

        <cfdump var="#arguments.CFEvent#" format="text"
➥output="/Users/styoung/Logs/WatchFolder.log" />
    </cffunction>

    <cffunction name="onDelete"></cffunction>

    <cffunction name="onChange"></cffunction>
</cfcomponent>
```

We've also leveraged ColdFusion on the back end of our LiveCycle Data Service (LCDS) destination. When metadata objects are added, modified, or removed from the managed collection, LCDS needs an "assembler" that handles the database operations to persist data.

To properly construct an assembler CFC, we must implement a number of methods that LCDS will expect to exist at runtime. Listing 26.3 highlights one of these, the fill() method. This function is invoked when an Adobe® Flex™ and/or Adobe AIR client initially connects to the data service to retrieve the existing collection.

LISTING 26.3   Fill Method Inside the Assembler CFC

```
<cffunction name="fill" output="no" returntype="unleashed.metadata[]"
access="remote">
   <cfargument name="param" type="string" required="no">

   <cftry>
      <cfif structKeyExists(arguments, "param")>
         <cfreturn variables.dao.read(param=arguments.param)>
      <cfelse>
         <cfreturn variables.dao.read()>
      </cfif>

      <!—- If the SQL failed, report the error, include SQL if debugging
►turned on —->
      <cfcatch type="database">
         <cfif isDebugMode() AND  isDefined("cfcatch.queryError") AND
►isDefined("cfcatch.sql")>
            <cfset msg = "Error during fill: " & cfcatch.queryError & ".
►SQL was :" & cfcatch.sql>
         <cfelse>
            <cfset msg = "Error during fill: " & cfcatch.message >
         </cfif>
         <cfthrow message="#msg#">
      </cfcatch>
      <!—- If anything else happened, report the error —->
      <cfcatch type="any">
         <cfset msg = "Error during fill: " & cfcatch.message >
         <cfthrow message="#msg#">
      </cfcatch>
   </cftry>
</cffunction>
```

For our example, we used the ColdFusion extensions inside of Adobe FlexBuilder to auto-matically generate the assembler CFC. This is done by simply right-clicking on a database table within the ColdFusion RDS view (see Figure 26.2) and selecting the ColdFusion wizard named Create CFC. The database table will be introspected and the accommodating CFC code generated for you within your project!

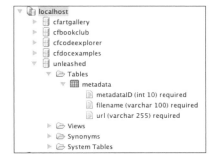

FIGURE 26.2   ColdFusion RDS view within Adobe Flex Builder.

NOTE

If you've previously installed Adobe Flex Builder without the ColdFusion extensions, you can download them from the Adobe website:

http://www.adobe.com/support/coldfusion/downloads.html

Working with LiveCycle Data Services

With regard to LCDS, we need to define our destination. Listing 26.4 shows the addition we made to accommodate our video distribution application. Because LCDS is integrated into ColdFusion, when adding new messaging destinations, we have to modify the configuration file under the web root of CF itself located at:

```
{ coldfusion.install.root }/wwwroot/WEB-INF/flex/data-management-config.xml
```

LISTING 26.4   Adding a New Management Destination to LiveCycle Data Services

```
<destination id="unleashed">
    <adapter ref="coldfusion-dao"/>
    <channels>
        <channel ref="cf-rtmp" />
        <channel ref="cf-polling-amf"/>
    </channels>
    <properties>
        <component>unleashed.metadataAssembler</component>
        <scope>request</scope>
        <metadata>
            <identity property="metadataID"/>
        </metadata>
        <server>
            <fill-method>
```

```
        <use-fill-contains>false</use-fill-contains>
        <auto-refresh>true</auto-refresh>
        <ordered>false</ordered>
      </fill-method>
    </server>
  </properties>
</destination>
```

A second change we need to make is in regard to channel definitions located in the
services-config.xml file located in the same directory:

{ coldfusion.install.root }/wwwroot/WEB-INF/flex/data-management-config.xml

By default, all references to the server location and port within this configuration file are
made via environment variables:

http://{server.name}:{server.port}{context.root}

That's fine for server-deployed Adobe Flex applications running on that same server, but
Adobe AIR clients are a different animal. Adobe AIR applications are not compiled in the
server environment, nor are they guaranteed to be delivered from that same server once
packaged. For this reason, we need to hard code the URLs of the endpoints in the configuration files so that these values are compiled into our Adobe AIR application. To avoid
changing the actual server files, you can copy the configuration files locally into your
project and hard code those values instead. When doing so, be sure to copy all the files
referenced by the services-config.xml file listed at the top of the file as follows:

```
<services>
   <service-include file-path="remoting-config.xml" />
   <service-include file-path="proxy-config.xml" />
   <service-include file-path="messaging-config.xml" />
   <service-include file-path="data-management-config.xml" />
</services>
```

NOTE

Alternatively, channel sets and data service destinations can be defined in ActionScript.
Your Adobe AIR application will still need to be aware of the correct server and port to
connect with, but that could always be listed in a property file distributed in the Adobe
AIR application itself—or perhaps even updated dynamically at runtime if the server
location ever needs to be changed.

The Adobe Flex part of the equation is remarkably straightforward. Listing 26.5 outlines
the basic wiring on the client side to connect and "fill" the data collection when the
application starts up.

LISTING 26.5   Connecting to a Data Service from Adobe Flex

```
<?xml version="1.0" encoding="utf-8"?>
<mx:WindowedApplication xmlns:mx="http://www.adobe.com/2006/mxml" layout="vertical"
applicationComplete="init()">

    <mx:Script>
        <![CDATA[
            import mx.rpc.events.FaultEvent;
            import mx.rpc.events.ResultEvent;
            import mx.collections.ArrayCollection;

            [Bindable]
            private var metadataCol:ArrayCollection = new ArrayCollection();

            private function init():void
            {
                metaService.fill( metadataCol );
            }

            private function onResult( event:ResultEvent ):void
            {
                metaService.autoSyncEnabled = true;
            }

            private function onFault( event:FaultEvent ):void
            {}
        ]]>
    </mx:Script>

    <mx:DataService
        id="metaService"
        autoCommit="true"
        autoConnect="true"
        autoMerge="true"
        destination="unleashed"
        result="onResult( event )"
        fault="onFault( event )" />

</mx:WindowedApplication>
```

When the init() function fires after the application has loaded, the client synchronizes
with the data service via the specified destination in the DataService tag. The fill method
accepts an array collection that will be used to populate the collection coming down from

the server. This local variable, metadataCol, can then be bound to various components within the application and render the elements of the collection as you see fit.

Where things get really interesting is that when elements of the array collection are updated on the client, the changes are automatically synchronized back to the server! For example, suppose the array collection is bound to a data grid component. When the application loads, a collection of objects will come down from the data service and, through data binding, populate the data grid. Now in addition to that, you might have an Add Record button on the interface that allows the user to type in a new record directly in the data grid (or perhaps edit an existing record). When those values are committed, it causes the client to synchronize to the server and relay changes to other connected clients automatically!

Although all this can execute automatically, you, of course, have the option to listen for and react to various events and invoke synchronization manually. There are also cases in which data conflicts might happen when more than one client changes the same record at the same time; these can also be caught and handled locally. What we've touched on in this sample application is truly the tip of the iceberg.

Summary

The combination of Adobe ColdFusion and Adobe LiveCycle Data Services serves as a powerful platform for today's rich applications. The data management facilities can drive synchronized data models across connected clients with very little code with no extensive knowledge of the plumbing behind the scenes.

As of this writing, Adobe LiveCycle Data Services version 2.6 was just being released. Be sure to look into the new features being offered around improved performance, protocol support, simplified Hibernate support, and offline syncing capabilities leveraging SQLite in Adobe AIR.

PART VIII

Adobe AIR 1.5 and Adobe Flash 10 Extras

IN THIS PART

Using Adobe Flash 10 Features in Adobe AIR

With the incremental release of Adobe® AIR™ 1.5, we developers now have access to most of the new features available in the Adobe® Flash® Player 10. If you are unfamiliar with the architecture of the Adobe AIR runtime, the Flash Player is one of its moving parts, which, of course, is used to render any Adobe® Flex™ application content.

The second major addition in this Adobe AIR 1.5 release is an update to the Webkit HTML engine, yet another major component of the runtime. The new version of Webkit contains a new JavaScript virtual machine (VM) called SquirrelFish. The SquirrelFish VM is a direct-threaded byte-code engine that interprets JavaScript at runtime, which makes this update important for Adobe AIR developers using HTML/JavaScript/AJAX in their applications. Webkit with SquirrelFish is, on average, over four times faster than recent versions (Webkit 3.0). You should notice significant performance increases if you are developing HTML-based Adobe AIR applications.

The inclusion of Adobe Flash 10 is a major leap forward—delivering a ton of new features. Some highlights include the following:

▶ 3D effects with accompanying application programming interfaces (APIs)

▶ Vector data type support

▶ Custom filters and effects

▶ New text rendering engine

▶ Drawing API enhancements

▶ Updated Saffron font rendering engine

▶ Enhanced sound APIs

▶ Dynamic video streaming

> **NOTE**
>
> For an in-depth overview of Adobe Flash 10 capabilities, visit the following websites:
>
> http://www.adobe.com/devnet/logged_in/jchurch_flashplayer10.html
>
> http://www.adobe.com/products/flashplayer/

The first question that might come to mind is, "What features can we leverage in our Adobe AIR applications?" The short answer is all of them! Anything accessible via ActionScript APIs is usable in Adobe AIR as the Adobe AIR runtime only *adds* new capabilities to Adobe Flash via Adobe AIR–specific methods and classes. This chapter focuses mainly on the new 3D effects, as this is the most consumable new feature with the biggest visual impact.

Using 3D Rotation Effects

The new 3D effects are going to have a significant impact on the visual aspects of Adobe Flex applications running in Adobe AIR.

Let me start by saying that although adding 3D effects to display objects is easy, it does not mean everything in your user interface should be rotating in funky 3D space! As developers we tend to gravitate toward new capabilities and start applying them to everything under the sun just because we can. However, this can have a detrimental effect for your users' experience. Remember the BLINK tag? Okay...enough said.

The 3D features stem from the new drawing APIs available in ActionScript that allow you to draw complex shapes and apply texture mappings. Luckily for us we don't have to go that deep to reap the benefits in Adobe Flex. Anything that extends `DisplayObject`, such as `Shape`, `HBox`, `VBox`, `Panel`, `VideoDisplay`, and so on, will now have a set of new properties that facilitate its positioning in 3D space, as follows:

▶ RotationX

▶ RotationY

▶ RotationZ

▶ Z (z-axis)

The rotation attributes specify the degree at which the display object should be rotated on the given axis. For example:

```
myImage.rotationX = 45;
```

If you can picture a graph with an x-axis and a y-axis, setting the `rotationX` of an object "swings" the display object 45 degrees on the x-axis. Another way to picture this effect in real terms is to visualize a tree branch hanging perpendicular to the ground (our x-axis). If you were to reach up with both hands and start to swing on the branch, you'd effectively be setting your rotationX in degrees. At rest, you'd be at 0 degrees while swinging right around the branch to 360 degrees would return you to your starting state. Figure 27.1 depicts the rotationX, rotationY, and rotationZ properties.

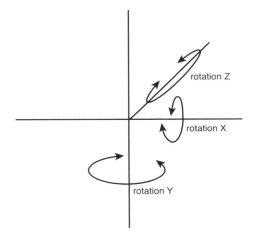

FIGURE 27.1   The x, y and z axis in 3D space.

Rotating on the y-axis is the equivalent of swinging around the tree trunk as opposed to the branch. Another example is the front door of your home; it swings on its y-axis.

The z-axis is where things start to get interesting. Using the tree analogy, the z-axis represents another branch perpendicular to the ground but resting 90 degrees from our x-axis (first branch). At this point though, perhaps a visual demonstration would be more effective! Listing 27.1 outlines a demo application that allows you to interact with the rotation of all three axes in real time with the option to animate.

LISTING 27.1   Visualizing the Rotation of a Display Object on the X-, Y-, and Z-Axes

```
<?xml version="1.0" encoding="utf-8"?>
<mx:WindowedApplication
    xmlns:mx="http://www.adobe.com/2006/mxml"
    layout="vertical"
    horizontalAlign="center" verticalAlign="middle"
    verticalGap="5"
    title="3D Demo"
    initialize="init()">

    <mx:Style source="styles.css" />
```

```
<mx:Script>
  <![CDATA[
    import mx.binding.utils.BindingUtils;

    private var isAnimatingX:Boolean = false;
    private var isAnimatingY:Boolean = false;
    private var isAnimatingZ:Boolean = false;

    private function init():void
    {
       BindingUtils.bindProperty( airLogo, "rotationX", xRotation, "value" );
       BindingUtils.bindProperty( airLogo, "rotationY", yRotation, "value" );
       BindingUtils.bindProperty( airLogo, "rotationZ", zRotation, "value" );
    }

    private function animateX():void
    {
       if( isAnimatingX )
       {
          isAnimatingX = false;
          buttonX.label = "Start X Rotation";
          removeEventListener( Event.ENTER_FRAME, onAnimateX );
       } else {
          isAnimatingX = true;
          buttonX.label = "Stop X Rotation";
          addEventListener( Event.ENTER_FRAME, onAnimateX );
       }
    }

    private function onAnimateX( event:Event ):void
    {
       if( airLogo.rotationX == 360 )
          airLogo.rotationX = xRotation.value = 0;
       xRotation.value = airLogo.rotationX += 10;
    }

    private function animateY():void
    {
       if( isAnimatingY )
       {
          isAnimatingY = false;
          buttonY.label = "Start Y Rotation";
          removeEventListener( Event.ENTER_FRAME, onAnimateY );
       } else {
          isAnimatingY = true;
          buttonY.label = "Stop Y Rotation";
```

```
                  addEventListener( Event.ENTER_FRAME, onAnimateY );
               }
            }

            private function onAnimateY( event:Event ):void
            {
               if( airLogo.rotationY == 360 )
                  airLogo.rotationY = yRotation.value = 0;
               yRotation.value = airLogo.rotationY += 10;
            }

            private function animateZ():void
            {
               if( isAnimatingZ )
               {
                  isAnimatingZ = false;
                  buttonZ.label = "Start Z Rotation";
                  removeEventListener( Event.ENTER_FRAME, onAnimateZ );
               } else {
                  isAnimatingZ = true;
                  buttonZ.label = "Stop Z Rotation";
                  addEventListener( Event.ENTER_FRAME, onAnimateZ );
               }
            }

            private function onAnimateZ( event:Event ):void
            {
               if( airLogo.rotationZ == 360 )
                  airLogo.rotationZ = zRotation.value = 0;
               zRotation.value = airLogo.rotationZ += 10;
            }

            private function reset():void
            {
               isAnimatingX = isAnimatingY = isAnimatingZ = true;
               animateX();
               animateY();
               animateZ();
               xRotation.value = yRotation.value = zRotation.value = 0;
            }
      ]]>
   </mx:Script>

   <mx:Image
      id="airLogo"
      width="300" height="300"
```

27

```
        maintainAspectRatio="true"
        source="@Embed(source='assets/air.png')" />

    <mx:Spacer height="60" />

    <mx:HBox>
        <mx:VBox>
            <mx:Button id="buttonX" label="Start X Rotation" click="animateX()" />
            <mx:Button id="buttonY" label="Start Y Rotation" click="animateY()" />
            <mx:Button id="buttonZ" label="Start Z Rotation" click="animateZ()" />
            <mx:Button label="Reset" click="reset()" />
        </mx:VBox>
        <mx:VRule height="100%" />
        <mx:VBox>
            <mx:HBox horizontalGap="20">
                <mx:Label text="Rotation X" width="70" />
                <mx:HSlider
                    id="xRotation"
                    tickInterval="10" snapInterval="10"
                    labels="['min', 'max']"
                    minimum="0" maximum="360" liveDragging="true" />
            </mx:HBox>

            <mx:HBox horizontalGap="20">
                <mx:Label text="Rotation Y" width="70" />
                <mx:HSlider
                    id="yRotation"
                    tickInterval="10" snapInterval="10"
                    labels="['min', 'max']"
                    minimum="0" maximum="360" liveDragging="true" />
            </mx:HBox>

            <mx:HBox horizontalGap="20">
                <mx:Label text="Rotation Z" width="70" />
                <mx:HSlider
                    id="zRotation"
                    tickInterval="10" snapInterval="10"
                    labels="['min', 'max']"
                    minimum="0" maximum="360" liveDragging="true" />
            </mx:HBox>
        </mx:VBox>
    </mx:HBox>
</mx:WindowedApplication>
```

If you've checked out all the projects from the Adobe AIR Programming Unleashed repository, go ahead and launch the project Chapter27-01 in either debug or run mode.

Figure 27.2 shows the application in various states as the Adobe AIR logo is being rotated on each axis. You can manually rotate each access by adjusting each of the slider controls on the right side. Next, select one of the start buttons on the left to have the image animate on a particular axis. While animating on a single axis, you can manually change the value of the other axes by adjusting the slider controls. Or for some real fun, start the animation on all axes and prepare to get a little dizzy.

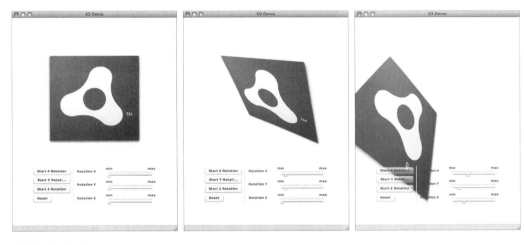

FIGURE 27.2   3D demo application in action.

As you will notice, the performance is quite impressive given that we're rotating a bitmap image through 3D space. We can chalk this up to the new capabilities of Adobe Flash Player 10 with its reliance on your machines graphics processing unit (GPU), that is, the processor on your video card.

Working with Display Objects and the Z-Axis

In Listing 27.1 we explored the new rotation attributes available on display objects. The advent of Adobe Flash Player 10 also gives us a new z property we can use to position display objects in 3D space.

Traditionally when using absolute positioning, we position objects by specifying their x and y coordinates. Specifying the z-axis changes the game. When the z attribute is given a value other than the default of 0, a Matrix3D object is created automatically. What this means is the x, y are no longer screen coordinates but rather relative positions to the parent 3D container.

If you've had any experience with 3D modeling tools, you might find this concept easier to grasp than most. A simpler way to visualize this idea is to think of a cube. When looking at it directly in 3D space, it looks like a square box. Moving it up or down, left or right equates to the x- and y-axis. Now consider if we rotate the cube a few degrees on the y axis. Changing the value of the x-axis by 10 pixels no longer moves the cube 10 pixels to the right, at least from the camera's perspective. The cube moves based on its axis, which is no longer directly in front of the camera. What this boils down to is that, when you move and object on the z-axis, the new x and y coordinates are then calculated based on the following equation:

```
(x*cameraFocalLength/cameraRelativeZPosition,
➥y*cameraFocalLength/cameraRelativeZPosition)
```

Listing 27.2 demonstrates this effect by adding new images at an incremental value on the z-axis. Notice that as additional images are added to the stack, each image in succession is larger (see Figure 27.3). That's because its relative positive to the camera is closer. This is done automatically via the Matrix3D object.

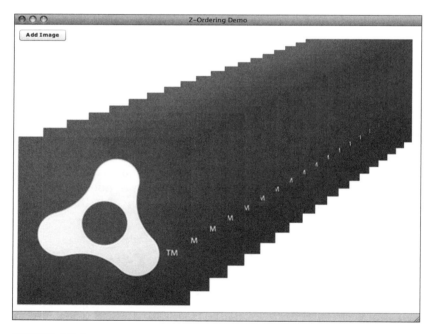

FIGURE 27.3   Visualizing display objects along the z-axis.

LISTING 27.2   Visualizing the Addition of Display Objects on the Z-Axis

```
<?xml version="1.0" encoding="utf-8"?>
<mx:WindowedApplication
    xmlns:mx="http://www.adobe.com/2006/mxml"
```

```
   layout="absolute"
   title="Z-Ordering Demo"
   creationComplete="init()">

   <mx:Style source="styles.css" />

   <mx:Script>
      <![CDATA[
      import mx.controls.Image;

      [Embed(source="assets/air.png")]
      [Bindable]
      private var image:Class;

      private var axis_y:Number = 20;
      private var axis_x:Number = 0;
      private var axis_z:Number = 0;
      private var childIndex:Number = 0;

      private function init():void
      {
         axis_x = nativeWindow.width - 220;
      }

      private function addImage():void
      {
         axis_x += -25;
         axis_y += 10;
         axis_z += -10;

         var img:Image = new Image();
         img.source = image;
         img.z = axis_z;
         img.x = axis_x;
         img.y = axis_y;

         addChildAt( img, childIndex );
         childIndex++;
      }
      ]]>
   </mx:Script>

   <mx:Button label="Add Image" click="addImage()" x="10" y="10" />
</mx:WindowedApplication>
```

27

One last thing to keep in mind is that the child order in a `DisplayObjectContainer` does not equate to the z-axis. For example, if we were to replace the following line in Listing 27.2:

```
axis_z += -10;
```

with the following:

```
axis_z += 10;
```

each new image would be further away from the camera and would appear smaller than the previous. Oddly enough, the last image added still appears to overlap all other images. We have to change our strategy such that the image closest to us remains the highest in the child order stack.

Summary

With the release of Adobe AIR 1.5, developers have access to all the new features available in Adobe Flash Player 10. This includes performance enhancements, 3D APIs, new font rendering capabilities, and custom filters, to name a few. Unfortunately not all of this new functionality is directly accessible from the Adobe Flex Framework—well, at least not until the next major release, which would, of course, be rolled into a future release of Adobe AIR. With that said, there is nothing stopping you from building you own Adobe Flex components that leverage Adobe Flash 10 Player features; in fact I expect a number of exciting projects to crop up from now until the next major release of Adobe Flex. In this chapter, we've touched on some of the new 3D capabilities. I hope this whets your appetite!

The 3D effects capabilities offer developers a whole new way to visually represent application states and data. Over time, we will likely see various third-party solutions leverage the underlying drawing APIs to offer high-performance 3D applications and ready-to-use components for the rest of us. (See papervision3d.org.)

PART IX

Appendices

IN THIS PART

APPENDIX A

Adobe AIR Resources for Developers

This appendix provides useful resources for developers.

IDEs

Although you are certainly free to use the development tools of your choosing, the following are the most common tools of the Adobe® AIR™ and Adobe® Flex™ trade:

▶ Eclipse

http://www.eclipse.org

▶ Flex Builder (standalone or Eclipse plug-in)

http://www.adobe.com/products/flex/flexbuilder/

Server-Side Technologies

Adobe AIR applications can communicate with a wide array of server-side technologies. Here are two specific technologies used in this book:

▶ Adobe LiveCycle Data Services

http://www.adobe.com/products/livecycle/dataservices/

▶ Adobe Blaze DS

http://labs.adobe.com/technologies/blazeds/

Security

In establishing trust between you, the application provider, and your users, consider investing in a certificate for signing your Adobe AIR applications from one of these authorities:

- ▶ Thawte—Code-signing certificates for Adobe Integrated Runtime (AIR)

  https://www.thawte.com

- ▶ VeriSign

  http://www.verisign.com

Mailing Lists

Invaluable resources whether you're a beginner or at the advanced level:

- ▶ Flexcoders (Adobe AIR topics as well)

  http://tech.groups.yahoo.com/group/flexcoders/

- ▶ FlashComGuru—Flash Media Server

  http://www.flashcomguru.com/flashmedialist/

Build Tools

Build tools of the trade. Resources for building Enterprise-level applications:

- ▶ Apache Ant

  http://ant.apache.org

- ▶ Home of Flex Ant tasks

  http://labs.adobe.com/wiki/index.php/Flex_Ant_Tasks

Testing

After you've experienced the benefits of a test-first methodology, you will never look back. FlexUnit tests are a great start:

- ▶ FlexUnit home

  http://code.google.com/p/as3flexunitlib/

- ▶ Borland Silk Test 2008 (now supports Flex)

  http://www.borland.com/us/products/silk/silktest/index.html

Continuous Integration

When your team is expanding, continuous integration is much more efficient in resolving conflicts quickly and early in the development process:

▶ Whitepaper on continuous integration

http://www.martinfowler.com/articles/continuousIntegration.html

▶ Home of CruiseControl

http://cruisecontrol.sourceforge.net

Version Control

An absolute staple for any developer, whether you're operating in a group or as an individual:

▶ Subversion

http://subversion.tigris.org

▶ Subversion plug-in for Eclipse

http://subclipse.tigris.org

▶ Concurrent Versioning System (CVS)

http://ximbiot.com/cvs/cvshome

▶ Perforce

http://www.perforce.com

▶ Google code

http://code.google.com/hosting/

Development Resources

Great articles and discussion on many related technologies and platforms:

▶ Inside RIA

http://www.insideria.com

▶ Both client- and server-side resources

http://www.infoq.com

▶ Server-side resource, some RIA

http://www.theserverside.com

Libraries Used in Our Projects

Free libraries we've used in our sample projects:

- ActionScript 3.0 Yahoo! Maps

  http://developer.yahoo.com/flash/maps/

- Flex components

  http://code.google.com/p/flexlib/

Blogs and Publications

Blogs are an essential tool in the developer's war chest. If we had to pick a single resource for you to take away out of this entire list, it'd be the MXNA blog aggregator. It provides continuous exposure to the heartbeat of the development community:

- Adobe blog aggregator

  http://weblogs.macromedia.com/mxna/

- Flex developer journal

  http://flex.sys-con.com

- Peter Martin, FlexUnit guru

  http://weblogs.macromedia.com/pmartin/

APPENDIX B

Adobe AIR API Reference Poster (Downloadable)

This appendix (a downloadable poster) is a chart outlining all the new capabilities in ActionScript 3 relating to Adobe® AIR™ for easy reference.

The poster can be downloaded from the book website:

1. Go to www.informit.com/title/9780672329715.
2. Click Downloads.
3. Click the link that appears, and the download should start automatically.

Downloading Source Code for *Adobe AIR Programming Unleashed*

The projects used throughout this book can be downloaded directly into Adobe® Flex™ Builder 3 by means of a source control client called Subversion. (The Eclipse plug-in version is aptly named Subclipse.) Or if you'd rather peruse the source files directly, a single Zip archive can be downloaded and extracted onto your desktop.

The advantage of using the Subversion plug-in is that you can "check out" all the projects in one shot and have them populated inside Adobe Flex Builder as Adobe® AIR™ projects. In addition, if any updates are posted, you can sync all the projects with a couple of mouse clicks.

Installing the Subversion Plug-In for Adobe Flex Builder

Whether you choose to use Adobe Flex Builder 3 standalone version or Eclipse plug-in, the procedure is virtually identical:

1. Visit the Subclipse site and copy the link for the "Eclipse Update Site" for the latest stable release:

   http://subclipse.tigris.org/

   At the time of this writing, that is

   http://subclipse.tigris.org/update_1.2.x

2. Open Adobe Flex Builder 3 or Eclipse if you have the Adobe Flex Builder plug-in installed.

3. Navigate to the Help, Software Updates, Find and Install menu option (see Figure C.1).

4. Select Search for New Features to Install.

5. Select New Remote Site.

FIGURE C.1   Installing new features in Adobe Flex Builder/Eclipse.

6. Enter **Subclipse** for the name and paste the Subclipse update URL into the second field. Click OK (see Figure C.2).

FIGURE C.2   Configuring the Subclipse update site.

7. You will now see your entry in the site list. Be sure it is the only one checked. Click Finish.

8. In the Search Results window, expand the Subclipse node and check Subclipse Plugin. The optional items should be unchecked. (They typically require additional installs.) Click Next (see Figure C.3).

9. You need to accept the terms and license agreement to proceed. Click Accept and click Next.

10. Click Finish to start the download and installation.

11. You are prompted with an install warning stating the feature is not signed. Click Install All (see Figure C.4).

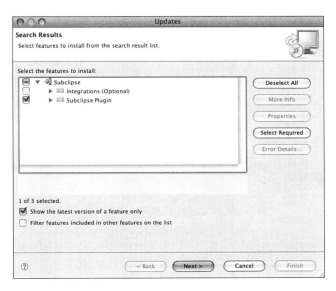

FIGURE C.3   Selecting Subclipse options.

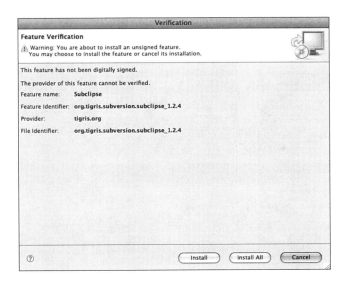

FIGURE C.4   Completing the Subclipse installation.

12. When asked to restart Eclipse or Adobe Flex Builder, select Yes.
13. After Adobe Flex Builder has restarted, navigate to the Window, Perspective, Other menu option.

14. Select SVN Repository Exploring and click OK. This opens a Subversion perspective within Eclipse or Adobe Flex Builder that enables you to connect and retrieve source code from a repository (see Figure C.5).

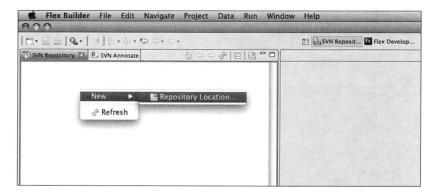

FIGURE C.5   Exploring the Subclipse perspective.

15. Paste the repository URL from the Google Code Project site for Adobe AIR Programming Unleashed (http://air-unleashed.googlecode.com/svn/trunk/). Click Finish (see Figure C.6).

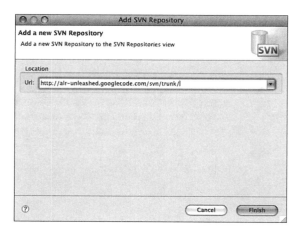

FIGURE C.6   Connecting to the Google Code repository.

16. If you are connected to the Internet, you should now see the repository on the left tab. Expand the node; all the projects for the book are listed (see Figure C.7).

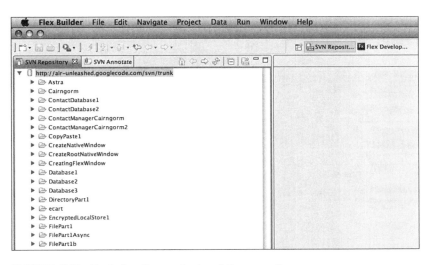

FIGURE C.7   Exploring the contents of the repository.

17. Now you can select the projects you want to check out. To retrieve them all, select all the subfolders, right-click the selection, and select Checkout (see Figure C.8).

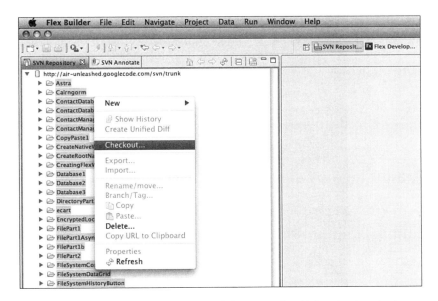

FIGURE C.8   Checking out Adobe AIR Programming Unleashed projects.

18. Keep the default options in the Check Out dialog. Click Finish.

19. After the projects have downloaded, click the Flex Development perspective on the top toolbar in Eclipse or Adobe Flex Builder 3 (see Figure C.9).

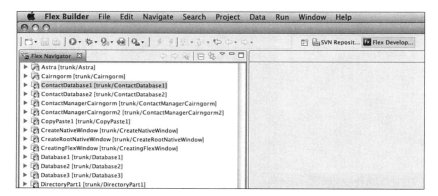

FIGURE C.9   Accessing projects from the Adobe Flex development perspective.

20. You can now open each project, inspect the code, and run/debug the applications.

Downloading the Zip Archive

Alternatively, you can download all the Adobe AIR Programming Unleashed projects as a single Zip file. You can then import projects into your favorite Integrated Development Environment (IDE). The Zip file is at this URL: www.informit.com/title/9780672329715.

Index

A

M

P-Q

parameters

FlashVars, 293

FlexUnit, 388

paste() function, 137-138

patch information, retrieving, 48-49

paths

directory paths, 102

file paths, 102

peer-to-peer networking, 421-422

photo-sharing example application, 422

Bonjour protocol, 422

Java Mini Web Server, 423

server sockets, 423-426

performAdd() method, 385

performance, 61-62, 64

persisting user login information, 277-279

perspectives

Adobe Flex Builder, 322

Eclipse, 22

photo-sharing example application (peer-to-peer networking), 422

Bonjour protocol, 422

Java Mini Web Server, 423

server sockets, 423-426

plug-ins, installing Subversion, 457-462

Pop-Up Menu, 169-170

positioning windows

based on Screen bounds, 93-96

relative to screens, 96-99

PrepAddCartCmd class, 345-346

primary keys, retrieving of inserted rows, 199-200

Product class, 336-337

ProductDelegate class, 341-342

Profiler button, 62

PromptingTextInput, contact manager with integrated Yahoo! maps application, 414

properties

currentTarget, 175

keyEquivalent, 173-175

proxy images, 115

publications, 454

R

re-encrypting databases with new keys, 208

reading

application settings, 43-45

data in encrypted local store, 275

data from tables, 200

files, 105-106

FileMode, 109

rebuilding CruiseControl, 406-407

records, inserting into database tables, 196-199

reducing coupling with design patterns, 325

references

Screens, obtaining references to the main screen, 91-92

SDKs (software development kits), 22

   installing

      Adobe Flex, 26-27

      Java, 23

   Java, adding to system paths, 24-26

seamless application installation, 292-299

   badge.fla files, 292

   badge.swf files, 292

   default_badge.html file, 293-297

   FlashVars parameters, 293

   getApplicationVersion() method, 298

   getStatus() method, 297-298

   installApplication() method, 298-299

   launchApplication() method, 299

   overview, 291

security, certificates, 452

security sandboxes, 263-265

   application sandboxes, 266

   bridges, 266-270

      UserAPI, 270

   types of, 264-265

selectDefaultRecord(), 199

self-signed certificates, creating for testing, 367-368

server sockets for photo-sharing example application, 423-426

server-side technologies, 451

servers, remote servers, updating Adobe AIR application, 314-316

Service to Worker pattern, 330

ServiceCapture, 57

ServiceLocator, Cairngorm, 332-333

ServiceLocator class, 340-341

services, interacting with design patterns, 325

setClipBoard() function, 136

setDataHandler() method, 154

setup(), test cases (FlexUnit), 378-379

Shockwave Flash (SWF), 213

Shockwave Flash (SWF) files, 68, 363

shopping cart application (Cairngorm)

   AddItemCmd class, 347-348

   AddItemView.mxml file, 353-355

   CancelAddCmd class, 346

   CartController class, 348

   CartItem class, 337-338

   CartModel class, 338-339

   CartView.mxml file, 350-353

   ecart.mxml file, 349-350

   Java server-side component, 335

   LoadProductsCmd class, 344-345

   LoadProductsEvent class, 343-344

   overview, 335

   PrepAddCartCmd class, 345-346

   Product class, 336-337

   ProductDelegate class, 341-342

   ServiceLocator class, 340-341

shutting down, application shutdown process, 41-43

signature.xml file, 302-303

signatures, digital, 34, 303-306

   Certificate Wizard, 304-306

   overview, 299-301

   signature.xml file, 302-303

W-X

UNLEASHED

Unleashed takes you beyond the basics, providing an exhaustive, technically sophisticated reference for professionals who need to exploit a technology to its fullest potential. It's the best resource for practical advice from the experts, and the most in-depth coverage of the latest technologies.

Adobe Dreamweaver CS3 Unleashed
ISBN: 978-0-672-32944-9

OTHER UNLEASHED TITLES

Microsoft XNA Unleashed: Graphics and Game Programming for Xbox 360 and Windows
ISBN: 978-0-672-32964-7

Windows PowerShell Unleashed
ISBN: 978-0-672-32953-1

ASP.NET 3.5 Unleashed
ISBN: 978-0-672-33011-7

PHP 5 Unleashed
ISBN: 978-0-672-32511-3

JavaScript Unleashed, 4th Edition
ISBN: 978-0-672-32431-4

Xcode 3 Unleashed
ISBN: 978-0-321-55263-1

Mac OS X Tiger Unleashed
ISBN: 978-0-672-32746-9

informit.com/sams

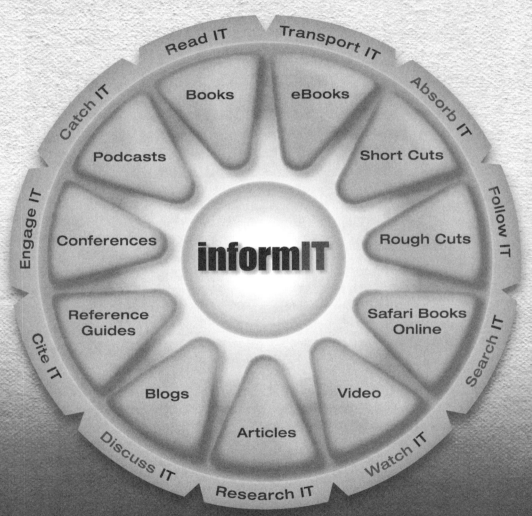

LearnIT at InformIT

Go Beyond the Book

11 WAYS TO LEARN IT at www.informIT.com/learn

The digital network for the publishing imprints of Pearson Education

FREE Online Edition

Your purchase of **Adobe® AIR™ Programming Unleashed** includes access to a free online edition for 45 days through the Safari Books Online subscription service. Nearly every Sams book is available online through Safari Books Online, along with more than 5,000 other technical books and videos from publishers such as Addison-Wesley Professional, Cisco Press, Exam Cram, IBM Press, O'Reilly, Prentice Hall, and Que.

SAFARI BOOKS ONLINE allows you to search for a specific answer, cut and paste code, download chapters, and stay current with emerging technologies.

Activate your FREE Online Edition at
www.informit.com/safarifree

> **STEP 1:** Enter the coupon code: 9FK7-S6MJ-CKX4-K6JF-VFR6.

> **STEP 2:** New Safari users, complete the brief registration form.
>   Safari subscribers, just log in.

If you have difficulty registering on Safari or accessing the online edition, please e-mail customer-service@safaribooksonline.com